Murder Town, USA

Critical Issues in Crime and Society

Raymond J. Michalowski and Luis A. Fernandez, Series Editors

Critical Issues in Crime and Society is oriented toward critical analysis of contemporary problems in crime and justice. The series is open to a broad range of topics including specific types of crime, wrongful behavior by economically or politically powerful actors, controversies over justice system practices, and issues related to the intersection of identity, crime, and justice. It is committed to offering thoughtful works that will be accessible to scholars and professional criminologists, general readers, and students.

For a list of titles in the series, see the last page of the book.

Murder Town, USA

Homicide, Structural Violence, and Activism in Wilmington

Yasser Arafat Payne,
Brooklynn K. Hitchens,
and Darryl L. Chambers

Rutgers University Press
New Brunswick, Camden, and Newark, New Jersey
London and Oxford

Rutgers University Press is a department of Rutgers, The State University of New Jersey, one of the leading public research universities in the nation. By publishing worldwide, it furthers the University's mission of dedication to excellence in teaching, scholarship, research, and clinical care.

Library of Congress Cataloging-in-Publication Data

Names: Payne, Yasser Arafat, author. | Hitchens, Brooklynn K., author. | Chambers, Darryl L., author.
Title: Murder town, USA : homicide, structural violence, and activism in Wilmington / Yasser Arafat Payne, Ph.D., University of Delaware, Brooklynn Hitchens, Ph.D., University of Maryland, College Park and Darryl L. Chambers, M.A., University of Delaware.
Description: New Brunswick : Rutgers University Press, 2023. | Series: Critical issues in crime and society | Includes bibliographical references and index.
Identifiers: LCCN 2022046048 | ISBN 9781978817364 (paperback) | ISBN 9781978817371 (hardback) | ISBN 9781978817388 (epub) | ISBN 9781978817401 (pdf)
Subjects: LCSH: Violence—Delaware—Wilmington. | Homicide—Delaware—Wilmington. | Gun control—Delaware—Wilmington. | Crime prevention—Delaware—Wilmington.
Classification: LCC HM886 .P39 2023 | DDC 303.609751/2—dc23/eng/20221227
LC record available at https://lccn.loc.gov/2022046048

A British Cataloging-in-Publication record for this book is available from the British Library.

Copyright © 2023 by Yasser Arafat Payne, Brooklynn K. Hitchens, and Darryl L. Chambers

All rights reserved

No part of this book may be reproduced or utilized in any form or by any means, electronic or mechanical, or by any information storage and retrieval system, without written permission from the publisher. Please contact Rutgers University Press, 106 Somerset Street, New Brunswick, NJ 08901. The only exception to this prohibition is "fair use" as defined by U.S. copyright law.

References to internet websites (URLs) were accurate at the time of writing. Neither the author nor Rutgers University Press is responsible for URLs that may have expired or changed since the manuscript was prepared.

rutgersuniversitypress.org

Contents

Introduction: Street Identity, Structural Violence, and Street PAR   1

Part I   Context of Opportunity and Violence

1. A City of Banks: A Long Legacy of Economic Violence and Crime   27
2. "Welcome to Wilmington—A Place to Be Somebody": Negotiating City Culture and Building Rapport   41
3. "Murder Town, USA": Reframing Gun Violence and Resilience in a Small City   57

Part II   Management, Containment, and the Social Control of Black Wilmington

4. "I'm Still Waiting Man . . . on That Golden Ticket!" Education and Economic Justice, a Dream Deferred—in Perpetuity   87
5. "F-ck the Police!" Standing Up to the Policing Machine   113
6. "I Don't Let These Felonies Hold Me Back!" How the Streets Radically Reframed Re-entry   135

Part III   Street Agency: Coping with and Ending the Structural Violence Complex

7. "Brenda's Got a Baby": Competing Roles of Black Women as Matriarchs and Hustlers   157

8	"Street Love": How Psychological and Social Well-Being Interrupts Gun Violence	181
9	"Winter Is Coming!" White Walkers, Revolutionary Change, and the Streets Call for Structural Transformation	196
	Conclusion: Calling for a Radical Street Ethnography: Street PAR, SOR Theory, and the Bottom Caste	217
	Notes	233
	Bibliography	263
	Index	287

Murder Town, USA

Introduction

STREET IDENTITY, STRUCTURAL VIOLENCE, AND STREET PAR

Capitalism was built on the exploitation and suffering of Black slaves and continues to thrive on the experience of the poor.
—Martin Luther King Jr., "The Three Evils of Society"

The quest for the emancipation of Black people in the U.S. has always been a quest for economic liberation.
—Angela Davis, interview with *Frontline*

All ethnographies are exploitative in nature, because . . . they advance professional careers and status on the backs of others, often the powerless. Researchers are notorious for going into poor communities and taking but rarely giving back—or, as local activists sometimes say, for "cutting and running."
—Timothy Black, *When a Heart Turns Rock Solid*

IT WAS OCTOBER 2009, and we had just selected fifteen research-activists for the Wilmington Street Participatory Action Research (Street PAR) Project to examine gun violence in the Eastside and Southbridge sections of Wilmington, Delaware.[1] Stakeholders were thrilled with the project's potential, but frankly, some were also concerned that some Street PAR Associates might embarrass them. Most Associates were only a year out of prison, and in Delaware, about 80% recidivated within three years of a serious offense.[2]

Theoretically, Delaware's rates of recidivism suggested that many of these Associates would recidivate, and for some stakeholders, a failing, widely supported re-entry program was risky or could easily tarnish their reputations. I am delighted to report that as a professional collective, we were able to deal with those concerns and remain committed to these Associates.

We held a three-hour group orientation in a large boardroom at the United Way of Delaware. After completing a written assignment on their personal aspirations and expectations of the project, several Associates shared their perspectives on homicide in Wilmington.

Melodie Robinson was a married, 28-year-old Black woman and the mother of four sons. Highly respected and cherished in Southbridge, Melodie understood well the needs and interests of street-identified young people in her community. Standing with her written reflection in hand, Melodie asserted, "I am a strong Black mother and I need my community to be much better than it is. And I want to play my part in helping. . . . Way too many in South(bridge) have been killed, and we doing this to each other, because we don't have much."

Thirty-eight-year-old Corry Wright was originally from Brooklyn, New York. In 2005 he relocated to New Castle, Delaware, to start "a better life" for himself and his daughter. Intrigued by our discussion on qualitative and quantitative research, Corry perked up when Yasser explained we were going to launch a multimethod street ethnography that centered on a large community survey sample. I also explained that all of the data were important but were valued differently depending on the audience.

"Why would [some] value quantitative research more than qualitative research?"

Corry responded, "They value numbers. Qualitative is emotion . . . quantitative is *quantity* or how much something cost? It's relative to power. They don't care about the feelings and emotions." With quick insight, Corry unearthed some of the ongoing tensions in the academy about research rigor.

Excited by the enthusiasm in the room, Charles Madden, executive director of the Wilmington HOPE Commission and institutional partner, added, "*Everybody has got to have a voice.* And the reason why it is important that we do this project and many more projects like this one, is so that we hear *those voices.* Many people in this room do not have a voice, *that gets heard.* Here is a platform for those voices to be heard."

The HOPE Commission was a nonprofit organization founded by Mayor James Baker in 2006 to address Wilmington's increasing rates of gun violence, incarceration, and recidivism. After a successful street outreach campaign on homicide in 2008, the HOPE Commission called for a Street PAR project in the Eastside and Southbridge. In June 2009, Yasser accepted the role of leading this study, which was strongly supported by an institutional partnership of three universities, five nonprofit organizations, and other public officials.

The State of Wilmington: Corporatocracy and Violence in a Small Black City

Wilmington is a small, deindustrialized town by national standards, but it is also Delaware's largest and most influential city. And Wilmington truly had a giant personality. Crowned the "LLC" and "corporate" capital of the United States, Wilmington is indeed a beacon of wealth, *at least for some*.[3] The underbelly of this corporate leviathan is extreme poverty and a vibrant street culture in the city's predominately poor Black neighborhoods. Truly a tale of two cities, Wilmington was also labeled "Murder Town, USA," the "Most Dangerous City in America," and the capital for teenage homicide.[4]

Extreme Black poverty festers alongside extreme white wealth in this divided town; and Wilmington's smallness made it impossible to escape this shameful reality. Higher-income white neighborhoods such as Cool Spring, Midtown Brandywine, and Downtown Eastside surround and cut through poor Black communities like West Center City, the Northeast, and the Eastside. White wealth gloriously thrives in Wilmington while thousands of Black bodies drown in structural violence. And all of this intersects in too normal a fashion. Very few ever appear to be disturbed by Wilmington's troubling racialized divide in wealth. Just under the blue skyline of the sterling Bank of America building in Downtown Eastside, poor Blacks struggle to survive on Ninth and North Pine Streets; Ninth and Lombard Streets; and Tenth and Bennett Streets in the Eastside.

Wilmington is nearly 60% Black and 32% white, with a total population of 71,000.[5] Black residents (30%) experience more than double the poverty than do white residents (11%), and joblessness rates are equally troubling. At the time of our study (2010–2013), unemployment among Blacks (22%) was over five times higher than that of whites (4%). On average, residents in the Eastside and Southbridge earned between $23,375 and $20,221, respectively.[6]

Wilmington was also the third-most violent city of its size, and its homicide per capita rates were consistently higher than those of Philadelphia, Baltimore, Los Angeles, and even Chicago.[7] Nationally, homicide declined considerably since the mid-1990s, but violent crime and especially homicide increased sharply during this same time period in small, Rust Belt cities like Wilmington.[8] City size contributed to why Wilmington remained so violent. Victims, perpetrators, and their respective loved ones all lived within minutes of each other, and this proximity pretty much ensured spates of retributive violence. According to Waverly Duck, limited public spaces, proximity between perpetrators and victims, and increased availability of lethal guns were key factors that explained higher homicide rates in small cities.[9] Smaller municipalities generally had fewer resources to address poverty and violence than larger cities.

Violence in Wilmington also had less to do with a budding drug trade with dealers squabbling over street territory, as was apparent during the 1980s and 1990s. Instead, violent crime had more to do with structurally dislocated young people from a small city avenging in concentrated ways the deaths of brothers, cousins, or close friends.[10]

While it was true that the Eastside and Southbridge sometimes grew drunk on cocktails of dis-opportunity, violence, and death, it is critical to underscore that these neighborhoods were concurrently and even more full of "love" or high levels of social cohesion. Violence sometimes erupted, but strong Black community pride also reigned here. Ironically, the threat and use of violence in the context of compounding inequality also shaped how well-being was achieved in the Eastside and Southbridge.[11] On most days, an invisible chessboard of strategic alignments kept the peace. Scores of residents and persons involved with the streets were "protected" by their family ties, by membership in street crews and gangs, or by knowing people who demonstrated a capacity for violence.

Also, violence was not always understood as a moral wrong by members of the streets and other local residents.[12] In fact, violence was sometimes considered to be a restorative mechanism for peace or relief from the daily hassles and accumulated strain of living in concentrated disadvantage.[13] Strain theory asserts that not all stressful events are perceived as the same, even within the same social group. When someone perceives their victimization as unjust, they can view violence as a way to "minimize the 'psychic toll of strain' because it enables people to avoid or escape strain, compensate for the negative effects of strain, and/or satisfy a desire for revenge or retaliation."[14]

This alternative perspective on violence was intuitive to local residents, but not so much to outsiders. It was just too difficult or not worth the intellectual energy to ascertain why a crack cocaine dealer exacted gun violence for what he deemed a just reason, or to understand the value in knowing how active gang members cared about their families and neighborhoods. But for "the streets," or persons involved in crime as a way of life, this aspect of their social identity did matter, and they did deeply care about their families, close friends, and neighborhoods. And they too abhorred the gun violence. Homicide was a complex social problem, and ameliorating it was possible only by working with the people most affected. It is through a critical, systematic examination of their lived experiences and coping and bonding mechanisms that we can better understand and ultimately help those affected by gun violence.

Sites of Resilience Theory: Reconceptualizing "the Streets" of Wilmington

This book conceptualizes gun violence as a feature of Wilmington's social identity or as a "site of resilience" (SOR) for people involved with the streets as a way of life.[15] From this perspective, resilience is not a value-laden construct that simply means "good" or ethical behavior.[16] Residents in the Eastside and Southbridge made personal choices that were always shaped by their structural realities.[17] For our study, resilience represents the process by which people with a street identity ensure notions of survival, meaning, and life purpose.

Diener, Sapyta, and Suh warned that it was dangerous to impose "universal" classifications of "good" and "bad" mental health outcomes and called for the "subjective well-being" or the person's own perspective on health to be incorporated in any "evaluation."[18] They argued: "By 'health,' [scholars] . . . mean a universally good life that can be objectively verified by scientists. . . . They follow in the footsteps of . . . Maslow in their search for universal and objective characteristics of mental health that are free of particular cultural values. ... Subjective well-being is a person's evaluation of his or her life. This valuation can be in terms of cognitive states such as satisfaction with one's marriage, work, and life, and it could be in terms of ongoing affect, i.e., the presence of positive emotions and moods, and the absence of unpleasant affect."[19]

Conservative understandings of universalism among groups have been problematized by others, most notably Aimé Césaire, founder of the Negritude movement in the 1930s and 1940s. African diasporic scholars and activists of the Negritude movement developed pan-African concepts of Blackness or Africanity, and they were deeply committed to challenging global capitalism. Césaire argued that Western colonial powers strategically used the discourse of "universalism," "humanism," and "nation" to repress the ethnic-driven political efforts of African and indigenous populations around the world.[20] In his seminal work, *Discourse on Colonialism*, Césaire resisted Western abstract or "disembodied" universalism that works to strip African and indigenous groups of all their "particulars" or unique social identities.[21] Regarding Césaire's argument on "universality," Robin D. G. Kelley writes: "He had practically given up on Europe and the old humanism and its claim of universality, opting instead to redefine the 'universal' in a way that did not privilege Europe. Césaire explains, 'I'm not going to confine myself to some narrow particularism. But I don't intend either to become lost in a disembodied universalism . . . I have a different idea of a universal. It is a universal rich with all that is particular, rich with all the particulars there are, the deepening of each particular, the coexistence of them all.'"[22] Universalism or "colorblind" analysis is a racist, insidious epistemological project that centralizes hegemonic, European ways of knowing at the expense of continental and diasporic African people.[23]

In concert with Césaire's rejection of "disembodied universalism," we argue that street-identified, Black American men and women craft a multilayered cultural identity and a worldview that resists traditional conceptualizations of "deviance" or "delinquency." Their cultural identity is anything but universal, and their rich identity cannot be easily classified or reduced to a label or diagnosis. As with most groups, their cultural identity is nuanced by a wide assortment of characteristics like race, ethnicity, gender, class, and social location. A street identity is a racial-ethnic and culturally situated social identity that centralizes and governs the group's attitudinal and behavioral expressions.

According to SOR theory, "street life," "the streets," and "street" identity is colloquial and agentic language that represents an ideology centered on personal, social, and economic survival. Street life is also a spectrum of networking behaviors, or bonding and illegal activities deemed to be empowering in distressed environments. Through examination of over four dozen voices and critical perspectives, we found that street life in the Eastside and

Southbridge was more aptly characterized as a racial-ethnic, multidimensional, and geographically bounded cultural identity.

Street life is more than just participation in crime. The "shooter," the crack cocaine dealer, and the gang member were also doting fathers and mothers, loving life partners, and someone's children and grandchildren. They knew their continued involvement in the streets could result in bodily injury, incarceration, and even death. Yet, given their life circumstances and commitment to family, taking these extreme risks was perceived to be worth the possible consequences.[24]

Most people in the streets of Wilmington actually endorsed the same values supported by middle-class white America.[25] They wanted to be educated and gainfully employed, they desired a healthy nuclear family, and they too were disheartened by the cycle of gun violence. However, many in the Eastside and Southbridge were not able to adhere to this traditional value system, not because they did not want to, but because of its impracticality in the context of extreme poverty. In agreement with this theoretical perspective, Wilson asserts: "The decision to act in ghetto-related ways, although not reflecting internalized values can nonetheless be said to be cultural. The more often certain behavior, such as the pursuit of illegal income, is manifested in a community, the greater will be the readiness on the part of some residents of the community to find that behavior 'not only convenient but also morally appropriate.' They may endorse mainstream norms against this behavior in the abstract but then provide compelling reasons and justifications for this behavior, given the circumstances in their community."[26]

To the naked eye, violence in Wilmington's neighborhoods appeared random and out of control. But Duck's "local interaction order" theory argues that street-identified environments are governed by a locally situated value system that evolved out of the neighborhood's socioeconomic and political context.[27] Over time, the Eastside and Southbridge organically developed informal or unspoken agreements with the streets. This agreement determined the level and degree as well as the location and duration of violence and crime tolerated. Tapping into this local order, street code or social balance required superior racial-ethnic and cultural competence, and understanding these experiences was typically beyond the outsider's capacity, but a requirement for local residents. Misinterpretation of the code sometimes meant the difference between life and death. Residents in the Eastside and Southbridge were compromised because they understood well what Duck described as the "profound contradiction"—the difference between what was *moral* and what was *possible* to achieve in poor small Black communities: "The locally situated character of the social order that composes daily life frames the choices and resources available to people. . . . A profound contradiction [exists] between the beliefs residents hold and the practices they engage in. . . . This fundamental contradiction between beliefs and behavior does not reflect on the moral character of individuals. The social order of such neighborhoods rests on

FUNDAMENTAL PRISM

I.1. Sites of Resilience Theoretical Framework, Fundamental Prism Model

the nature of the underground or illegal economic enterprise and the orderly practices necessary to succeed in it, not on what people believe, value, or want for themselves and others."[28]

A street identity was also an intergenerational experience that contained fundamental and cultural components.[29] Core individual and structural conditions frame at least five fundamental mechanisms of resilience (see figure I.1). These mechanisms are presumed to be the foundational characteristics that drive all forms of resilience: (1) phenomenology or intersectional standing; (2) relational coping (i.e., key support networks); (3) racial-wealth standing; (4) exposure to structural violence; and (5) exposure to injustice.

The cultural component represents the racial-ethnic dimension of a street identity (see figure I.2). Urban ethnographers,[30] journalistic ethnographies,[31] and autobiographical accounts[32] have documented the wide use of race, ethnicity, and culture in street-identified communities. Jackson, for example, found the intersectionality of race, ethnicity, gender, and class was interwoven in the cultural fabric of Black Harlem.[33] He warned that race, ethnicity, and gender "are not only epiphenomena of truer class realities but important life-structuring social variables in their own rights, variables that help organize people's everyday lives and group affiliations in fundamental ways."[34]

SOR and the Cultural Fabric of Black Wilmington

The Black American experience deeply informs much of the Eastside and Southbridge and larger Black Wilmington. African-centered charter schools, soul food restaurants, blues and jazz events, hip-hop music and culture, grassroots organizations, Black American mosques, as well as rich African Methodist Episcopalian and Baptist traditions all thrived in Wilmington. The streets of the Eastside and Southbridge also took race, ethnicity, and culture seriously. Race was the primary factor by which they assessed their street environments and the people within them. Temperament, personality traits, behavioral mannerisms, and a person's overall potential and motivations were all tied to racial-ethnic and cultural background. In an effort to evaluate or learn about someone's intentions, Black residents eagerly inquired about the family lineage and ethnic backgrounds of people they did not know. A small town like Wilmington affords easy opportunities to track down someone's personal history, social standing, and kinship network—and street-identified Black men and women in Wilmington took every opportunity to do so.

Many in the streets were practicing Black American Sunni Muslims. Men dressed in white thobes with big beards, "prayer bumps," and bald heads, and fully garbed women with black burkas, hijabs, or veiled faces populated a large segment of Black Wilmington. Sunni Muslim Black men in the streets also struggled over the Qur'an's mandate against harming Muslims. Others were followers of the Nation of Islam, Black Moors, Hebrew Israelites, or Christianity, and some just believed in God.

Most Black residents in the Eastside and Southbridge considered the "militant" activism that poured out of some religious and grassroots organizations to be a notable feature. Reverend Derrick "Pastor D" Johnson, Imam Abu Maahir, and Bishop Aretha Morton regularly used their platforms to indict white supremacy. They were clergy *and* activists who had close relationships with the poor, and because of this they were able to engage with Wilmington's establishment on their behalf.

Much of Wilmington's present-day militancy emerges from a long grassroots legacy dating back to the late 1700s.[35] Richard Allen, Absalom Jones, Harriet Tubman, and especially the lesser-known figure Peter Spencer were key community leaders responsible for cultivating a thriving climate for Black empowerment in Wilmington, Delaware.

After purchasing their freedom, Delaware's former slaves Richard Allen and Absalom Jones jump-started the first major Black social movement by establishing the African Methodist Episcopal Church (AME) in 1787. The AME tradition presently remains the most dominant Christian denomination in Black Wilmington. Wilmington's grassroots, activist legacy was also reinforced by the pan-African messages of Marcus Garvey that spread into Wilmington in the 1920s, and the presence of Malcolm X and Malik Shabbazz in nearby Philadelphia in the late 1950s and 1960s is responsible for large numbers of Black Wilmingtonians converting to the Nation of Islam.[36]

PSYCHOLOGICAL AND PHYSICAL SPACES OF RESILIENCE. Sites of resilience theory argues a street identity is composed of psychological and physical spaces or "sites," and these sites are utilized by street-identified Black people to cope and become resilient (see figure I.2). Resilience is achieved through key ethnic- and culturally based relationships with people in particular psychological and physical spaces. Such coping experiences create the intimacy needed for the establishment of resilience.

CULTURAL PRISM

Street Code
- Economic survival
- Personal survival
- Social survival

⟷ Psychological SOR

Physical SOR ⟷
- Planning spaces
- Active spaces
- Intimate spaces
- Social spaces

STREET LIFE
- Bonding
- Illegal

I.2. Sites of Resilience Theoretical Framework, Cultural Prism Model

Psychological sites of resilience are the core values, belief systems, rules, or "code of the streets" used to guide the multiple negotiations and interactions (e.g., drug dealing) that occur within street-identified spaces. *Physical sites of resilience* are geographically bonded and diasporic places where the streets congregate to bolster personal and group levels of meaning. Franklin and Keyes refer to these spaces as "gathering places."[37] Basketball courts, local bars, street corners, and "the trap" are not arbitrary spaces, but examples of gathering spaces that have historical, emotional, and psychological significance for street-identified Black men and women.

Psychological and physical sites are typically coordinated around particular street hustles, and the crack cocaine trade is one key example of how these sites speak to expressions of resilience within a particular hustle. For many in the streets, the hustling of crack cocaine has a cultural ideology or code attached to it that is separate but also overlaps with the codes of other street hustles (e.g., gambling, armed robbery). People who sell crack cocaine or other hard drugs typically come from more violent and structurally challenged neighborhoods, which in turn influences how they navigate and think about the streets.[38] Motivated by financial desperation, members of local drug networks formulate a set of adaptive ethics designed to guide daily operations in chaotic locales. Physical spaces used by people who sell crack cocaine usually mirror their own traumatic experiences: street corners or alleyways, abandoned or boarded-up locations, or run-down city parks. In turn, members of these networks often embrace these structurally hardened spaces as empowering locations.

There were at least four types of overlapping spaces used by the streets of Wilmington: (1) *planning spaces*—spaces where illegal activity is contrived; (2) *active spaces*—spaces where street activities occur; (3) *intimate spaces*—spaces to bond with family members and other loved ones; and (4) *social spaces*—spaces to connect with peers and other community members. Psychological sites of

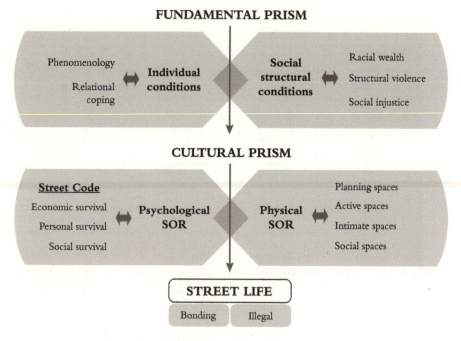

I.3. Sites of Resilience Theoretical Framework, Full Model

resilience constitute the ideology or the code attached to physical spaces, which gives these spaces special meaning. It is through the merging of psychological and physical dimensions that the use of a street identity is enacted as a site of resilience (see figure I.3).

THE STRUCTURAL VIOLENCE COMPLEX

The structural violence complex is a nefarious web of legislation, policies, laws, institutions, and structural systems designed to privilege whiter and wealthier communities at the expense of the poor and most vulnerable.[39] This complex is also an extremely racialized meta-system that targets particular racial-ethnic groups for various forms of exploitation. Undocumented Mexican Americans or Vietnamese street gangs in Southern California, low-income urban and rural Black Americans, and even the white coal-mining communities in West Virginia, have all been uniquely impacted by the structural violence complex.

What cannot be underestimated is the intentionality of the complex—a complex that is fully committed to an agenda of "structural genocide," or systematic harm of vulnerable groups. Structural systems are not arbitrary forces that sometimes produce unintended consequences.[40] More precisely, the structural violence complex is the embodiment of "empire," or the interests of white supremacy and the larger Western world.[41] Modern capitalism was conceptualized out of a slave labor financial model where production and wealth relied on African slaves.[42] Slaveholders borrowed from banks to buy slaves, roughly worth about $1,000 or $250,000 in current value, and then they borrowed against those new slaves to purchase more. Insurrection and life insurance policies on slaves were also honored, which secured their value in life and death. Alexander argues that U.S. capitalism was always fundamentally a "racial caste system" anchored in the most criminalized segments of Black America.[43] The impression of change via the Civil War and the civil rights movement disguised but never thwarted our economic system's requirement for poverty, unemployment, and cheap labor. Delaware's financial system shares in this shameful legacy of capitalism, slavocracy, and continued structural racism.[44]

Structural violence theory argues that street violence is the result of vicious social and structural forces.[45] According to Galtung, predatory institutions and structural systems harm groups and communities by preventing them from meeting their basic needs and "realizing their potentialities."[46] For Galtung, structural violence is synonymous with "social injustice" and is a cruel embodiment, or expression of "imperialism."[47] He also theorized violence as an interconnected triad of "structural," "cultural," and "direct" forms of violence.[48] *Cultural violence* refers to how broader society normalizes violence, or how most people are generally indifferent to the suffering experienced by poor people.[49] *Direct violence* includes "verbal" and lethal forms of violence such as homicide. Cultural and structural forms of violence are argued by Galtung to be greatly responsible for direct violence.[50]

Sites of resilience theory also draws on *Black Marxism theory* to contextualize the oppression of the Black working class;[51] *general strain theory*'s analysis of criminal adaptation to structural inequality;[52] *critical race* and *racial capitalism theory*'s emphasis on the ruling elite's need for a racialized, economic outgroup;[53] and *critical criminology*'s perspective of crime as resistance.[54] SOR theory contributes to this rich legacy the concept of a street identity that is anchored in a racialized, ethnic, and cultural worldview. Not enough attention has been placed on how racial-ethnic and cultural identities are embodied by street-identified communities to cope with and respond to an insidious structural violence complex.

Street PAR in the Streets of Wilmington
Reflections from Yasser

Murder Town, USA is a street participatory action (Street PAR) project that organized fifteen residents formerly involved with the streets and criminal legal system to document the relationship between economic well-being and street violence in Wilmington's Eastside and Southbridge neighborhoods. From 2010 to 2011, this multimethod study collected the following data from

TABLE I.1
Survey Design: Quota Samples (N = 520)

Age Group	Male	Female	Total
18–21	73	96	169
22–29	88	119	207
30–35	54	90	144
Total	**215**	**305**	**520**

Quota samples were determined by 2000 U.S. Census data based on race, sex, and age in the Eastside and Southbridge. Based on the total survey sample (N = 520), each cell represents the number (or percentage) of that particular race, sex, and age reflected in 2000 Census data.

TABLE I.2
Interview Design: N = 46 (28 men, 18 women)

Age group	Individual interviews	Dual interviews	Group interviews	Total
18–26	12	—	1 (4 participants)	16
27–33	10	2	1 (3 participants)	15
34–40	5	6	1 (4 participants)	15
Total participants	**27**	**8**	**11**	**46**

a community sample of street-identified Black men and women, ages 18 to 35: 520 surveys, 27 individual interviews, 4 dual interviews, and 3 group interviews (see tables I.1 and I.2).

Street PAR is an ethnographic method of collecting and analyzing data, but it is also an intervention for Street PAR Associates and local communities. Dr. Marlene Saunders, chair of the Department of Social Work at Delaware State University, and her graduate students provided individual and group levels of case management to Associates to troubleshoot any daily concerns that may have interrupted their participation (e.g., transportation, childcare). Associates were also paid biweekly and they earned $17 to $20 per hour on other research projects during and after our study's conclusion. Six Associates enrolled in college during and after the project's initial funding period. Three graduated with their bachelor of arts degrees (BAs), three completed their master of arts degrees (MAs), two pursued their doctorates, and only one Associate from this inaugural group has completed their doctorate. We also orchestrated dozens of community-based programs on gun violence, police misconduct, re-entry, and structural inequality.

People who are actively or formerly involved with the streets are best poised to critically examine the individual and structural experiences of street-identified populations.[55] Equipped with a unique cultural worldview, they can more credibly critique misinformed perspectives and they also can conduct analysis and propose solutions that would be better received by the streets. Long Incarcerated Fraternity Engaging Release Studies (LIFERS) is a scholar-activist group of men serving life sentences who have remained determined to offer analysis and recommendations for addressing the detrimental aspects of street culture.[56] Central to the LIFERS argument is their call for community-centered interventions to be interwoven through the perspectives of those incarcerated and active in the streets. According to the LIFERS, "It is unrealistic to think that any serious efforts to address the problem of drug addiction could be successful while simultaneously excluding drug users, who consume illegal substances and drug dealers, who market them, from such efforts. It is logically inconsistent, therefore to expect a reduction in crime simply by galvanizing law enforcement, legislators, and a few select community groups, while excluding those deemed to be criminal elements from the process."[57] The Street PAR model takes this inclusion seriously, and we recognize that any violence reduction efforts must center the perspectives of those most affected or involved with street violence.

RECRUITING THE TEAM. Three universities and five nonprofit organizations provided technical, infrastructural, and financial support to the project, as well as employment and educational opportunities for Street PAR Associates. Nonprofit organizations also networked our project into city and state leadership, including the city council, the state assembly, and the governor's office.

The Wilmington HOPE Commission (a nonprofit partner) issued a citywide call for residents with experiences in the streets and criminal legal system to apply for a yearlong, part-time position on the Wilmington Street PAR project. Residents were informed about the position via (1) job postings at nonprofit and other agencies, (2) street outreach efforts on the ground, (3) email and social media blasts, and (4) word of mouth. We were most interested in applicants with a desire to gain research experience, obtain secondary or postsecondary education, or work in a research-related field. Within a week of the release of the posting, we had received about 150 applications. Approximately seventy-five applicants were invited to a half-day group meeting at the Neighborhood House (a nonprofit partner) in Southbridge. Applicants participated in group activities designed to elicit attitudes on violence. From this group, thirty were invited for one-on-one interviews held at Christina Cultural Arts Center (a nonprofit partner) in the Eastside. Fifteen Associates were selected from this final group.

MEET THE WILMINGTON STREET PAR FAMILY. Street PAR Associates were a self-proclaimed "family," not simply a research team. This was a romanticized view perhaps, but their solidarity was genuine, and it benefited greatly by distinguishing the project from traditional research—it was a people-centered study that truly embodied a political pursuit committed to grassroots change.

Twenty-one-year-old Dubard "Dubie" McGriff was one of our youngest members; he had recently completed a four-year sentence for robbery, drug possession, and firearms possession. One morning at methods training, Dubard mentioned that "even when I made a $1,000 a day [in the streets], it didn't match the feeling I get when we see each other at a meeting." For them, the most valuable part of Street PAR was the social-support network it offered. Street PAR created a safe space for its Associates to think through many of their concerns. Before, during, and after meetings, they feverishly updated each other on their parole status, barriers to childcare, housing challenges, job opportunities, or recent news in the streets. The energy among this team was always electric, as we challenged each other to become better researchers and citizens.

Based on my prior research experiences in Harlem (New York City) and north New Jersey,[58] I realized I needed to forge an authentic relationship, months in advance, with someone from the Eastside and Southbridge. I needed the guidance of someone who understood Wilmington's street politics well enough to steer us around problematic personalities. Frankly, I needed someone I could trust who had high social capital—someone who could also be my eyes and ears in the communities. The only way Street PAR could happen in "Murder Town, USA" was through and with the permission of the streets.

Forty-year-old Darryl "Wolfie" or "Wolf" Chambers was my chief street liaison, guide, and mentor in the Eastside and Southbridge.[59] Recently released from prison, he was now an outreach consultant at the HOPE Commission. In 1996, Darryl was sentenced to thirty-five years for running a major drug organization. This was his only conviction, and this charge was a nonviolent felony. He had a bachelor of arts in sociology from the University of California–Davis at the time of his arrest. Darryl appealed his sentence and was later released after serving twelve years.

Over the next few months, Darryl and I got to know each other well. Sometimes we spoke for hours on the phone. One evening, I doubled down on the concept of structural violence. Intrigued, he pressed the point that inequality in Wilmington was racialized: "In Wilmington, it's always been like this, in terms of who got resources and power. Blacks have always been trapped out here. And white folks have always run the city, you here? Yeah, yeah, yeah . . . Dr. Payne, if we're going to being honest about it all, what's really going on in Wilmington is structural genocide."

Given that Darryl was very private, I was honored to meet his wife, Nikki, and his 18-year-old son, Muhammad, or "Dom" (Dominique). They were a stunning and proud Black Sunni Muslim family. Darryl's wife always wore a hijab but rarely covered her face. Nikki's bright smile and light spirit tempered Darryl's sterner disposition, and their son Muhammad just adored Nikki. I was grateful to meet Darryl's loved ones because he rarely invited anyone to his home or around his family.

One afternoon, Darryl took me to James and Jesse's Barber Shop in the Eastside. Located in one of the poorest parts of town, this shop was still a social hub for many on the corner of Tenth and Bennett Streets. Although this is one of the city's most violent neighborhoods, on this warm spring day children, teenagers, and adults were grateful to escape their winter-induced cabin fever. They chatted away and huddled around stoops and cars.

Four men stood near the entrance of the barbershop. As we approached, one looked our way and said: "Wolfie! Hey man. That's my *ba-aby*, right here!" The others turned around mid-sentence and joined in, "Wolfie!!!! Hey ba-aby!" Stunned at their casual use of the word "baby" for another man, I learned that many young Black men in Wilmington used "ba-aby" as a term of deep endearment.

"I want to introduce you guys to somebody. This is Dr. Payne and he is a professor at the University of Delaware, you hear? In a few months we are going to start recruiting for people to work on a research project with the mayor's office to help stop the violence, or at least to try and slow it down. We could really use your help in the Eastside."

"We there, Wolfie. We got you! So y'all are really going to be hiring people from out here [the streets] to do research?"

"And activism," I added. "We want to launch a study with the community and use that data to fight back. It is time for the streets to do research and activism."

My casual experiences in barbershops, on street corners, or in people's homes were necessary for recruitment of Associates and study participants. Darryl also knew that with each resident who could match my face to this new project, I was building rapport in the community.

Across multiple conversations, Darryl learned more about the concept of Street PAR and the types of residents that would best fit the mission and goals of our study. Darryl's work ethic and command of community concerns were impressive, and he later became the Senior Research Associate of our project. His thirty-hour schedule included recruitment and management of the team, attendance and payroll, data collection, management and analysis, writing contributions, and public presentations.

Darryl and I determined it was best to recruit Associates who already knew each other, or at least were connected by their social and family networks. We also thought a lot about their temperaments, personalities, and street backgrounds. These factors were important to consider when recruiting in a small city. A small city had a long memory, and the streets were too territorial in Wilmington to just haphazardly throw people together. Darryl made sure applicants with existing beefs did not move ahead in the interview process.

The saddest interview was with 38-year-old Kenyatta Brooks, a longtime friend of Darryl's. Kenyatta insisted, "This project was made for me. I need something like this in my life right now. If anyone knows about gun violence in Wilmington, it's me." To confirm this sentiment, Kenyatta shared that his brother was killed in 2008. Although he had been shot in the head and declared "brain dead," Kenyatta and his family spent a week with him in an induced coma before he was removed from life support. Matter-of-factly, Kenyatta recounted that "part of his brain . . . was hanging out of his head on the pillow in the hospital." After his interview, we wondered to what extent was Kenyatta still grieving his brother's death.

The newly recruited fifteen research-activists hailed from some of Wilmington's most hardened neighborhoods. Some were the "shooters," and most had been shot at. Only four Associates had ever been shot, and all of them had loved-ones who were shot and killed. Some were even major drug dealers or "bosses" of Wilmington's street corners and housing projects, and some even amassed a small fortune while in the game. At the risk of sensationalizing them, Street PAR Associates engaged in nearly every street crime conceivable—from prostitution to drug use and sales to violent crime. This broad array of experiences in the streets was integral for a diverse research team. But most importantly, they truly desired and were capable of extraordinary change, particularly when provided the resources to do so.

Twelve Black men and three Black women, ages 20 to 48, were selected for the Wilmington Street PAR project. Five were married, thirteen had at least one child, and eight identified as Sunni Muslim (see table I.3). Most of the male Associates had big beards, bald heads, and/or dark skin.

Six were originally from the Northside of Wilmington, and Patrice Gibbs (age 48) was from the Westside (see table I.4). Louis Price (34) was the only Associate originally from the Eastside, while Melodie Robinson (28), Dennis "Feetz" Watson (39), and Tianna Russell (29) were the only Associates that hailed from Southbridge. Kenyatta (38) and Earvin "Swearve" Griffin (26) actually lived in nearby New Castle, Delaware. Ashley Randolph (21) was originally from Chester, Pennsylvania, but relocated to New Castle at age 12. At the start of the project, however, Ashley lived in a small apartment on Ninth and Kirkwood—a hardened and gritty neighborhood in the Eastside. As a teen, Jonathan "Runn" Wilson had lived in San Diego, California, Yaden, Pennsylvania, and Southwest Philadelphia. After he was shot for a third time, Jonathan relocated from Southwest Philadelphia to Eastside, Wilmington in his mid-thirties.

Educational status varied greatly for the Associates (see table I.3). Ten dropped out of high school and at least nine eventually secured their GEDs. Five earned their high school diplomas (HSDs), five had some college experience, and two had earned BAs prior to the start of our project. Two Associates had military experience, but only one was officially a military veteran.

TABLE I.3
Backgrounds of Street PAR Associates in December 2009

	Males	Females	Total
Number	12	3	15
Race and ethnicity	Black American: 12	Black American: 3	Black American: 15
Age	41 (age range: 20–48)	25.6 (age range: 21–28)	X = 33.3 (age range: 20–48)
Socioeconomic status	Below poverty line	Below poverty line	Below poverty line
Employment status	All unemployed	All unemployed	All unemployed
High school diploma or GED	12	2	14
College degree	2	0	2
State felons/felony convictions	10	0	10
Sunni Muslim	7	1	8

All Associates were unemployed and lived below the poverty line. Ten had felony convictions, most of which were nonviolent convictions. No female Associate was ever incarcerated, but all three played a significant role in the streets of Wilmington, including in drug sales and prostitution.

From November 2009 to January 2010, we trained the Associates in research methods in the Neighborhood House in the Southbridge. We met three or four times per week for three or four hours per session in the center's multipurpose room. Associates completed eighteen research methods workshops with a focus on critical theories, methods, analysis, and activism. Reading and writing assignments were completed during workshops, and the team discussed and wrote about a range of topics (e.g., inequality, violence, and research methods).

In late December, about 100 people attended a graduation ceremony for the Associates at the Neighborhood House.[60] Family, friends, and city officials cheered when they received certificates of completion, a binder with a Street PAR curriculum, how-to books, and other gifts. In the new year, we reconvened in January 2010 to review what we learned in November and December 2009. With fresh eyes, we also critiqued the original design we had developed and assembled the materials needed for data collection. In February we began interviewing young people and by June we were hitting the streets to collect survey data.

Starting in February, we separated the fifteen Associates into four working groups: literature review, data collection, data analysis, and action subteams.

TABLE I.4
Street PAR Associates: Neighborhood location

Name	Title	Location
1 Brooks, Kenyatta	Research Associate	New Castle, DE
2 Chambers, Darryl L., aka "Wolfie," "Wolf," or "Gang"	Senior Research Associate	Riverside/Northside
3 Chambers, Derrick, aka "Der Der"	Research Associate	Riverside/Northside
4 Copeland, Kontal, aka "Gates"	Research Associate	Northside
5 Cornish, Bernard aka "Pooh John"	Research Associate	Northside
6 Gibbs, Patrice aka, "Dark Vadar"	Research Associate	Westside
7 Griffin, Earvin aka "Swearve"	Research Associate	New Castle, DE
8 McGriff, Dubard, aka "Dubbie"	Research Associate	Northside
9 Price, Louis	Research Associate	Eastside
10 Randolph, Ashley	Research Associate	Eastside
11 Robinson, Melodie	Research Associate	Southbridge
12 Russell, Tiana	Research Associate	Southbridge
13 Watson, Dennis, aka "Feetz"	Research Associate	Southbridge
14 Wilson, Jonathon, aka "Run"	Research Associate	Westside
15 Wright, Corry	Research Associate	New Castle, DE

The literature review team learned how to conduct searches, review scholarly arguments, and prepare basic written summaries. The action team executed our activism agenda. We planned dozens of action events on homicide and structural inequality between 2010 and 2015. Yasser supervised the data collection subteam, and the data analysis team learned about data management and basic analysis. The data analysis subteam also entered survey data into SPSS and critically reviewed for accuracy, or "cleaned," all professionally transcribed interviews. Associates laughed when transcribers misspelled the names of rappers like Meek Mill and Oschino, and they found it amusing that educated transcribers did not know how to spell well-known hip-hop clothing brands like Sean John and Rocawear. The Associates also occasionally launched into soliloquies about why transcribers had typed "[inaudible]" when confused by the participant's use of colloquial "street" language. Catching these mistakes and inconsistencies made Associates even more suspicious about how outsiders interpreted their concerns. A feedback loop also existed between the data collection and data analysis subteams. After they had closely listened to and read interviews, the data collection team was informed of emerging themes.

We convened in our subteams for fifteen to twenty hours per week, and every two weeks we met as larger group at the Neighborhood House for about three hours to update each other on the progress of our subteams.

REFLEXIVITY IN THE ERA OF RADICAL STREET ETHNOGRAPHY
Reflections from Yasser

Radical street ethnography recognizes how race, ethnicity, gender, class, and community of origin are consequential in shaping the ethnographer's intentions or overall analysis. Deep critical reflexivity also reminds the street ethnographer that our work is a "political" project that must move beyond documenting people's suffering.[61] Randol Contreras warns of the lure of "cowboy" ethnography, intellectual "exoticism," or an empirical voyeurism that ultimately denigrates the character of street-identified communities.[62] Grappling with this topic of exploitative ethnography, L. J. Dance argues that urban Black voyeurism is fueled by an "essentialist gaze."[63] Inspired to write *Tough Fronts* after conservative scholars Stephan and Abigail Thernstrom spoke on "Black progress" at the Ninety-Fourth annual American Sociological Association conference, Dance wrote: "It is from such elite and lofty points of view that scholars have gazed upon Blacks in general and *urban* Black Americans in particular. This gaze has often degraded; other times it has flattered. But most of the time, it has been an essentialist gaze. I deliberately choose the words 'essentialist' and 'gaze' to characterize the academic enterprise of studying urban Black Americans. Disregarding contradictions and hybridity, as well as eclectic and syncretic practices, scholars have taken a long, fixed stare and found urban Blacks essentially inferior, or mainstream, or victims, or virtuous, or oppositional."[64]

To confront this essentialist gaze, we argue that no street ethnographic study is immune to it. Academic research and especially street ethnography are inherently exploitive enterprises born out of, and dependent on, this gaze. And while deep reflexivity is necessary, it can only (at best) disrupt, not eliminate, the gaze. For the street ethnographer, the streets or the "exotic" possess an irresistible and commodifiable set of tales.

Intense critical awareness forces ethnographers to account for the strengths and limitations of their standpoints and the impact of their personal experiences in the development of analysis. Thus, I had to acknowledge how poverty and violence shaped much of my early life and especially my point of view. Hard times provided a unique window to peek through—a window that filters my analysis on trauma, crime, inequality, and especially resilience from the perspective of poor Black Wilmington.

My immediate family were "the streets"—including my mother. The youngest of four boys with married Black American parents, I was raised by successful street hustlers in Harlem, New York City. When I was two, we moved from a crowded, three-bedroom apartment in Harlem River Houses (or housing projects) to a predominantly white and upper-middle-class section of Englewood, New Jersey. In Harlem, my parents owned two high-end boutiques and an arcade in Harlem's historic downtown epicenter—the corner of 125th Street and Seventh Avenue. Payne's Ladies Wear, Payne's Lingerie, and Payne's Outlet and Arcade sat on this corner from the 1970s to early 1990s. Scores of patrons swept through my parents' businesses, especially the arcade, which effectively operated as a community center. Local hip-hop and R&B artists, teenagers, street hustlers with shell-toe Adidas and Cazal shades, and even some politicians and neighborhood organizers stopped by. The arcade's walls were lined with eight-foot machines with the likes of Donkey Kong, Dungeons and Dragons, and Centipede. At the back of the arcade, glass cases were filled with well-designed "freebase" pipes for customers in need of a device to smoke cocaine. And on a warm summer day, a community bonanza covered the front doors as radio speakers blared the latest urban music.

James Payne was my father, and he was a dominant force in Harlem. He wisely used his social capital to enrich the community by bringing together nonprofit, religious, grassroots, and street leadership to sponsor local events and provide resources to residents in need. It is only in writing this introduction that I am able to fully grasp how instrumental my father's civic experiences were to my own personal and professional development. His constant messaging on Black empowerment seeded me with the inspiration and grassroots strategies needed to organize a research-activist program.

The streets of Harlem called him "Payne" or "Chief," and he was a very violent man. In fact, he was the most violent man I ever knew. And like many in the streets of Wilmington, my father was also socially progressive. Many of his sociopolitical positions took root when he was a bodyguard for Malcolm X and under the mentorship of Malcolm's sister Ella L. Collins. These early experiences with Malcolm and Ella inspired him to organize community programs in Harlem, including several voter-registration campaigns. Also, every Easter, Thanksgiving, Christmas, and New Year's Eve, my parents gave away hundreds of free turkeys, liquor, and other gifts to the people of Harlem.

The ups and downs of my formative experiences also led me to the streets, at least for a brief period in my life. In short, I sold large quantities of marijuana, dabbled in selling crack, and owned illegal guns. I was arrested several times but never convicted of a felony. I was an angry teenager and young adult who had acquired a small taste for violence. I had also been assaulted on a few occasions. Once I was jumped by fifteen to twenty street rivals, and on another occasion I was almost shot. I can still feel the bullets whistling by my right ear.

Now, as a full professor, I think very differently about my previous experiences. I am most surprised that I actually survived the social-structural traps that destroyed so many others. These transformative experiences ignited a critical awareness in my soul that compels me to this day to reach far into the streets, and to radically reframe opportunity and violence *with* them.

OUR STUDY WAS FUNDED IN 2009 by a state block grant from President Barack Obama's American Recovery and Reinvestment Act. Additional financial support was provided by the United Way of Delaware and a matching grant from the University of Delaware (UD)'s Office of the Provost. *Murder Town, USA* is written for academic and lay audiences, policymakers, grassroots organizations, people identified with the streets, the incarcerated, and the formerly incarcerated.

The first author, Yasser Arafat Payne, is the lead author, and *Murder Town, USA* is written from his first-person perspective. Brooklynn K. Hitchens and Darryl L. Chambers are also full authors and greatly aided in the substantive development of the book. Given the participatory nature of this project, each author contributed significantly to the development of both this manuscript and the overall research program.

Originally from the Northside neighborhood of Wilmington, Brooklynn K. Hitchens joined the study in 2010 as an undergraduate assistant at UD. While pursuing a PhD in sociology at Rutgers University, Hitchens rejoined our research program as a project director in 2016. She is now on the faculty at the University of Maryland, College Park. Darryl L. Chambers (aka "Wolfie" or "Wolf") was an original Street PAR Associate for this study. He later acquired his master's degree in criminology at the University of Delaware, where he works as a research associate for the Center for Drug and Health Studies. Mr. Chambers is also the executive director of the Center of Structural Equity in Wilmington, the center where our research program is housed.

Murder Town, USA: The Fundamental Outline

In December 2014, *Newsweek* released a fiery article, "Murder Town USA (aka) Wilmington, Delaware." Abigail Jones's examination of gun violence in Wilmington opened up a larger discussion about a city of two tales: how a small city's identity was forged and sustained by white wealth and by Black poverty. The publication of Jones's news story greatly disrupted this city's sociopolitical climate.[65] After 2014, city officials were forced to reckon with structural racism and the role it played in the maintenance of poor Black neighborhoods. Websites, conferences, newspaper and magazine articles, local residents, political platforms, nonprofit leadership, and local musicians all debated the extent to which Wilmington actually fit the moniker "Murder Town." Public officials worked hard to invalidate this framing. But many in the streets marveled at it, particularly when "Murder Town" was used to describe the connection between extreme white wealth and Black poverty, or how white wealth was tied to gun violence in Wilmington.

Our book project, *Murder Town, USA*, expands on Abigail Jones's core argument on race, wealth, and crime with a deeper analysis led by the people most affected by poverty and gun violence in Wilmington.[66] Missing from broader discussions is the analysis of voices most likely to perpetuate and be victimized by gun violence. It is only through and with those in the streets that it is possible to fully understand and develop interventions to improve their neighborhoods.

Part I, "Context of Opportunity and Violence," examines how structural violence has always contributed to homicide in Wilmington. Looking back to the 1800s, chapter 1, "A City of Banks," situates violence and crime within the financial or economic context of Wilmington. Chapter 2, "'Welcome to Wilmington—A Place to Be Somebody,'" describes how trust was established with three segments of the community in the Eastside and Southbridge: larger neighborhoods, street-identified environments, and community professionals. This chapter also outlines the sociocultural backdrop of Wilmington. Chapter 3, "'Murder Town, USA,'" addresses how street-identified Black men and women understand violence as an adaptive feature of life or an expression of resilience in local environments with little chance for mobility. In response to the anointing of Wilmington as "Murder Town, USA," formal leadership rushed to disavow this characterization. Young people in the streets, however, argued that this news coverage finally brought national attention to the violence and stark poverty generally experienced in Black Wilmington. This chapter also reveals that most participants did not experience violent victimization. Most argued that exposure to violence, or witnessing and hearing about others being assaulted or killed, were larger issues than being directly victimized.

Part II, "Management, Containment, and the Social Control of Black Wilmington," consists of three chapters that document the street's negotiation of economic survival with punitive opportunity, policing, and judicial environments. Chapter 4, "'I'm Still Waiting Man . . . on That Golden Ticket!,'" examines how joblessness, dilapidated housing, and poor schooling conditions contribute to gun violence. Given the structural obstacles they experienced, both men and women—but women more so—expressed concern about the well-being of their families. And for most men, it was a choice between engaging in crime and its collateral effects of physical injury, incarceration, and death or simply doing nothing and residing in extreme poverty. Chapter 5, "'F-ck the Police!,'" captures street-identified Black men and women's experiences with police. Everyone interviewed shared stories about either observing or personally experiencing negative contact with police. Many reported being disrespected, harassed, and brutalized. In addition, this chapter explores how the police murder of wheelchair-bound Jeremy McDole led to a long-lasting uneasiness in Wilmington.[67] In fact, in the subsequent weeks and months, several volatile interactions with police would be tied to McDole's murder. Chapter 6, "'I Don't Let These Felonies Hold Me Back!,'" unearths how many in the streets cared deeply about people returning home from prison, largely believed in their potential to thrive after incarceration, and often provided support to returning citizens. Re-entry programs were perceived to be complicit in the widespread system of structural oppression. Felony convictions, parole violations, unemployment, and poor housing were noted as key features of a larger structural violence complex. Boxed into disenfranchisement, returning citizens used a range of illegal and legal strategies to navigate re-entry.

Part III, "Street Agency," consists of three chapters that describe how the streets coped with and fought back against structural oppression. Chapter 7, "'Brenda's Got a Baby,'" focuses on how women kept Black families together in the wake of the incarceration of their men. Structural forces removed Black men from the home and made heterosexual marriage almost unobtainable, which perpetuated female-headed Black homes in Wilmington. As a result, the women were caught between participating in crime or low-wage work to provide for their children. This chapter also highlights how incarcerated women used street participatory action research to fight against sexual abuse in Baylor Women's Correctional Institution. Chapter 8, "'Street Love,'" reveals that street-identified Black men and women had high levels of psychological and social well-being. While they are often described as having low self-esteem or poor self-worth, we found that men and women in the streets thought highly of themselves and their families, and they often contributed positively to their communities. For most, "street love" represented the way they bonded with each other and gave back to their neighborhoods. Chapter 9, "'Winter Is Coming!,'" analyzes the anger that resulted in Wilmington from poor political leadership and deep structural inequality. Now more than ever, we heard calls for the streets to stand up to police violence, joblessness, or poverty.

We conclude *Murder Town, USA* with an argument for a radical shift in the field of street ethnography. Street ethnographers must collaborate more seriously with poor Black residents to harness their data in service of sociopolitical power. The data on poor Black people are invaluable, and residents have to be trained in how to access it and how to analyze and profit from their own information. Research institutions are well positioned to launch these kinds of translational research programs, given their wide network of private, foundation, and federal funding sources, as well as their relationships with state, county, and local governments.[68]

Many in the academy are beguiled into believing that the mere documentation of poor people's suffering is a form of help or real justice. Wade Nobles's concept of "scientific colonialism" rejects the colonization of data from Black communities.[69] Street PAR aligns with Nobles's argument and offers a reciprocal, research-activist paradigm that benefits poor Black American communities first, followed by traditional researchers.

Without more effective interventions, street-identified populations will continue to experience academic failure, drop out of school, be among the chronically unemployed, be victims and perpetrators of gun violence, and crowd our prisons at alarming rates.

To transform the people most ensnared in the criminal legal system, public leadership must believe in this group's potential and treat them with dignity by providing quality opportunities. Community professionals should learn how to engage street-identified Black men and women through research and activism—this undertaking would produce an inestimable return to schools, society, and the streets themselves. Like all of us, the streets deserve to live secure and fulfilling lives, and they deserve nothing short of our best efforts in helping them to do so.

Part One

Context of Opportunity and Violence

Chapter 1

A City of Banks

A LONG LEGACY OF ECONOMIC VIOLENCE AND CRIME

There has long been a thorny relationship between Wilmington's mostly Black, impoverished center and its largely white, wealthy suburbs. Riots that erupted after the 1968 assassination of the Rev. Martin Luther King Jr. devastated the downtown, and the nervous governor at the time set a nationwide record by deploying National Guard troops for nine months.
—Neil MacFarquhar, "After Centuries of Obscurity, Wilmington Is Having a Moment"

In Wilmington, where about a quarter of the population lives in poverty and many lifelong residents barely make more than their parents, the American Dream has remained just that—a dream.

...about 60 percent...in Southbridge are employed. About 86 percent...are from low-income families who have never left Wilmington....

Nowhere else in Delaware is there so little economic mobility. It's hard to find many places in the United States where those who grew up in low-income families are making as little as $14,000 a year.
—Jessica Bies, "Wilmington: One of the Hardest Places to Achieve the American Dream"

IT WAS FRIDAY, and I looked forward to spending the evening with my childhood friend, Tommy (a pseudonym), who now lives in Middletown, Delaware, a fast-growing, middle-class suburban town. Like me, Tommy was originally from Harlem, had relocated to Englewood, New Jersey, and then later moved to Delaware to start his professional life with the New Castle County Police Department. Tommy's father was a local drug dealer who was shot and killed in Harlem when Tommy was nine. Emotionally broken, Tommy's mother used crack cocaine to cope with his father's death.

"She already was playing with that powder [cocaine]," Tommy said. "My father's murder sent her over the edge, though. That's why she got strung out."

His father's homicide worsened the poverty and addiction already affecting his home in Harlem. Tommy soon moved in with his uncle in Englewood, New Jersey, a nearby small town. Although Tommy and I were both from Harlem, we actually first met in Englewood, where he lived with his uncle, aunt, and two older cousins in a subsidized apartment complex called King Gardens. Tommy had a child by the time he was in eighth grade, and in eleventh grade Tommy left his uncle's apartment. Tommy moved in with our mutual friend Scott. Eight months later he was kicked out after his relationship with Scott's younger sister was uncovered.

After a decade or so, Tommy and I reconnected in Delaware. He was unemployed and divorced, with six children with five different mothers. Tommy explained that he had recently resigned from the New Castle County Police Department.

Tommy tried his best to hold onto his four-bedroom home in Middletown. No longer able to afford the mortgage, he moved to a smaller three-bedroom home nearby. Both homes fell into foreclosure. After a few months at a friend's home, Tommy was able to save enough to secure a townhouse in another area of Middletown.

On that Friday evening, Tommy, his friend Herman, our mutual friend Scott from New York City, and I celebrated at an unofficial housewarming of Tommy's new townhouse. At first, Herman was standoffish, and Scott was slightly offended by his "dark energy." In any case, after Herman and Scott relaxed, the four of us had a ball in Tommy's mostly unfurnished home. We downplayed Tommy's hard times with laughing, eating, and drinking the night away. And Herman stole the evening with his humor.

Herman was a 47-year-old Jamaican American who I learned later was well known in the streets of Wilmington. That evening he was dressed in all black, and his giant smile exposed a few of his sparkling gold-capped teeth. He was slightly pudgy and had caramel-brown skin, a "low Caesar" haircut, and a trimmed slim mustache. A rhythmic patois spilled from his mouth as he filled Tommy's empty place with joke after joke after joke. Elated to meet Herman, I looked forward to enjoying his friendship.

Three weeks later, Herman Curry was shot and killed in Eden Park on a Saturday afternoon in July 2012.[1] Eden Park was located in Wilmington's Southbridge neighborhood, with a large, looming, and rusted traffic light at the park's narrow entrance. Much of the land surrounding the ten-acre park was closed to the public. Abandoned by industry, these lands were generally considered to be contaminated. Eden Park was fenced in and its entrance was encased in stonewall. Lumpy dried soil, crabgrass, dandelions, and patches of sun-burnt grass blotted most of the park. Gravel and dirt pits were interspersed throughout. In the center of the park sat a worn-down basketball court with loose sand under both rims.

"This couldn't be the Herman I met at Tommy's," I thought as I read this news article. I took a seat after reading about Herman's Jamaican background. Before I could digest the news any further, my eyes ran across an indisputable photograph of Herman Curry.

Otis Phillips (age 34), Jeffrey Phillips (no relation, 22), and Sheldon Olge (43)—three reputed members of Wilmington's Sure Shot Jamaican-based street gang—slowly approached Herman seconds before his public remarks at the well-attended Marcus Garvey Soccer Tournament. Since 1996, people from near and far had attended this annual soccer tournament and Caribbean picnic, which lately had been organized by Herman.

Otis Phillips gently tapped Herman on the shoulder and whispered, "Ninja, run, p-ssy, today you are dead." Unknowingly, Herman turned around into gunfire. He was shot six times in the chest, in front of hundreds gathered in Eden Park. A shoot-out ensued between the three gunmen and Herman's "shooters," or unlicensed bodyguards. Hyperaware that his life was under threat, Herman had made sure to keep security around him at public events. But on this day, his security was unable to prevent his murder.

Herman lay on the grass grasping for breath, with blood spilling out of his chest and mouth. Amid the melee, Herman's shooters shot Sheldon Olge multiple times and also shot each of the other two gunmen, Otis Phillips and Jeffrey Phillips, in their legs. All three gunmen managed to escape in their car. Olge, the getaway driver, succumbed to his bullet wounds and crashed a few blocks away, near the Henrietta Johnson Medical Center in Southbridge. Ironically, Olge crashed into the center's large sign that read, "Helping, Healing, Caring." Otis Phillips and Jeffrey Phillips made a run for it, but they were tracked down by police dogs. Behind bushes in a vacant lot, their bullet-riddled legs were mauled until police arrived.

During the shoot-out, two bystanders were also shot. Sixteen-year-old Alexander Kamara, a resident of the nearby upper-middle-class Pike Creek community, was shot in the head and killed, and a 33-year-old man from Baltimore received a minor gunshot wound in his shoulder. Both Otis Phillips and Jeffery Phillips were charged with two counts of first-degree murder in the deaths of Curry and Kamara, one count of first-degree, attempted murder for the injured man from Baltimore, and conspiracy and possession of a firearm during the commission of a crime.

I soon found out that Herman's death was a result of witness retaliation. Prior to the shooting, police were looking for Otis Phillips, who was on the run for several years. Otis was a suspect in the 2008 murder of 40-year-old Chris Palmer, a bodyguard at a local nightclub in the Eastside. Herman threw a birthday party at the nightclub, and Chris would not allow Otis to enter the club because he was armed. Otis felt disrespected and shot up the birthday party in a fit of rage, killing Chris Palmer. It was unclear whether Chris's death was intentional, but Herman had witnessed the homicide and was prepared to testify against Otis. The 2008 slaying of Chris Palmer was the primary reason Otis ordered the public execution of Herman. In an effort to prevent Herman from testifying, Otis returned to Southbridge in 2012 to kill Herman. Jeffrey and Otis received life sentences, and Otis also received the death penalty.

I knew Herman for one evening. He was the proud father of six children, and he bragged about them that evening at Tommy's. Very little suggested he had only a few weeks to live. Maybe there were signs. Herman was noticeably guarded when Scott and I arrived. Maybe a prescience of death explained why he did not drink alcohol that evening. Perhaps the threat of death explained why he wore all black with a thin leather jacket on a warm summer night. I now wonder if he had a concealed firearm on his person. Given the danger he faced, having a firearm would have been wise; it made good sense in the context.

That night at Tommy's home, I was oblivious to Herman's behavioral subtleties. But Scott was not, nor was he surprised when informed about Herman's death.

Neither was Tommy when I called him, in disbelief.

"Hello."

"Did you hear what happened to Herman?"

Calm and undaunted, he chuckled, "Yeah, I did. That's how it goes down in Wilmington sometimes."

"What happened? Why was he killed?" Conjecture surrounding Herman's death was rampant at the time.

"My understanding was, Herm was into some things he shouldn't have been. And they say he was about to snitch."

I didn't understand Tommy's causal response and why he appeared unalarmed. After all, Herman was his friend, and we'd spent the evening laughing in Tommy's home just weeks earlier. But Tommy sounded more concerned about returning to whatever my phone call interrupted.

A lot of time passed before Tommy and I reconnected in Delaware. He had changed considerably and was not the Tommy I knew in Englewood. Hardened and much angrier, Tommy blistered with a selfishness and stiff meanness. Tough times changed Tommy. Although he promised to, Tommy never called me about Herman's funeral arrangements. Tommy's coarse treatment of Herman's death was strangely common in the streets of Wilmington. Particularly for those who did not retaliate, immediately detaching from deaths was quite adaptive to surviving. The smallness of these neighborhoods forced rivals to quickly demonstrate, rather than conceal, their intentions toward one another. Tommy and several others stood down. If you did not have the resources to leave town, then there were few places to permanently hide. Wilmington's Sure Shot gang's brazen swarm on Eden Park strongly suggested they were prepared to do whatever they considered necessary to resolve a dispute. From their perspective, pre-emptive displays of murderous rage were protective mechanisms against snitching, or a suitable strategy to ensure their survival.

Herman's death, like so many other homicides before his, reverberated for months inside Southbridge and larger Wilmington. Slayings of Black boys and men were frequent and particularly disruptive to Wilmington's social order. A breakdown in cultural values was often claimed to be the cause of these homicides. But from our perspective, violence metastasized from concentrated disadvantage, and both ills were tied to Wilmington's structural arrangement of white wealth and Black poverty.

STRUCTURAL CONTEXT OF THE EASTSIDE AND SOUTHBRIDGE

Wilmington's wealth ensured that the city remained the social, political, and economic engine of Delaware. Dover was Delaware's capital, but Wilmington was the state's effective capital. Politicians and local news often touted, "As goes Wilmington, so goes the state of Delaware."[2] The social and structural winds or forces in Wilmington were so strong and centralized that nearly all major stakeholders in Delaware had an office in Wilmington, including the governor and both U.S. senators.

Given the centers of power and opportunity nestled in Wilmington, thousands commuted into Wilmington each day. During the five-day work week, Wilmington's population doubled, to about 130,000–150,000.[3] Wilmington's professional community sprawled throughout the downtown area, and most businesses closed by 7:00 P.M.

Wilmington's seventeen square miles consisted of forty-two recognized small neighborhoods located in five major sections of the city: Northside, Northeast, Westside, Eastside, and Southbridge. The Eastside and Southbridge were much smaller sections than the other three, and as a result, only three small neighborhoods in the Eastside and two small neighborhoods in Southbridge were officially recognized by the City of Wilmington. While there was no formal consensus on the ground, local residents did not necessarily agree with the city's demarcations of neighborhoods.

Black residents in the Eastside and Southbridge perceived those who lived in their housing complexes, stretches of row houses, and streets to be a "local community." In general, a neighborhood was perceived to be a small collective of families ranging from several dozen to a few hundred. Largely due to structural vulnerability, most people in these small collectives were also bounded to one another for social, political, and financial support.[4] For the purposes of our study, and given the smallness of these communities, the Eastside (5,000) and Southbridge (2,000) were conceptualized as "large neighborhoods," or city sections with small communities inside them.

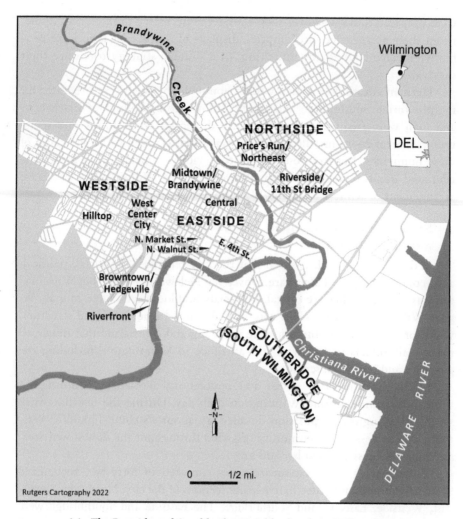

1.1. The Eastside and Southbridge Neighborhoods in Wilmington

The Eastside and Southbridge were adjacent sections or large neighborhoods, or were juxtaposed in the most eastern and southeastern corner of Wilmington (see figure 1.1). The Eastside (7%) and Southbridge (3%) together accounted for only about 10% of all of Wilmington's residents. There were approximately 7,000 people between these two neighborhoods, and young Black adults (ages 18–35) roughly accounted for 1,600 of them in the Eastside and Southbridge. Both the Eastside and Southbridge were primarily populated by low-income Black residents, although Black middle- and upper-middle-class niches were nestled in small neighborhoods like Downtown Eastside and Christina Landing in Southbridge.

TABLE 1.1
Demographic Characteristics: Survey Sample

	Males	Females	Average
Age	24.8	25.5	25.2
Married*	5%	5.4%	5.2%
Low-income housing**	61%	66%	64%
Employed	32%	39%	36%
Completed high school	53%	59%	56%
Trade experience	28%	38%	34%
Incarcerated	65%	34%	48%

*Calculation includes participants that are legally married, married but separated, and widowed.

**Low-income housing includes multifamily homes.

But for the most part, adverse conditions cut across large swathes of the Eastside and Southbridge. Southbridge's housing project and the Eastside's Compton and Bethel Villa housing projects were among the larger tenements in these communities. Late-night shootings sometimes occurred outside of Southbridge's Marvin's Casbar Lounge on Lobdell Street and City Tavern Bar on the corner of A and South Claymont Streets.[5] Two blocks away was the intersection of New Castle Avenue and A Street, a well-known social space in Southbridge that was rowdy on some evenings. Several impoverished corners also blotted the Eastside, including Bennett and Taylor Streets, and North Pine and Lombard Streets.

Median household incomes in the Eastside and Southbridge were $23,375 and $20,221, respectively.[6] The Eastside comprised three census tracts (9, 17, and 20); tract 17 was the poorest and had the largest concentration of low-income Black Americans. Sixty percent of household income in tract 17 made less than $15,000 per year; 44% lived below the poverty line; and the median income for tract 17 was $11,500. Nearly 40% of household incomes in Southbridge (tract 19) made less than $15,000, and 40% lived below the poverty line.

Based on our survey data of street-identified Black men and women in both the Eastside and Southbridge (N = 520), 44% did not have a high school diploma and nearly two-thirds were unemployed and lived in poor housing (see table 1.1). Only 34% had any trade experience, and the women (38%) surprisingly reported more trade expertise than the men (28%). Also, nearly 50% were incarcerated, with the number of men (65%) almost double the number of women (34%).

The Eastside

The Eastside was made up of three small neighborhoods: Downtown Eastside ("the mall" or downtown location of Wilmington); Upper Eastside;

and the larger and poorer Eastside. Delaware's white elite lived and worked in the Downtown and Upper Eastside, and Upper Westside; or on any given workday, these three areas teemed with a predominantly white professional class. This part of the Eastside and Westside also held a sizable banking district, dozens of law offices, and a smattering of churches, restaurants, shops, and condominiums. Bragging about Wilmington's wealth and the city's strong potential to get more, Mayor Dennis P. Williams said, "There's approximately $500 million worth of private and public investment taking place in our city. Specifically, the 380 downtown apartments, Woodlawn Flats, Residence Inn Marriott, Christina River Bridge, South Wilmington Wetlands Park, Wilmington Skate Plaza, Sacred Heart Village II, and Harper Thiel are just a few projects that will continue to spark job creation. In addition, the arena I proposed to be created on the Riverfront will make Wilmington even more competitive as a destination for meeting, conference, and convention business."[7]

Walnut Street was the major dividing line between poverty and wealth in the Eastside. On one side of Walnut Street was the ultraprivileged in Downtown Eastside, and on the other side was the larger Eastside with some of Wilmington's poorest Black neighborhoods.

Southbridge

Called "the South" by the streets, Southbridge was the smallest and most isolated section of Wilmington. Within Southbridge was a small, gentrified neighborhood (Christina Landing) near the John E. Reilly drawbridge. The larger Southbridge community, however, was predominantly low-income and Black. On most days, one could find several homeless Black men asking for change to pump gas or clean car windows at the BP gas station on New Castle Avenue. A few businesses thrived in Southbridge: a local clinic (Henrietta Johnson), a barbershop (Runn Way Unisex), a convenience store (K-N-F Market), a liquor store (Dugan's), a gas station (BP Gas), and two local bars or lounges (City Tavern Bar and Marvin's Casbar Lounge). At the time of our study, Southbridge had no grocery stores, few recreational spaces, and no restaurants.

History of Crime, Poverty, and Wealth

Black Wilmington has always been poor. This racialized poverty can easily be traced back to Wilmington's post-Reconstruction period in the late 1800s, when brutal forms of economic deprivation impacted the well-being of Black Wilmington.[8] In 1889, two white reporters from the *Evening Journal* were escorted by police into the "darker side of Delaware's Metropolis," where recently freed Black Wilmingtonians dwelled. The reporters described a grim scene of "slums" full of "misery," overcrowded homes shared by "twenty-five families," and a "stream of dark humanity" plagued by blight and disorder.[9] Through the 1900s, economic conditions for Blacks in Wilmington remained bleak. Despite being more educated than white immigrants, Blacks were the most "invisible" of Wilmington's ethnic groups—employed in the least desirable industrial jobs as unskilled laborers, or as service workers such as laundresses or domestics, and excluded from the clerical, managerial, and technical jobs available only to whites.[10] Poor Black residents continued to dwell in "shacks" in back alleys that were "unspeakably unsanitary, with open sewerage . . . floating on the stagnant water of the swamps," and were disproportionately susceptible to tuberculosis, rheumatism, and typhoid.[11] Remarkably, conditions remained unchanged through the twentieth century. Over one hundred years after Emancipation, Black Wilmingtonians suffered in "rat-infested homes torn apart with age" and from the stressors of city living: "over-crowding, dehumanization, loss of community, [and] loss of compassion for one's fellow beings."[12] Concentrated disadvantage shaped the economic deprivation of Black Wilmington, and for some, street life was and is an unfortunate by-product of living in spaces with scarce resources.

Black poverty in Wilmington, both then and now, existed alongside an overwhelming concentration of white wealth or immense corporate greed and political power. One of the wealthiest families in the United States, the du Ponts, first rose to power in Wilmington. In 1802, E. I. du Pont de Nemours developed gunpowder mills that revolutionized U.S. military warfare, soon obtaining a "near monopoly of the munitions market," a position the family currently maintains.[13] Manufacturing explosives during World War I, the du Ponts became the major supplier of military powder to the Allies, which catapulted the wealth of the family.[14] Largely as a result of the family's prosperity, by 1918 Wilmington was called a "Magic City," the "Wealthiest City per Capita in America."[15] Soon, the du Ponts expanded from gunpowder to other chemical products for World War II: nylon, Teflon, ingredients for the drug industry and the atomic bomb, and other war-related products.[16] They transformed Wilmington into one of the "Chemical and Corporate Capitals of the World," and continued to dominate nearly every aspect of Delaware life, including politics.[17] The du Ponts were even known to manipulate the votes of poor Blacks (who largely voted Republican until the 1960s) to keep the Republican Party in power.[18]

With a current net worth of over $14 billion, the du Ponts continue to be key members of the corporate ruling elite. They helped position Wilmington as a corporate welfare state and a central hub for the banking and credit card industries.[19] In fact, Wilmington's downtown area is home to the headquarters of nearly two-thirds of all Fortune 500 firms and nearly half of all publicly traded U.S. companies—including shell companies for corporate giants like Apple, Bank of America, Google, Coca-Cola, the New York Stock Exchange, NASDAQ, and Walmart.[20] Drawn by Delaware's relaxed domestic and foreign tax regulations, businesses flock to the state, where they are able to shift revenues to holding companies in Delaware and then minimize taxes paid to other states.[21] Delaware secures an 8.7% corporate income tax rate from all domestic or foreign corporations that conduct business in the state. Large businesses and chain stores pay royalties to sister companies in other states, which allows Google, for example, to avoid paying millions of dollars in California income tax. Thus, Delaware has easily become the "biggest state provider of offshore corporate secrecy."[22] And Wilmington has transformed into a "corporate haven" for national and international businesses alike, filtering millions of dollars through the city and concentrating wealth for privileged residents and financiers.[23]

Most infamously, Delaware's tax code does not require limited liability companies (LLCs) to report "beneficial ownership information," or the legal names and addresses of persons who own and profit from the LLC. As a result of this loophole, LLCs in Delaware have been used to launder and hide money in shell companies.[24] For instance, drug trafficker Joaquín "El Chapo" Guzmán's tequila company, as well as nine companies owned by Paul Manafort (former campaign manager to Donald Trump) were registered in Wilmington. All of these businesses were believed to be used to launder tens of millions of dollars.[25]

Wilmington is also a city of banks. Its ruthless financial culture was seeded by the state legislature in the late 1970s and then solidified by former governor Pierre "Pete" S. du Pont IV.[26] In 1981, Governor du Pont ratified the Financial Center Development Act, which established Wilmington as one of the largest and most influential banking districts in the country. Wilmington's elevated banking stature has more to do with its credit card division than with investment banking, which still is firmly headquartered in New York City.[27] According to Wink, this form of "high-stakes economic development" is significantly responsible for Americans' "ballooning credit card debt."[28]

Such corporate and political wrangling—and the resultant wealth—comes at the expense of poor, mostly Black families who have historically been an exploited labor force in this country, and in Wilmington specifically. Despite being the home of wealthy leaders like President Joseph R. Biden, Wilmington remains a tale of two cities, where wealth germinates blocks away from concentrated poverty. The city's racial wealth gap has created two Wilmingtons: one for the "haves," who are mostly white, middle- and upper-middle-class residents, and one for the "have-nots," who are mostly Black, lower-income residents. Leafy, million-dollar estates with "manicured lawns . . . enshrouded in a peaceful cocoon" sit near housing projects and vacant and "rundown, two-story brick row houses."[29] The city's white-Black dissimilarity index of residential segregation is 55.4 according to 2010 U.S. Census data, which suggests that at the time of the study, over 55% of Wilmington's white population would need to move to another neighborhood to make whites and Blacks evenly distributed across the city. This index is comparable to those of Minneapolis (50.9), San Francisco (52.8), and New Haven, Connecticut (50.7), though not as high as hypersegregated cities like Chicago (82.5), Flint,

Michigan (65.9), and Philadelphia (73.4). Concentrated disadvantage, residential segregation, and unemployment exacerbate economic stressors, particularly in small, interwoven cities like Wilmington. These inequities also increase the likelihood that people will embrace street life, crime, and violence in urban communities.[30]

When Everything Hit the Fan

Street violence has always been a historical feature of Wilmington. For over a century, Black Wilmington was cast as a "bad place to be alone in," "danger[ous] to life and pocketbook," "reeking of filth," with "iniquitous dens" of sex and crime.[31] The framing of poor Blacks in Wilmington during the 1800s suggested violent lawlessness: "a colored woman who periodically beat her little daughter," "blacks who stand on the corners and fight among themselves," and "many people in the vicinity who teach their children to steal."[32]

Poor Black women and girls were also framed as illiterate, "genus of 'Chippie,'" or cheap and sexually promiscuous, and prone to violence and vulgarity.[33] A 1930s report on Wilmington concluded that "although they made up only 11 percent of the city's population, blacks accounted for 35 percent of those convicted of crimes . . . [but] since most of the victims were black, too, whites were apathetic."[34] Alongside this criminal framing came an onslaught of race-based practices designed to oppress Black Wilmingtonians, notably through Jim Crow laws in housing and urban renewal, policing, and state-sanctioned violence.

Prior to the 1930s, most Blacks in Wilmington were segregated to slums in the Eastside and Southbridge neighborhoods. There they paid more than poor white immigrants for their "paltry housing," and 1930 data suggest that almost half of Wilmington homes had no indoor plumbing.[35] Particularly in the Eastside, blight persisted through the mid-1900s, with "broken windows, unhinged doorways, collapsing plaster ceilings, dilapidated [and] overused wooden privies."[36] To contain the growing Black population and meet working-class whites' need for public housing, Wilmington created the Wilmington Housing Authority in 1938.

Following years of rising socioeconomic instability, Wilmington reached a boiling point in the 1960s, when it "unmistakably entered a spiral of decline."[37] Scholars have well documented how police used surveillance and racial coercion to suppress and criminalize Black militant groups and gangs.[38] The Wilmington Police Department (WPD) have historically used violent coercion to monitor and oppress "lawless gangs," even if it meant that "several heads were broken."[39] Lynching of Black men, once a legalized form of racial terror, occurred under the watch of the WPD into the 1900s.[40] Delaware was also the last state to outlaw whipping posts—in 1972—and posts were still on public display until 2020.[41]

State violence against Black Wilmingtonians continued until conditions exploded in the 1960s. A racially volatile decade, the 1960s represented the apex of racial, economic, and political injustice in inner cities across the country. Hundreds of "race riots" swept the nation from 1964 to 1971, as poor Blacks grew frustrated and resentful of living in poverty and the false promises for change.[42] Indeed, as Dr. Martin Luther King Jr. adeptly warned in 1967, a "riot is the language of the unheard," and the result of centuries of impeded racial progress. Sick of outrageously high rents for "atrocious" housing, slum landlords, blocked access to unions and jobs, inferior schools, and inadequate social services, Black Wilmingtonians joined this fight, leading the 1967 riots in the Westside.[43] Blacks destroyed and looted white-owned stores, bricked police cars, and lashed out with violence until Mayor John E. Barbiarz "restored order" by instituting a curfew.[44] He and Governor Terry threated Black residents with the National Guard if residents did not squelch all unrest.[45]

Police aided in this political repression. Under the pretense of suppressing "Black gangs" who supposedly posed a moral, quality-of-life threat to Wilmington, the WPD decimated "grassroots leadership of the ghetto" through police surveillance, raids, brutality, and incarceration. Police infiltrated the Wilmington Youth Emergency Action Council (WYEAC), a social justice organization with street-identified Black members known to be politically active.[46] Federal and local funds were then cut for WYEAC, which usurped a lifeline of Black cooperative economics and resistance in Wilmington.[47] The Delaware state legislature even threatened to cut welfare payments, and when a group of poor Wilmington residents went to protest in Legislative Hall, they were met with state policemen and National Guardsmen.[48]

The assassination of Martin Luther King Jr. in 1968 was the final straw: Wilmington and cities all over the nation again erupted in violence. Black Wilmington was fed up with a "disregard for Black life" through institutional failures and generational traumas.[49] The small city amassed about $250,000 in property damage (or about $2.2 million in today's value) from dozens of fires, firebombed police cars, sniping incidents, and injuries—and police arrested hundreds of residents.[50]

Though this outbreak of violence was mild in comparison to that in surrounding cities like Baltimore, Washington, DC, and Newark, New Jersey, the state government's reaction was extreme. Declaring a state of emergency on April 9, 1968, Governor Charles Terry brought about 3,500 National Guardsmen into Wilmington, whose population then was merely 95,000.[51] Donning M1 rifles, automatic shotguns, Thompson submachine guns, steel helmets, and body armor, the National Guard primarily patrolled the city's Black neighborhoods of West Center City, Northside, Eastside and Southbridge in "radio-equipped jeeps" alongside local and state troopers.[52] With this act, Wilmington succumbed to racialized state violence never seen before. Months after rioting stopped in Wilmington and other cities, Wilmington was still under the control of an armed, mostly white and male occupying army. The National Guard occupation of Wilmington lasted over nine months, which remains the longest guard occupation of any U.S. city since the Civil War.[53]

The fallout was catastrophic. Black Wilmingtonians were embittered: left with riot-torn neighborhoods, white Wilmingtonians began to relocate en masse, and the WPD maintains a tense relationship with Black residents to this day. Neighborhood instability, along with the violent occupation of the National Guard, also facilitated an increase of street violence between Black residents in Wilmington.[54] In May 1968, the murder of Leonard Flowers, a prominent gang member and one of Wilmington's "modern-day Robin Hoods," debilitated the city's Black neighborhoods further, because the informal community leader had been gunned down by another gang member.[55] Black gangs began to war, fighting each other for the limited territory and resources available to poor people in Wilmington.[56] Now pointing inward, violent street life increased as a consequence of the decimation and weakening of Black Wilmington.

The Making of Murder Town, USA

Through the 1960s, police warred with Black Wilmington, and youth responded to the criminalization and oppression by embracing street life. Long a feature of Wilmington's neighborhoods, poor Black gangs such as the Jayhawkers, Mountain Dew Gang, Romans, Stompers, and Blackie Blacks "often attacked police with bricks and bottles" and were supposedly "hostile" and "highly territorial."[57]

Violence in Wilmington escalated in the 1990s, though larger cities experienced a dramatic decline in violent crime beginning in 1991. In 1996 and 1997, Wilmington broke its first records in shooting victims and homicide, with 108 and 107 shooting victims, respectively.[58] Between 1993 to 1996, 911 calls increased by 83%, specifically for assault, burglary, drugs, and homicide.[59] The majority of shooting victims and suspects were Black males under the age of 25, and most had at least one violent felony arrest.[60] By 1997, Delaware responded to this spike in violent crime and open-air drug markets with Operation Safe Streets and the Governor's Task Force, a statewide crime reduction initiative that targeted Blacks deemed "high risk probationers," through police surveillance, sweeps, arrest of curfew violators, and even special operations with the FBI; the Drug Enforcement Administration; the Bureau of Alcohol, Tobacco, Firearms and Explosives; the U.S. Marshals Service; and the Secret Service.[61] This large-scale infiltration of Black neighborhoods resulted in a power vacuum in the streets that many believe partly explains the current elevated rates of gun violence in Wilmington. Children and grandchildren of former hustlers were left without role models or leadership, leading to a "resurgence of new emerging street groups."[62] Wilmington, now routinely called one of the "most dangerous small cities in America," had a violence problem that cost the state $611 million per year.[63]

Wilmington remains a hearty tale of two cities. The minority is ruthlessly ambitious, wealthy, and generally white—and the majority is a predominantly Black American community that faces the long intergenerational wrath of crime and structural violence. Smaller, whiter Wilmington has always been dependent on the social-structural dislocation of poor Black Wilmington, including its cheap labor, unemployment, and poverty. White Wilmington is dependent on poor Black Wilmington as an employment source for a cottage industry of public safety, social and medical services, and schools—all created and maintained for mostly white professionals living in and outside the city.

Wilmington is also a prideful, tribal, and territorial town—and this city's territorialism is interlaced along racial, ethnic and class lines, from Wilmington's corporate sectors to its street corners. Street PAR Associates and the institutional partnership guarded us—the university researchers—against this abrasive cultural dynamic. The program partners' professional capital eased challenges with Wilmington's bureaucratic or corporate arm, and the Associates' social capital provided ground-level legitimacy, which translated into wide support for the project in the community.

Wilmingtonians are also very appreciative of their city's smallness. Surrounded by big corporate cities (e.g., New York City, Philadelphia, Baltimore, and Washington, DC), Wilmington's small but thriving corporate sector means they have fewer people to compete with, as compared to bigger cities. But while small city size means more white wealth, this further constricts resources for poor Black Wilmington. Small city size ensured a greater concentration of poverty, crime, and especially violence inside communities like the Eastside and Southbridge.

Black Wilmington leverages what positive advantages it can from its smallness, relying on its social networks in a city where it is possible for most to connect in person. Social capital and a vibrant social network have significant value in a small state like Delaware and a "big small" city like Wilmington. Delawareans treasure their smallness and commonly refer to the advantages of a small space as the "Delaware Way"—the ability for most in a state of only 1 million, and 71,000 in Wilmington, to personally reach out to one another.[64] But while smallness created a level of cultural intimacy that many embraced, small city size also exacerbated violent inequities in the Eastside and Southbridge.

Wilmington's historical record on poverty and violence was invaluable to our Street PAR project. Admittedly, the city's record was overwhelming to process and strongly suggested little would or *could* change. But the political stars had aligned for us. A small window of opportunity to push back opened for men and women from the streets of Wilmington. And we were in! No matter what it meant. Whether we could resist or not, we organized as if we were going to change the world. As far as we were concerned, what other choice did we have?

CHAPTER 2

"Welcome to Wilmington—A Place to Be Somebody"

NEGOTIATING CITY CULTURE AND
BUILDING RAPPORT

> This is the crime of which I accuse my country and my countrymen, ... that they have destroyed and are destroying hundreds of thousands of lives and do not know it and do not want to know it. —James Baldwin, *The Fire Next Time*

> I noticed [another researcher] employed the term "peer researchers" to refer to participants he had trained to conduct surveys and to enter quantitative data in Excel. His idea of using program participants was quite intriguing.... Still I wanted to go beyond employing them merely to do routinized activities such as conducting surveys someone else had created and entering data into a computer. I wanted to use their intelligence and to cultivate their practical and critical skills.
> ... community members control a valuable resource for knowledge that is not easily matched by what the sociologist can gather or observe.
> —Joshua M. Price, "Conflict over Approaches to Social Science Research"

DELAWARE IS ONE of the original thirteen colonies, and this ambitious small colony despised British rule so much that it joined the American Revolution to secure its own political and economic fiefdom. Because Delaware was first to ratify the U.S. Constitution on December 7, 1787, Delaware is affectionately regarded as the "First State." Delaware's nickname is so catchy that "The First State" is stamped on various social and professional paraphernalia, from T-shirts, hats, and coffee mugs to license plates and even local hip-hop mixtapes.

Delaware was colonized first by the Dutch in 1631, then the Swedish in 1638 and the British in 1664.[1] The founding colonizers determined that

Delaware had great trading capacity and the potential to become a small financial paradise. Delaware occupies the northeastern section of the Delmarva Peninsula, a 180-mile landform that includes Delaware, Maryland, and Virginia. Delaware's close proximity to the Chesapeake Bay, Delaware River, and the Atlantic Ocean gives the state a unique advantage in domestic and international maritime trade. When the Swedish arrived in Delaware in 1638, they developed a trading colony they named Fort Christina. Under British rule, Fort Christina was renamed Wilmington in 1739. Since its early eighteenth-century origins, Wilmington was considered a prosperous "river city" that sat between the Christina and Brandywine Rivers.[2] One of Delaware's major ports, the port of Wilmington, is the state's largest container port and controls about 2 million tons of cargo annually.[3]

Delaware's ports were also used to traffic thousands of enslaved Black bodies from Africa through the Delaware River. The Swedes first introduced African slavery to Delaware in 1639, but slavery increased exponentially under the British.[4] By the early 1700s, Wilmington and larger Delaware had a critical mass of free, enslaved, and legally incarcerated Black people.[5] By the early 1800s, slaves accounted for one-third of Delaware's total population, and Black men and women made up one-third of Delaware's incarcerated population.[6] Southbridge was also a major post on the Underground Railroad for runaway slaves until 1860, when slavery officially ended in Wilmington.[7] According to local historian Harmon Carey, Southbridge was the "cradle of Black political leadership" because of its strong abolitionist movement, and the subsequent Black activist movements that also emerged from this small neighborhood.[8]

Wilmington slowly evolved into "A Place to Be Somebody," and corporate industries prospered in this city between the post–Civil War period and World War I (1865–1914). Bustling industry drew large numbers of Europeans immigrants, Black families, and aspiring professionals and their families. In 1860 there were 21,250 residents; by 1920, Wilmington's population had increased to over 110,000.[9]

Delaware has three counties—New Castle, Kent, and Sussex—and over half of the state's population (550,000) lives in its northern county, New Castle. New Castle County hosts a majority of the state's progressive organizations (e.g., Pacem in Terris and Delaware Coalition of the New Jim Crow), and central (Kent County) and southern (Sussex County) Delaware are much more rural, white, and conservative. Given the groundswell of residents in north Delaware, economic and political power ultimately rests in New Castle County. And at the heart of New Castle County is Wilmington, the largest city, with the densest concentration of people in Delaware.

Black Wilmington is also negatively affected by poverty and crime, and especially distressed by gun violence. In 2010, at the start of our study, Wilmington recorded 197.5 violent crimes per 10,000 people, a 3.3% overall increase

TABLE 2.1
Crimes in the Eastside and Southbridge

	Eastside	Southbridge
Assault	547 (7%)	406 (5%)
Aggravated assault	151 (6%)	145 (6%)
Kidnapping	8 (6%)	9 (6%)
Drugs	444 (6%)	209 (3%)
Weapons	140 (5%)	129 (5%)
Robbery	82 (5%)	51 (3%)
Stolen property	19 (5%)	16 (4%)
Burglary	129 (4%)	168 (6%)
Theft	379 (4%)	537 (5%)
Prostitution	4 (13%)	3 (10%)
Homicide	2 (5%)	2 (5%)

Crime reported to police between January 1, 2007, and November 12, 2010. Numbers in parentheses are the percent of those total Wilmington crimes. Southbridge accounts for 2% of Wilmington's population, while the Eastside accounts for 7% of Wilmington's population. Also, these crime rates do not reflect crimes committed by Eastside and Southbridge residents in other parts of the city.

SOURCE: Ira Porter, "Hope Where Others See None. Project Goes Straight to the People to Cut Crime, Poverty—My Neighborhood: A Special News Journal Report," *News Journal*, November 21, 2010, A12.

in violent crime from the prior year, as well as a 13% increase in property crime.[10] Most of the violence in Wilmington actually occurred in the Northside and Westside, or not necessarily in the Eastside and Southbridge. But this did not mean that poverty and violence was not rife in the Eastside and Southbridge—it was. The types of crime the Eastside and Southbridge struggled with mostly were assault and the use and possession of illegal drugs and weapons (see table 2.1). Crimes in the Eastside and Southbridge accounted for nearly 30% of Wilmington's overall crime rate.[11] Further, it should be noted that nationally, violent crime and especially homicide has declined over the last thirty years, but homicide rates have been particularly high in small and medium-sized cities like East St. Louis, Illinois; Trenton, New Jersey; Chester, Pennsylvania; and Wilmington, Delaware.[12] Also, while our study focused on the Eastside and Southbridge (7,000 people in total), homicide and other forms of crime in other parts of the city (Northside and Westside) also greatly impacted the well-being of the Eastside and Southbridge, given how small Wilmington was as a city.

The gift and curse of "the Delaware Way" is that everyone presumably "knows" each other. This small-town, folksy mantra is often repeated, and even if someone did not know you personally, there is a very good chance they know someone who *does* know you personally. Condensed degrees of separation or the perceived distance between two people, along with close-knit networks, also potentially alter the social proximity of violence in a small city. Scholars argue that the "six degrees of separation" or "small-world phenomenon" links individuals through a "short sequence of intermediate acquaintances," such that they are merely a few steps from each other in a network.[13] Papachristos, Braga, and Hureau propose that these degrees of separation are even smaller for those involved in violent crime; they found that the "shortest path" between any individual in a gang network and a gunshot victim is 4.69, or roughly five "handshakes" removed from a gunshot victim.[14] Given this notion of degrees of separation, it does not take much for larger segments of a small city to be more tightly connected than in larger cities. We found similar network affiliations in Wilmington, as perpetrators, victims, and associated loved ones frequently saw each other in public spaces. These collisions sometimes led to vicious waves of retaliation.

The Eastside and Southbridge and other poor communities in Wilmington were easily filled with a dozen or two "gangs," crews or groups ranging in size and influence. The younger street collectives kept sprouting up but generally lacked the older, stable leadership that was more typical of gangs or street crews during the 1980s, 1990s, and early 2000s. This new crop of youth had also become much more violent as they contended for what remained from a previously thriving drug trade. Further, although the term "gang" has grown in popularity among younger generations, national street gangs (e.g., Bloods, Crips, and Gangster Disciples) did not dominate in Wilmington. Wilmington's preference for localized street identities extended out of a fierce pride and city-based territorialism. Street collectives in Wilmington were generally made up of local crews or gangs in the forms of housing or project gangs, neighborhood gangs, block or street corner gangs, and prison gangs. Some of the more hardened crews in Wilmington included the Hill Top Boys, Baby Yellow Gang, Elm Street Boys, STK (Shoot to Kill), OMB (Only My Brothers), TMG (Touch Money Gang), Riverside Project's Gang, 300 Gang, 27th Street Gang, and the Wilmington Trap Stars.[15]

Becoming "Somebody" in "The First State"

Wilmington was "A Place to Be Somebody," and it held golden opportunities for incoming professionals savvy enough to navigate the city's territorialism. For the aspiring colonizers of the 1600s, the ruling white elite in post–Civil War Wilmington, and the large numbers of financial interlopers in the late nineteenth and early twentieth centuries, Wilmington continued to be a city where outsiders were able to come in and establish themselves. This was also true for outside street hustlers, particularly hustlers from surrounding, larger cities like Philadelphia, New York City, and Baltimore. Outside hustlers who were interested in leaving a saturated big-city drug market were able to come to Wilmington for more opportunity in a small town with an active street environment.

"Welcome to Wilmington: A Place to be Somebody" was the city's official slogan. Like "The First State," this slogan was also printed on various city paraphernalia and used as the name of many city programs. This slogan was also carved on several red wooden billboards in Wilmington. As the slogan promised, Wilmington provided me with an unbelievable scholarly opportunity "to be somebody." Wilmington was also an ideal city or social milieu to develop a Street PAR program, and we did so during a period of burgeoning progressive reform in the state. This small city's legacy of crime and poverty, deep-rooted Black activism, corporatization, and white wealth—in conjunction with the "right" set of local residents and my northern, big-city approach—all converged to create the ideal sociopolitical climate for our Street PAR project to thrive.

The Wilmington Street PAR project was a collective of Black men and women from the streets working alongside university researchers, students, and some of Wilmington's most prominent politicians, bankers, and nonprofit executives. We grounded our unyielding activism in rich high-quality data to ultimately spread a message on structural violence and crime in a small city. Thus, we created a base of support that had to be reckoned with.

Building Rapport with the Partnership, Community, and the Streets

Crucial to the success of any Street PAR project is the development of rapport with three core groups: the local neighborhood, street-identified environments within these neighborhoods, and service providers who work in these communities. While the support of the larger community is needed, Street PAR especially requires buy-in from the leadership ranks of the streets. Ethnographers typically refer to this buy-in as "entrée" from a key set of community "gatekeepers."[16] It was the buy-in of the streets that guaranteed strong support from the larger neighborhood, and later, with community professionals. The streets of Wilmington may have had little wealth and limited sociopolitical power, but they did have a social standing that was large enough to sway public opinion. Professional support alone could not carry a Street PAR project, and neither could general public support. It was strong support from the streets that activated, consolidated, and emboldened overall public support for our project.

As the official leading partner, the Wilmington HOPE Commission was responsible for identifying other organizational partners we needed to navigate Wilmington's temperamental political environment. Charles Madden, executive director of the commission, introduced me to various nonprofit and banking executives and other public officials. Charles knew that in a small city where social networks ruled, it would be ill advised not to "make the rounds" with city leadership. Community professionals in Wilmington were a tight-knit group, and like most groups in this town, they, too, were very tribal. City leadership were very selective about the people, groups, and programs they supported. But with their support, it was much easier to gain access to vital resources like media coverage, free space to utilize in nonprofit offices, and consideration for funding. Wilmington is so small that it would be very easy for leadership to hamper community projects. Leveraging their institutional capital in Wilmington, nonprofit executives like Charles were able to rally staff, government officials, and banking executives around issues like re-entry and gun violence.

Building Rapport with a Corporate Gatekeeper

One afternoon, Charles and I met with Michael Purzycki, an esteemed corporate executive and longtime member of Wilmington's establishment class. Mike was chair of the HOPE Commission's board of directors and he firmly directed the vision of this nonprofit. Mike held so much power that he later became the mayor of Wilmington, in 2017. Through interactions with Mike and Charles, I learned about the power of the white elite in controlling a small town and how Black professionals clamored to get a piece of the pie.

Born in 1945, Mike was a white Irish American man raised in a working-class community in Newark, New Jersey. After graduating from Seton Hall Preparatory School, a private all-boys Roman Catholic high school in nearby West Orange, New Jersey, Mike received an athletic scholarship to play wide receiver at the University of Delaware (UD). By his senior year in 1966, Mike had broken every Blue Hen receiving record at UD. After graduating, he played for the New York Giants for only five months in 1967, and then he was permanently sidelined after a major knee injury. Although he never played professional football again, Mike was paid for the rest of the season, receiving "$15,500 . . . at a time when you could buy a beach house for $8,400, and tuition, room, and board at a four-year college averaged $1,064 a year."[17]

Now in his early seventies, Mike was corporate royalty in Wilmington. Worth untold millions, Mike was a big whale in a small rich pond. He ran a successful law practice and served as an attorney for the Delaware Senate. In 1982, Mike was also elected to the New Castle County Council, where for nine years he was the chairman of the county's finance committee. His claim to wealth, however, rested in real estate. As a thriving developer, his portfolio even included Ivy Hall Apartments at UD. Just in Wilmington, he owned three personal homes and residential properties: a single-family home in the wealthy Highlands neighborhood bordering the Westside, a row house near Canby Park, and a condominium in the wealthy Happy Valley neighborhood, minutes from the residence of President Joseph Biden.

In 2009, Mike became the executive director of the Riverfront Development Corporation, and his office was located in the 90,000-square-foot Chase Center on the Riverfront. The Chase Center hosted numerous events for large audiences such as concerts, high-end car shows, weddings, and major political events including President Joe Biden's victory speech in November 2020. However, before Mike developed the Wilmington Riverfront, the area was considered a city dump or "swamp." But by 2017, the Riverfront had accrued $1.2 billion in investments.[18]

Mike was very personable and approachable. He was also the quintessential embodiment of Wilmington's ruthless white wealth. His trademark smile and gregarious personality enchanted most and masked his partiality for Wilmington's corporatocracy. Towering at six foot one, Mike was lean in build and clean-shaven, and his stark-white hair was always perfectly coiffed. He exuded confidence and competence and walked with an air of well-connected privilege. Mike was on a first-name basis with the state's elected officials, and even casually referred to President Biden as "Joe." People's characterizations of Michael Purzycki varied greatly, or depending on the side of town where the person resided. People in Black neighborhoods and more progressive circles often described him as a "controlling," "condescending," and "arrogant" neoliberal white man, while the affluent and other professionals generally exalted his business acumen, political competency. and personal wealth. Whatever you made of him, he was a key player in Wilmington's financial and sociopolitical scene.

What distinguished Mike as a corporate bulwark was his open advocacy for poor Black Wilmington—at least rhetorically. Often, he called for improved economic and educational opportunities, police and criminal legal reform, and violence intervention in neighborhoods like the Eastside and Southbridge. Mike was even rumored to spontaneously give cash to people in need, or on a whim, jobs to unemployed young Black men.[19] Mike and his wife also adopted a Black son whose biological parents struggled with drug addiction and incarceration. Yet despite these acts of kindness, reactions to Mike were mixed.

One afternoon, Charles and I drove to Mike's office for a meeting.

"I'm glad you're finally meeting Mike. Just know, there are times when Mike has gotten a little pushback from the community. I mean, in some ways, he's comes off like a lot of powerful white men. But in other ways, he's not. Yas, trust me, Mike is a good guy. Plus, he can help us in Wilmington."

"I understand. If you trust him, I trust him. Plus, we're going to need some real help in Wilmington."

Then we both started laughing. We implicitly knew a cutting-edge project could rub some of the city's more traditional stakeholders the wrong way. Arming some of the most marginalized people with an empirical and activist skill set and platforms to challenge traditional power was, for some, a risky endeavor.

"I don't talk too much about my background, but I'm from Detroit. My family is messed up with all of the same issues that Black people in Wilmington are struggling with. I know a lot about how poverty and addiction f-cks a family up. Yas, when I got a chance to make something of myself, I jumped at it. Plus, Yas, it's my values. I really want more than we had in Detroit. As a people, we need to start thinking about wealth. I want to leave something to my family. That's another reason why I make sure to be around people like Mike."

Mike mentored several young Black professionals, and Charles was clearly someone he treasured. With the support of Mike and other members of Wilmington's establishment, Charles was publicly and professionally elevated in Delaware. Charles's reception in the Eastside and Southbridge was generally lukewarm, but he was savvy enough to leverage key relationships with the right set of residents who had high social capital. While people like Wolfie provided cover for Charles, many in the Eastside and Southbridge were still very suspicious of him. Some even taunted Charles at public events, chastising him for "selling out."

THE HOPE COMMISSION, new and struggling to connect with residents, wanted to elevate their footprint in Black Wilmington, and the Wilmington Street PAR project was one means by which the commission sought to establish themselves in the Eastside and Southbridge. The HOPE Commission was also poorly resourced and understaffed, but they still had a well-paid executive director in Charles, and a very powerful board filled with nonprofit and banking executives and prominent academic and political leadership. And Mike was the chief among this professional bulwark.

The passage of then-senator Joseph Biden's Second Chance Act in 2007 ushered in a windfall of funding for re-entry programming and research. The HOPE Commission was a re-entry nonprofit and well poised to receive support. Mike, Charles, and the board viewed the Wilmington Street PAR project as one of several key projects that could garner the support the commission needed to become the state's first "one-stop re-entry center," a place where returning citizens could get most of the resources they needed.

Charles and I finally reached Mike's office. After shaking hands and a quick introduction, we sat down to speak for about an hour. Mike said,

> I think a lot of our problems in Wilmington with unemployment and violence would be solved if we got a better handle on re-entry. Yasser, our recidivism rates are out of control. A lot of these guys, when they come home, they are left to fend for themselves. Our system has made it much too difficult for them to navigate the re-entry process. If you want your ID, you have to go here. If you want to take care of housing, then you have to report there. If you want to look for a job . . . well, you get

my drift. We have to do something different. These guys need a one-stop re-entry center. It's time to think outside the box. . . . The PAR project, we think, is an opportunity to do just that, to work in partnership with the community.

I replied, "Wow! It's so refreshing to hear your perspective on re-entry. To be honest, I'm a bit surprised . . . but I'm also very happy to hear it . . . and to be able to come to a city where it is possible to do real PAR work."

Mike and Charles nodded in agreement, and Mike continued with his critical thoughts on re-entry. Mike reiterated how poor services led to an increase in unemployment, violence, recidivism, and broken families. For Mike, quality services were the linchpin in making Wilmington a better place for everyone, including Black men and women in the streets.

After our discussion, we shook hands, said our goodbyes, and parted ways. Charles and I chatted further in his car. We both knew that in a small place like Wilmington, Mike's approval meant we were moments away from launching a groundbreaking project.

The following week, I met Charles in his office to take a tour of the Eastside and Southbridge. Downtown Eastside was the buffer neighborhood between West Center City and the larger Eastside, both of which are low-income Black neighborhoods. The HOPE Commission was located at 625 North Orange Street, just a two-minute drive from one of the United States' most infamous addresses: the Corporation Trust Center (CT Center), 1209 North Orange Street. The Corporation Trust is a subsidiary of Wolters Kluwer, a Dutch multinational services firm.[20] Because of Delaware's loose tax laws, the CT Center is presently home to 300,000 businesses, over 1 million business entity registrants, and over half of the companies on the Fortune 500 list.[21] This corporate mammoth sat walking distance from the Eastside, one of the poorest neighborhoods in the state.

Charles and I hopped into his car, and after two right turns we arrived at the Downtown Eastside's major intersection: Fourth and Market Streets. We drove down this small hill into the larger, poorer, and darker-skinned Eastside community. Directly across the street from the Wilmington Police Department (WPD) were two public housing complexes: the soaring Compton Towers and the sprawling Bethel Villa Apartments. Near the WPD were several boarded-up row homes. Famous Liquors was next to Miracle Tabernacle Church on the corner of Fourth and North Lombard Streets. So much life and diversity of social experience was on this small stretch of Fourth Street. As we continued on Fourth Street, we crossed over the William J. Winchester Bridge into Southbridge. In 1945, Winchester was the first Black member of Delaware's state legislature.[22] The bridge was symbolic of Black life in Wilmington, in that it connected Wilmington's two oldest Black communities: Eastside and Southbridge. At the other end of the bridge, Fourth Street changed into

South Heald Street, and we continued driving. We made a right on A Street and then a left onto Townsend. Small homes packed these narrow blocks. We stopped at Townsend and C Street, at one corner of the historic Elbert Palmer Park. Continuing down Townsend, we drove down a narrower, one-way street that looped around the large rectangular park. We parked in front of the HOPE Zone office near Southbridge–Wilmington Housing Authority (or housing projects), which was on the other side of Elbert Palmer Park. We sat quietly in the car and absorbed the moment. A few small children played outside, not too far from the car. A group of five young Black men in front of a nearby building laughed. Staring out his car window, Charles quietly acknowledged, "As you can see, Yas. It's basically one way in, and one way out." Then he pulled off and drove us back into the Eastside.

DEVELOPING RAPPORT IN A SMALL TOWN meant that repeatedly I had to be introduced to people. There was a lot of handshaking and hugs, sitting in on meetings, and attending local events. I couldn't tell you how many times I said, "Hello!," "How are you?," or "Nice to meet you!" There was also a general expectation for me to remember at least some names. To my surprise, many remembered mine. A hospitable decorum and general acknowledgement of one another were interactional and cultural traits required in a place like Wilmington. Also, I quickly became aware that local residents were constantly evaluating the way I interacted with them and my comfort level inside their neighborhood spaces. How I interacted in real time, over time, was the best way for them to critically examine my intentions. Thus, I had to be evaluated and re-evaluated to determine whether I would be allowed to lead the Wilmington Street PAR project in their communities. All bets were off if I appeared aloof or disconnected, too uncomfortable, inauthentic, or opportunistic. Cultural authenticity and the proper level of sensitivity to their concerns was the only way into the hearts and underbelly of the Eastside and Southbridge. The right people vouching for you went a long way with all strata of Wilmington, but particularly in the streets. The way I was introduced—the slow rolling out of me and the project to the community—was crucial to the development of ground-level support. Wolfie, Charles, and I knew the project could not be quickly forced into these neighborhoods. Furthermore, a rolling introduction to the community slowed the project down enough to adequately contemplate how Street PAR could work in Wilmington.

Charles and Wolfie continued to take me to the community over the coming months while Charles and I also worked on several grant applications. Two applications and about seven months later, Charles met me in Southbridge, showed his cell phone, and said, *"We got it!"* Flashing on his cell phone was the email confirming that we had received a state block grant under President Barack Obama's American Recovery Reinvestment Act.

WILMINGTON STREET PAR METHODS TRAINING

After winning the grant, the partners and I started outlining a strategy for recruitment of Street PAR Associates, while my graduate students and I began developing a two-month curriculum for a research methods training. Although there are nine principles that guide Street PAR projects, there is no standardized curriculum, given the breadth of topics, methodology, and forms of analysis.[23] My graduate students and I had to think deeply about a curriculum that would be sensible for fifteen Associates in the Eastside and Southbridge.

Street PAR is a phenomenologically based research orientation and intervention that spans the theoretical, methodological, and empirical arguments in the literature. PAR and other cooperative methodologies have long been identified as excellent strategies to work with active, street-identified populations, or people involved with the criminal legal system.[24] Street participatory action research is the iteration of PAR designed to directly work with the streets to provide them with rigorous educational, vocational, and sociopolitical training.

Our core assumption is that with these skills, our Street PAR program can achieve its chief mission: the mobilization of men and women in the streets to secure sociopolitical and economic power. Technical skills will also foster their ability to economically thrive while fighting for their communities. A compounding, consistent empirical message generated by Black men and women in the streets is an extremely effective strategy to challenge traditional power. By mastering their own data, Street PAR puts local communities in a position to frame or control their public narrative.

Nine Dimensions of Street PAR

Street PAR is grounded in nine core dimensions (see figure 2.1), and these dimensions inform methods trainings and guide the overall direction of Street PAR projects.[25] These dimensions are markers or principles implemented in varying ways to gauge the progress, degree, and impact of a Street PAR project. These nine dimensions are also conceptualized within the framework of two subareas: project organization; and community and advocacy.

The project organization subarea flushes out all technical and operational features of the project. This larger, organizational principle charges Street PAR teams to critically think through use of resources, power dynamics, project design, and the ethical implications of the study. Project organization is also guided by the following five dimensions: (1) project identity, (2) ethics, (3) resources and incentives, (4) timeline, and (5) methodological design. The Community and Advocacy subarea grounds the project in the culture of the street environment and larger neighborhood(s), or within the study context. This subarea is guided by these four dimensions: (1) local history, (2) the

Project Organization Subarea	Community and Advocacy Subarea
• Project identity • Ethics • Resources and incentives • Timeline • Methodological design	• Local history • Audience • The PEOPLE • Action plan

2.1. Nine Dimensions of Street PAR

audience, (3) the *people* (or neighborhood's perspective on study), and (4) the action plan.

Street PAR methods training was held over two months in two locations: the Neighborhood House (a nonprofit) in Southbridge and UD's satellite campus in Downtown Eastside. Training involved eighteen research methods workshops, and each workshop was four to five hours in duration. The first nine sessions taught Associates the basic concept of theory and worked with Associates to develop our study's theoretical framework. The remaining nine workshops taught Associates the basic concepts of methods, analysis, and activism, and focused on co-designing with them our methodology, identifying forms of analysis, and developing an action plan for our Street PAR project. After a graduating ceremony, we reconvened during the third month to review what we had covered in the initial two months of training.

Workshops were led by a mix of guest facilitators such as professors, graduate students, politicians, police officers, and social workers. The curriculum was interdisciplinary and spanned several disciplines including criminology, social psychology, sociology, public health, history, film, and the arts. Each Associate received a large binder filled with hard copies of all workshop materials including PowerPoint presentations, academic journal articles, book chapters, white papers, reports, and newspaper articles.

Long workshop sessions (four to five hours) provided an uninterrupted and highly structured learning environment for persons with varying living circumstances, many of which were not conducive to focusing on research methods. Therefore, all readings, activities, and other assignments were covered during workshop hours. Passages from carefully selected readings, with targeted questions for Associates, were covered individually and in small- and large-group formats.

Fran Baum, Colin MacDougall, and Danielle Smith's "Participatory Action Research," published in the *Journal of Epidemiology and Community*

Health, for instance, is a good journal article to use in a large group activity to teach the concept of PAR to Street PAR Associates.[26] During training, I projected Baum et al.'s three-page paper on the room's LCD screen.[27] Of the nine subsections in their paper, we focused on "Definition of PAR," "Distinctiveness of PAR," "Methodology/Method," "Power/Empowerment," and "Lived Experience." I called on various Associates to read aloud selected passages, and for other Associates to critically respond to what was read.

Given that our study was focused on gun violence, John Rich and Courtney Grey's "Pathway to Recurrent Trauma among Young Black Men: Traumatic Stress, Substance Use, and the 'Code of the Street,'" in the *American Journal of Public Health*, was another article that worked well in training.[28] Responding to Rich and Grey's findings on shooting victims in Philadelphia, Jonathan (Associate) said, "It's kind of hard hearing Swearve [Associate] read that part about who is most likely to get shot." Then Jonathan looked at the screen and read three passages he highlighted from Rich and Grey's paper:

- "Violent injury is also a chronic, recurrent problem. Previous studies have revealed recurrence rates of between 5% and 45% over the 5 years subsequent to the initial injury.... After victims leave the hospital, most return to communities where violence is all around them and where they feel especially vulnerable."
- "Victims, who have a heightened sense of danger, feel even more pressed to protect themselves, a posture that may place them at risk for recurrent violence."
- "Faced with these realities, they may feel they have few options other than obtaining a weapon to stay safe. Studies have shown that carrying a weapon raises the risk of reinjury, perhaps because it emboldens the victim to confront potential victimizers."[29]

After pausing for five to ten seconds, Jonathan said, "Where this study is taking place, this is where I'm from. I'm from Philadelphia. Done did anything you can imagine out there. I am who this guy is writing about. The reason why I moved to Wilmington was to get away from those streets, the violence, and going to prison. I'm 38 and I'm tired, man. Look, I am who he is writing about. I was shot three different times in Philly. I am who he is writing about."

We concluded this workshop with a writing assignment in which the Associates responded to three questions: (1) What do you think about Rich and Grey's study? (2) What were some strengths and limitations of this study? (3) In what ways can survey and interview methods be useful to our study in the Eastside and Southbridge? Graduate students and I reviewed their journal entries that evening and we returned them at the next workshop with extensive feedback.

To teach interviewing or qualitative methods, we reviewed chapter 3, "Field Work," and chapter 4, "Qualitative Data," in Robert Bogdan and Sari

Knopp Biklen's *Qualitative Research for Education: An Introduction to Theory and Methods–Field Work* (5th ed.).[30] To better inform the African-centered features of qualitative and ethnographic methodology, we paired these readings with Diane D. Turner's "The Interview Technique as Oral History in Black Studies"; and Adeniyi Coker's "Film as Historical Method in Black Studies: Documenting the African Experience," in Molefi Kete Asante and Maulana Karenga's *Handbook of Black Studies* (5th ed.).[31] Bogdan and Biklen's work offered clear arguments on building rapport, organizing field notes, triangulation of data, conducting research in "politically charged and conflict-ridden" environments, and interviewing techniques, including "visual recording." Turner's four-page chapter concisely outlines how to develop a culturally competent interview with Black Americans, while Coker's chapter focuses on film as an African-centered method.

Next, I played video clips of individual, dual, and group interviews from a previous film-based street ethnographic project. We focused on the fundamental mechanics of the interview such as type of interview, social desirability, interview location, type of interviewee, and semistructured features including establishing rapport and conversational tone. One-on-one interviews are better for gathering sensitive information on violence or for personal conversations about getting jumped, stabbed, or shot. Dual interviews, held with two participants, provide participants with joint support for a delicate discussion on violence. Group interviews generate group-level data or the target group's collective framing and cultural perspective on violence. After a small break, we ended our discussion on interviewing and ethnography with a role-playing activity.

To review survey methodology, we gathered in small groups to review Bruce W. Tuckman's "Constructing and Using Questionnaires and Interview Schedules," chapter 10 in his book *Conducting Educational Research* (5th ed.).[32] We then reported back as a team to discuss. Associates also conducted descriptive analysis and basic significance tests including correlations, t-tests, analyses of variance, and simple regressions. We even discussed scale development and basic psychometric concepts including reliability, validity, and factor analysis.

In the next methods workshop, Street PAR Associates critically reviewed and revised a twenty-page questionnaire. After each Associate reviewed the survey, we debated the utility of some items. This debate led to substantive changes—we added, reworded, and deleted several items. The final outcome was an eighteen-page survey packet that spanned nine conceptual domains: psychological well-being, social well-being, and experiences with and attitudes toward crime, violence, employment, educational opportunity, police, and re-entry. The survey packet concluded with a demographic inventory. As with our interview protocol, we role-played how to approach study participants with a survey in the field.

Research methods training was designed to be challenging and, at times, difficult for the Associates. The training had to be rigorous if we were going to make the case that Black men and women from the streets were genuinely interested and capable of doing research. We knew they would succeed, particularly if the workshops and overall research experience were anchored in their racial-ethnic and cultural orientation—an orientation that required a focus on social-structural empowerment. Rigorous training also offered Associates the skills to transition into more traditional forms of employment and educational opportunity.

The first step in creating an academic setting for Associates to do well began with the formal partners actively disrupting the implicit bias we all have regarding the learning aspirations and potential of street-identified Black Americans. We recognized that no matter how progressive we were as professionals, it was nearly impossible to not be affected by the persistent negative framing of street-identified Black populations.[33] We increased our awareness of this bias by regularly discussing the topic, even though it was uncomfortable.

In one session, we discussed the implications of teacher expectation theory.[34] Teacher expectation theory, or what Rosenthal and Jacobsen originally described as the "Pygmalion effect," refers to teachers' attitudes toward their students and how these attitudes are powerfully predictive of student's academic performance.[35] Teachers' negative characterizations of their students, for instance, are enough to undermine the performance of high-performing students.

With this argument in mind, we expected the best of Street PAR Associates and truly believed they wanted to do well. We also created the necessary conditions for them to thrive. From our perspective, high rigor demonstrated how seriously we respected them and how committed we were to the positive development of their communities. Our explicit goal was to provide Associates with "doctoral-level training," or to "bring the doctoral student (research) model to the street corner" as a community-level intervention. Tough, culturally competent teachers and curriculums increase school performance even among street-identified Black students.[36] A galvanizing research training also motivated Associates in the same way.

"PAR is so empowering!" Ashley cheerfully said. "We've learned how research can affect communities and change communities."

Jonathan stunned me when he said, "First of all, PAR is the first time I saw qualified African American people studying African American people."

Pat added, "PAR are researchers from your own community. You get someone outside the community that comes in and does the research, they're not going to get the answers we got. We are the voice of the voiceless. Soldiers without swords. . . . The training that Dr. Payne gave us was on a graduate level. He didn't downgrade the training. He realized just because we had street experience, that didn't mean we didn't have the wherewithal to understand what we learned."

Corry stated, "Knowledge is power . . . and what you do with that power is your wisdom. Because knowledge without action is wasted. So, PAR gives you the opportunity to gain wisdom with action."

Street PAR Associates knew wholeheartedly that we believed they were "Somebody" and could professionally "Be Somebody" in a city intent on denying them the opportunity they always deserved.

CHAPTER 3

"Murder Town, USA"

REFRAMING GUN VIOLENCE AND
RESILIENCE IN A SMALL CITY

> The main social and economic causes of violence . . . are those that divide the population into the superior and the inferior, the strong and the weak, the rich and the poor, the more highly unequal a society is, the higher its rates of violence. For example, the most powerful predictor of homicide rates throughout the world, and this has been repeated in dozens of studies, is the size of the gap between the rich and poor.
> —James Gilligan, "Dr. James Gilligan on Violence"

> There is a population in Wilmington who aren't doing as well. They're struggling. Their kids are dying. They have no money and very little voice. This show is about them. It's not about those of us who are doing well, who happen to be the only ones who had their feelings hurt by the title [*Remaking Murdertown*]. . . . Wilmington is not a scary place. There's nothing to be afraid of. Nothing. In fact, it's this fear that keeps our communities separated, isolated and makes it super hard to try anything to change that.
> —Zach Phillips, in "Tidal Wave"

OVER THE YEARS, Wilmington has been slapped with negative descriptors, from the "meanest" and "unfriendliest" to the "most violent" and "most dangerous" city in the United States.[1] In 2017, Wilmington was declared the "most dangerous place in America for youth," given the city's elevated rates of violent crime per capita.[2] Alarming language typically framed the public discourse on Black Wilmington. Yet, local viewpoints, particularly from residents and members of the streets, provided more nuanced explanations of the violence. But outsiders still controlled the public narrative with ham-fisted or uncritical and alarming language, and often that language was used to enforce punitive solutions.

Although negative media characterizations proliferated about Wilmington, it was *Newsweek*'s front-page article on violence that had the greatest impact.

Newsweek crowned Wilmington "Murder Town USA" in December 2014, drawing national attention to conditions in the small city.[3] The ABC network began development on *Murder Town*, a television series starring Jada Pinkett Smith, who was cast as Wilmington's first Black female district attorney.[4] Local residents were excited, but Delaware's establishment class wasn't and instead quickly moved to shut down plans for the TV series. Mayor Dennis Williams, the Wilmington City Council, Senator Chris Coons, Richard Smith of the Delaware NAACP, and Rabbi Michael Beals of Beth Shalom protested against the making of *Murder Town*.[5] Leadership argued that the TV series and its provocative title would chase out residents, businesses, and corporations or discourage them from relocating to a city perceived to be too violent. In a scathing critique on Facebook, Mayor Williams responded, "That's unfortunate. A bunch of has-beens playing in different roles to try to rebuild their acting careers. That's OK. If they want to come into Wilmington and spend some of that money, go to the West End, the Hotel du Pont, bring in 500 people to spend at our restaurants. I'll take their money. I just hope they get somebody good-looking to play me."

Unlike public leadership, most Black residents did not feel embarrassed by *Newsweek*'s article. Instead, they felt affirmed by this reporting, and as a result, many embraced the attention. Residents were actually surprised that Wilmington's story of violence and structural oppression had landed on the national stage; thus, they enthusiastically welcomed ABC and Jada Pinkett Smith's interest in Black Wilmington.

One Saturday afternoon, I sat with Lou (Associate) and his 20-year-old son Idris in their home in Wilmington. It was not uncommon for me to visit Lou's home to watch a game, or for him, his wife Ivy, and their three children to visit my home to barbecue. And Lou and I always made sure to sneak in time for a hearty conversation on the state of Black America.

On this Saturday, our conversation drifted to white and Arab supremacy, the role of Black revolutionaries and grassroots organizations, Black Americans' attraction to the Abrahamic religions (i.e., Christianity, Islam, and Judaism), and the unwillingness of city leadership to address Black Wilmington's war with the structural violence complex. For Lou and Idris, these issues had everything to do with why Wilmington was labeled "Murder Town, USA." They also asserted that negative media portrayals at the behest of Black political leadership (whom they perceived to be controlled by Wilmington's white corporatocracy) were helping to sabotage the Black communities they were elected to protect. From their perspective, negative media made it easier for city leadership to justify opening up their communities for gentrification, or to make a profit from the banishment of generations of Black families. Lou and Idris argued that Black Wilmingtonians desperately needed a radical Black social movement to stop their erasure in or removal from Wilmington.

They also believed that outsiders' fear of Wilmington was offensive, irrational, and fueled by the media's stereotyping of poor Blacks as a racialized "other."

For Lou and Idris, the violence that occurred typically took place between a set of individuals with an identified and seemingly irresolvable conflict, as opposed to a random set of "gun-toting predators" seeking a violent "thrill kill." Lou and Idris did not feel threatened by the city's violence, as they had key community relationships, cultural adeptness, and the ability to read the verbal and nonverbal interactions or group dynamics surrounding street violence.

"What does 'Murder Town, USA' mean to you? Is it a fair description of your city?" I asked.

Lou responded, "I definitely don't embrace it *and* I am not offended by it.... The way it [violence in Wilmington] is viewed, I don't see it that way.... I work around Blacks that live in the suburbs and whites that live in the suburbs. And they might ask you, 'Do you live in the city [Wilmington]?' And I'm like, 'Yeah, I live in the city' ... and they be like, 'Oh my god, you live in the city! [*laughter*] And I be like, 'What the hell?' I often think to myself, 'What are they seeing that I am not?' At work, they be like, 'Oh my God, it's so dangerous, I avoid the city at all cost.' This is how they talk. Even the young Black ones that live in the suburbs, they avoid the city at all cost."

"What do you think they are afraid of?"

"I think the sensationalism of the newspaper articles is making them have the wrong impression.... To them, people are just being walked up on and being shot. Like, without purpose, you can get killed. They think if they come to the city to watch a movie, they might get their head blown off. Or they think if they come to the Riverfront, they might get killed ... and that's just not the case. To me, I look at it like, especially coming from the streets, there is always two or three sides to that story. Now, it's messed up that the person got shot or killed.... We see the vigils, and there is a few innocent victims, but for the most part, I always ask, 'What role did that person play in becoming victimized?' ... The mothers of sons lost to the streets never talk about the things their sons did in the streets.... A lot of times, all we see in the public is just the tears."

"Does small city size play a role in why the violence has spiked here in Wilmington?"

"Chicago is huge! LA is huge! New York is huge! So, if you have an enemy there, it could be years before they run into each other. But if you have an enemy in Wilmington, I could run into you by accident.... And just because I slapped you don't mean when you catch me in my vulnerable state, you are going to slap me.... Every side of town is only five minutes away, as opposed to a Chicago, or LA, or New York, where we might be an hour away from each other in the same city.... But here in Wilmington, I can hop in my car real quick and drive somewhere to knock somebody off."

"Is the city safe for you and your Black son?"

"I think it is safe for someone that is not in the streets. It's all how you move. Like my son, a lot of his friends are in the streets, and a few of them just recently got locked up. . . . So yes, I think the city is safe for me and my son. It's all how you move out here. I taught him how to move. I think it is safe for him because he knows how to move."

I asked Idris, "Do your friends sometimes embrace the language, 'Murder Town, USA'?"

"Yeah."

"Do you think they still love their community?"

"Some of my friends say that, but they do love their families and their communities. Some of them do have real love for their community, but some of them don't, though."

"Does your friends' embrace of 'Murder Town, USA' have anything to do with the poverty?"

"Yeah! The poverty is real out here. And yeah, it make people sometimes be violent. . . . And being young without much, you looking for something, for an identity. The name [Murder Town, USA], for some, do mean a lot, because it gives them that, you know that, validation. . . . Some of the kids are really in the street life, selling weed and dope to take care of their little brothers and sisters. . . . Some of my friends might not have their mom and dad. . . . Some of them got to live with their aunt, with like eight other people. . . . The words 'Murder Town, USA' do make us [Wilmington] more respected in the streets, but it is also bad for us to be called that, too. It do make some people feel like you shouldn't want to move to Wilmington, like you might get robbed or killed, or it's not safe for your kids."

Lou added, "As far as the city's leadership, they don't like 'Murder Town, USA' because it's bad for business. They want more whites to move in, because this is a banking city. All the banks are in Wilmington, so they now want to move the Blacks and Puerto Ricans out and bring in more whites, so they be closer to the jobs. . . . Trying to get in the city at 8:00 A.M. in the morning, it's hard! . . . Black leadership ain't doing nothing with the city. The Arabs, the Chinese, they got all of the stores in Black communities. So where do we fit in? There ain't really no Black-owned businesses in the city. We here, but we just existing."

ALTHOUGH WILMINGTON is a tough town, with spells of extreme violence, very few understood Wilmington only as a grim "Murder Town" swamped with nihilism. Even in the streets, they mostly understood their communities to be a set of loving or socially cohesive neighborhoods. But many in the streets still embraced the hyperbolic language of "Murder Town" because it ripped the scab off an often-ignored discussion on the relationship between structural violence and crime. For the streets, a discussion on violence was inextricable from a discussion on extreme poverty. Poverty and violence were assumed to be concepts that were inherently linked. Still, it was much rarer for leadership to comprehend the totality of poverty and/or address violence in this way, at least publicly. City leadership, in one speech after the other, claimed that it had to first get control over the gun violence by advancing one policing initiative after another, before it could muster resources to address the impact of structural violence in neighborhoods like the Eastside and Southbridge.

For the community, the shock value of "Murder Town, USA" pulled the blinders off and shone a national spotlight on the concentrated poverty, massive unemployment, school inequality, and poor housing that undergirded gun violence in Black Wilmington. Residents were not naïve about the city's violent reputation, and sometimes young people in the streets even co-opted "Murder Town, USA" for use on social media or in rap songs. Other refurbished names used by the streets to describe dis-opportunity and violence in Wilmington were "Kilmington" or "Killington," "Little Fallujah," "Savage Land," "Savage Life," and "Hellaware."

Ferguson's school-based ethnography examined Black masculinity as a social identity and form of coping in two groups of sixth grade boys: "Trouble Makers" (lower-performing Black boys) and "School Boys" (higher-performing Black boys).[6] Among the Trouble Makers, Ferguson found a group of boys who strongly identified with their street-oriented group, N———s for Life (NFL). Coping in a radically reframed way, these boys used the word "n———" to bond and resist school mistreatment. Like the streets of Wilmington in their use of street terms, NFL snatched the sting off the intended denigrating insult of "n———" by reinterpreting this term to be a very racialized, ethnic, gendered, classed, and resistance-based concept. NFL reappropriated "n———" as a territorial, cultural space and used the word as a litmus test to evaluate others who were perceived as unworthy of using it (e.g., School Boys). Identification with the word "n———" was useful for NFL to know, who was in or out of their group, and the guarded posture around the use of this word was a clever way to secure their group identity. How they used "n———" was also how they maintained dignity and challenged an oppressive school environment.

Though many from Wilmington's establishment class resisted negative descriptions of "Murder Town, USA," the reality still remained that sections of Delaware and Black Wilmington struggled with violence. According to Sumner et al., "The growth in Delaware's homicide rate has outpaced that of every other state," and Wilmington vacillated between being the third- and fourth-most violent city of its size in the United States.[7] Wilmington comprised only 8% of the state's population but accounted for 25% of crimes in Delaware, nearly half of the state's shootings and homicides, and over one-quarter of all violent crimes.[8] Wilmington amassed thirty-two murders and 197 shootings in 2017, breaking its 2010 homicide and shooting records.[9] In the minds of most, thirty-two murders did not equate to an epidemic, but in a small city of 71,000, this number was enough to cause great alarm. Thirty-two homicides converted to a per capita rate of forty-four murders per 100,000 people, which makes Wilmington's rate higher than that of most big cities, including Baltimore, New York City, Philadelphia, Los Angeles, and even Chicago, for at least the previous ten years.

CITY LEADERSHIP AND THE COMMUNITY CHARGED our project with the task of framing an analysis on violence through the perspectives of street-identified Black men and women in the Eastside and Southbridge. Street PAR Associates and institutional partners were clear that a study that did not achieve this goal, or only championed the efforts of university researchers, would not be tolerated. Further, all parties agreed that not only were the voices of the streets missing from systematic analysis, their direct participation was usually missing from analysis *and* policy recommendations. They insisted that our project respond accordingly!

To accomplish this ambitious feat, we had to leverage the Associates' analytical insight, passion for activism, and social capital to make real sense out of the violence without demonizing the people mostly responsible for it. This was easier said than done. Some felt that because we worked so closely with the streets, we neglected to hold them sufficiently accountable for their behavior. Some even believed that we legitimized, if not romanticized, their experiences. However, we knew that condemning street-identified populations or recommending punitive strategies would only destroy our project and contribute to the exacerbation of Wilmington's problem with violence. We also knew that those most likely to perpetrate the violence also desired a more cohesive community. *But how were we going to adequately grapple with the tensions of violence and a call for a better community*—a question that also concerned most street-identified Black men and women in the Eastside and Southbridge?

We were at an ethical crossroads, and we struggled with how to tell an empirical story without harming the communities we wanted to serve. What analysis could we possibly provide that would be considered useful by all stakeholders, including the streets? How could our project actually lead to significant levels of change? How were we going to study communities rife with violence, and also make clear that these communities were not solely defined by violence? More precisely, how were we going to tell a story about crack cocaine, heroin, "dippers" or "wocky-tock" (PCP) dealers, sex workers, and "shooters" or murderers without castigating them?

After three months of rigorous methods training, the team decided our core questions would be these:

1. To what extent was gun violence tied to economic and educational inequality?
2. To what extent were socially and structurally disrupted neighborhoods like the Eastside and Southbridge a desired outcome for city leadership and corporate institutions?

3. To what extent was violence understood as coping and used as a site of resilience?
4. To what extent did the streets care about contributing to the uplift of communities they sometimes caused havoc in?

Wilmington was not Murder Town, USA, particularly if this language was intended to crudely disparage Black Wilmington, which often was how public leadership tried to spin *Newsweek*'s coverage. But if a news article could expose how a wealthy city exploited its most vulnerable citizens and triggered the very gun violence it promised to alleviate, then from the perspective of the streets, the sensational language of "Murder Town, USA" was spot on. According to Abigail Jones, small city size forced people to reckon with the coexistence of structural suffering and grand opulence.[10] Unlike in bigger cities, it was impossible to overlook the obscene inequality in Wilmington. Wealthy areas like the banking district, Downtown Eastside, or "the Mall," upmarket neighborhoods like Trolley Square, Brandywine, and North Wilmington, as well as Greenville were constant reminders of the structural inferiority of poor sections of the city like the Eastside and Southbridge. The more affluent neighborhoods are plush with upper-middle-class-ness and extraordinary wealth, such as beautiful tree-lined streets, well-stocked grocery stores, boutiques, manicured country clubs, and even a sprawling golf course.

Jones deftly articulated the inhumanity of the stark two-tale-ness of Wilmington:

> Drive 15 minutes outside the city center and you'll find sprawling landscapes studded with du Pont mansions, including Winterthur, a 1,000-acre preserve with a 175-room house; Longwood Gardens, which draws more than 1 million people each year; and Nemours Mansion, which has been called a "mini Versailles." . . .
>
> This other Wilmington is blighted with rundown, two-story brick row houses in high-crime neighborhoods like Hilltop, Eastside, and Browntown. Some homes are vacant, their doors and windows boarded up. Many are rentals, which tends to attract a transient crowd, including drug dealers. Stoop after stoop, porch after porch, young black men sit and pass the time.[11]

WILMINGTON'S CULTURE OF VIOLENCE

At its essential core, Wilmington's street code on violence was an intergenerational and organic ideology steeped in principles of personal, social, and economic survival. This nimble street code or cultural value system was crafted around particular street hustles to guide illegal activities like drug dealing, robbery, and violence. Violence more often thrived in the Eastside and Southbridge when there was little street order, or when less of a relationship existed between younger and more established street figures. Street leadership, ironically, was the buffer between the power vacuums in these two neighborhoods. Power vacuums in drug markets and street gangs often leave voids in the lives of Black youth, which increases the likelihood they will usurp power using violence.[12]

Older street veterans typically held the social capital and economic resources to stabilize these communities. They also were more likely to model for younger street generations the code of violence; according to Richard from Southbridge, "It was passed on from fathers to sons." The code was also passed from peer to peer and sometimes from younger to older street generations. The culture of the streets was also modeled by seasoned members of the streets more than it ever was articulated by them, especially in the absence of established, long-standing, or older hustlers. Although plans were crafted for particular street hustles that led to making money, hustlers rarely adhered to a grand formulaic street paradigm or set of static rules on violence or other activities. There was not necessarily an official rule book. Rather than learning an established framework of street-identified how-to steps, hustlers gained a mastery of street culture—such as when and how to be violent—primarily through personal experience. The dynamism of Wilmington's younger street generations consisted of a wide assortment of individuals and crews with varying motives and levels of experience, making it nearly impossible for them to conform to a rigid code of ethics. Also, young street groups were born out of a "deeply racialized context" that was shaped by a desire for collective identity—even if that meant using violence.[13]

The truth is, we never encountered anyone who viewed violence as an essential, treasured feature of their communities. However, strategic use of violence was still widely considered to be a suitable method for avoiding and settling otherwise irresolvable conflicts.[14] Part and parcel of the code was the belief that physical injury, incarceration, and/or death were probable and worth the risk. Extreme poverty necessitated a street code on violence that made these undesirable outcomes socially acceptable or permissible, at least for persons seriously involved in the streets. As a result of this context of violence, there was more outrage than surprise when people were harmed. Hard times, including deaths, were expected, and most braced themselves for this unfortunate news. Venkatesh found that residents in the South Side of Chicago also mourned in a genuine but adjusted way for their loved ones in the streets.[15] Venkatesh says, "Any loss of life is mourned in the projects, but there are degrees. Young men and women who choose a life of drugs and street gangs may, understandably, not [live] long [in] this world. When one of them dies, he or she is certainly mourned, but without any great sense of shock; there is a general feeling that death was always a good possibility."[16]

When violence took place, it often sucked the life out of the Eastside and Southbridge. For weeks, these communities would reel in disbelief. Numerous homicides languished in the long memories of these small communities, which also exacerbated violent conflict. Yet, the size of these small neighborhoods also increased the robust forms of social cohesion in times of tragedy. Dozens of informal social networks emerged during times of distress, which spoke strongly to the resilience of local residents. Low-income Black men and women lived and loved hard in Wilmington, and they found innovative ways to survive not only homicide but also the massive inequality that assured continued violence.

A single homicide was enough to bring Wilmington to its knees. Community centers sometimes closed for the day following a homicide. Nearby street corners grew desolate, and parents encouraged their children to stay close to home. Many tried, but in a small city the impact of lethal violence was impossible to escape. Family members of the slain were forced to tolerate the presence of family members of the perpetrator at convenience stores and local parks. A homicide in Staten Island, for instance, did not typically impact the social equilibrium of Harlem or New York City overall, but in Wilmington, it was very possible for one homicide to negatively affect most residents in the city. All residents lived within a fifteen-minute drive of each other, and their collective memories of homicide victims kept this small city poised for rashes of retaliatory violence.[17]

Seventeen-year-old Dayveair Golden's untimely death provided a great example of the good and bad of a small city struggling with violence and poverty. His homicide spoke loudly to the racialized poverty that proliferated across generations in Southbridge.

Coping with Dayveair's Passing

Dayveair Desmond Lamonte Golden was killed during the second month of our research methods training, and most Associates and some partners knew him well. They were deeply affected by his death, so we had to suspend and then extend our schedule by two weeks. It was apparent that they needed time to mourn and provide support to Dayveair's family.

Speculation about Dayveair's murder commanded Wilmington's attention, especially in the Southbridge community where he lived. Dayveair was a 17-year-old Black boy who fought and beat up his friend, Marquis Wing.[18] Marquis returned with his 18-year old brother Daniel, and in a fit of rage they shot Dayveair. Found slumped over in the front yard of his home on the 500 block of Townsend Court, Dayveair was rushed twenty-five minutes away by ambulance to ChristianaCare Hospital, where he was pronounced dead at 6:15 P.M. on Wednesday, December 9, 2009. Shooting victims cannot be admitted to ChristianaCare Hospital's Wilmington campus, which is approximately five to ten minutes away from where Dayveair was shot. The Wilmington campus is not equipped or resourced to be a level 1 trauma center, which is needed to treat violent injuries. Gun violence victims must be transported to ChristianaCare's campus in Newark, Delaware. At least forty-five minutes to an hour elapsed from the time he was shot until Dayveair made it to the Newark campus. And although he had been shot, he likely died from hemorrhaging or bleeding out, which could have been avoided if he had been transported to the Wilmington campus.[19] One of the most frequent causes of preventable death following injury, bleeding out is a significant example of how Black Wilmington struggles with structural violence.

Dayveair's funeral was held under the direction of the House of Wright Mortuary at Ezion Fair Baptist Church, a beautiful center of worship with a well-manicured estate in Southbridge. Ezion was also an appreciated refuge for the needy, including Dayveair's mother Yadira, who could not afford to pay for her son's funeral. Funeral and burial services for homicide victims in Wilmington could easily reach $8,000 to $10,000, a steep price for poor Blacks who made less than $20,000 a year on average. Many in Southbridge coped with homicide by relying on religious institutions for both spiritual guidance and material support.

After picking up Tiana (Associate) from her home in Southbridge, she and I drove over and arrived at Ezion by 10:00 A.M. Cars and people packed the parking lot on this Saturday morning. A long line of loved ones streamed into Ezion, while a critical mass remained in the parking lot. A small camp of fifteen to twenty young people curled up in a territorial space. Only members of Dayveair's inner circle were allowed entry. The Wilmington Peacekeepers formed the core of another cluster in the parking lot. Created in 2008, this group was comprised of mostly older Black men, many of whom were formerly incarcerated. With their earned social capital or street credibility, the Peacekeepers routinely canvassed Wilmington's toughest neighborhoods, dressed in orange paraphernalia including t-shirts, hoodies, jackets, fitted sports hats, and winter "scullies" (or skull caps) with their logo. They spoke, prayed, handed out pamphlets, and comforted victims of violence on street corners, in local parks and family's homes, and at funerals. Their director, Brother Lamonte X, described the Peacekeepers as "an interfaith group. . . . We go out at least one hour a week to promote peace and unity. . . . We need a spiritual awakening."

Curious, I asked, "Why are the Wilmington Peacekeepers made up of mostly men?"

"Man is the key in the community . . . and Black men need to be more of an integral part of the community and . . . mentor to our children. . . . Who are the ones causing the havoc in the community? Men! Our boys are in the streets because the men aren't there."

As men, they were also more skilled than women on how to be hands-on with street-identified Black boys and men. Their masculinity and former experiences in the streets allowed them to competently respond to the sensitive natures of Black boys and young men under duress. Women were a part of the Peacekeepers, but they yielded to the men's use of their Black masculinity and street capital when engaging young men in public environments. Brother Lamonte X described for us their somewhat tense interaction with Dayveair's friend who had witnessed the homicide. He was wildly incensed and ready for retaliation on the night of Dayveair's murder, but the Peacekeepers convinced him and the young men that stood nearby to join them in prayer. After praying with locked hands for about fifteen minutes on a street corner in Southbridge, the young men promised they would not retaliate. They agreed it made little sense to do so, since Marquis and Daniel had already been arrested.

Another Peacekeeper noted that positive change was very possible, even for the most hardened. We were encouraged to understand the humanity of these boys as a window of opportunity or a means to positively engage their vulnerability; it was in this fragile emotional space that change was most possible. The streets were most likely to listen or "be talked down" from entrenched retaliatory positions once their vulnerabilities were honored. After the prayer, the Peacemakers engaged further. Dayveair's friends were still angry and some even had guns, or "heat," on them, but according to this Peacekeeper, these boys still cried together: "These are boys. These are somebody's babies. . . . These young boys were crying like the babies they are."

A public viewing of Dayveair's body preceded his funeral. Youths engulfed Dayveair's casket. They cried, moaned, sat and stood still in silence, and prayed over him. Young people wore sweaters and hoodies creatively airbrushed with Dayveair's name, face, and a message to "RIP" (Rest In Peace). Dayveair's thin, dark-skinned body lay peacefully in his gray casket. Attached to the casket was a large bouquet of flowers that hung over him. His eyes were closed and both hands were gently crossed over his waist. He wore a black hoodie with a silver pendant attached on the right side of his chest, a pair of blue jeans, and a white T-shirt.

Dayveair's crowded funeral was filled with sadness and celebration. Religious leaders, executives from nonprofits, politicians, educators, family members, and others sang, shouted, and truly worshiped Dayveair's life. In Black religious communities, death is seen less as a cause for sorrow and more as an opportunity to give thanks to God for the life of the slain. Cultural mores permitted close family and friends to be visibly vulnerable. Cathartic outrage was socially acceptable, and loved ones were expected to "keep an eye on" or protect the enraged from making poor reactionary decisions. Strident expressions such as crying, screaming, and physical convulsions—particularly from Black women—were tolerated as adaptive and even necessary methods to drain victims of their wrath. Girls and women were more likely to scream and cry out, while Black boys and men, at least inside Ezion, were generally expressionless. Pastor Lynette Trayvor shook the congregation with her rendition of the gospel ballad "Never Would've Made It." Her soulful voice and impeccable range stirred many to clap, stand up, and engage in the call-and-response tradition of the Black Baptist Church.

Senior Pastor Christopher T. Curry gave the eulogy. Pastor Curry was a dark-skinned man with short hair and a full beard peppered with patches of gray. Dressed in clerical vestments, he wore a satin royal purple robe with sizable beige crosses stitched on each side of his chest. Pastor Curry was a fiery orator who was short in height but a giant in his ability to preach. He understood all too well the social-structural conditions Black residents faced in Southbridge. Raised by a single mother in public housing, Pastor Curry revealed that his two brothers were killed seventeen years ago. He also shared that he, too, ran in the streets before his calling to the Lord. Pastor Curry leveraged his previous experiences in the streets to change or appeal to the minds and hearts of young people in Southbridge.

Pastor Curry begged everyone to resist the perpetual framing of Black people as uneducable, unemployable, prone to violence, hypersexual, and bound for arrest and prison. And then he lashed the congregation.

"Young people, let me appeal to you, it's time to do something different. . . . If you continue to do what you always did, you going to continue to get what you always got. At what point are you going to get mad? . . . At what point will we say that life is worth living? There is a term called a "self-fulfilling prophecy." That's when a person tells you something and you start acting it out. The system has told you that you are slow, you're stupid, you're dumb. . . . The system told you that you will never be nothing. So now we acting it out! Based on your zip code, we can tell when you going to prison! At what point will you say enough is enough? I am somebody! I can make it! I can make it! At what point will you wake up?"

Shouting and a roaring applause followed. "Yeah! Thank you, Father! Let's go!" Pastor Curry asked the streets to "stop trying to be tough" and also chastised city leadership for their role in Black youth becoming a "forgotten generation."

Pastor Curry embodied the perspective of an older Black boomer generation that emphasized self-determination and personal responsibility over arguments on the impacts of structural violence.[20] And with this individualistic perspective, most boomers have lost faith in, and a connection with younger Black generations. Black boomers often castigated and tried to guilt-trip the impoverished, particularly those involved in the streets. This rhetoric was an adaptive strategy used by professional Black boomers to survive in a stratified society. They encouraged the use of sheer will, individualism, and bootstrapping to fight off systemic racialized genocide. Blaming poor Black people for their social and structural problems had become an effective way to relieve themselves of the responsibility and call to action needed to curb the structural violence crawling over Black Wilmington. By placing significant blame on Black Wilmington, Black leadership abdicated their role in challenging the structural systems and institutions that were actually sabotaging the communities they were employed to protect. Although they knew of no way to repair the structural rot, Black leadership still tried to convince the most vulnerable that there was enough opportunity to successfully bypass poverty en masse.

According to Pastor Curry, success in poor Black communities required learning how to transfigure pain into happiness and pleasure, or to use the strictest form of discipline to conquer a web of structural violence.

"Discover joy in your difficulty. . . . The reality of humanity is that life is tough. . . . We will continually experience struggle . . . but as the people of God, we are spiritually wired in such a way that we will always successfully go through our difficulties, without our difficulties going through us."

At the end of his sermon, Pastor Curry left the podium and preached among the pews. He convulsed as he sang, paced, and preached. The congregation, choir, and organ player chimed in. Most congregants stood, and their increasing excitement led to more shouting and screaming. Pastor Curry walked over to Dayveair's family in the front row and preached some more. He stood in front of Dayveair's mourning mother, who continued to sit.

Dayveair's family huddled near his casket as the church emptied out. Most family members wore airbrushed black clothing and footwear in tribute to Dayveair—T-shirts, sweaters, hoodies, pants or jeans, sneakers, boots and shoes. All of the items were black, and most were airbrushed with their last words to Dayveair.

Thirty-one-year-old Yadira Golden stood somberly in front of her son's casket, with a small toddler on her shoulder. Yadira wore thick black shades and a long-sleeved black button-up shirt with Dayveair's picture and the words "Mommy's 1st Baby" airbrushed on back. Dayveair's father, Roger Hall, was incarcerated at the time and was not permitted to attend the funeral.

One block away from Ezion, Dayveair's funeral repast was held in the multipurpose room at the Neighborhood House. A long walking procession stretched between the church and community hub. Most middle-class and/or professional funeral-goers did not attend. But this multipurpose room was filled to the doors with younger, middle-aged, and older local residents.

At the repast, local activist Lynette Williams sarcastically criticized Charles Madden, whom Lynette considered part of the Black elite. An embarrassed younger man stood quietly beside her as she questioned the HOPE Commission's impact in the community. Lynette's brother Vaughn Allen Williams had been shot and killed in Wilmington in March 1998. Stirred by her brother's passing, Lynette began organizing residents and was drawn in by the HOPE Commission's call to address violence and re-entry.

Lynette chided, "My boy [Charles Madden] right here. I haven't seen him [in the community] since last year." Confident that his nonprofit was more involved than she suggested, Charles politely smiled and did not respond.

Driven by blistering anger, Lynette employed grassroots activism to challenge formal leadership about violence in the city, along with the status of her brother's unsolved murder. Her approach was a bit unorthodox and brusque, but no one questioned her commitment. Instead, they grimaced or discreetly shied away from her at public events.

"We need a homicide unit in this city." Looking back at Charles, she yelled, "He don't speak out about how we need a homicide unit! It's time for the chief of police [Michael J. Szczerba] to go home [resign].... We need a homicide unit!"

I was surprised to learn that Wilmington did not have a homicide unit or any special unit to investigate violent crime. Leadership thought it was unwise to assign additional resources, in a city struggling for resources, to a police unit dedicated to solving homicides.[21]

The national clearance rate for homicides was 61%, but in poor Black communities this rate was considerably lower.[22] In 2014, the clearance rate for homicides in Wilmington was only 14%.[23] Poor Black bodies were expendable in this city. Lynette and many others like her fought back by doing their best to shame neoliberal politicians, many of whom accepted the disposability of Black bodies.

More people arrived at the repast. Most were there to support the family, but many were also there to dine. A large number of residents who otherwise would not have eaten much that day were fed. A long line snaked around the multipurpose room, leading to the food trays. Family members and friends of Dayveair's family enthusiastically served a seemingly endless supply of chicken, whiting fish, collard greens with smoked turkey bones, string beans, and macaroni and cheese. I secured a plate and was fortunate enough to find a small space at a nearby table.

Unknowingly, I sat next to Dayveair's 19-year-old friend Richard, his mother, and his younger sister. At first, the four of us ate quietly. Then Richard, out of curiosity and a need to crack the silence, asked who I was and what I did for a living. Delighted that he and his family had made me feel welcomed, I explained that I was conducting a study on violence in Southbridge. Richard wanted to know more, and his mother looked on approvingly as I talked about the project and my trajectory from Harlem and Englewood, New Jersey, to Wilmington and the University of Delaware. Richard ended our conversation with the caveat and call for our project to document his community with integrity: "Just make sure your study talks about how we're good people, too. Make sure to tell them that a lot of us don't got food in the refrigerator. That's why we in the streets. A lot of us are living with nothing. Living in straight poverty.... Make sure your study talks about that."

I left the repast with Richard's words swirling in my head and heart. We agreed to speak later, and I prayed that evening to live up to his expectations.

Speaking with Yadira: Street PAR, Social Capital, and Dayveair

We interviewed Dayveair's mother, Yadira Golden, about three months after her son's funeral. Yadira was especially close with Melodie (Associate), and it was mostly because of their relationship that Yadira agreed to speak with us. At age 31, Yadira had lived in Southbridge for ten years. She had a GED and was unemployed since the passing of Dayveair, and now she focused on being a mother to her a 15-year-old son and 8-year-old daughter.

Yadira was a thin, dark-skinned woman who wore a small black leather jacket and white t-shirt with abstract patterns of butterflies. She sat with her hands in her jacket pockets for most of the interview, and amazingly smiled and laughed throughout.

Yadira was age 14 when she gave birth to Dayveair, age 16 when she had her second son, and age 23 when she had her daughter. She described the average woman in Southbridge as a "single parent, mother, raising children on their own." Yadira also cited poverty, joblessness, "boredom," few mentors, and even fewer constructive youth activities as key factors leading to street violence. She blurted out that children were "disrespectful" because "there is nothing for them to do!"

Wolf was on staff in the HOPE Zone (HZ) office, which was strategically located in Southbridge's housing projects. Dayveair was a registered member of the HZ's afterschool program. Staff at the HZ took an interest in Dayveair after noticing his obvious signs of trauma and increasing involvement in the streets. He had a severe learning disability and a penchant for violence, and also was rumored to hustle drugs. Like other mothers in Southbridge, Yadira had repeatedly asked Wolf to assist her with Dayveair. However, Wolf's schedule was already overwhelmed.

Perhaps feeling guilty that he was not able to intervene in Dayveair's life, Wolf asked Yadira, "One time you mentioned . . . that you needed me to talk to Dayveair. . . . We all feel saddened by his death, but if Dayveair's father [Roger Hall] was home [from prison] . . . do you think it would have made a difference [prevented him from being killed]?"

Puzzled by the question, Yadira dove into a soliloquy that rejected the assumption that Dayveair would be alive if Roger had been active in his life. After all, Roger was in prison, which suggested to Yadira that his involvement with crime on the outside had a negative influence on Dayveair. I also sensed that Yadira wondered if we questioned her fitness as a mother. Clinging to her dignity, Yadira attributed Dayveair's behavioral problems to the absence of a positive Black male role model. For Yadira, it was obvious that a single mother raising a teenage Black boy and two other younger children in a neighborhood rife with violence could not provide the Black male mentorship Dayveair so desperately needed.

Yadira declared, "Dayveair wasn't a bad kid. He was just caught up in the neighborhood or everyday lifestyles. I wanted better for him. . . . It's hard when you are a single mother trying to raise three kids and trying to be a mother and father, or trying to be everything to your children."

Staring at Wolf, Yadira said, "It's hard. I asked for help. I'm not sure if his father would have made a difference. . . . Dayveair having his father around could have harmed him. His father may have not been the right person for him. His father could have led him down the wrong path, too. I think a child still needs some type of male role model in their life, regardless if it is their father, uncle, friend. . . . They need somebody there to teach them how to be a man, not just negativity. And I was screaming out for Dayveair to get help!"

Residents with an established relationship were allowed to critically evaluate the conditions surrounding a homicide. Therefore, it was not inappropriate for Wolf to carefully challenge Yadira on the circumstances of Dayveair's life and death. Indeed, this delicate conversation traversed sensitive emotional terrain, but local cultural mores allowed for this moment to take place. Small-town dynamics could exacerbate the violence, but the advantage of Wilmington's small neighborhoods was that they also facilitated lasting and interwoven relationships that were drawn on during dark periods. Collective memories and key relationships were cultural currency in a small city, as revealed in Yadira and Wolf's terse exchange. Their textured relationship spanned at least twenty years. Wolf and many of his friends were from the Riverside neighborhood in Wilmington's Northside, but they socialized with Dayveair's father Roger, who was from Southbridge. Consequently, Wolf had spent considerable time around Yadira and her friends. Wolf and Yadira's friendship was shaped by overlapping relationships that, across time, coalesced to produce a safe moment for Yadira and Wolf to engage in a sensitive and frank conversation about Dayveair.

There were five of us in this closed space with Yadira, and I was the only outsider or noncommunity member in attendance. At this point, I asked no questions; I just sat there and absorbed the exchange. The high social capital of the Associates eased the potential for an explosive conversation with Yadira. Our discussion with Yadira was obviously more than a standard interview. Because of the Associates' social standing in the Southbridge, our interview was re-invented into a space of group bonding, in search of greater insight about violence in Wilmington. Yadira had at least a dozen of these same talks with close family and friends since the passing of Dayveair. Cathartic conversations like these were how she managed the pain of her son's death. Black men and women in Southbridge relied heavily on key relationships to soften the enduring sting of violence. Social networks and support from religious and other nonprofit institutions were among the most valuable resources residents like Yadira had available to cope with homicide. Southbridge's capacity to cope with homicide was also anchored in racial-ethnic and cultural forms of mourning. The way close family and friends convened on street corners and inside homes, the religious rituals bestowed at funerals, and the gendered methods of mourning were all particular expressions of how Black people in Southbridge survived homicide.[24]

Dayveair's tragic death confirmed for me that Wilmington was a tough city, but it was by no means the embodiment of gun violence. One homicide in this small town, however, was enough to suck out the city's oxygen, making the Eastside and Southbridge feel more unsafe than it actually was. To the surprise of many who lived outside of these neighborhoods, most residents who were street-identified were not violent as a form of identity, or violent as a primary hustle. The "muscle," "street fighter," "hired gun," "shooter," or so-called violent sociopath represented the smallest slice of Wilmington's street-identified community.[25]

Street communities in the Eastside and Southbridge were insular spaces, and their members often worked hard to prevent community activities, and especially crime, from spilling outside of their borders. Upper-middle-class people were generally the safest or the least likely to be physically harmed. Ironically, it was still the outsider's outrage and fear that typically framed the public narrative and policy responses to violence in Wilmington.[26] Unable to properly interpret the violence, outsiders often conflated victimization and perpetration, thus greatly misrepresenting the danger in Wilmington.

Most members of the streets were not violent as a form of identity (i.e., "the shooter"), and an even smaller segment of the street was repeatedly victimized by violence. More often, we found that most street-identified Black men and women suffered from being repeatedly exposed to co-victimization or vicarious incidents of violence.

Exposure versus Victimization

Virtually all participants in our study suffered from chronic exposure to street violence. Exposure to violent crime and poverty is also linked to the psychological and social well-being of low-income Black neighborhoods. Family dynamics or dysfunction,[27] general fear and anxiety related to personal safety,[28] and concern for more safe places for children to play[29] are well cited in the literatures that address the relationship between violent crime, inequality, and well-being. Jones's African-centered project, for instance, examined how exposure to street violence negatively affected the psychological, family, and social well-being of a community sample of seventy-one low-income urban Black children (ages 9–11) in Houston, Texas.[30] Nineteen percent witnessed someone they knew being stabbed or shot, and 10% reported seeing someone they knew being killed. Jones also found that formal kinship networks improved psychological, family, and social well-being.[31]

Most survey participants in our study had witnessed people being threatened with assault, robbed or mugged, chased by a group of people, or seriously injured by an act of violence (see table 3.1). A majority of participants also reported losing a friend or relative to gun violence. And the men, unsurprisingly, were much more likely to be exposed to all forms of violence. Our data have significant implications for the psychological and social well-being of our participants and residents of the Eastside and Southbridge, who are pummeled by chronic exposure to street violence.

TABLE 3.1
Exposure to Violence

	Male	Female	Low occurrence (1–4 times)	High occurrence (9+ times)	Total sample
I saw someone threatened with serious violence	73.8%	66%	24.7%	34.7%	68.2%
I saw someone beaten up or mugged	64.7%	51.2%	25.4%	28.4%	62.2%
I saw someone being chased by a group of people	65%	49.2%	25%	22.4%	55.5%
I saw someone seriously injured after an act of violence	66.5%	54.3%	28.4%	21.8%	59.8%
I have a relative who was killed with a gun	56.3%	53.5%	—	—	54.6%
I have a friend who was killed with a gun	57.8%	60.1%	—	—	59.2%

About 62% of participants had observed someone being beaten up or mugged at least once, while 12% had observed such street activities more than twelve times. In fact, 81% noted that they had seen someone robbed before, with at least 27% witnessing this in the week prior to completing the survey. This overall pattern of exposure to violence coincided with other indicators of victimization, as most were exposed to various forms of violence, with a smaller group being repeatedly exposed to these specific acts. For instance, nearly 60% reported viewing a "seriously injured person" after an incident of violence, and 16% reported observing this more than twelve times. Eighty percent admitted to ever seeing someone seriously harmed, with at least 19% reporting observing this a week prior to completing this survey.

The most poignant of the data on the exposure to violence were people who had lost a loved one to gun violence. Chillingly, more than half of our survey sample had lost a family member or a close friend to gun violence. About 55% reported at least one relative killed with a gun; of these, 70% specified decedents who were cousins, while 15% were brothers. Sixty percent had lost at least one close friend to gun violence.

Unlike in the exposure data, most participants did not report being repeatedly victimized by street violence (see table 3.2). However, persons who were victimized generally fell into one of two groups: periodically victimized or repeatedly victimized. Although relatively few were occasionally assaulted, robbed, chased by a group, attacked with a knife, or shot, the men in this

TABLE 3.2
Violence Victimization

	Male	Female	Low occurrence (1–4 times)	High occurrence (9+ times)	Total sample
I was threatened with serious violence	52%	43.4%	23.2%	26.8%	52.2%
I was slapped, punched, or hit by someone	45%	41%	23.7%	22.5%	42%
I was robbed	34%	19%	16.2%	11.1%	25%
I was chased by a group	27.5%	16%	8.8%	9.6%	20.6%
I was stabbed	32%	20%	13.4%	9.2%	25.2%
I was shot	29.2%	13.4%	9.8%	10%	20%

sample were much more likely to be victimized by all forms of violence. Also, most (55%) did experience low-level, simple assaults like being "slapped, punched, or hit by someone." Almost 25% admitted they had been assaulted one to four times, and 16% had been assaulted more than twelve times.

About 30% were mugged; of these, 16% were robbed one to four times and 11% were robbed nine or more times. Similar outcomes emerged for stabbings and shootings. It is important to underscore that the vast majority of street-identified persons in our sample had never been stabbed or shot. Generally, people who experienced this level of violence experienced either few or many instances of stabbings and shootings. Approximately 25% reported being stabbed, and of those attacked, 13% were knifed one to four times, and 8% were stabbed more than twelve times. Younger participants (18–21) were also more likely than older age groups (22–29 and 30–35) to report being stabbed one to four times or repeatedly knifed more than twelve times.

As with the reported stabbings, most (80%) street-identified persons had never been shot. About 10% reported being shot between one to four times, and 6% had been shot more than twelve times. Younger participants (18–21) were again more likely than older ones (22–29 and 30–35) to report being shot more than twelve times.

MOST STREET-IDENTIFIED Black men and women in the Eastside and Southbridge were not victimized by extreme violence, nor did they routinely perpetrate violence. Instead, most struggled with chronic exposure to violence, the effects of which were likely heightened in a small city. Violence was less of a social norm than publicly portrayed, but one vicious incident in Wilmington was enough to permeate its social environment for weeks. The social intensity of the homicide sometimes outgrew the actual demography of Wilmington's violent crime rates. Some homicides more acutely and negatively affected Wilmington's social equilibrium. A single homicide sometimes had more impact than three to five homicides over the same six-week period, particularly if the victim was well known or in the streets, or considered to be an unfortunate or undeserving victim.

Researchers and public officials generally did not account for the intensity of homicides—this was a mistake. The deeper stories that surrounded the homicides always grounded the perspectives of Black residents in Wilmington, and oftentimes, these stories were morbid and very difficult to absorb. To our surprise, however, most victimized persons we spoke with did not allow their experiences to stifle their well-being or future aspirations.

Eighteen-year-old Shaq from the Eastside was viciously beaten at age 14 by a group of older men. Walking home, exhausted from football practice, Shaq was accused of breaking into their car and stealing a Playstation (video game console). Confused and shocked, Shaq tried to explain that this was a case of mistaken identity, but "they just started hopping on me. They just started swinging but I'm fighting back. . . . It was going on for like a good five or ten minutes and then they left. My shirt is ripped. I was limping. My lips was bleeding and [I had a] swollen eye. . . . I didn't feel it, but my jaw was fractured and . . . I had to get it wired shut for like two months. But it was in the past, I'm not gonna worry about it now." Undeterred by this event, Shaq enrolled in art school and he looked forward to becoming a filmmaker.

Thirty-year-old Husk had retired from the streets and now was a youth counselor in Southbridge. Given his new position, he was a bit guarded about sharing his previous experiences with gun violence. In his early twenties, Husk had been shot in his liver, collarbone, pancreas, chest, and head. After waking up from a two-month coma, it was difficult for him to come to terms with shrinking from 230 to 95 pounds. Greatly challenged by "learn[ing] how to walk again, [and] write" again, his new reality not only frightened him, but it exacerbated his paranoia so much so he would "snap." "It looks crazy! The look is different. Scars on you that you [never seen before]. . . . It does something [to you]. Like one day, you might wake up and snap. [I was shot] everywhere . . . just missed this artery right here. . . . You know, if you get shot under your collarbone, it hit an artery, you're done. . . . I still got a [bullet] fragment [lodged inside of me]."

Again, relatively few in the Eastside and Southbridge were victims of repeated violence. But a single episode of homicide was enough in a small city to permanently disrupt family and neighborhood dynamics. Homicide sometimes positively mobilized Wilmington with vigils, forums, or rallies—but it also ate away at the city's social resolve. Put simply, the streets and local residents were emotionally broken by the violence while simultaneously and miraculously finding ways to survive it.

DUBARD AND STREET PAR: SURVIVING VIOLENCE AND INEQUALITY

The lives of Street PAR Associates mirrored how other residents experienced violence in Wilmington. Almost all Associates had been shot at or were victims of gun violence, and/or all Associates had close family members and friends who were victims of gun violence. Like many in the community, they also experienced the complexity of emotional and physical recovery.

Dubard "Dubie" McGriff (Associate) had never been shot, stabbed, or jumped by a group, but he had repeatedly witnessed people being seriously injured. And admittedly, the impact of these events has permanently affected him. Hard drugs were regularly used and sold in the basement of his grandmother's house, the home he was raised in. Most of his aunts and uncles struggled with addiction, and according to Dubard, "The only thing we worried about was if we got caught, was the State going to take us away? That was a constant worry for me as a child." Dubard was selling drugs by age 12, which in some ways made him extremely popular as a youth. Dubard's mother also routinely hosted house parties for him, even during the weekdays, "and then [he'd] get up the next morning and go right to school like it wasn't nothing." Sometimes at high school he purchased pizza for the entire school.

And then it ended. Charged as an adult at age 17, Dubard was later sentenced to four years in Howard R. Young Correctional Institution for drugs, robbery, and possession of firearms. We met a year after his release from prison in 2008. He was now age 21.

During the project's first year (2010), Dubard's mother died from complications from substance abuse and his grandmother passed away from natural causes. Two or three hundred attended his grandmother's funeral. She was clearly the family's matriarch and a beloved community staple. In the second year, his 22-year-old brother, KaBron Rykard, was shot and killed. Dubard had a total of ten siblings—seven on his father's side and three from his mother. He also had two daughters, and Dubard was the primary caretaker of one daughter and his younger sister. At 23, he was a rising patriarch, and I was unsure how he kept himself together while focusing on his re-entry into Wilmington.

When I first met Dubard, he was withdrawn. He later said his "numbed" disposition shielded him from impending trauma. His former use of "Xanies" (Xanax) also helped deaden the sting of "bad news." Admittedly, he loved many but trusted few. Pain had taught him to guard his emotions. Violent trauma had even forced Dubard to be worried about his daughter's future, because he wanted to insulate her from the inevitable experience of "loss."

"That's what we do—we live, we die, and we kill each other.... I'm numb. My numbness is how I deal with it. I want to care, I want to love, I even want to cry sometimes, but I don't know how.... I think about my daughter all the time.... I worry about her and how she will experience loss. Loss is inevitable, though. Everybody loses at some point. But I don't want her to lose, though. I seen so much loss and death that I am not even surprised when someone dies. Sometimes you can tell when somebody is about to get killed. The way they moving in the streets, the way they talk, the way they act, you can just tell when somebody's about to get killed. It's like you can smell it or feel it in the air. That's why I don't trust nobody. I want to trust people, but I can't right now."

At a meeting in January 2010, Dubard matter-of-factly explained that the night before, he witnessed the death of 9-year-old Tommy White Jr. The city reeled from this Black boy's torturous death. Unlicensed 17-year-old Latika Wright accidently drove over Tommy at Twenty-Fifth and Jessup Streets.[32] Tommy was struck while he rode an electric scooter recently purchased for him by his father. He was lodged beneath the vehicle, and Latika unknowingly dragged him for at least five blocks. Dubard and several friends driving on Twenty-Third and Lamotte Streets saw Tommy's body dangling from the back of Latika's car. They immediately gave chase to inform her. Onlookers also screamed and ran to the vehicle to alert Latika. At a stop sign, she finally rolled down the window to make sense of the commotion. After comprehending the gravity of the circumstance, the shocked Latika turned off the car, took the keys, and bolted on foot from the vehicle. Dubard and others worked tirelessly to lift the vehicle off of Tommy. They were unsuccessful. Dubard knelt down and tried to convince Tommy "that it was going to be alright. I just kept hearing, 'huh, huh, huh.' I can still hear his voice to this day. And then blood just started oozing out everywhere." Tommy died before paramedics arrived. Latika was arrested nearly a month later. The influence of drugs and alcohol were rumored to have blunted her sensibilities that afternoon. Dubard said, "She was on pills, Xanies most likely. At least that's what she was known for doing. But I don't think she did that on purpose. It was really an accident. But she might have been high. She was the type of girl that grew up rough. She had low self-esteem and fought a lot. She's the type that would get upset at people when they question her about it [driving over Tommy], . . . That was her way to cope with some crazy shit. I honestly think she feels f-cked up for killing that little boy. Funny thing is, her baby father got killed a block away from where she ran over that boy."

Judge Oliver Toliver sentenced Latika to serve six months of a suspended two-year sentence in home confinement. She was also required to pay restitution for failure to report the fatal crash; to participate in 200 hours of community service; to have no contact with the victim's family; to undergo alcohol abuse and mental health treatment; to not drive or take any drugs or alcohol for the period of her sentence; to obtain her GED certificate; and to participate in an "enhanced supervision program."

STORIES FROM THE PERSPECTIVE OF DUBARD and other Associates were authentic examples of how the concentric cycles of violence linked residents together.

For this reason, our project was more than a study to the Street PAR Associates. The more they did to reduce violence, the more enthused they became. But Wilmington's epidemic of violence was so ubiquitous that Associates were not immune to its impact. No matter how much change they created, gun violence still found ways to seep into their lives.

"CODE BLUE, IT'S A CODE BLUE!" HOMICIDE HITS THE STREET PAR FAMILY

In September 2010 we interviewed Wolf's son, Muhammad. His birth name was Dominique Helms, and most in Wilmington knew him as "Dom." Muhammad was his Islamic name, and it was generally used by close family, friends, and his Muslim community. Muhammad was a 19-year-old, thin, dark-skinned male with prescription glasses and thick sideburns. Melodie, Kenyatta, Louis, and I spoke with him on a basketball court in Southbridge's Elbert Palmer Park—a park that had its fair share of violence, including street fights and shoot-outs. We sat near one of the court's backboards, which had the word "Southbridge" sloppily scribbled in black spray paint.

Muhammad described the Eastside, a neighborhood he lived in as a small boy and still frequented, as being more affected by "juvenile violence" than "adult violence." "Juvenile violence" represented less lethal forms of violence like teenage bullying, low-level assaults, and sale and use of narcotics, while "adult violence" referred to shootings or homicides. Overall, Muhammad attributed involvement in crime to structural inequality: "I've always been a firm believer [that] if you don't have money to throw around, life is very hard for normal people.... If you don't have the financial stability to survive, you're going to end up doing something inappropriate [to make ends meet]." He blamed Delaware's elite for the striking impoverished conditions found in the Eastside and Southbridge. For Muhammad, it was the economic "hoarding" of mostly white elites that prevented these communities from rebounding. Muhammad concluded that city leadership had no intentions of rectifying the extreme poverty experienced by thousands. Passionately, he reminded us, "They [city leadership] don't help my community. They might help the overall city's wealth ... but they don't help the places that really need help.... It's really a lot of issues out there that people don't realize.... People really live in poverty.... It's really horrible in some houses. *I'm talking like, really bad!*"

Much of Muhammad's structural awareness was taught to him by his mother and father, and he also learned from his personal observations of Black Wilmington. Although Wolf was incarcerated for much of Muhammad's early life, he still remained in consistent contact with him throughout his incarceration. And it was in these moments that Wolf skillfully imparted a critical analysis of structural violence, or how formal leadership targeted their family and Black Wilmington for structural devastation.

Wolf had completed most of the requirements for his Bachelor of Arts degree in sociology at the University of California–Davis prior to his incarceration in 1997, and he was awarded the degree right before his release from a halfway house in January 2009. In November 2008, while at the halfway house, he began as an outreach worker for the HOPE Commission and a research assistant for Dr. Karen Parker at the University of Delaware (UD), who was contracted by the HOPE Commission to lead a street outreach project on violence. After reviewing Wolf's CV, I encouraged him to apply for the sociology doctoral program at UD. In the next few months, Wolf completed his GRE exam and applied to the PhD program in fall 2010. In April 2011, he received his acceptance letter for fall 2011. Classes were months away from starting, but he immediately began collecting publications on Marx, Engels, Durkheim, and Weber, among other classic and contemporary scholars. It looked to me like he had about four or five dozen printed readings, not to mention what he may have also downloaded. I said to him, "This is too much. Maybe read some of this, but there is no need to try and master all of this material before late August. The average first-year doctoral student is not prepping like this. Relax. You will be fine."

It was early September, and we were elated during our research meeting at UD. Our progress was notable, and we had a lot to be proud of. We were in the middle of analysis and still very active on the ground with programming. We also had at least four Associates enrolled in college, and most were employed. We were also ecstatic that public officials and, most importantly, the community took our project so seriously. We left this meeting at UD in such high spirits.

Later that evening, I received a blunt text from Wolf: "My son's been shot. He's dead. I'm at ChristianaCare." I called back but he did not pick up. A flood of phone calls and texts followed from others. Dumbstruck and shaken, I gathered myself and hastily drove to ChristianaCare Hospital. I stumbled into a waiting room where I saw throngs of Black people. Everyone stared at me. Thinking I was in the wrong location, I decided to search elsewhere. While I was walking out, someone shouted, "Dr. Payne?" I did not recognize him, but he graciously pointed to his right and said, "Wolfie is outside." I rushed out of the waiting room and slowly approached Wolf, who was in the middle of a conversation with two people. Derrick, Wolf's younger brother and Associate on the project, walked in circles about 75 to 100 feet away, flailing his arms and spouting obscenities.

Dominique Muhammad Helms was shot and killed by 26-year old Lynell Tucker on September 14, 2011.[33] Muhammad was just shy of his twentieth birthday on September 23. Lynell had arrived at his grandmother's home to see Muhammad and Shakeem laughing on the porch. Muhammad and Shakeem were cousins, and Shakeem and Lynell were also cousins and grandchildren of the same grandmother. By way of his uncle Derrick, Muhammad was technically related to Lynell's family, and he enjoyed spending time at the home of Lynell's grandmother. The grandmother and matriarch of the home also considered Muhammad her grandson.

Irritated, Lynell exploded and banished everyone from his grandparent's property: "I want everybody off my grandma's step!" Clinically diagnosed with a "lower IQ" and impulsive behavior, Lynell was known to bully youth in Wilmington.[34] He was even rumored to have stripped a young boy of his clothes and forced him to walk home naked.

As Lynell drove away to park, Muhammad yelled back, "I know you are not talking to me. This is my family!"

The argument sharpened and then they fought. Muhammad, who was younger, got the best of Lynell. Lynell's father stormed out of the house to break up the fight but ended up getting into a physical skirmish with Muhammad. Muhammad said to Lynell before he walked away, "You're lucky your pops just saved your life." Muhammad returned home, which was a few minutes away by foot. He made it to the front steps, turned around, and Lynell was behind him waving a gun. Words were exchanged, and Muhammad tried to flee, but he was shot once through his back. Clutching for breath and coughing up blood, he made it through his front door and collapsed in his mother's arms.[35]

THAT EVENING AT CHRISTIANACARE HOSPITAL, a staff member in the emergency room yelled over the intercom, "All doctors, Code Blue! It's a Code Blue! All doctors and staff report to room 4."

"Code Blue" is the most urgent distress call to all available hospital staff for assistance to resuscitate. After hearing these clarion words, Wolf looked over to his wife Nicky and calmly said, "You know our son just died?" Muhammad was pronounced dead soon after the Code Blue announcement.

Lynell left town the night of the murder. Captain Nancy Dietz promised Wolf that she would bring Lynell to justice before she retired. It rained on September 23, Muhammad's twentieth birthday. It was twelve days after his murder, with no word of Lynell. Wolfie had just left UD to drive home to Wilmington. Captain Dietz called him on his cell phone. Wolfie recalled, "It was raining. I was in my car and Nancy called. I picked up and she said, 'Wolfie! We got him!'"

Marshals found Lynell on the 2300 block of North Jefferson Street in Daytona Beach, Florida. He was later convicted of first-degree murder and possession of a firearm during the commission of a felon and was incarcerated for life without the possibility of parole.

Muhammad's funeral was held at Darul-Amaanah Mosque near the corner of Fourth and Delmore Streets. Darul-Amaanah is a small, quaint, and humble Black American Sunni Muslim mosque, deeply cherished by the surrounding neighborhood. Darul-Amaanah was filled beyond capacity. About one-third of mourners sat in chairs; the rest stood against the walls, sat on the floor, and spilled outside of its doors. The locally revered Imam Abu Maahir (née Ishmael Hacket) presided over Muhammad's funeral. Afterward, family and friends in large numbers chatted outside. An elongated procession of about seventy cars, vans, SUVs, and pickup trucks turned on their hazard lights and honked their horns as we followed Muhammad's hearse. At the Fourth and Church Streets intersection, Captain Faheem Akil—a Sunni Muslim, police officer, Black man, and dear friend of Wolf—was proud to wave the procession through. We drove twenty minutes away to Hunt Irving Chapel at Haven Memorial Cemetery in Chester, Pennsylvania.

Sunni Muslims are buried in highly ritualist cultural form. Only the men were allowed to physically bury Muhammad; the women remained far on the periphery or in the parking lot. Upward of fifty to seventy Black men surrounded Muhammad's gravesite. A line formed and one by one, Black men jumped into Muhammad's grave and used their bare hands to dig dirt out of the bottom, most eastern section of the grave. Then Muhammad's body, wrapped in white cloth, was lowered. Autopsies are not allowed on Muslim corpses, so some blood spilled out as his body was positioned to face the East.

Tears streamed down my face and I kept shaking my head in disbelief. I was the only man in tears. Most were silent, and the mood was grim. These men were deeply sad, but they had learned how to numb that part of themselves in order to endure. I suppose death, and more specifically, murder, were too common to emotionally lose yourself. But I could not help myself. Wolf was silent, tearless, and as strong as ever, with beads of sweat streaming down his bald head and face. Many relied on him for help with food, paying bills, or resolving conflicts. Wolf was used to being a weighted-down community pillar, but I now wondered who would truly be there for him.

Muhammad died almost one year to the day after we last interviewed him. His magnificent spirit was the epitome of unrealized Black male greatness that was stolen from Wilmington. He was a part of the ROTC program in high school and was months away from joining the army—he just needed to retake his eye exam. After the army, Muhammad aspired to enroll in college, like his father.

EVERY YEAR, I call Wolf on Muhammad's birthday (September 23) and passing day (September 14). Sometimes I think it is best to leave him alone, but he insists that on those days he needs to be around "good people."

What Wolf and his family were faced with was unimaginable, but what was even more disturbing was his decision to return to the doctoral program about a month after Muhammad's passing. I encouraged Wolf to take the year off and relax—"UD will maintain its commitment to you," I tried to reassure him.

"I would love to take a year off to reflect, but becoming a doctoral student also means this is how I am going to feed myself. I'm a take a year off to go where, and do what?"

The lives of Associates mirrored what families struggling with homicide dealt with—limited opportunities. The added stressor of a homicide easily overwhelmed their daily schedules. Finding time to adequately mourn or cope with homicide was a luxury afforded only to the fortunate or privileged.

Violence saturated Wolf's life. He had lost countless friends and now his son to gun violence. Prior to his incarceration, Wolf was also shot on two separate occasions, once in his back and once in his leg. Even with great loss, he has proudly held onto his roles as family patriarch and trusted community pillar. But most were unaware of how Wolf concealed his growing emotional and psychological troubles. Although he was never clinically diagnosed with post-traumatic stress disorder, he now had high blood pressure, bouts of insomnia, violent dreams, a touch of ADHD, and general anxiety. Exposure to street violence and its resultant psychosocial symptoms deeply impacted him.

In 2014, as part of his strategy for coping with Muhammad's death, Wolf led a gun violence outreach program with ChristianaCare Hospital, the City of Wilmington, and the State of Delaware. Wolf had been involved with gun violence prevention since 2009, but it was in 2014 that he was able to get stable resources for this prevention program. To date, Wolf and several Associates have visited over 90% of shooting and homicide crime scenes. When appropriate, they offer support to enraged loved ones either at the scene, at emergency rooms, and/or at their homes. They also sat with youth to "talk them down" from committing retaliatory gun violence.

The Wilmington Street PAR Project went far beyond an empirical investigation. For the Associates, their participation in activism was as equally important as the analysis. Associates also appreciated how the project blended warmth with serious academic focus. They coalesced into a social and professional network they could actually rely on for guidance and material support. In addition, this unity of men and women, formerly involved with the streets, vis-à-vis a research-activist project quickly represented a beacon of hope in a small city environment. Taken seriously by leadership, they now represented a radical, refreshing and durable example of change in Wilmington.

Furthermore, although small city size was useful for building relationships, small size also influenced why overlapping or concentrated relationships sometimes spiraled out of control with violence. Outside of police interventions, relatively few well-resourced programs existed in Wilmington to offset violent crime and the reality of extreme poverty. From our perspective, or in this social-structural context, violence was adaptive, not only to survive the streets but also to provide material resources. Most were not regular victims of violence, nor were they violent as a form of identity—but most were willing to be violent if they deemed it necessary. And nearly everyone we encountered in the streets was overly exposed to the outcomes of gun violence. Witnessing and hearing about friends and family being robbed, assaulted, and killed was too difficult for them to continually absorb.

VIOLENCE REDUCTION PROGRAMS would greatly benefit from accounting for the *social intensity* of shootings and homicides. Chronic exposure to gun violence was a certainly a problem in Wilmington, but the intensity of one homicide sometimes had a more negative impact than multiple homicides over the same time period, particularly in a small city with really small neighborhoods. For example, the brazen murders of the brothers of Kenyatta and Dubard (Associates), Herman, Dayveair, little Tommy, and Muhammad cut so deeply into Black Wilmington's soul that for months, these homicides overshadowed much of the subsequent, unrelated violence in the city.

Therefore, to reduce gun violence, it is necessary to *culturally* evaluate *all incidents*. This variation indicated that to reduce gun violence, it was necessary to *culturally* evaluate *all violent incidents*. Street PAR Associates filled this void because they possessed the cultural awareness and capacity to evaluate the violence and work with the streets. Community professionals generally did not understand the underlying stories at the center of the shootings. But residents and especially Street PAR Associates knew the people and surrounding stories well, and as a result, they knew how to navigate the violence. Typically, outsiders merely reacted to the reported raw numbers and the media's salacious language with punitive policy.

Contrary to prevailing messages, we found that street-identified Black men and women in the Eastside and Southbridge wanted what most Americans wanted: safe communities, quality jobs and schools, and stable housing. Everyone we encountered in the streets also treasured their connection with their community. The right set of relationships was a cultural currency that was cherished and traded in neighborhoods with few material resources. The Eastside and Southbridge consisted of an inherently interdependent body of social networks that required some degree of real co-operation with each other. And because of this complex, intergenerational interconnectedness concentrated in a small city, poor Black Wilmington was much more a loving community than it ever was a stereotypical "Murder Town, USA."

PART TWO

*Management,
Containment, and the
Social Control of Black
Wilmington*

Chapter 4

"I'm Still Waiting Man ... on That Golden Ticket!"

EDUCATION AND ECONOMIC JUSTICE,
A DREAM DEFERRED—IN PERPETUITY

> We are nothing more than modern-day slaves living on a modern-day plantation. It was that speech, "The Other America," that broke it down when MLK said, "What does it matter if I have the freedom to sit at the lunch counter as my white counterpart, and I cannot afford the same hamburger?" And it was then I realized the matrix, which is ... as African Americans, primarily we don't have access ... to jobs. You don't have access to opportunity. We don't have access to capital that is not predatory.... That leaves you in an environment where we're surrounded with drugs, gangs, guns, alcohol, and bullets. You are surrounded in a war zone ... and basically this is economic genocide.... We are positioned to die! We are positioned to kill. We are positioned to be killed—thus all the violence.... That's what you're going to get ... when you don't have access ... to [opportunity].
> —Byron Allen, "Billionaire Byron Allen Talks Black Wealth with Antonio Moore"

CHRIS ANDREW COONS is a U.S. senator and one of Delaware's most charismatic personalities. Originally from Hockessin, a wealthy white suburb in New Castle County, Coons now lives with his wife and their three children in Wilmington. The church's messages on virtue, love, and justice that he received as a child inspired him later to incorporate these values as core part of his political platform. His early church experiences had made such an impression that Coons became an ordained elder at West Presbyterian in Wilmington.

Senator Coons easily adapted to different audiences or circumstances. He effortlessly held one-on-one conversations on a street corner or inside a coffee shop, and he also connected with churchgoers while giving sermons on Sundays at both Black and white churches. Without breaking a sweat, Coons had the ability to grab the hearts of small crowds, and then shift gears and provide articulate commentary on CNN or at a press conference. His calm and caring demeanor surfaced during public moments, and he made everyday people feel like they really mattered. Coons's consistent professionalism also satiated the ruthless appetites of Delaware's predominantly white establishment, which was a difficult social chord to strike. His political acumen made him a public darling in and outside of Delaware.

The quintessential politician, Senator Coons is a well-educated, wealthy, and extraordinarily ambitious politician who, by all accounts, is committed to the public good. Senator Coons earned his JD from Yale Law School and a master's degree in ethics from Yale Divinity School. Prior to becoming a U.S. senator, Coons had a relatively short life in politics. In 2000, he was president of the New Castle County Council, and in 2008, he became county executive of New Castle County. In 2010, Coons took over Joe Biden's old senatorial seat in Delaware.

Senator Coons is also a part of the "top 1%" of Americans.[1] In fact, Delaware's U.S. senators, representative, and governor were all members of this top 1%. While most sources could not confirm how he amassed his wealth, some estimates put Senator Coons's net worth between $6 million and $15 million.

In a post–Great Recession environment, employment became a major part of Coons's platform. In fact, his first bill in 2011 was the Job Creation through Innovation Act. This bill was intended to provide tax credits for small businesses, encourage companies overseas to return to the United States, and incentivize green energy markets. Coons's legislation died in committee, but in a city where Black men hungered for work, the whiff of "job creation" was still a breath of fresh air.

Our Street PAR project began in 2010, the same year Coons won his senatorial seat. And with our repeated messages on structural violence, we managed to grab his attention. In a small town, it was possible to create a messaging vortex on racial inequality.

In September 2013, we unveiled the first iteration of our study, *The People's Report*, as a feature-length documentary, an interactive website, a 173-page report, and three social media platforms.[2] Thousands attended dozens of viewings of the documentary in Delaware, and countless numbers read our report and listened to our presentations. We cultivated a strong base of support in the Eastside and Southbridge and also outside of these neighborhoods, including support from a large segment of white liberals in Wilmington and throughout Delaware.

Later that fall of 2013, Senator Coons's office requested a copy of the documentary. Excited, we dropped one off at his office the next day. A few months later, we met with Senator Coons, and he validated our message on structural violence. And then he promised to do something about it.

"Winning the Fight against Urban Unemployment"

In February 2014, Senator Coons established an employment commission to reduce high levels of unemployment in Delaware's "urban" communities. "Urban" was really a euphemism for poor Black people. Though it was attacked for being too exclusionary, the mandate's language was flexible enough to include other low-income populations. This was one of my first major lessons on navigating Delaware's political winds, and the winds here were strong and very resistant to structural change. Delaware's liberal identity was a superficial branding that never reflected how truly racialized or conservative the state was on issues like opportunity, poverty, and crime.

Senator Coons convened the first of four meetings, which together were called the "Winning the Fight against Urban Unemployment Discussion Series," on Wednesday, February 19, 2014, at Wilmington's historic Goodwill of Delaware and Delaware County Building. Bold political gestures like this were rare from mainstream candidates in Delaware. Coons's threatening of the status quo was risky and potentially career ending. But the young senator still went forward, promising to bring greater opportunities to poor, urban, and mostly Black residents. Right before this first meeting, Senator Coons boldly said to a reporter,

> Chronic urban unemployment is an epidemic that is tearing at our communities and eroding our neighbors' quality of life. Unemployment rates in Delaware's urban communities are significantly higher than in other parts of the state and have been for years. Crime, poverty, chemical dependence, and lack of educational opportunity all contribute to stubborn jobless numbers that have confounded elected officials and community leaders for decades. The goal of this series is to confront the problem head-on, generating actionable ideas for addressing it locally in our community and legislatively in Washington. . . . We cannot let the complexity of this challenge scare us away from confronting it. . . . As elected leaders, we need to keep trying and we have to come together as a community to find solutions.[3]

On the morning of February 19, an impressive group of grassroots leaders and public officials assembled for a ninety-minute meeting at the Goodwill Building. Formally dressed professionals clamored for entry, and I was among this designated group of stakeholders. Security was tight. After our photo IDs were cross-referenced with a master list, we passed through a metal detector and were directed to a large conference room.

JP Morgan Chase's vice president of global philanthropy and community relations, the president of the Metropolitan Wilmington Urban League, representatives of the mayor's office, the Department of Labor, Wilmington Job

Corps, and the Challenge Program, along with a cadre of well-paid nonprofit executives, all piled into a large conference room for a discussion on improving employment in Delaware's "urban" communities.

Senator Coons and Goodwill's director of workforce development, Zanthea Nichols, moderated the discussion on topics ranging from crime and job training to recidivism. Senator Coons emphasized, "If we're going to overcome the chronic unemployment that is holding back Delaware's urban areas, it's going to be because we came together as a community to do it."[4] Senator Coons went on to distinguish the causes of "urban unemployment" and "unemployment more broadly." Until he noted this distinction, I had never thought about unemployment in this way. Skillfully, he articulated that a "big box store," "reopening a factory," or an infusion of quality employment could not, on its own, improve unemployment in Delaware's urban communities.

"Is that right?" I thought to myself. I also scribbled on my notepad, "An infusion of high-quality jobs was exactly the kind of structural remedy, communities like the Eastside and Southbridge needed. What could be more useful?"

For Coons, "urban unemployment," or Black joblessness, had to do with structural racism and a history of slavery, but it also had to do with poor values, or what Oscar Lewis called a "culture of poverty."[5] Lewis argued that about 20% of poor Black Americans (among other racial-ethnic groups) internalized negative characteristics associated with being impoverished, like laziness or a poor work-ethic, family dysfunction, and social vices (e.g., drug use, hypersexuality, or aggressive and violent behavior).

Senator Coons never actually defined or explained the causes of "general unemployment," or how "general unemployment" differed from "urban unemployment." Itching in my chair, I longed to hear what the different factors were that explained the intergenerational poverty in nonurban places like coalmine West Virginia and white rural Louisiana, or the drugs and violence that are part of life on Native American reservations in Arizona, New Mexico, and Utah. Senator Coons continued, "The causes and symptoms of urban unemployment are historically and fundamentally more complex than for unemployment more broadly. Solving it just isn't as simple as attracting a big box store or reopening a factory. Crime, poverty, chemical dependence, and lack of educational opportunity all contribute to stubborn jobless numbers and struggling communities trapped in a painful cycle."[6]

Senator Coons continued on the need for better employment for returning citizens. Somberly, he said, "It is really challenging to get folks who have spent time in prison employed." Coons was aware of the barriers returning citizens faced in Delaware, but he also believed there was some opportunity to develop a functioning re-entry program centered on quality employment. Senator Coons further argued that "small businesses" inside poor urban Black neighborhoods, or "mom-and-pop shops," needed the financial capital to hire more returning citizens, because these were the businesses that were mostly likely to readily employ them. This was a great idea, and these "small businesses" definitely deserved the support, but this suggestion still fell far short of the structural change needed to address Black unemployment in Wilmington. Equipping the few Black businesses that existed with the capital to hire people with felonies would be a drop in the bucket in terms of the opportunity needed to reverse the immense poverty and joblessness in the Eastside and Southbridge.

Before I could finish scribbling down the questions "What about big businesses in Delaware? Could something be done to make them hire more people with a felony record?" Coons responded, "It was much less likely . . . [for returning citizens] to be employed by major companies or by international companies."[7]

I was not disappointed in Senator Coons's remarks. I deeply appreciated the attention he brought to this matter. Coons sincerely tried to move the ball forward on a court designed to let only some players win.

Most attendants in the room were quiet and reserved. When called on, they either recited empty platitudes or supported a culture of poverty thesis. No one offered any structural explanations.

One Latina woman, an executive director of a nonprofit in Southbridge, argued that "the men" needed to better understand "personal responsibility." This woman's organization was not a re-entry center, nor did she have any formal expertise in this area. But like other nonprofits, it was able to secure a city grant contract to provide job training and free professional attire to returning citizens.

An Arab man who was formerly incarcerated for homicide and now a re-entry specialist in Delaware for the U.S. Probation Office agreed with her framing of returning Black men. He added, "I think the problem with employment, has a lot to do with the motivations of the men." The Latina woman nodded in agreement. A few others nearby also agreed. He continued: "My program has gotten a few guys with felonies, good jobs with construction. Jobs that would help them get on their feet and make good money. They might be on time the first few days. Or, if they don't come in, they won't call to inform their supervisor. Then they still might show up the day after. . . . Some just stop coming, altogether. So, I would say, to improve things, we first need to focus on the true motivations of the men."

Senator Coons added that barriers to employment were further compounded by a failing economic system and the fact that poor Black men had to compete with more qualified applicants in search of work. "Providing the resources for real employment is a challenge. Particularly at a time when we have state and federal budgets that are really constrained and where there are other folks who don't face those challenges who are eager and ready to enter the work force."[8]

I continued to sit quietly. But when he closed out, Senator Coons looked my way. "Dr. Payne, before we wrap up, I wanted to offer you an opportunity to share some final thoughts about employment in urban communities."

Surprised, I quickly gathered my thoughts. "I think, as community professionals, we need more of a realistic understanding of people returning home from prison. I would argue that often, the way we think about employment for this population is not based on what they are actually experiencing. The help is out of context with their reality.... At some point, we have to account for the structural violence that's destroying their communities and making it almost impossible for Black men with a felony to get work."

Then I slowly turned in the direction of the Latina and the Arab man and said, "Yes, at least for me, it does make sense for some men to go to work for a few days and then show up late or not show up at all. When you take into consideration their reality—the low-wages and long hours . . . the disrespect and the loss of dignity that many of them go through on the job, not to mention what they go through outside of the job, then yes—it makes a whole lot of sense that some don't show up on time or up to work. And yes, those same men do really want to work, and they do really care about their families and their communities."

Unexpectedly, a number of people in the room smiled and agreed. Senator Coons and his staff also appeared to be pleased. Shortly after, he ended the meeting with promises to schedule a second one.

A cheerful, murmuring crowd formed, greeting each other with handshakes, hugs, and multiple exchanges of contact information. Two of Senator Coons's aides waved me over and expressed their support. "Dr. Payne, that's why we wanted you here. We knew in this charged atmosphere, some would be reluctant to say what needed to be said, to say what you said, Dr. Payne."

I admire Senator Coons. He is very smart, and this meeting was a bold first step for a U.S. senator to take. In effect, he risked his political career by raising a serious conversation on Black urban unemployment. This is a no-no for mainstream politicians. That said, it is important to note that this esteemed group of stakeholders never met again. This was the first and last time we convened, although Senator Coons said he "looked forward to continuing the dialogue" in at least three other discussions. On its face, our gathering could be criticized for being a well-produced meeting with a great attendance list. No concrete suggestions, recommendations, or agenda were ever nailed down.

But for me, this was a great meeting for different reasons. It is true that no clear solutions were ever identified by the group, but we still had a giant platform to air structural grievances rarely voiced in Delaware's conservative circles. Coons also legitimatized a sensitive conversation on structural violence that so many in the corporate and political sectors wished would quickly disappear. He gave us the political cover or public shielding we so desperately needed to shift the narrative in this city of banks.

Reframing the Narrative about Chronic Black Unemployment

Severe unemployment best explains why so many Black men and women hit the streets. Serious concern about this group's access to opportunity is typically ignored in national, state, and local debates. There are long-standing and widely held beliefs about "the undeserving poor," or the argument that low-income Blacks, especially those who break the law, are culpable for their experiences with unemployment and poverty.[9] These negative beliefs about poor Black people are reinforced by depictions of them as lazy, irresponsible, criminally inclined, hypersexual, and disdainful of traditional middle-class values. Because these stereotypes are deeply embedded in the public's consciousness and street-identified people often lack political power, formal leadership were often reluctant to advocate for greater opportunity for them.[10] As reflected in President Obama's 2012 State of the Union address, which focused on economic opportunity, political and public sympathies lie with those Americans who are believed to "work hard and play by the rules."[11]

We strongly challenge the argument that street-identified Black populations are at fault for their lack of opportunity. Instead, we frame a street identity as sensible, functional, and resilient, or an adaptive means for coping with extreme poverty. Structural barriers were foundational to study participants' experiences with unemployment and poverty. And we found that they genuinely wanted to be educated and gainfully employed, but their opportunities for doing so were severely limited. In general, both liberal and conservative scholars believe that poor Black people's negative experiences with opportunity, and especially the experiences of those who are male and street-identified, are largely due to internationalizing "dysfunctional" social values.[12]

The assertion that low-income Black people are disproportionately unemployed due to their lack of effort or a negative emotional and social outlook on life is absurd. Black people have actually been more willing to accept low-wage jobs than whites, and a higher proportion of Blacks than whites in the labor market are actively looking for work.[13] Other studies clearly reveal that Black men and women in the streets do want legal jobs.[14] Thus, as with education, there is no evidence that a street identity precludes valuing or participating in formal employment.

Structural violence, or the intentional effort by the state to destabilize communities like the Eastside and Southbridge, better explained why so many young Black people went to the streets. Nationally, Black Americans had poorer economic outcomes and less accumulated wealth than any other racial-ethnic group.[15] The median household wealth for whites was twelve times that of Blacks, and while white wealth has increased since 2010, Black wealth has steadily declined since 2002.[16] Among 16- to 19-year-olds, unemployment rates were even more disparate—31.7% for Blacks, 21.2% for Latinos, and 14% for whites. Sum reported a staggering 95% jobless rate for low-income, Black 16- to 18-year-olds who dropped out of school.[17]

Wide-scale deindustrialization beginning in the 1960s prompted a mass exodus of manufacturing firms from urban cities with large Black populations, especially in the Midwest and Northeast, like Wilmington. Factories were sturdy forms of employment for generations, and when these companies left, Black men without a high school diploma or college degree were the most likely to be without a job.[18] As solid working-class jobs went away in urban Black communities, service- or office-related employment dramatically increased in urban and suburban communities. Many, then and now, believed that low-income Black men lacked the "soft" technical or professional skills to do well in this "new" service economy.[19]

Since the Great Recession ended in 2009, the widely reported "new" jobs are more likely to be low-wage jobs that require little skill or experience, such as Uber drivers, cashiers, parking attendants, and fast-food workers.[20] The U.S. Department of Labor projects that of the ten occupations expected to have the most job openings through 2022, seven require less than a high school education.[21] And although most available jobs don't require a high school diploma, Black boys and men are still largely prevented from obtaining them. While a lack of education skills play a role in Black male unemployment rates, hiring discrimination is also a major factor. Employers often view Black men as hostile, lazy, and irresponsible; they instead are much more likely to recruit and hire Black women, men and women of other racial-ethnic groups, and immigrants.[22]

Dis-opportunity in Black Wilmington

For the streets, stable structural opportunity meant access to quality employment, housing, and culturally anchored schooling. For them, jobs, housing, and schools (usually in this order) were the three core pillars that any thriving community required. Sufficient resources, particularly in these forms of opportunity, were believed to create the support needed to take on and navigate a structural landscape of predatory lending, punitive laws and policies, hostile policing, and hyperincarceration. They were also convinced that quality jobs, housing, and schooling would be a fail-safe intervention to eradicating street violence.

During some time period, each study participant struggled with some combination of hunger, substance abuse, neglectful and abusive parenting, substandard living conditions, failing schools, and widespread unemployment. An astonishing 64% reported being unemployed (see table 1.1). Notably, 68% of men reported being unemployed, with 57% actively looking for work. About 63% of women were unemployed, with 54% actively looking for work. In general, employed participants held low-paying jobs in low- or semiskilled employment sectors. Fifty-one percent (N = 134) of all reported jobs were manual labor (17.3%), retail cashier (17.3%), and clerical work (16.5%); while nearly one-third were in food service (9.8%), health care (8.3%), social work (7.5%), and domestic work (6.8%). For many in our study, low wages or too few hours prevented them from meeting their day-to-day material needs, which contributed to a cycle of debt and poverty, and then to their eventual involvement in the streets to supplement their legal incomes.

Richard (age 19) said that Southbridge's isolation from the larger city significantly contributed to its concentrated poverty. Southbridge was separated from greater Wilmington by the Christina River, and only two of its three drawbridges could be used by residents to drive into other sections of the city. Richard also said that many in Southbridge were so poor they did not have internet access, making it very difficult to apply for jobs online and for some children to complete their schoolwork. "In Southbridge . . . I could name . . . two people [with] computers in they crib [home] . . . that have working internet. . . . It's hard to look for a job when you ain't got no money, you gotta get on a bus, you gotta go here and there to fill out applications. . . . When I lived in Southbridge, I never left Southbridge. . . . [There are] no real good payin' jobs unless it's in the middle of the city [Downtown Eastside], where you working in a big building or whatever, or construction."

According to William Julius Wilson, joblessness in poor urban communities have skyrocketed because "two-thirds of employment growth in metropolitan areas has occurred in the suburbs."[23] Mass movement of jobs to the suburbs has also concentrated poverty and forced poor Black Americans into structural isolation.[24] The "job spatial mismatch" found in Southbridge and the Eastside blocks residents like Richard from developing the necessary informal job networks that shape who gets employed.[25] "Opportunity hoarding" accelerated in small cities like Wilmington, so residents had to both have the proper credentials and know the "right people" to obtain decent work in Wilmington.[26]

Access to a car has the greatest impact on significantly reducing the job spatial mismatch, but maintaining a functioning and registered inexpensive vehicle was a luxury that many like Richard did not have in Southbridge. If you lived in Southbridge and did not have access to a vehicle, then your transportation choices were by unreliable car and bus services, or walking a few miles into greater Wilmington.

Southbridge was the most cordoned-off section of Wilmington, and because of this isolation, a palpable air of abandonment existed in Southbridge, leaving many to feel neglected and sometimes disrespected by the rest of the city. For this reason, many in "the South" were prideful, standoffish to outsiders, or had a chip on their shoulder.

Richard also explained there was a strong relationship between low economic well-being and participation in the streets. Economic well-being captures how people perceive and how their behavior is informed by their socioeconomic standing.[27] Knowing whether someone is employed is important, but employment status does not reflect an individual's experience with material resources, and it is this particular experience with resources or wealth that is most predictive of involvement in the streets.[28] According to the Council on Social Work Education, economic well-being is "the ability of individuals, families, and communities to consistently meet their basic needs (including food, housing, utilities, health care, transportation, education, childcare, clothing, and paid taxes), and have control over their day-to-day finances. It also includes the ability to make economic choices and feel a sense of security, satisfaction, and personal fulfillment with one's personal finances and employment pursuits."[29]

Economic well-being probably mattered more than unemployment in terms of why some went to the streets in the Eastside and Southbridge. The vast majority of poor and unemployed Black people were not street identified, but most in the streets were poor and unemployed. Often, what better explained why poor Black people in Wilmington became street identified was their subjective well-being with opportunity or how they internalized trauma during periods of extreme poverty.[30]

Richard also reminded us that Blackness and maleness or the intersection of race and gender explained why large numbers of Black males in Southbridge were unemployed while most white males in Wilmington were employed. "You know, it's [employment] crazy! . . . I don't really got no friends in the city that got a job, 'cept my white friend. . . . Even some of the older (Black) people, man, don't even got jobs. . . .'Cause like I said, we born into poverty, dog. We born into this game [of poverty and the streets]. I wasn't in this game for fun."

Felony records also barred many of Wilmington's Black men from many types of employment, such as jobs in education, health care, and human services.[31] Like Richard, Anthony B. (age 33) was a returning citizen who struggled with obtaining work. Anthony has been convicted and re-entered the community from prison at least ten times, and in each case, employment was his most difficult challenge in avoiding recidivism. Anthony also said that employment was the only safety line for people growing up in communities saturated with poverty and violence. Employment was so important to his ability to change his life and yet, so evasive and uncertain, that Anthony likened job hunting to playing the lottery. "Every time I re-enter, I kept doing the same things that got me in jail. . . . Last time I got out of prison . . . I waited for that job to come . . . and it was hard. I wanted to go back to hustling. . . . I knew then if I didn't do what I used to do, I'd be all right. . . . I'm saying to you, if you hang in there . . . it'll come to you. . . . I ain't going to tell you it's easy; it's hard. . . . I always tell myself . . . a lot of people get killed, there's more bodies [homicides] being dropped for like little crazy stuff. . . . I've been looking for a job for four or five months now. I'm still waiting man, I'm waiting on that golden ticket!"

Unemployment, poor housing, and bad schooling, in addition to harmful policing and overincarceration, ultimately made residents of the Eastside and Southbridge the bottom caste, or an economic outgroup in Wilmington.[32]

Home Conditions and Poverty

Two-thirds of survey participants lived in public housing or multifamily homes (see table 1.1). When asked to describe their living conditions, most shared a troubling picture, but they also stressed that varied conditions were a more realistic portrayal of housing for people in the streets. They came from a spectrum of home conditions ranging from extremely poor and unsanitary living circumstances to stable, lower-middle-class home conditions. Although the majority were poor, many in the streets also came from "clean homes," "church backgrounds," and "good families."

When we asked Adil (age 18) to describe poor homes on the Eastside, he answered, "It depends. 'Cause everybody live different. I want to say it's different. . . . It depends on the people that live in the house. Everybody's place don't look chaotic. Like, it depends." Again, everyone including Adil offered distressing characterizations, particularly of people involved with the streets, but they also stressed that living conditions were varied (even in public housing) and not a monolith of extreme poverty.

Some did admit that a significant segment of the streets lived in squalid conditions, but they often tied this level of poor housing to drug addiction. These kinds of distressed homes were described as untidy, unsanitary, having little food, or sometimes infested with roaches or other insects. According to Jerome (age 31), "You could walk in a motherf-cker's house, [and] see nothing but baking soda sitting in the refrigerator . . . and that's probably 'cause momma's getting high with it. Other than that, you ain't got nothing. You got a living room, a black-and-white TV, and that's it. Probably two or three chairs and a couch. . . . Shit at the kitchen table, all over the kitchen table. Shit like the bathroom's f-cked up."

Rennie Rox (age 35) grew up in a home with similar living conditions. Rennie's childhood home on Ninth and Pine Street in the Eastside was plagued with poverty, substance abuse, and the effects of an incarcerated father. Poverty also played an instrumental role in why he and other family members got involved in the streets. "There wasn't nothing new [in the home]. . . . You talking about books holding up couches . . . you might not have a bed frame. Your mattress and your box springs on the floor. The typical poverty Wilmington situation. But I never take nothin' away from my mother. . . . She tried everything she could to make sure that we had a hot meal every night, even if it was just breakfast food. . . . We're . . . gonna make some French toast or somethin' tonight [laughter].... I love my mom to death. She's the inspiration for me!"

For Rennie, the streets and the internalization of its core values was the only way to make it out of extreme poverty. Rennie became street identified during his early teenage years, and selling drugs was his primary hustle. Drug dealing and drug possession resulted in two stints in state prison for a total of thirteen years.

Rennie also believed racist laws and policies were responsible for the mass incarceration of Black men, which on the back end fueled a rash of street violence. In Wilmington, mass incarceration of Black men, caused a power vacuum that began in the early 2000s and later resulted in structural fallout for neighborhoods like the Eastside and Southbridge. Rennie admitted that he had almost "given up" on trying to reach youth in the streets. His optimism to help youth was stifled because a few weeks prior to our interview, he was robbed at gunpoint of "$30 and a cell phone" in front of his home. "You might get shot. You might get robbed in front of your very own house. It happened to me before.... I don't trust nobody after dark. I don't even like walkin' after dark. Like, literally. And these are my own people. People that I would have considered my little brothers in another time of life ... they'll take my life for $30 and a cell phone. Absolutely savage, ignorant, animal behavior."

How School Policy Punishes Black Students

President Barack Obama's $100 billion America Reinvestment Recovery Act funded the Race to the Top national program, the largest K–12 educational initiative, with $4.35 billion distributed to nineteen states.[33] These awards promised to positively impact 22 million students or about 42% of the country's poorest students. Grant recipients were expected to address four "areas of reform": (1) rigorous standards and better assessments; (2) data systems tracking student progress; (3) support for teachers and school leaders; and (4) interventions and other resources for low-performing schools.

The Delaware Department of Education (DDOE) received $120 million between 2010 and 2015 to reform all of its early care and education programs and produce "great outcomes for all children."[34] About 28,022 low-income children from birth to kindergarten in Delaware qualified for at least one of four areas of support: (1) health and developmental needs, (2) early childhood workforce, (3) high-quality programming, and (4) school readiness for children from birth to 8 years old. The U.S. Department of Education, and especially Secretary Arne Duncan, lauded Delaware's Race to the Top program. Still, many Delawarean parents, educators, and state leadership viewed the program with great disapproval. Delaware's secretary of education, Mark Murphy, was subjected to a stiff "grilling" from the state's legislature after bravely requesting an additional $7.5 million for Delaware's "educational sustainment fund" to maintain programs funded by the Race to the Top grant, which ended in 2015.[35] Many did not understand what was accomplished with the $120 million, not to mention why an additional $7.5 million was needed. Murphy argued that taxpayers needed to fund ten positions in his department that were previously funded by Race to the Top to maintain the positive gains made under the grant. State Representative Karen Peterson responded: "One of the biggest complaints I hear from my constituents is that education is just loaded down with all these administrators. Here we have $1.5 million going to ten people. And in some places, we've got schools trying to scrape up one more teacher? It just seems so out of whack." Peterson also noted that two of the ten positions would make more in a year than several state cabinet secretaries. In addition, far too many residents and the state legislature accused Secretary Murphy's department of irresponsibly allowing "millions . . . [to go] to state bureaucracy [while] too little has actually helped teachers in classrooms," said Representative Joe Miro. He continued, "You may have a view of the wonderful things Race to the Top has done, but the public does not appear to share that view." Representative Harris McDowell added, "Most races have a tape that the racers get across, a finish line. When is the finish line for Race to the Top? When do we finish this, or are we just building a permanent bureaucracy?"

Secretary Murphy resigned in 2015 amid the Race to the Top controversy and the debacle over implementing the Priority Schools plan, which many considered an insensitive program for failing schools.[36] Under this plan, six high-poverty schools with extremely low test scores were identified in Wilmington for a structural overhaul. The terms of the overhaul, however, proved to be Secretary Murphy's professional death knell. As a function of the Priority Schools' plan, Secretary Murphy unsuccessfully called for these six schools' principals to be fired and all of the teachers to re-apply. Two school districts' local unions and all 200 Delaware State Education Association delegates who represent the state's nineteen school districts voted no confidence in Secretary Murphy and the DDOE. Some believed that the Priority Schools plan was a failed attempt to cover up the mishandling of millions of dollars provided by Race to the Top funding. Although Secretary Murphy and others claimed that targeted students and parents benefited from Race to the Top, this was not firmly supported by schooling outcomes in Wilmington. This criticism could be made just about anywhere that Race to the Top was implemented in the country.

Although Delaware hit a thirty-year low with dropout rates in 2014, dropout rates were still twice as high for Black youth than for white youth.[37] For the years 2009 and 2010, only 47% of Black males in Delaware graduated in four years, in comparison to 52% of Latinos and 68% of white males.[38] In fact, the Schott Foundation ranked Delaware as the seventh-worst state in the nation with respect to Black male graduation rates.[39] In 2015, Delaware was declared the second-worst state for the school-to-prison pipeline phenomenon.[40]

According to the DDOE, in the period from September 2011 to June 2012, a total of 1,527 students dropped out of school statewide. Blacks accounted for 43% and Latinos 13% of Delaware's dropout rate, and most were ninth and tenth graders. Delaware dropouts are overwhelmingly male, and 403 Black males and 111 Latino males dropped out during that period. Blacks represented 31% (480) of all dropouts in New Castle County. Nearly 58% of Wilmington youth, overall, failed to graduate from high school, and less than one-third had the skills necessary for gainful employment.[41] School dropout rates for Black youth in Wilmington were at about 60%, and for Black male youth, dropout rates were at approximately 65%.[42] Poignantly, the Black male dropout rates for some Wilmington neighborhoods like Southbridge were 100% between 2006 and 2009.[43]

Wilmington was brought under federal investigation by the Department of Education's Office for Civil Rights (OCR) for the disproportionately "harsh" and excessive rates of remedial tracking, suspensions, expulsions, and other disciplinary outcomes for Black children, and Black boys specifically, in the Christina School District.[44] The Christina School District enrolls most of Wilmington's low-income Black children, and it is also the largest school district in Delaware. The ACLU of Delaware and the Metropolitan Wilmington Urban League developed the Coalition for Fairness and Equity in Schools in 2014 to oversee recommendations made by the OCR. In defense of Wilmington's most vulnerable children, this coalition wrote:

> Delaware ... is part of a disturbing national trend known as the school to prison pipeline. In the 2012–2013 school year, 39% of public-school students in Delaware received in- or out-of-school suspensions. Students with disabilities are being suspended from school at about twice the rate of their peers. Astoundingly, while only about 10% of the children in Delaware's public schools have an identified disability, over 70% of juvenile offenders struggle with behavioral/mental/emotional issues and/or substance abuse, and almost 50% have serious learning disabilities. The odds for suspension and expulsion soar even higher depending on the students' race. African American and Latino students are suspended 3–4 times more than their white peers, even when they represent a substantially low enrollment rate overall.

In 2012, U.S. Education Secretary Arne Duncan announced that the Christina School District had reached full "resolution of a compliance review" with the Department of Education's recommendations for Christina.[45] As part of its compliance, Christina determined and promised to allocate $1 million to address school climate and to rectify the excessive disciplining of its students. This new agreement also required Christina to comply with seven major changes:

- Ensure to the extent possible that student misbehavior does not require school removal;
- Collaborate with experts on strategies to prevent discrimination in school discipline;
- Provide disruptive students with support services to improve behavior;
- Revise disciplinary policies, and implement practices that promote equity in discipline;
- Provide training to staff on disciplinary policies, and implement programs for students and parents/guardians that explain these policies to them;
- Effectively address school climate issues; and
- Improve the disciplinary data collection system.

Governor Jack Markell, "the Education Governor," responded to Wilmington's educational meltdown by legislating and instituting the Wilmington Education Improvement Commission (WEIC). Surrounded by Delaware's top lawmakers in an elaborate press conference, Governor Markell signed into law SB122 and HB148, which authorized and funded WEIC, on August 4, 2015. WEIC was chaired by Dr. Tony Allen, a middle-aged Black man and senior executive at Bank of America, and data analysis and research oversight was provided by Dr. Daniel Rich, an older white man, a former provost and distinguished faculty member in urban affairs and public policy at the University of Delaware. Almost two dozen residents and some civic leaders populated WEIC's five subcommittees: (1) Redistricting Committee; (2) Charter and District Collaboration Committee; (3) Meeting the Needs of Students in Poverty Committee; (4) Funding Student Success Committee; and (5) Parent, Educator, and Community Engagement Committee. WEIC's formal charge was to rigorously evaluate and reform educational policy for Wilmington's Black children in pre-K through twelfth grade. WEIC was an enormous undertaking, as leadership and thousands of residents came together in what they believed would be real educational change for poor Black youth.

In April 2015, WEIC released a 245-page report titled *Strengthening Wilmington: An Action Agenda*.[46] Featuring WEIC, Governor Markell hosted a widely publicized educational summit at the Chase Center in 2016. Approximately 1,000 attended, with the promise of sound educational reform.

WEIC's most controversial proposal was a redistricting plan which, if approved, would move Wilmington's youth from the Christina School District to the Red Clay School District, another of the four districts that served Wilmington. Dr. Mervin Daugherty, the superintendent of Red Clay, was tacitly supportive, but his core constituency was annoyed if not irate at the suggestion. WEIC assured Red Clay and other districts that they would be provided with adequate supplemental funding to serve large numbers of students from low-income families, English-language learners, and students with special educational needs from kindergarten to third grade.[47] The state legislature, however, was unconvinced of the viability of WEIC's proposal and instead chose to stall and underfund WEIC. Although Markell had promised $7.5 million, the state legislature rebuffed what was really only a request for WEIC to receive support for their redistricting plan.[48] WEIC's proposal failed 6–15 in the state senate, but the state legislature approved $200,000 for WEIC to take an additional year to develop a "more detailed plan."

Some thought Governor Markell's effort to address Wilmington's educational crisis was just smoke and mirrors or performative because Markell never strongly expended hard political capital for significant school-based structural change. Others thought Markell intended only to create the impression of major change, to preserve his legacy.

Extreme poverty and poor educational outcomes continued to snuff out the potential of Wilmington's Black children. Delaware had become exhausted by the enormous amounts of social, intellectual, and political capital it exuded over these children. After all, between 2009 and 2016, the state and especially Wilmington spent well over a $100 million as a result of Race to the Top, were forced to comply with Arne Duncan's federal investigation and recommendations, endured the Priority Schools debacle, transition from the removal and replacement of Cabinet Secretary of Education Dr. Mark Murphy, and executed what they could from WEIC. Most disturbing, however, was that with all this energy, these grand interventions produced very little change for poor Black youth in Wilmington.

Seven months into the new 2017 term of Governor John Carney's administration, the six "priority schools" in Wilmington identified for improvement were faring even worse.[49] Bayard Middle School, for instance, remained at 3% proficiency in math and 8% to 9% proficiency in English, while Highland Elementary School's poverty rate was 74% and Warner Elementary School's was 83%.

Leaving School: Cultural Limitations, Homelessness, and School Exclusion

Although schooling difficulties have been attributed to a criminal culture that openly rejects formal education, we argue that street life is more of a response to poverty, unemployment, unstable housing, and poor treatment inside schools.[50] Also, we believe that street-identified youth do in fact value education.[51] Mateu-Gelabert and Lune found that "the concerns expressed by the students were not that educational attainment in general would not pay off in life, but that the education that *they* got was not worth the effort."[52] Students typically resist schooling processes that they feel violate their intellects, culture, and personal dignity.[53] Rather than rejecting education in general, many street-identified students are likely skeptical of the value of the education that they have access to in school and are resentful of the conditions under which it is offered.

Even amid great educational inequality, most study participants demonstrated positive attitudes toward formal education, though their level of optimism did not necessarily translate into school success. Forty-four percent of participants had not earned a high school diploma, and two-thirds reported no trade or construction experience. Results also suggested that high school noncompletion was an intergenerational problem in the Eastside and Southbridge. About 42% reported that their mother had not graduated from high school, and 60% reported that their father had not graduated or they did not know his educational status.

Cultural Competence and Motives of White Educators

Khiry (age 18) believed that most teachers and school administrators were not equipped to effectively work with Black children from Wilmington. He believed that his white male principal's default response to behavioral troubles was to suspend or expel students. According to Khiry, his principal privately admitted he did not know how to create a positive learning environment for poor Black children. When asked if teachers were sincerely interested in educating Black youth, Khiry responded, "Not really. . . . I just think they're there just to be there. . . . My principal told me . . . he really don't know how to deal with . . . African American kids [or] like the urban kids. . . . He just don't like tolerate it, he just like get rid of them and he was like other principals. If you . . . like to fight, he probably talk to you, . . . but [if] you got in a fight, he'd probably just like suspend you, for like the maximum days he could."

Mike (age 27) echoed similar cultural concerns that young white teachers in particular were not prepared to work with Black children and were even complicit in the elevated suspension rates. "Teachers don't care." Mike, with a tremor in his voice, said that many white teachers held antagonistic attitudes toward these children. Mike believed that for many white teachers, teaching Black students was simply about a "check," or getting paid rather than helping poor children reach their full potential. Mike believed that students also recognized disingenuous teaching, and that this problematic educational practice actually prompted misbehavior by students as an indication of their dissatisfaction with teachers. "The teachers are young, white, and they don't care, so they figure well, 'I ain't got to put up with this, so I don't give a damn if you learn or not. . . . That's up to you, or you going to get suspended.' And them kids know that . . . a lot of the teachers, they don't want to deal with nobody else's kids. . . . They come to get a check and that's it."

Kevin (age 35) worked as a janitor in an elementary school in the Riverside neighborhood of Wilmington. Like Khiry and Mike, Kevin also underscored how school staff did not have the sociocultural and class competencies to effectively teach children from Wilmington. Trying to get our attention, Kevin impressed on us that "they can't relate," and that teachers' educational training did not prepare them for "how to even teach a Black child." For Kevin and almost everyone else we interviewed, inadequate teaching was primarily responsible for the breakdown between white teachers and Black students from Wilmington. "So what does it look like for the kids? It looks real grim.... The teachers now don't understand it, they can't relate. So, I go through all these classrooms throughout this building and I'm seeing a teacher teaching but they don't understand how to even teach a Black child. It's a method; it's a strategy. You just can't come in here with your book knowledge. Book knowledge is not working. You have to have that feel, that understanding of the child, the community, and the families."

Gender and Experiences with School

Women in our study were more likely to express concerns about their own children's schooling opportunities. Dionne (age 29) admitted that she preferred to send her children to "white schools" because "I know they are going to get a better education.... The curriculum is different." She and other women believed that white schools were more rigorous and had better resources, and they wanted their children to receive the same quality education. Dionne also believed that school officials and politicians were very aware of the disparities between poor Black and wealthy students, which she described as the racialized "politics" of education.

Lanise (age 34), a devout Sunni Muslim, had four Black boys, and they resided in the Southbridge housing projects. Lanise was just as hands-on as Dionne was with her children's education. Lanise also believed that teachers were disrespectful and underprepared and that they contributed to learning environments that were hostile to Black children. "When you live in a certain area [poor neighborhood], you're going be treated a certain way by the teachers, whether they ... have PhD's, master's, bachelor's ... they automatically assume they [children] have no values, they have no moral conduct, they're not being raised right, they're out of control, they're unruly.... That's just not the case for all of the children in this environment.... Because this environment is impoverished ... they automatically ... have a lack of patience ... for the children in these school districts.... There's some disrespect. But for the most part, I don't think that they're taught adequately."

School exclusion is typically based on how students are perceived and treated, conflicts between schooling and street life, and out-of-school factors. Street-identified youth often face environmental conditions that hinder school success, such as poverty and parents who are overburdened or absent from the home.[54] Valdez's study of 150 gang-involved girls reported violence and substance abuse in their households, and other studies show that street-identified youth are overly exposed to gun violence.[55] These conditions cause distress and lead to in-school difficulties, which are sometimes exacerbated by school staff. Dance found that teachers perceived street-identified Black male adolescents as "irrationally disruptive and uneducable."[56] Similarly, Rios found that white educators viewed street-identified Black and Latino male youth as threats to the school environment.[57] In general, these youths' schooling troubles were met with distain and sanctions.[58] For many participants, educators were simply and solely punitive in their approach with youth.

- Doc (age 34): "They don't know what to do, but keep suspending them!"
- Anthony (age 33): "Some of them [teachers] come to school with their personal problems and take it out on other children.... Some of them already have a bias, ... Somebody that lives in the suburban community [and] comes to the hood and teach, they already got a mind frame like, 'I ain't got time for these n——s. I'm just gonna let them run loose. I'm getting a paycheck at the end of the day.'"
- Mike (age 27): "If they can get you out of their classroom in order for their class to run smooth, that's what they're gonna do.... Now you [students] got an attitude 'cause you've been embarrassed, so every time you come in class you got beef, you understand? Then the crib [student's home] is not right. We be barely eating, subsidized housing."

After being removed from school in tenth grade for making a "terroristic threat," Shaquille (age 18) registered for Job Corps and eventually completed his GED. Shaquille's negative experiences with school also did not negatively affect his college aspirations.

Ashley (Associate) asked Shaquille, "Do you think that the public educational system in Wilmington is adequately preparing its Black children?" "Not all the schools are bad," he replied. "Some schools are preparing kids more well than other schools are for college. Like Concord, that's a good school ... if you want to go to college. Dickerson, um, maybe, [but] Brandywine and Mount Pleasant, no."

Curious and taken by his response, Ashley wanted to know more about Shaquille's schooling background. "What is your current educational level?" He replied, "I don't got my high school diploma. I got my GED, though. I'm in the transitional period to get into Delaware College of Art and Design. I'm trying to get into photography, 'cause I'm into cameras.... It's a two-year course to get an associate's degree in photography."

Although he truly valued a quality education, Shaquille, like other men in the Eastside, was unable to escape the criminal legal system. Unable to get his social-structural footing, in 2016 Shaquille was sentenced to eighteen years in a nearby Pennsylvania prison for a string of armed robberies and conspiracy to commit robbery.[59] What's more, the terms of his sentencing require

Shaquille to serve an additional five to ten years for armed robberies in Delaware after 2033—his earliest opportunity for parole in Pennsylvania.

Addiction, Home Life, and School Violence

Leslie (age 31) was a single Black woman with three children, two girls and one boy, ranging in age from 3 to 12. Her skin, particularly the creases on her face, carried deep fatigue. For the last four years Leslie had been homeless, staying with her children in a variety of places in the Eastside, sometimes on the living room floor in her mother's home. She attributed her son's misbehaving in school and also her daughter's negative behavior to her unemployment and unstable housing. Leslie said, "One woman [at a social agency] . . . told me . . . that if I don't find housing, she was going to call . . . DFS [Department of Family Services] . . . [to] take my kids away because I don't have housing."

When asked to describe the conditions of her last apartment, Leslie disclosed, "There was cracks in the walls. . . . The ceiling started to leak in the kitchen and the dining room area. . . . The landlord was told about the situation and it was like, she didn't even care. . . . The pipes had to be removed from underneath the sink. . . . The drains would clog . . . The refrigerator . . . like, pieces were missing on the inside. And it worked well, but there was just pieces that were missing."

Louis (age 29) admitted that he "grew up in a crack house" and his mother struggled with a crack cocaine addiction. The emotional strain he experienced as a function of his mother's addiction was exacerbated in the school environment. Teachers read about a "drug raid" at his home in newspapers and inappropriately handled this information, embarrassing Louis in front of his classmates and making it difficult for him to focus academically. According to Louis, the reporting of his mother's addiction caused students to make fun of him, which led to fights and disciplinary problems at school. "Holes on the wall. Um, clothes everywhere. And I came from a clean family, but addiction . . . will break anything down. . . . Paranoia [and I had] . . . no trust [in school officials]. . . . You're going to middle school and your teacher has a newspaper with your mom's name on it: 'A Drug Raid!' . . . That's embarrassing . . . coming out of school on the bus and coming home and people point at you, 'Ain't that your mom right there buying drugs?'"

Louis's mother's addiction and his difficulty in school increased after they witnessed his father being killed in front of their home. Louis's challenges eventually caused him to leave school in the tenth grade. Louis said he never felt school was a supportive place, and he claimed teachers were very "disrespectful" and even told him he would not be successful in life. More troubling were his accounts of physical abuse by teachers, which went unreported because of his lack of support at school and home: "A lotta my teachers . . . were disrespectful. Some teachers, told me that . . . I wouldn't be, 'successful.' . . .

I've always been a very smart, educated kid. I had good grades and everything, but I would always get into it with teachers.... I've even been hit a couple times. I've been choked by teachers. I've been hit. I've been disrespected.... And I wouldn't say nothing to my mom or nobody [about it]. I would just take it to the chin."

One of the most heartbreaking examples of difficult home conditions and its effects on schooling was Byron's case. According to Byron (age 20), his father denied paternity, and his mother told him he was a "mistake" when he was 11 years old, causing him to contemplate suicide. After years of poor treatment, Byron's mother kicked him out of the house on a rainy night, at the age of 13, with only the shorts and tank top he was wearing. Byron became homeless, and as he described it, he often resorted to "anger and aggression" to cope with the severe distress caused by his parents' rejection and his need to survive on the streets. Not surprisingly, Byron became completely disconnected from school. "Experiencing homelessness at the age of 13, sleeping in the park.... I had to go to the store every day, dog, and steal just to eat.... Sleeping on my people's back porch, asking for covers and blankets.... That shit hurt. Real talk, it hurt.... That's why I be ready to put a n—— under [kill someone] with no problem, no remorse, 'cause I done been through it, you feel me?"

Aaron (age 29) was formerly involved with the streets and able to transform his life. Ironically, the impetus for positive change was the murder of his close cousin "J. R. the Beast" or Jerome E. Perkins Sr. J. R. also left two sons and a daughter behind. J. R. and Joseph Rogers were both "under-bosses" for Wolf's street organization prior to his incarceration, and it was during Wolf's incarceration that J. R. was killed, on October 18, 2005. J. R. was so beloved in Wilmington that he is the only known major street dealer to receive a front-page story in the *News Journal* when he was murdered.[60] According to reports, J. R. tried to drive himself to the hospital after being shot but crashed into a nearby house and succumbed to his injuries.[61]

Joseph Rogers was incarcerated for life in November 1997 for shooting and killing a security guard who was an off-duty probation officer working as a bouncer at Gotham Nightclub on Delaware Avenue in Philadelphia. It was because of this case with Joseph that Wolf popped up on the FBI's radar. Although Wolf was the boss, he had miraculously evaded federal authorities. Against his better judgment, Wolf dropped off money to the mother of Joseph's children while Joseph was on the run. Since Wolf stopped by the home, the feds immediately started investigating him. Shortly after, Wolf was arrested for running a multimillion-dollar criminal enterprise.

Aaron, J. R., Joseph, and Wolf all ran together in the streets. And now Wolf and Aaron were among a few, a rare cut of Black men from the streets of Wilmington, that were not in jail or dead. Aaron became a schoolteacher, and at the time of his interview, he had taught in a charter school for six years. As an educator, he never understood why schools were so ill equipped to address race and poverty and resistant to properly educating poor Black children. Aaron spoke earnestly about the number of hungry children who arrived each morning at his school with unwashed underwear or dirty socks and school uniforms. Aaron also recognized that several of the children's parents struggled with addiction. "Sometimes you have kids come to school and tell you they didn't have lights on [in their homes] or they didn't have food, or their mother or father didn't come home [last night]. Or all week, they wore the same uniform to school, because they couldn't get their clothes washed. They didn't have clean underwear and clean socks to wear."

School Violence

Negative experiences with teachers and other students, coupled with the threat of school exclusion, explained why some students were violent. Cultural incompetence, underpreparation, and excessive punishment were specific factors that caused some students to internalize a street identity to protect themselves from students and educators. Some students were also violent to preserve their dignity inside precarious or unsafe schools.[62] From this perspective, it made sense to be volatile or street-identified in dangerous schooling environments.

Almost 70% of survey respondents "often saw physical fights in high school," and women (67%) were much more likely than men (60%) to witness student violence. According to other researchers, boys overall are much more likely than girls to fight inside schools.[63] This may be why men (41%) in our study were more likely than women (33%) to report not feeling safe in school. Also, 62% reported that "the police or security officers in my school made the school safer," with women (56%) being more likely than men (47%) to agree that "police or security" increased school safety.

According to Gloria (age 35), rates of student violence and leaving school altogether was sometimes a form of coping with unsafe and intellectually nonnurturing schools. Instead of dealing with the needs of impoverished students, student overcrowding and transactional teaching, Gloria's high school decided to address its challenge with violence by militarizing itself with "security guards" and "police officers." From Gloria's perspective, a toxic institutional or school culture caused students and teachers to disengage from the learning process, thus increasing the potential for violence to take place. "Because it's [school] so large and there's so many students . . . fights are gonna break out. . . . I'm gonna bump into somebody. . . . There's so many kids out there that are just angry and want something that they don't have, the materialistic stuff. . . . Then fights start and now they have police officers there, they have security guards there. . . . Teachers are afraid of the students. Like I said, they [teachers] come in, get a check, and they leave. They clock in and they clock out. . . . [The] first day of school was always a fight, drugs. . . . I couldn't wait to bolt out of that school. It got to the point where I was like, 'Do I want to go to school?'"

School performance was also tied to whether the student's basic material needs were met. Attentiveness, behavioral comportment, and respect for academics were greatly affected by whether students had clean clothing, school supplies, and respectful and safe learning environments.

About 68% reported that "I cared a lot about my clothes or how I dressed in high school," and approximately 65% agreed that "in my high school, it was important to have name-brand clothing." Students who struggled with poverty often came to school tired, hungry, or with tattered clothes, and as a result they were often shamed and bullied by other students. For some, it made sense to participate in crime to cope with extreme poverty, embarrassment, and being bullied in schools:

- Pop-Pop Solid (age 18): "[Anyone's mother] who don't work, or just get food stamps and a check [public assistance], . . . it's kind of hard to tell those students not to go out there [in the streets] and try and make some type of money. . . . You can't really tell a kid who, when he go to school, everybody's talking bad about him and he can't concentrate on his work. . . . You can't tell no student like this not to go try and get some new sneakers and clothes, just so [students] will leave him alone and stop bothering him."
- Byron (age 21): "I got raked on [teased], picked on. I didn't have [good] clothes. . . . I didn't have the Rocawear [popular clothing brand] shit other students had. My thread count was low [I didn't own many clothes]. I know [my clothes were cheap] 'cause [my clothes] ripped easy. . . . I didn't have his [a more privileged student's] mom. . . . He going on field trips, he got lunch money. . . . I didn't have what they had."

L. Johnson (age 18) was about four months from graduating high school, yet he recognized he could still be victimized in school before graduation. Of most concern was that being seriously threatened and attacked could lead to suspension or expulsion. But from L. Johnson's perspective, he did not have a choice to ignore a serious threat or opt out of defending himself. Not doing so in an already volatile schooling environment would weaken his social status and increase his vulnerability or the likelihood of being victimized. Although L. Johnson possessed the grades and motivation to thrive in college, practically, it still made sense for him to risk his college future. He insisted, "I don't like it [student violence]. That's why my goal is to finish school. . . . I'll be done in June, and I want to be a criminal justice major."

L. Johnson further recognized that he was in the crosshairs of the school-prison nexus in that removal from school would increase his likelihood of participation in the streets. But he intended to graduate, enroll in college, and return to his community to be a mentor to young Black boys given he was also a victim of gun violence.

Corry (Associate) asked L. Johnson, "How did violence in your school affect you?" He replied, "Most of the violence that's going on . . . is between the ages 14 to 20. . . . Every time you look in the paper, a 16-year-old just shot an 18-year-old. Or a 17-year-old was shot at a high school basketball game. A 15-year-old just got shot while skating. . . . Young people don't have nobody to look up to. They don't have no more leaders or mentors like when I was coming up. . . . Ain't nobody looking out. . . . I think I can help out a whole lot, because I done seen and been around everything. I've been shot. I done been through a lot . . . since I was young, I could relate to them more, to help them out."

Violence at Howard High

Howard was the only public high school any Black student in Delaware could attend until 1978, and now, as Howard High School of Technology, it remains a highly competitive, predominantly Black vocational school in the Eastside of Wilmington. Howard was front and center in *Gebhart v. Belton* (1952), a desegregation court case combined with four other cases into the landmark *Brown v. Board of Education* (1954), in which the U.S. Supreme Court overturned the "separate but equal" doctrine and ruled that state laws establishing racial segregation of public schools were unconstitutional. Howard High School was the only school desegregated by court order at the state level. Because of this legacy, Howard was made a National Historic Landmark in 2005.

Despite its academic prominence, Howard still faced challenges with school violence. Sixteen-year-old Amy Inita Joyner-Francis was brutally punched and stomped to death in the bathroom of Howard in April 2016.[64] Some watched inside, and dozens of students listened outside the bathroom. Video postings of the fight emerged from the onlookers. Amy later died from cardiac arrest due to a rare heart condition.

Family Court judge Robert Coonin in April 2017 found Trinity Carr guilty of criminally negligent homicide.[65] The 17-year-old faced eight years in prison as an adult, but as a juvenile she received supervision until age 19. Carr and another 17-year-old girl were found guilty of third-degree criminal conspiracy for Amy's death. A third teenage girl was charged but found not guilty of conspiracy.

Brandon Wingo's murder was another shocking homicide of a Howard student.[66] At four foot ten, Brandon was a clean-cut and biracial 15-year-old freshman at Howard, where he played basketball for the high school team. One afternoon after Brandon left school, he was shot three times and killed on Clifford Brown Walk in the Eastside. The public was shocked to learn that Brandon was an active member of Only My Brothers (OMB), a local gang warring with the Shoot to Kill (STK) gang. The murder of 16-year-old STK member Jordan Ellerbe in January 2015 was rumored to be the motivation for Brandon's homicide over a year later. About a year prior to his murder, Brandon was charged with second-degree attempted robbery, second-degree conspiracy, and third-degree assault. The charges were dropped when the victim did not appear in court. Months before his death, Brandon was also charged with motor vehicle theft and receiving stolen property.

Kevon Harris-Dickerson, age 20, Zaahir Smith, age 19, and Diamonte Taylor, age 19, were members of STK, and these three young Black men were convicted of first-degree murder and conspiracy not only in Brandon's death but also in unrelated cases. Harris-Dickerson testified against Smith and Taylor, saying they killed Brandon for disrespecting their murdered friend on Facebook.[67]

According to Harris-Dickerson, after sitting in a car on Clifford Brown Walk, Taylor, wearing a trench coat and carrying a handgun, got out and approached an unsuspecting Brandon, chased him around a car, and shot him in the head.[68] Taylor and Smith later returned to the scene to view and laugh at Brandon's dead body. Taylor posted a photo of the nine-millimeter weapon on social media, describing it as the "Wingo dropper."

Brandon Wingo's death and the beef between STK and OMB was at the center of a three-day national news series that declared that Wilmington was the homicide capital for youth ages 12–17.[69] Three out of 1,000 youths were likely to be hurt or killed in Wilmington, almost double the rate of youth violence in Chicago. Only sixteen arrests were made for the sixty-four Wilmington youths that were shot and the five killed between January 2015 and Labor Day 2016. Four more homicides and over a dozen shootings were tied to the OMB and STK rivalry.

Conclusion

> Millions ... find themselves walking the streets in search for jobs that do not exist. In this other America, millions ... are forced to live in dilapidated, substandard housing conditions where they do not have wall-to-wall carpet. Where they all too often have wall-to-wall rats and roaches.... Unemployment is still wide in the Black community.... Underemployment is just as great.... Because of this economic deprivation, there is a great deal of bitterness; a great deal of despair; a great deal of anger.
> —Martin Luther King Jr., "The Three Evils of Society"

Employment, housing, and educational barriers lock Black Wilmington into a pattern of intergenerational poverty. As a result, many Black males in Wilmington left or were forced out of schools. Those without a high school diploma struggled to find work, and in the absence of legal work, many used the streets to meet their basic needs. This was particularly true for the men, reflecting the fact that job prospects were poor for people with low levels of formal education.[70] Many Black men in Wilmington also had criminal records, which exacerbated their employment difficulties in ways that were permanent and severe. And for many Black men in Wilmington, deciding to participate in the streets was a choice between crime and its collateral effects of physical injury, incarceration, and death, or simply stewing in their extreme poverty.

Moreover, the mistreatment in schools many experienced and witnessed strongly suggested that this problem was not limited to a few "bad actors." Creating a nurturing learning environment for Black children requires systemic changes in the policies, practices, and cultures of pre-K–12 schools and the institutions that train educational practitioners. Drug addiction also impairs some parents' ability to adequately supervise and provide for their children, and as a result, some youth turned to the streets to meet their material needs and to emotionally cope. Under such conditions, it is extremely difficult, if not impossible, for young people to focus on schoolwork, and schools were largely unprepared to support students with these kinds of troubled home environments.

People with low levels of formal education in these communities, both with and without criminal records, have an immediate need for quality employment. If we are truly committed to the upward mobility of all, then we must ensure that the most disenfranchised among us have access to livable wages. This will require a shift away from blind faith in capitalistic market forces toward a belief that all citizens have value.

Chapter 5

"F-ck the Police!"

STANDING UP TO THE POLICING MACHINE

> To many American[s] the police are the government, certainly its most visible representative. [The] ... evidence suggests that the killing of Negroes has become police policy in the United States and that police policy is the most practical expression of government policy.
> —William L. Patterson et al., *We Charge Genocide*

EVERYONE WE SPOKE to shared that either they themselves or someone else they saw was treated unfairly by police. In the Eastside and Southbridge, many felt disrespected and harassed, and some even spoke of being physically brutalized by police. Late arrivals and no responses to 911 calls were also common.

Although they were enraged, Black men and women in the streets still wanted effective community policing programs, which strongly suggested they and the larger community were hopeful for an improved relationship with police.

Disgusted by the Wilmington Police Department (WPD), Pop-Pop Solid (age 19) shouted, "F-ck the police!" Pop-Pop, the nickname for Wolf's son Dominique (or Muhammad), recounted a story of a young white man in Wilmington who was shot trying to purchase drugs. What alarmed Pop-Pop most about the shooting, however, was the quick police response. In Pop-Pop's experience, cases of violence experienced by Black substance abusers, and especially Black male victims, were not cases generally prioritized by the WPD.

"F-ck the police! I never liked the police. . . . I could never understand how the police in Delaware work. Like, I don't get it."

Surprised by the sharpness of the outburst, Louis (Associate) asked Pop-Pop, "What happened to make you so angry at police?"

"A white junkie got shot . . . two days ago. I think somebody had bodied [killed] him. I looked outside and there was cop cars everywhere. . . . I done seen brawls. I'm talking about real brawls of ten or more people, like, fighting against each other for . . . two, three hours on end. And then I only seen one cop car, like two and a half hours after the fight was over [just] to say, 'Is [there] anything still going on?' Do you see the [racial] inequality of things? . . . I'm not saying the police don't do their part because to a point, to an extent, they keep chaos under a minimum. But they definitely have personalized opinions on what they will and won't come for. If they hear, 'There's two Black kids in Southbridge running around shooting at each other,' don't be surprised if they take their time."

The criminal legal industry was big business in Delaware, and this social control machine rarely stifled the increasing rates of shootings and homicides in Wilmington between 2010 and 2020. Some years were less violent than others, but overall, shootings and homicides steadily increased. Wilmington was rocked by gun violence, and to worsen matters, the WPD had only a 14% homicide clearance rate in 2014.[1] Due to mounting public pressure, clearance rates did improve, hovering between 38% and 50% in the following years.[2]

Police and residents—especially Black men in the streets of the Eastside and Southbridge—maintained a severely strained relationship. Outside of major structural change, it was difficult to even imagine what could be done to improve a relationship that was so inherently adversarial.

Racial composition of police departments has been linked to overpolicing. Duran's study of Latino gang members and police in Denver, Colorado, and Ogden, Utah, found that not only were most police deployed to low-income Latino and Black neighborhoods, but the "diversity" of these two city's police forces "paled in comparison to [the diversity of] these neighborhoods."[3] Ferguson, Missouri, and Baltimore, Maryland, are also cities with police forces that do not reflect the racial compositions of their cities. The Ferguson Police Department is 87% white, although Blacks comprise 67% of the city's population.[4] Black residents in Ferguson accounted for 85% of vehicle stops, 90% of citations, and 93% of arrests between 2012 and 2014.[5] Similarly, the racial composition of the Baltimore Police Department does not reflect Baltimore, as 48% of officers were white in a city that was 63% Black.[6]

Black residents in Wilmington also believed that the strained relationship was attributable to multiple forms of bias on the basis of race, ethnicity, gender, age, and class. The WPD was 70% white and only 21% Black, and this predominantly white department primarily stopped, arrested, and investigated young Black men in a city that was nearly 60% Black.[7] The WPD also consisted of 320 sworn personnel and 64 civilian support staff, with only 286 dispatchable officers. In theory, a city the size of Wilmington required 20 police officers per 10,000 people, or about 140 officers.[8] However, due to Wilmington's challenges with violent crime, the WPD's authorized strength was deemed an appropriate size.[9] Relative to the population, Wilmington has one of the highest numbers of police officers per 1,000 residents of any city in the nation. According to the FBI's report *Crime in the United States 2013*, the average number of officers per 1,000 residents for cities of 50,000 to 99,000 is

1.6 (or 1.9 for cities in the Northeast).[10] The WPD's current strength of 286 puts Wilmington at 4.0 officers per 1,000 residents. By comparison, of the 405 cities nationwide having a population of 50,000–99,999, only three cities have an officer-per-population ratio of 3.6 per 1,000 residents or higher. In addition, for all cities having a population of 50,000 or more, only 13 out of 671 cities examined nationwide have an officer-per-population ratio of 3.6 or higher. At that level, according to the FBI report, only one out of nearly 700 cities had a higher ratio of officers per 1,000 residents than Wilmington.[11]

Wilmington had high levels of street violence, but there was little evidence that more police in Wilmington ever correlated with less violence or crime. More police generally resulted in more arrests and incarcerations, and this policing dynamic largely destabilized thousands of Black families and neighborhoods. It was true that violent crime steadily increased and needed to be slowed. But most residents did not believe that more police was the panacea for gun violence.

Public leadership were generally indifferent to outcries about joblessness, poor housing conditions, or extreme poverty—the key factors residents argued were most responsible for gun violence. Wilmington's three previous mayors, dating back to the Honorable Mayor James Baker, all acknowledged that the city could never police itself out of its extreme poverty and violent crime problem. However, each still ramped up and rolled out aggressive policing initiatives. There was strong rhetorical support for enhanced social service programs, but rarely was this call for new programming properly planned or resourced. Aggressive policing was Wilmington's primary go-to intervention to stem the tide of gun violence.

Mayor James Baker took office in 2001 and green-lighted the police "jump-out squads" program, but violent crime still rose throughout his twelve-year tenure. Under Baker's administration in 2010, Wilmington broke its homicide record. Mayor Dennis Williams launched a multitude of policing initiatives between 2012 and 2016, but violent crime still increased. Michael Purzycki became mayor in 2017, and he immediately moved forward with finding a new chief from outside of Delaware to lead a bold policing campaign. But 2017 proved to be the most violent year on record in Wilmington's history.

The Williams administration (2012–2016) was arguably the most criticized for the WPD's handling of gun violence. Embattled for most of his term, Williams staked his political legacy on reducing violent crime. If there was any politician that could succeed, it was assumed to be Williams. The former detective vowed to never "hug a thug" (i.e., be soft on crime), and although he aimed to be tough, his "law and order" platform promised the police would be "fair." He reminded audiences that he authentically understood their concerns and could reach many in the streets, because he, too, was a former gang member, and was raised in "Riverside's housing projects" or in the Riverside-Wilmington Housing Authority.

In one press conference after another, the Williams administration announced new or revised policing initiatives. On June 30, 2014, the WPD started using ShotSpotter, at the cost of $415,000 over three years. ShotSpotter was surveillance technology that scoured the community for sounds of gunfire to target the likely locations of shootings. Wilmington's ShotSpotter program could track gunshots in a three-square-mile radius, and its targeted range in the city covered the Eastside and two other violent communities. According to Mayor Williams, 231 shootings were tracked during the first six months, and after tactical adjustments, shootings were reduced by 42% (135) over the next six months.[12]

The city argued the 42% reduction in shootings was accounted for by its "multifaceted" policing initiative. Operation DISRUPT (Dealing with Issues of Stabilization through Respect, Understanding, and Promoting Trust) began in January 2015. Operation DISRUPT reassigned thirty officers, sixteen of whom were from the desperately needed Community Policing Unit, to aggressively "flood the streets five nights a week with more patrol officers than normal, specifically in hot-spot areas."[13] The Community Policing Unit was responsible for checking in or proactively engaging with residents in some of the toughest communities. Officers cooked breakfast, installed bulbs in street lamps, tutored students, gave away books and toys, and helped residents with groceries.[14]

In 2015, Mayor Williams finally created Wilmington's first homicide unit and crime reward fund.[15] He finally capitulated to a call that had been resisted by city leadership since 2009. Though this improved relations with the community, Williams was still at odds with the Drugs, Organized Crime, and Vice Division and the Fraternal Order of Police (FOP). Tensions flared, and the FOP withdrew their support and voted "no confidence" in Mayor Williams's administration and in Chief Bobby Cummings.[16]

To the extent he could, an arrogant Williams shrugged off the criticisms by orchestrating a ninety-one-count indictment against thirteen Black male youth from the Touch Money Gang (TMG).[17] All thirteen TMG members were convicted for six homicides, possession of illegal weapons, and other violent crimes. The community's response to the mass arrest was mixed and even caustic at times. City leadership, Attorney General Matt Denn, and members of the state legislature still tried to pass mandatory minimum legislation set to target Wilmington's Black youth.[18] Although most of their overall efforts were defeated, they hailed the TMG convictions with Mayor Williams as victories and evidence in support of the strict legislation they espoused. Policing the violence was supposed to be Williams's strength, but the political grounds had shifted in Wilmington. Neither Williams or Denn had noticed this in time to recover. This mistake would cause them both to be one-term office holders.

Operating from a dated political rulebook, Williams championed a "tough on crime" platform at a time when the public pushed back against hardened policy. Majority-Black cities like Wilmington were now more critical of the impact of aggressive policing initiatives. A growing number of white liberals had also joined in the fight against mass incarceration. Williams had not realized that he could no longer rely on the old guard's discourse of personal responsibility. Williams's predecessors Sills and Baker, as Black men, were able to get away with their harsh characterizations of the social failings of Black Wilmington. Sills's and Baker's unforgiving analyses of street violence and poverty was widely supported by older and upper-middle-class Black Americans. From their perspective, the sharp criticism was the help they needed to improve their structural conditions. Sills and Baker spared no opportunity to remind Black Wilmington that the spread of violence and disopportunity was their own making, the result of negative choices. But times had changed. If Williams was to survive, he had to abandon this position or the classic respectability politics held firmly by Black boomers.

The 2014 Crime Commission

In 2014, Governor Jack Markell convened nine community policing experts to be a part of the coveted Wilmington Public Safety Strategies Commission—a "crime commission" established to make key recommendations for swift and major police reform in Wilmington.[19] And to our grand delight, Governor Markell selected Wolfie as one of the nine experts. Other members of this exclusive commission included Wilmington's chief of police, Delaware's top state prosecutor, the governor's chief of staff, and the vice president of Capital One Bank.

There was a charged atmosphere around the "crime commission," which absorbed much of Delaware's public attention from 2014 to 2016. The nine members received no financial support, but the governor's office did pay $200,000 to the Police Foundation to do a full evaluation with concrete recommendations to reduce crime and improve policing. The nine-person commission only monitored the process and approved the Police Foundation to conduct the evaluation; it had very little to do with the evaluation itself. The Police Foundation interviewed dozens of community and professional stakeholders over six to eight months to quickly spit out a 200-page report with 111 targeted recommendations.[20]

This glossy report debuted in 2015 in the main auditorium of Bayard Middle School. This three-hour event included a press conference, a brief presentation of the report and its core recommendations, a public ratification by the nine-person commission, and a contentious public hearing or response period. Residents and news cameras filled the auditorium. The commission's nine members sat on stage.

During the public hearing period, one white woman shouted, "Where's the mayor at? Why isn't he here? We are talking about a problem that's in his city, and he is not here. This is unacceptable!"

Chief Cummings looked uncomfortable but continued to smile. From the mayor's perspective, Governor Markell had encroached on his territory by developing the commission without sufficient direction from the mayor's office.

Moreover, the well-produced and lengthy report made it possible for the Police Foundation to receive $200,000 upfront and receive additional funding to implement their recommended changes. And after receiving the report, the state legislature approved $1.5 million to move forward with their recommendations. But due to an ongoing feud with the governor, Mayor Williams delayed the new policing initiative Governor Markell sought to implement. The mayor's firm position against the governor's plan for police reform further hurt the mayor's approval ratings. Also, the stalemate over the $1.5 million earmarked for police reform solidified Governor Markell's defeat on policing and crime in Wilmington. They both insisted they were doing everything they could; and they both also blamed each other for the policing problems in Wilmington. But Markell and Williams were unaware that the worst of 2015 had not yet arrived. This embarrassing public feud would soon take a back seat to something far more sinister.

Jeremy "Bam Bam" McDole

Tensions with police erupted after officers murdered wheelchair-bound, 28-year-old Jeremy "Bam Bam" McDole, who was paralyzed from the waist down from a previous shooting.[21] On September 23, 2015, four officers surrounded an aloof-looking McDole, sitting in his wheelchair behind a grey sedan. Some claimed McDole had a gun on his person and shot himself accidentally, while others said he was "high on dippers [PCP]." The McDole family contended that Jeremy was unarmed and police later "planted a gun" on him.[22] No gun was ever confirmed by onlookers, but McDole's hands later tested positive for gunshot residue.

Uploaded video footage detailed the officer-involved shooting. Senior Corporal Joseph Dellose yelled, "He is over here! . . . Show me your hands!" Literally two seconds after warning McDole, Dellose fired and hit McDole with a shotgun blast.

One young male in great disbelief calmly muttered, "Oh shit."

The same officer shouted again, "Drop the gun! Drop the gun!" But no gun was visible. Many onlookers wondered what exactly was perceived to be a gun.

Still alive, McDole remained largely unresponsive to the demands. It did not appear that McDole was hurt or that he understood the commands. He just sat there and looked on. If anything, he shrugged his immobile legs a few times to get more comfortable. I recognized this unique shrugging of paraplegics from observing Jonathan (Associate). After being shot in 2011 he was paralyzed from the waist down, and he fidgeted in his wheelchair the same way McDole did before and after he was shot the first time by police.

Soon after joining the Street PAR project, Jonathan opened a barbershop and salon in Southbridge. One Sunday morning in 2011, Jonathan stopped by the shop to tidy up for the upcoming week. A man knocked on the door, but Jonathan waved him off. The shop was closed, and he needed to finish sweeping. The man remained, and with his body language he signaled he needed a quick word. Aggravated by the stranger's insistence, Jonathan slowly walked to the front door to unlock it.

The man pulled out a gun. In a fit of rage, Jonathan punched him in his face, which was a grave mistake. Jonathan was shot three times in the torso, with at least one bullet piercing his spine. After falling to the floor, he immediately lost the feeling in his legs. Bleeding profusely, he whispered to the man, "Please pull me by the front door. Don't let me die, . . . I have kids." Surprisingly, the shooter pulled Jonathan to the door so he could flag down someone for help.

That evening, I visited him in the intensive care unit at ChristianaCare Hospital. Jonathan's mother called me over and explained his condition. They learned he would make it, but he was permanently paralyzed from the waist down. After our exchange, she permitted me to spend time with him alone. The feeling and mood in the room was almost indescribable. He was in state of strange calmness. Heavily medicated, he came in and out of consciousness. A big tube ran down his throat, and smaller ones pierced other parts of his body. At his bedside, I placed my hands in his, and prayed. Shortly after, I cried.

I visited Jonathan again about a week later. Amazingly in good spirits, he had a way of making light of a tough situation.

"You got a lot of love here." I said to him. "And everybody is rooting for you. Just take your time, rest, and get stronger."

"Thank you, Doc, for stopping by. It means a lot to me, my brother." He smiled and looked down, below his waist. "Doc, look at my legs. They feel all wiry." He giggled some more. "They feel like spaghetti." We both burst out in a surreal laughter.

"It was good to see you, Mr. Wilson, and I will make sure to stop by soon." Once again, he looked at his legs and we laughed some more. Giggling, I jogged into the waiting room where his family was. They were pleased we had a positive interaction, but were not quite sure how to interpret my laughter.

In any case, my experiences with Jonathan informed how I understood McDole's fatal interaction with police. Many believed that McDole wanted to die, that he committed suicide by a cop. For many, McDole gave police the permission they needed to satisfy their blood lust for poor Black men.

While McDole sat in his wheelchair, police screeched commands.

"Drop the gun!" Other officers chimed in, "Drop the gun!" But where was McDole's so-called gun? "Drop the gun!" "Drop it!" "Drop the gun!" One officer hovered near McDole with a shotgun pointed at him. Then this officer shot him and then walked away.

McDole just sat there, almost as if he wasn't shot. Other officers began yelling, "Let me see your hands!" "Hands up!" "Put your hands up!" Jeremy was paralyzed from the waist down.

A younger officer now hovered near McDole, screaming, "Hands up!"

Another resident said, "Put your hands up, cous[in]. They shot his ass. He's bleeding. He's bleeding." McDole was still conscious but had already been shot once by Captain Dellose. McDole sat quietly.

"Hands up!" "Put your hands up!"

McDole shrugged himself one more time, now putting his hands near his thigh area, or deeper in the crevices or corners of the chair, which was enough for officers to shoot and kill him. De-escalation was never an option.

McDole's murder was so jarring that rumors of killing an officer were dispatched over the neighborhood grapevine, and this new "beef" with police nearly erupted into an uprising.[23] By October, there were "three incidents in five days—one involving hundreds . . . with some throwing rocks and bottles at officers, and two more in which residents charged or yelled at police."[24] Residents felt they had little to lose in fighting back, especially since police had become more militarized and increasingly reliant on intrusive surveillance technology. They were already distrustful of police, and this deep distrust only exploded with McDole's murder.

Rios found that police in Oakland brutalized street-identified youth by roughing them up, punching them unconscious ("knocking them out"), and "almost breaking their limbs."[25] In response, youth resisted by being disrespectful to or even spitting on officers. Such actions were considered authentic expressions of resilience, "infrapolitics," or everyday enactments of resistance, and getting assaulted by police or jailed was thought to be worth it.[26] Aggravating police was an adaptive way to deter them from harassing disaffected youth.[27] Rios also reported that police generally avoided youth perceived to be too difficult.[28]

In any case, just when we thought the resentment couldn't get any worse, it did. So many were crushed when no charges were filed by the state against the officers who killed McDole. In January 2017, Lorretta Lynch's U.S. Department of Justice also declined to pursue civil charges, stating that they found insufficient evidence to prove officers used "excessive violence."[29] Yet, McDole's family did win a $1.5 million civil suit against the City of Wilmington.

VICARIOUS EXPERIENCES of police brutality and murder like the public lynching of Jeremy McDole negatively impacted the well-being of poor Black communities across the country.[30] And the compounding effect of observing and hearing about police killings greatly disrupted the social equilibrium of the Eastside and Southbridge.

Delaware is one of three states that makes it extremely difficult to access police misconduct data.[31] Law enforcement agencies are not required to report these data, and fewer than 3% of the country's 18,000 police departments or agencies actually report fatal shootings to the FBI since 2011.[32] Reported data are also largely unreliable.[33] But from the available data, we know that fatalities committed by police occur at an alarming rate in Black communities.[34] Blacks are three times more likely than whites to be killed by police, when adjusted for population rates.[35]

"Why I Can't Stand Out in Front of My House?" Harassment and Disrespect

Perceptions of police were generally negative. Reported experiences ranged from extreme physical abuse to some positive interactions, but overall, the streets felt they were unfairly targeted, stopped, harassed, frisked, arrested, and convicted for minor crimes, and for crimes they did not commit.

Richard felt "disrespected" by police, and he claimed he never witnessed any officer fairly protect and serve residents in Southbridge. According to Richard, police expected Black men to "bow down," or be docile in their presence. Frustrated with reliving experiences of degradation, Richard admitted he was eager to fight a police officer. For Richard, police were formidable only because they had laws to protect them. But officers lacked the heart of a warrior, which is how Richard evaluated a man's standing in or out of the streets. As far as Richard was concerned, police were "soft," "chumps," and "nothing to be afraid of going to war with. . . . They're just protected by the badge." From his perspective, police were actually more afraid of the streets than they were of the police.

"I've never seen a cop protect. . . . I never seen it! Cops do a lot of stuff they don't gotta do. . . . They so forceful, . . . they know they got that badge and that gun and that taser gun. . . . They got the whole unit behind them. Take all that off and see me in the streets! I'm not no disrespectful person, dog. But when I see you with that badge and stuff, I ain't gonna say, 'What's up?' but I ain't gonna disrespect you, neither. And I think the cops disrespect us!"

The men were extremely angry with police, and few of the police realized how serious they were. The men also had few opportunities to constructively process their displeasure and hold police accountable.

MEN IN OUR SURVEY SAMPLE had slightly more negative attitudes toward the police than women (28.6 and 27.1, respectively) (see table 5.1). Older participants also had more negative attitudes toward police; and the difference between the three age cohorts were small: (1) ages 18–21 (27.4), (2) ages 22–29

TABLE 5.1
Gender and Age Groups: Attitudes toward Police

Gender	Age Group	Mean
Male	18–21	27.4
	22–29	28.7
	30–35	30.0
Male subtotal		28.6
Female	18–21	26.8
	22–29	27.4
	30–35	27.3
Female subtotal		27.1
Total		27.8

Scores range between 12 and 40, with higher scores representing more negative attitudes.

(28.7), and (3) ages 30–35 (30). Also, the oldest men, ages 30–35, had the most negative attitudes toward police (30.0), while women ages 18–21 had the least negative attitudes (26.8).

Disappointment in the police's overall job performance was also very high. About 75% disagreed with the statement "Police do their jobs well" and 58% agreed with "Police sometimes allow crime to occur without stopping it." Most also reported that police "harassed" and "bothered" them in ways that made them feel "unsafe." Almost 61% agreed that "I worry that the police I see on the streets might bother me or my friends," and 80% agreed that "The police give people a hard time for no reason."

Leondrei (age 35) from the Eastside and Erica (age 22) from Southbridge represented well how men and women across age were very resentful of police.[36] They believed that overpolicing was a racialized and classed practice used to sustain the current structural arrangement of Black poverty and white wealth. Leondrei and Erica also argued that overpolicing was such a problem that many people were uncomfortable with relaxing in public. Leondrei also was especially offended when he perceived that police harassed law-abiding residents. He shouted, "They're locking you up in the streets [i.e., public spaces].... It's summer time! Why I can't stand out in front of my house? You ain't riding out in Greenville [wealthy Wilmington neighborhood] talking about, 'What y'all doing out here?' *It don't matter what I'm doing out here!* 'Did you hear any gunshots? Is any bottles being busted? Did any ... neighbors ... call ... and say it was a ruckus out here?'"

Leondrei's frustration with the police was valid and had a lot to do with him being a Black man with little sociopolitical power or ability to change anything. More frighteningly, this was the lens he believed police viewed him through, which stoked his anger. Leondrei was unemployed and formerly incarcerated, and he struggled with addiction. Dignity was the one thing he had some control over, but even that felt compromised by the police. Leondrei also believed that the aesthetics of their deeply impoverished neighborhoods lulled police into having a subtle disdain for them. Leondrei emphasized that neighborhoods like Greenville were policed with more respect because they were whiter and wealthier sections of Wilmington. Aggressive surveillance of the Eastside and Southbridge signaled to Leondrei that police were mostly there to marshal and manage as opposed to protect and empower them.

Moreover, street-identified Black men and women in the Eastside and Southbridge generally thought police could care less about the structural factors leading to crime. The hardships associated with poverty or poorly performing schools for example, were perceived to be irrelevant to the police, and this prevented any opportunity to develop a meaningful connection. Instead, street-identified young people believed that police instinctually assumed that residents were up to no good and it was their duty as police to hold them accountable.

Frustrated, some salvaged some degree of integrity by openly calling out or challenging police for perceived indiscretions. In this spirit, Leondrei mimicked for us how he loudly questioned police for "harassing" him and friends in front of his home in the Eastside. He yelled, "It's summer time! Why I can't stand out in front of my house? . . . *It don't matter what I'm doing out here!*" Leondrei's response to police demonstrated how he and his friends on that day maintained their respect in a neighborhood where respect was hard to come by. This moment with police not only provided a cathartic platform for Leondrei, it was also a way to restore dignity and receive validation as a Black man with little sociopolitical power.

Erica never observed police do anything positive beyond shaking a resident's hand, and she, too, berated them for not respecting Black residents. She further contended that the lack of a cultural understanding of poor Black people clouded the police's judgment and interactions with people they had little respect for. A distorted cultural perspective, according to Erica, led to knee-jerk and clumsy police initiatives such as "jump-out squads," which were designed to stop poor Black residents from congregating in public spaces, or sitting in front of their homes.

Melodie (Associate) asked Erica, "What does law enforcement look like in Southbridge?"

"You can't sit on the step and talk . . . without them telling you, 'You got to move!' 'You live here?' 'What's your name?' 'You got ID?' It's horrible!"

"How does that make you feel?"

"It's uncomfortable. Their attitude is ignorant. It's not like you see every day [that] somebody is selling drugs or playing dice."

Reporting and Late Arrivals

Both men and women agreed that the police's late arrivals and failures to respond contributed to Wilmington's increasing rates of gun violence. But only the women admitted that they had called the police and personally experienced late arrivals or no responses. Men and women generally spoke about contact with police in the same way, although no male interviewee admitted to ever calling police for assistance. Street culture was harder on street-identified Black men than it was for street-identified Black women for reaching out to police for support. Any cooperation with police could be interpreted as "snitching"—the deceitful sharing of information about crimes with police. Street culture tolerated women requesting support from police, primarily because they cared for children and were anchors for families.

Angel, a 24-year-old Black woman and mother from Southbridge, blamed police for fostering a climate of mistrust by not responding to calls for assistance. Angel angrily said it was common for police to arrive late, even if they were notified of a fight or gun violence.

To learn more about her perspective, Wolfie asked, "What kind of relationship does the police have with residents?"

"Around here? None!"

"No relationship?"

"Say you fighting or somebody got shot, you call the cops, they be here in like twenty minutes or half an hour if they really want to come over here."

In their dual interview, Kendre (age 27) and Michelle (age 31) said it was common for police to respond late to emergencies in Southbridge. Both women had reached out to police in times of distress, and both claimed they were ignored after reporting that their car was broken into, and even that gun-toting men were chasing their children. Kendre also said that thirty minutes was the quickest time she could recall police arriving in Southbridge.

KENDRE: My car got robbed . . . right in broad daylight. . . . I called [the police], they told me, "[I] have to have a cop call you back to take a report over the phone." I'm like, "Don't y'all need to come out here to do fingerprints and something like that? Someone was all in my car." . . . The cop didn't call me until 6:00 P.M. that night [and] I called them at 1:00 P.M. . . . They don't care about Southbridge. . . . They just don't care.

MICHELLE: At least you got a call. They ain't never show up when I said I got robbed. They ain't show up 'til hours later after my son and his friends got chased by the guy with the gun. . . . No, Wilmington's finest. [And] I called them twice.

Kendre and Michelle felt Southbridge was valued far less than white communities. They believed their neighborhoods were not a priority for police, and negative interactions with police were deeply systemic or more prevalent than acknowledged by public officials. Kendre and Michelle remained optimistic or just had to believe that positive change was on its way. Until then, they intended to be vocal advocates for better policing.

Louis (age 31) expressed that police repeatedly harassed customers in his barbershop in the Eastside. Police believed he was selling drugs inside the business, given his previous felony conviction and the company he sometimes kept around the barbershop. Police once raided during work hours, and according to Louis, neither he nor anyone else were arrested. During this raid, Louis was also shot at by cops because they mistakenly believed he had a firearm. This enraged Louis, and he sometimes responded to these raids by inviting even more people to his shop on Friday or Saturday evenings to show up police, or preserve some semblance of dignity: "I was harassed for a long time. For a long time! Maybe it was 'cause of the company I [kept] but . . . I wasn't doing nothing wrong and they were still harassing me. . . . They would come to my place of business and do raids and not find nothing and embarrass the crap out of me. . . . I have even been shot at by the cops before . . . they supposedly thought I had a gun on me. . . . They're very . . . disrespectful. . . . They think everybody's a criminal. They think everybody's doing wrong."

After moving around in her chair and slowly collecting herself, Ashley (Associate) asked Louis, "Would you say that police don't see residents as humans?" He replied, "Yes! Police see wrong every time they drive up and down these streets. And they're very abusive out here. I've seen them beat a lot of people up. . . . I've seen them . . . hurt a lot of people. And they get away with it."

A SMALLER, CRITICAL MASS of Black youth and young adults were repeatedly stopped, arrested, and incarcerated in the Eastside and Southbridge. Relatively few, perhaps a more hardened or active strain of street-identified Black men, had chronically experienced negative contact with police in the previous twelve months. Younger men were much more likely than Black girls and women or older Black men in the streets to occupy public spaces, particularly for purposes related to crime.[37] In our survey sample, the youngest men (ages 18–21) were more likely to have negative contact with police and the oldest women (ages 30–35) were the least likely to have negative contact (see table 5.2). Also, the men nearly doubled the women in this area (2.6 and 1.7, respectively).

Both men's and women's negative contacts with police declined for older age cohorts, and most negative contacts were accounted for by our "stopped," "frisked," and "summons" data.

- *Stopped by police.* Forty-two percent were "stopped by police." On average, they were stopped four times during the previous year. About 61% of men and 29% of women reported being stopped.

TABLE 5.2
Gender and Age Groups: Negative Contacts with Police in the Past Twelve Months

Gender	Age Group	Mean
Male	18–21	2.8
	22–29	2.6
	30–35	2.4
Male subtotal		2.6
Female	18–21	2.0
	22–29	1.6
	30–35	1.5
Female subtotal		1.7
Total		2.2

Scores range between 0 and 7, with higher scores representing more negative contacts with police. Contacts include seven types: stops, frisks, given a summons, detainment without arrest, arrests, picked up in a sweep, and incarceration. Most participants generally reported, or most of the variance for this scale is accounted for, by only three items: being stopped, being frisked, and being arrested.

- *Frisked by police.* Twenty-nine percent were "frisked by police." On average, they were frisked about four times in the last twelve months. Men made up 70% of those who were frisked.
- *Given a summons.* Twenty-two percent were "given a summons," and 60% of them were men. On average, they received three summonses during the previous year.

Of those previously arrested, one-third reported being arrested between one and four times, while approximately 13% were arrested or taken away by police more than twelve times in their lives.

"Action" and Policing in Wilmington

Prior to data collection, we started developing a working relationship with the WPD, the Public Safety Office, and the Wilmington City Council. Also, we scheduled two officers to lead a two-hour community policing workshop for methods training. We made it clear to city leadership that training formerly incarcerated people did not mean we were opposed to the WPD or the practice of ethical and sometimes tough policing. And while we supported good policing, we still underscored that we could never share with them any incriminating information about anyone involved with our study.

Over a two-year period, we led a set of diversity, culture, and implicit bias trainings for the WPD, Youth Rehabilitative Services, the Division of Prevention and Behavioral Health Services, and administrators of Delaware's juvenile justice system and the Red Clay School District. Other programs included organizing and sitting on panels with the chief justice, the attorney general, and the chief of police. Even when it was difficult to do so, it was important to show the public that we were on the same team. For us, however, this did not mean we would soften our message. If real change with police was to occur, it could only be accomplished with the people and by working through hard truths.

In 2013, we called for a street outreach program on gun violence, and by 2014, the Wilmington Cease Violence program was finally formed.[38] The national Cease Violence program is based in Chicago, and this office works with low-income neighborhoods across the country to develop Cease Violence chapters and train "violence interrupters" to tackle gun violence in their communities.

Under the leadership of Darryl "Wolf" Chambers, the Wilmington Cease Violence's inaugural group of interrupters included four other Street PAR Associates and six other Honorary Associates recruited from Wilmington.[39] Research Associate Patrice Gibbs was this program's first operational director. Darryl's brother, Derrick "Der Der" Chambers (Research Associate) was also hired as a "violence interrupter," and in 2016, Derrick received the first Willis Young Memorial Award at the meeting of the National Network of Hospital-Based Violence Intervention Programs in Baltimore. Further, by 2017, Wilmington's thriving Cease Violence program evolved into the Community Intervention Team—a violence prevention program that is currently housed in Darryl's nonprofit, the Center for Structural Equity.[40]

The Mayor and the Governor in the Eastside

In 2015, Darryl and I received an email from Drew Fennell, the chief of staff for Governor Markell, requesting that we arrange a meeting with the governor and residents—*in the Eastside*—on policing and violence. We only had a week to pull it off, but our experiences with programming in these neighborhoods prepared us well to meet this ambitious timetable.

We hit the ground and got the word out. Somewhat apprehensive on the day of, I sent Facebook and Twitter messages out three hours before the event. Minutes after, I received a text from Drew reminding me not to promote this event in any "major way." We were aware that the governor's office and other offices followed us but did not realize how closely they monitored our social media platforms. A widely promoted event would force them to rearrange with stricter security measures.

It was 4:30 P.M. and time to go. The event was scheduled at 6:00 P.M., and I had to pick up my good friend Fr. David Andrew, senior pastor at the Episcopal Church of Saints Andrew and Matthew in Wilmington.

Father David and I arrived at Rashad's Barbershop in the Eastside at 5:30 P.M. At age 67, Rashad had owned his barbershop for about thirty-five years. Rashad had a freshly lined gray goatee, and he wore a black Muslim prayer cap and a black barber apron draped over his plaid shirt.

Rashad's Arabic name meant "thinker" or "counselor," and he was a very respected mentor to Black youth in the Eastside. And much of his wisdom spoke to the importance of Black entrepreneurship.

"What does Black business mean to Black people in the Eastside?" I asked him.

"It means stability. It models for them how we can create our own."

I followed up with, "I am sure you could open this business anywhere. Why is it important for you to be in the Eastside?"

"What I'm trying to do is to, first and foremost, [provide] some kind of structure. A lot of kids in the Eastside that come to my barbershop don't really have a lot of structure."

"As an elder in the community, what do you think about the violence?"

Rashad said, "Some of the stuff . . . really concerns me. . . . like kids shooting each other. Just the behavior of our young folks. We need parents to teach our children how to be respectful and how to carry themselves. . . . To be honest with you, I think they [parents] are doing all that they can do, but we have been doing that for a long time."

Rashad's Barbershop stood on the corner of Seventh and Pine Streets in the Eastside in a small but lively brick building. The shop was packed. Standing room only. At about 5:45 P.M., two tinted black SUVs and one car parked in front of Rashad's. About two minutes to the hour, Governor Markell exited one of the SUVs and walked into the barbershop. Dressed in a smoky gray suit with a blue shirt and no tie, Governor Markell walked in and immediately started shaking hands and saying hello. Behind him followed Drew and one plainclothes security officer.

After a brief opening, I thanked and introduced Governor Markell. The barbershop applauded, and he warmly addressed everyone. "I'll be the first to validate the state can and will do more to revitalize the Eastside. In times of financial instability, it's no excuse, but your community has been neglected. But tonight, I want to listen and hear the concerns of the Eastside or from people that's most affected by unemployment . . . the crime, problematic policing. We can't arrest ourselves out of this, and we will do our best to bring real opportunities back to the Eastside." Looking to Drew, he added. "My staff and I are constantly thinking through how to develop more impactful job training programs, stable housing, and better schools."

About ten minutes into his address, Mayor Williams walked in, fashionably late. Dressed in his customary well-tailored suit with a bright white and pink tie, long black dress jacket, and black skull cap, Williams strolled in with a small entourage. When Markell finished, Williams took over, reminding everyone of his neighborhood roots and firm commitment to improving Black Wilmington.

Excited and genuinely happy that the governor and the mayor had come to visit, residents leaped in with questions about jobs, violence, and police and prison reform. After an hour and half, we departed for James and Jesse's Barber Shop and Maude's Beauty Shop on Tenth and Bennett Streets in the Eastside. Tenth and Bennett was in one of the most violent neighborhoods in Delaware. Wolf selected this location because it was important for Markell to observe firsthand the impoverished conditions of places where the "bodies were dropping at." We parked a block away from Jesse's, which gave the governor and me an opportunity to walk and chat about the poverty tearing apart the Eastside. "Governor Markell, I just want you to know we are so happy you came out tonight to meet with the people. We are grateful you and Drew made it a point to finally to come out to these neighborhoods. This means a lot to the Eastside to see you out here. Not too many of your stature would be willing to do so. This is Tenth and Bennett, a real hot spot in Wilmington."

Slightly puzzled and maybe even annoyed, he responded, "I've visited communities like these before. . . . No, no, no. I've met with folk in this community before and I looked forward to meeting with them tonight."

When we walked in the barbershop, Mr. Jesse greeted us with a giant smile and an overflowing shop. Governor Markell and Mayor Williams did their one-two punch again, but this time the question-and-answer period became more combative. Dubard (Associate) and others candidly asked questions about police misconduct. They insisted that at least three officers "had to go!" To my surprise, Mayor Williams was aware of these officers and appeared to side with Dubard's criticisms. Williams promised justice would be dispensed if evidence supported the claims against these officers.

Dubard said, "Mayor Williams, a lot of these police don't respect us in these neighborhoods. Sometimes they be busting us in our heads and shaking us down for money. They grab some of these guys up and take 'em in the alleyway." The mayor replied, "My office has been informed and I assure everyone, we are on the case. You know, I'm a former detective, and I'm very supportive of the WPD, but this issue has our attention."

Markell was quiet on police misconduct, and when the moment was right, he changed the conversation. "How many of you read Dr. Payne's post on social media about tonight's event?" Most were silent. I jumped in, "For the record, it's not me who got the people here tonight. It's them (Street PAR Associates). They are *that good*. They are the reason why everyone is here." Pointing to the crowd, I said, "It's the high social capital of people like Wolfie, Lou, Ashley, Kontal, and Dubard, and also the promotional efforts of Tyerin (Honorary Associate), that made tonight possible. It's all them, not me."

As the Q&A continued, Drew waved me over and requested to meet Tyerin. Tyerin A. Griffin (age 33) was a charismatic figure in Wilmington, and he also was one of the city's most successful promoters. Tyerin promoted this meet and greet on his social media platforms, where many were informed about the event. Politicians were always interested in who could get the word out to large numbers of people. Tyerin was especially great friends with Kontal and Dubard (Associates), and the three of them had organized local parties and concerts with hip-hop artists like Meek Mill, Jadakiss, Yo Gotti, Scoot Luv, and Trey Songz.

Tyerin was a proud Sunni Muslim, and his religious identity was reflected in his long, well-groomed beard, thin mustache, and pronounced zebiba (prayer bump) on his forehead. Tyerin also had been previously incarcerated, but he was on the upswing, and now he successfully ran several businesses including a barbershop and hair salon.

One afternoon, Dubard and I spoke with Tyerin in a small park in Southbridge. Sitting on a park bench, slowly looking from left to right, Tyerin shared how gun violence had rocked his life. Like so many others, he had been made numb by the murders of friends, but his detachment more accurately was the way he coped with the pain. Murder had also raised Tyerin's awareness about how just one homicide was enough to greatly disrupt the city of Wilmington. "I have seen a lot of violence [and] it affected me. It takes a part of your life. Sometimes I think seeing so much violence, [or] being exposed to it, desensitizes you. If you are around so much hurt and pain and you see so much of it, [you become] desensitized to violence. . . . I am used to it."

Dubard asked, "Have you lost anyone to the streets, like to a violent crime?" Tyerin replied, "I lost a lot of people to the streets . . . but one was like my homie, my best friend. . . . Like, certain people [who were killed] that you know and just, like, hung out with, and it [their death] don't really mean nothing to you, until it is someone special. And that one person was Jerome Greene, that I lost."

Jerome "Boomer" Greene was tragically killed in front of his 9-year-old daughter in February 2008 while walking out of the corner store on the 300 block of East 23rd Street.[41] Boomer was also the father of four other children. Tyerin took a moment to gather himself. He had not planned on speaking about Boomer.

"That was like my best friend. He was like a brother to me."

Dubard followed up, "How was he murdered?"

"He was shot coming out of a store in front of his daughter. He was shot several times."

"In front of his daughter? How is his daughter doing now?"

"She is going through a lot, as far as being a kid growing up and having to deal with the constant reminders of her dad not being in her life. Her dad was real active in her life. He was always there. . . . She is going through the natural struggles of growing up without a father that was a part of her life. He wasn't a distant father to her. He was a good father. Also, for her to witness that, she is just going through the behavioral problems that any child would be going through dealing with that."

After noticing a somber shift in Tyerin's mood, Dubard asked him, "How has Boomer's murder changed your life?"

"At some point in your life [after] being around [so many] murders and being in the streets, you become desensitized. You never really think about the aftermath of you taking a life or life being taken until it really hits close to you. . . . I think it kind of affected me in a positive way. . . . You always hear jokers say, 'I'm a kill him,' but like you never think about them kids that you be leaving behind. It made me realize, if you do take a life, you not just affecting that person you kill . . . you really affecting them kids, the mothers. . . . It never should get to that point where you feel like, 'I'm a take his life.' Because really, you're taking that kid's life. You are messing up that mother's life. You're not just affecting that person that's in the grave. You're affecting so many others."

Boomer was killed on a Sunday afternoon when then-senator Barack Obama campaigned for the presidency at Wilmington's Rodney Square. Tyerin heard about Boomer's murder while in the Plummer Community Corrections Center (PCCC). The PCCC is a correctional facility that supervises male and female offenders on work release. PCCC inmates are allowed time out to search for employment before returning to PCCC to check in for the evening. While on his two-hour break, Tyerin ran over to where Boomer was shot, to see if he could speak with him. Tyerin was under the impression that Boomer survived, because

> he was shot before. . . . Shootings is, like, common. So, I still rushed over there. I'm looking at the crime scene. "This ain't a normal crime scene," I thought to myself. It was awfully quiet. . . . They took him away, but there was no sirens. I noticed they were not trying to rush him to the hospital. The next day, I got the newspaper to learn more about what happened. . . . My man just got shot in front of his daughter, broad daylight, Obama in town—this should be front-page news . . . this should be something big, I thought. There's was no article, no nothing. I'm like, "Wow." This ain't even important to some people. . . . The way I became desensitized, they [the public] became desensitized to broad daylight shootings.

Approximately one year later, after the governor's and mayor's visit to the Eastside, an undergraduate student at University of Delaware who lived in the Westside of Wilmington stopped by my office, in great alarm.

"Dr. Payne, did you hear what happened to Mase?"

"No, I didn't. Who is Mase?" I learned that Nathaniel T. Mangrum, aka "Mase," of the West Center City neighborhood, was well known in the streets of Wilmington.

"They say Tyerin killed Mase at this club on Governor Printz."

"Are you sure about this?" In my mind, Tyerin left the streets alone and was on the verge of becoming a business mogul.

"Yes, Dr. Payne! I am sure. Tyerin killed Mase, and the city is going crazy!"

Tyerin shot and killed Mase and then shot and attempted to kill Mase's friend who stood nearby, on Friday, April 1, 2016, at the Shades of Blue Bar and Lounge in the Edgemoor section of Wilmington. Purportedly, Tyerin and Mase's beef stemmed from a promotional dispute over Mase's birthday party at Shades of Blue. Mase hired Tyerin to promote his party, and at some point, they couldn't see eye to eye about proceeds from the party. Unable to peacefully resolve their differences, some onlookers claimed that Tyerin was warned he would be attacked after the bar closed. It was rumored that Rihanna's song "Man Down" ominously played at 12:30 A.M. when Tyerin approached Mase and made one last overture to peaceably settle their disagreement. Some say Mase's friend "mushed" (shoved with an open palm) Tyerin's face. During this final dispute, Tyerin shot and killed Mase first and then shot his friend, who was believed to be the instigator of Tyerin and Mase's beef. After the shooting, Tyerin quickly escaped and went on the run for five months.

City police, state troopers, and emergency medical technicians descended on Shades of Blue. Their beaming red, blue, and white lights sprayed the melee of bar patrons in the parking lot. Mase was beloved, if not worshipped. Many that night openly cried and shouted profanities. Men walked around flailing their arms, vowing revenge. Heartbroken women fell to the ground and were comforted by friends. Police stood out of the way as loved ones mourned. One man was so angry that after failed attempts at controlling him, nearby friends just encircled him so he would not endanger himself with police.

Sites of resilience theory explains why Tyerin determined that his brazen display of gun violence was adaptive on this ominous Friday night. Most likely, from Tyerin's perspective, he had no choice but to make the decision he did. After all, Mase reputedly was a much more dominant force in the streets. But Tyerin was formidable, too; he came from a strong line of shooters and drug dealers. Tyerin was also desperately trying to transition away from the streets, which ironically made him vulnerable to violence. Although Tyerin was successful, his business was still growing, and he had not yet made enough to remove himself from the neighborhoods that would eventually consume him. Tyerin was also a felon, which meant he was barred from most legal employment with any financial promise. Opening a business in the neighborhoods where violent crime was most likely to occur was arguably his best option. Furthermore, Mase was a daunting challenge, and it was apparent that he was willing to be lethally violent. But Tyerin would not be bullied or physically harmed, even if it meant risking incarceration. Doing so would also compromise his standing and safety in Wilmington. Discussions with Mase had clearly broken down, and perhaps, from Tyerin's perspective, he had to be pre-emptive, because his experience and capacity to be resilient required him to be so. He had no choice. Wilmington was a small city, and going back and forth with Mase was untenable, so settling this dispute now was probably Tyerin's best option.

A warrant for Tyerin's arrest for first-degree murder was immediately issued. Police claimed he had close ties to Philadelphia's underground community, and they encouraged the public to report any information of his whereabouts. By the next morning, a street memorial with stuffed animals and lit candles was set up for Mase outside of Shades of Blue and near his Westside home. It is common in Wilmington for street-identified groups and related loved ones to display street memorials in this fashion to mourn publicly or establish resilience during tragic moments.[42]

Shortly after Mase's murder, a press conference was held by Wilmington's city council. Councilwoman Sherry Dorsey Walker furiously said, "I'm asking for a cease violence. I am asking all the young men who feel it necessary to kill someone in retaliation for what has been taking place in the streets of Wilmington to stop and put your guns down. I'm asking you, right now, if Black lives matter, then why are you killing one another? . . . We have to stay prayed up!"

Council President Theo Gregory spoke next. "Let us not retaliate. This has to stop at some point in time. We are all brothers and sisters in this. We have to reach some common ground of understanding and learn how to resolve our differences, different than just killing."

Councilwoman Sherry and Council President Gregory were wise enough to know that in addition to Tyerin's pre-emptive strike and the deep mourning for Mase, retaliative violence, too, would be considered a site of resilience by Mase's camp, or an appropriate way to resolve this matter.

As the press conference concluded, a nearby incident on Elm and Harrison Streets forced the police in attendance, including Chief Cummings, to quickly leave. It was unclear why, but police chased, tackled, and arrested a young Black man.

Hundreds poured into the streets to view Mase's funeral procession. Like in the famous 1998 hip-hop song "Horse & Carriage" by Cam'ron, featuring the rapper Mase, the casket of Nathaniel "Mase" Mangrum was escorted through Wilmington by a white, horse-drawn carriage. In the weeks following, Mase's loyalists not only continued to make threats to Tyerin's friends and family, they allegedly shot up of Tyerin's barbershop, where his girlfriend worked and daughter played. Dubard and Kontal (Associates) were among Tyerin's close friends that were repeatedly threatened. In response to the shootings and death threats, Tyerin eventually released the following Facebook post, while on the run:

> In this world I guess it's OK to bully people, make attempts on innocent people lives, threaten people lives. . . . A lot of yall think yall know the

story but don't.... A lot of yall knew what was going on but made no attempt to intervene.... All of yall sitting and watching my family, daughter, mother, girlfriend, sisters lives and friends life get threaten but once again yall ... are not saying anything about that.... Justice will be served and the whole truth will come out. I will turn myself into the police once I'm assured every person in my life ... [is] protected. But once again most of yall think it's OK to threaten people's lives.... And yall threating my daughter. Smh [shaking my head].

Tyerin's Facebook account was removed soon after this message was posted.[43] Marshals had trouble tracking him down, and this post flew in their faces. Rumors also flew that he was "probably walking around as a fully covered Sunni [Muslim] in Philly." In turn, the police focused on Philadelphia and alerted the public.

Due to the repeated threats to his loved ones and after five months on the run, Tyerin turned himself in to the Delaware State Police on Sunday, September 4, 2016. He was later sentenced to ninety years in prison as a habitual offender.[44]

Chapter 6

"I Don't Let These Felonies Hold Me Back!"

HOW THE STREETS RADICALLY REFRAMED RE-ENTRY

You already crippling them at [age] 17.... You say you want them to "reintegrate into society." But you want to chop off two legs and an arm. What do you want them to do? They're just young people trying to find their way through the mess that we created. At the end of the day, these kids are made by us.
—Corry Wright (Street PAR Associate), in "Upstream"

They returned to neighborhoods plagued by violence, households prone to financial crises, a legal labor market offering low-paying, degrading jobs.... The cultural and developmental adaptions to these conditions, are the real reason why young men began offending in the first place and why so many continued to offend. Because the juvenile justice system is ill-equipped to restructure the labor market to create better jobs, allow young people the financial freedom to invest in higher education, dismantle racial discrimination or residential separation, or fix families struggling with poverty or addiction, it must recast the problem in terms of poor decision making, as a matter of individual deficits on the part of the young men who are part of the system.
—Jamie Fader, *Falling Back*

DELAWARE'S 2017 CORRECTIONS BUDGET to supervise 6,140 inmates in four state prisons and seven other facilities totaled almost $300 million.[1] Each inmate cost the state about $41,000. This budget was also used to supervise 17,220 probationers and parolees in thirteen community corrections offices or centers.[2] Of the four state prisons, Delores J. Baylor Women's Correctional Institution (BWCI) is the only women's prison in Delaware. BWCI housed approximately 400 women, both pretrial and sentenced women. About

40% of women were "detentioners," or held in the pretrial phase.[3] In 2010, of the 1,113 individuals released from Delaware prisons, over half were Black men and 3.8% were Black women.[4] The three-year recidivism rate for Black men in Delaware was 78%, and Black men age 24 and younger had a staggering recidivism rate of 93%.[5] Including juvenile detentions and jail incarcerations, approximately 1,200 residents returned each year to three zip codes (19801, 19802, and 19805) in Wilmington. In these zip codes, "more than 50 percent of men—7,200 men out of 14,000—are on probation."[6]

Due to the hordes of returning and recidivating Black men, re-entry was a priority for Wilmington when I arrived in 2008. Re-entry funding poured into Wilmington, and nonprofits such as the Wilmington HOPE Commission and Delaware Center for Justice (DCJ) were among its primary beneficiaries.

Re-entry reform was even a priority for judicial leadership including Delaware's Office of the Attorney General. Joseph Robinette "Beau" Biden III was the attorney general (AG) in Delaware from 2007 to May 2015, when he passed away from a brain tumor. The AG's main office was located in Downtown Eastside on French Street in the Carvel State Building. Wilmington did not have a district attorney, so the AG's office was responsible for prosecuting homicides and other serious crimes for the entire state. During his 2006 campaign, Beau promised to improve the AG's office relationship with Black Wilmington. He recognized that rhetoric around hyperincarceration was less common and tolerated in a progressive era. Under Biden's direction, Delaware's AG office became more open to public discussions and community meetings on overpolicing, incarceration, and poor re-entry services.

With the support of progressive talent like Deputy Attorney General Dan Logan and State Prosecutor Kathy Jennings, Biden ushered in what some considered landmark justice reform. Biden's office was chiefly responsible for ending Delaware's mandatory life sentence for three felony drug convictions, and for restoring voting rights and driving privileges to convicted felons. Biden's office also developed Delaware's Crime Strategies Unit, a state division that focused on violent crime.

The young AG was a decade ahead of his time. Biden was arguably the forerunner to a wave of progressive prosecutors, AGs, and district attorneys who "vow[ed] to fight the system."[7] Biden's most radical prosecution was of Delaware's banks (and other banks in the country), which he proved had disenfranchised Black homeowners during the 2008 Great Recession.[8] In what was called the National Mortgage Servicing Settlement, Biden was instrumental in securing $180 million that he promised to return to the families and communities taken advantage of by various financial institutions. Biden said, "The mortgage crisis wrecked our economy and devastated families and neighborhoods throughout Delaware and the nation. We cannot allow the mortgage crisis to be a man-made disaster for which there is no accountability. The funds we have secured in these settlements are being put to work helping thousands of Delaware families avoid foreclosure, strengthening communities hit hard by the fallout from the housing crisis, holding banks accountable and reimbursing government losses. Our work is not done."[9] However, after Beau Biden passed away, the decision to return this settlement to the community was rescinded.

I FIRST MET BEAU BIDEN in January 2011 at the Delaware State Bar Association's Dr. Martin Luther King Jr. Breakfast and Statewide Day of Service. This was a grand annual event held at the Chase Center at the Riverfront. Dozens of Black church congregations and a diverse cadre of professionals attended this breakfast every year. After breakfast, on my way out, Beau Biden and I ran into each other.

Extending his hand, Biden exclaimed, "Dr. Payne! How are you?"

Delighted to finally meet him, I said, "I'm fine. How are you?"

"I have heard so much about you. I'm looking forward to catching up sometime."

"Let's do it. I am looking forward to catching up with you, too."

Before he passed away on May 30, 2015, he opened his office to several groups like ours to engage in deeper discussions with the community. On a few occasions, Darryl and others met with Biden and members of his office to discuss how they could be more proactive and supportive of their neighborhoods.

After Beau's passing, we continued to meet with his office.

Ashley Blazer Biden is the daughter and youngest child of President Joe Biden. Beau was liberal for an AG, but by Delaware's standards, Ashley was radical. And for some in Delaware's establishment, this was problematic. Ashley was outspoken, a great public speaker, and a rising giant in the field of re-entry. And her uncompromising advocacy forced Delaware to pay attention to poor Black Wilmington, and especially the concerns of the streets.

Beau was the doting son, poised to carry on his father's legacy. Ashley was daddy's little girl—she and her father adored each other. Yet, Beau's and Ashley's perspectives on the structural needs of Black Wilmington couldn't have differed more from their father's. Very few in Black Wilmington ever condemned Ashley for President Biden's legacy or record. Given cultural norms around family, most of Black Wilmington understood how Ashley could cherish her father while advocating for change that effectively challenged his record. In fact, Black Wilmington probably would have trusted Ashley less if she had openly disrespected her father.

Senator Joe Biden's criminal justice record was tied to a troublesome legislative legacy that stemmed from the 1914 Harrison Narcotics Tax Act.[10] Following the convict lease system—a prison system later declared unconstitutional for its cruelty—the Harrison Act was used to hyperincarcerate Black men for sales and use of hard drugs like cocaine and heroin.[11] The Harrison Act applied a "special tax" and/or up to ten years imprisonment for "opium and coca products" that required a doctor's prescription.[12] To usher in the Harrison Act, Congress and media outlets like the *New York Times* argued that an ever-growing scourge of "Negro Cocaine Fiends," or Black men addicted to cocaine, were raping unsuspecting white women and otherwise hurting "innocent" or law-abiding citizens.[13] Cocaine was believed to induce in Black men such a supernatural frenzy or "craze" that their bodies could withstand gunfire. Intensified white hysteria about cocaine-addicted Black men also expedited the passage of the Harrison Act, which was ultimately responsible for "establishing the foundations of federal drug law enforcement."[14]

Senator Joe Biden contributed to this racist legislative legacy, with his roles in (1) the Comprehensive Control Act of 1984, (2) the Anti–Drug Abuse Act of 1986, (3) the Anti–Drug Abuse Act of 1988, (4) the "Crime Bill," or the Violent Crime Control and Law Enforcement Act of 1994, and (5) the RAVE Act of 2003.[15] The Anti–Drug Abuse Acts of 1986 and 1988 and the Crime Bill of 1994 are the most damaging and best known. The Anti–Drug Abuse Acts are responsible for the major sentencing disparity for possession of powdered cocaine versus crack cocaine. The 100-to-1 sentencing ratio derived from this law established a mandatory minimum of five years imprisonment for five hundred grams of powdered cocaine or five grams of crack cocaine.

Both Anti–Drug Abuse Acts facilitated the hyperincarceration of millions and destroyed the families and communities of millions more. Black communities were assumed to have more of a "drug problem," or, given their poverty, they were believed to abuse the cheaper and supposedly more dangerous crack cocaine. This supposed drug problem was fueled by racist media images of "crazed" Black men who randomly assaulted people.

The political war on drugs of the 1980s and 1990s were deeply tied to these images, though their underlying logic and rhetoric were faulty and profoundly racist. From the 1980s to the early 2000s, whites comprised two-thirds of all crack cocaine addicts.[16] White Americans were more likely to use and sell crack cocaine, but the public face of crack was still Black. Blacks were more likely to be incarcerated and have their personal lives destroyed for a drug that whites actually had more of an issue with. The Crime Bill, which Biden famously touted as "Biden's Bill," reinforced the devastation created by the Anti–Drug Abuse Acts. Politicians, academics, and the media again invoked narratives about the "criminal Black man" and "super predator."[17] In a 1993 speech on the Senate floor, Biden passionately made the case for the Crime Bill:

> We must take back the streets. . . . It doesn't matter whether or not they were deprived as a youth. . . . It doesn't matter whether or not they are the victims of society. . . . I don't want to ask, "What made them do this?" They must be taken off the streets! . . . Unless we do something about that cadre of young people, tens of thousands of them, born out of

wedlock, without parents, without supervision, without any structure, without any conscience developing... because they literally have not been socialized.... If we don't,... a portion of them will become the predators fifteen years from now. And Madam President, we have predators on our streets that society has, in fact, in part because of its neglect, created.... They are beyond the pale, many of those people.... Beyond the pale.... We have no choice but to take them out of society.... You cannot make rehabilitation a condition for release. That's why... in the federal system you serve 85% of your time.... I don't care why someone is a malefactor in society. I don't care why they are antisocial. I don't care why they've become a sociopath.... But they are in jail!

Senator Biden, Bill and Hillary Clinton, and even elitist members of the Congressional Black Caucus liberally invoked this brutally racist language to seal the deal on the "Biden Bill." Once it was passed, the national government required federal inmates to serve 85% of their prison time, and it provided $1.3 billion in grants to hire 100,000 police officers and militarize police departments. Moreover, nearly $10 billion was earmarked for new prisons.[18]

These laws ravaged Black America, leaving it in an almost irreversible state of structural disrepair. Draconian policies such as those advocated by Senator Biden have led to the mass removal of at least "1.5 million missing Black men."[19] Yet, even in the wake of this social and structural devastation, Black men and women in the streets still found ways to be resilient when coming home from prison.

Sites of Resilience and Re-entry in the Streets

Race and gender were central to how incarceration and re-entry were experienced in Wilmington and throughout the country. Black men are grossly overrepresented in most federal, state, city, and county facilities, and they have the highest rates of incarceration among all racial-ethnic-gender groups.[20] About 93% of state and federal inmates are male, and Blacks comprise about 40% of prison and jail detainees.[21] The number of incarcerated Black women is comparatively smaller, but Black women are incarcerated at twice the rate of white women.[22]

Black Americans are also overrepresented among the approximately 620,000 individuals released yearly from state and federal prisons, and most returning citizens are released conditionally, under community supervision (probation or parole).[23] In 2016, over 4.5 million adults were under community supervision, the vast majority (81%) on parole.[24] As with incarceration, Blacks are overrepresented in community supervision, making up 55% of probationers and 38% of parolees.[25] Probation and parole often mandate engagement in re-entry activities, as opposed to providing voluntary re-entry services.

Despite growing efforts to improve services, recidivism rates remain high. Approximately 68% of all prisoners and 72% of Black prisoners released in 2005 were rearrested within three years, which strongly suggest re-entry programming lacks effectiveness for many former prisoners.[26]

Shortcomings of services, the sabotaging practices of re-entry officers, and the limitations of family support create a context in which many returning Black men feel they can rely only on themselves. We address this missing perspective in the academic and public discourse by examining experiences with and attitudes toward re-entry among street-identified Black men and women.

Attitudes toward Returning Citizens

Street-identified Black men and women in Wilmington understood well the negative impact of re-entry, as many were either returning citizens themselves or had family and friends ensnared in the criminal legal system.

Incarceration rates were high in our study, but not as high as we initially suspected for people who were street identified. About 48% of our survey sample— 65% of men and 34% of women—reported they had been incarcerated. Some 28% were incarcerated for a violent crime, while most were last incarcerated for nonviolent, often minor or low-level crimes, including 17.6% for fines and 8.1% for violations of parole.

In general, participants held positive attitudes toward returning citizens. About 85% agreed with the statement "People who come home from prison deserve another chance." And nearly 70% believed that returning citizens "did not want to return to the streets and prison." We also found that attitudes toward returning citizens became more positive as participants got older.[27]

BLOCKED OPPORTUNITY. Men and women across age groups felt that returning citizens' experiences with unemployment and poverty had little to do with a poor work ethic and professional skills and more to do with structural violence. Participants also believed that returning citizens preferred legal employment over participating in crime.

Louis (Associate) spoke with Jerome (age 31) about a returning citizen's capacity to navigate legal work and the draw of the streets.

LOUIS: Do you think most guys coming out of prison want to work a legal job? Or do you think they would rather go back to the block [selling drugs]?
JEROME: A lot of people would rather work. . . . Ain't nothing out here no more. This shit (street life) is dead. . . . Motherf-ckers getting killed every day over this kind of shit.

For Jerome, the financial rewards gained in the drug trade during the 1980s and 1990s were over. What remained were devastated Black communities like the Eastside and Southbridge, which were now overwhelmed with concentrated poverty, overpolicing, arrest and incarceration of mostly Black boys and men, and a violent power vacuum filled with disaffected Black male youth.

Moreover, women were just as supportive of returning citizens as the men. Previously active in the streets, Toni (age 18) was now a young mother who recognized how returning Black men uniquely experienced structural violence. Toni believed the community had a responsibility to better comprehend the structural challenges facing its returning men, and she expected the Eastside and Southbridge neighborhoods to provide these men with material support. "I mean, everybody deserves a second chance. Just 'cause he messed up there once, and went to jail, and did whatever he did, that don't mean you can't let him in. Because, say if he . . . never went to jail, . . . [they] still have a system in place to block him. . . . His stuff may not be up to par, [but] that still don't mean to kick him to the curb. You will want somebody to help you out, . . . give you what you need."

Relationships with returning citizens were complicated and often fraught with painful memories. As supportive as participants were of re-entry, they were also very critical of returning citizens. Overall, returning citizens were characterized as a varied group who experienced re-entry mainly as a function of their socioeconomic circumstances.

Many recognized that some returning citizens internalized the racial oppression or structural barriers put in place against them. Although Banks (age 27) had been previously incarcerated, he was among the most critical of returning citizens. He believed that Wilmington's high recidivism rate was the result of "giving up." He even held himself most accountable for his recidivism. Banks had two drug felony convictions and acknowledged that he "made some wrong decisions" after his second stint in prison. He received a second chance from the Plummer Community Corrections Center (PCCC), a transitional minimum-security facility. He was especially grateful that PCCC helped him regain full custody of his son.

Structural criticism related to re-entry was the most dominant perspective, but structural analysis never eclipsed their agency. It was impractical for them to merely ponder a structural analysis, or the negative impact of structural violence, given their daily needs. More accurately, participants advanced both individual and structural explanations on re-entry.

Returning Black people are fully aware there are multiple structural forces working against them.[28] Despite the prevailing view that these men and women fail to take personal responsibility, evidence strongly suggests that Black returning citizens ultimately hold themselves most accountable for their failures.[29]

According to Arditti and Parkman, the "developmental paradox" recognizes that while successful re-entry requires dependence on others, this perspective conflicts with Black men's expectations of themselves as adult men.[30] Indeed, studies of Black men's perspectives on re-entry show their profound desire to be self-sufficient and able to support their families, which conflicts with the structural barriers they face.[31] Research suggests that Black men view successful re-entry as primarily a matter of self-reliance, discipline, and perseverance, even if they and most other returning citizens they know fall short of these goals.

Attitudes toward Re-entry Programs

Most were disappointed with Wilmington's re-entry services; many expected them to offer more substantive employment and educational opportunities to reintegrate into society. About 63% of those we surveyed disagreed with the statement "There are good prison re-entry programs in the city of Wilmington," 58% disagreed with "Most people returning home from prison can find a job, if they really want to," and 57% reported that there were not "enough educational programs available for people incarcerated in prison."

Terrel (age 27) lived with his wife and four sons in Southbridge, and he argued that service providers needed to rally around providing quality employment. For Terrel, high rates of unemployment in Southbridge were mostly tied to hiring discrimination against individuals with felony convictions. Unable to comprehend how one legal infraction could harm someone's life chances, Terrel insisted that most returning citizens were talented and hardworking: "There should be more programs helping [Black men] to get a job . . . because it's literally impossible [after incarceration]. They might have made a [bad] decision . . . [and now] the decision they made when they were 16, has affected . . . their lifetime. . . . *It shouldn't be a felony that's stopping someone to be productive!* . . . You got people with felonies that got all types of brains, education, talents."

Discriminatory hiring policies and "anti-Black racism" make securing employment particularly difficult for returning Black men.[32] People with felonies are often legally banned from occupations in fields such as health care and education, and many other employers will not hire Black men with criminal records.[33] Pager's research on hiring practices shows that employers are significantly less likely to hire Black men with criminal records for entry-level jobs than similarly situated white and Latino men.[34] In fact, Pager found that white and Latino men *with* criminal records were more likely to secure jobs than Black men without a record. Such biases reflect perceptions of not only Black former prisoners, but Black men overall and especially low-income Black males, as unreliable, criminally inclined, and contentious.[35]

Anthony B. (age 33) shared that self-reliance was the best strategy to offset the inadequacies of Wilmington's re-entry programs, which he believed generally fell short of the claims they touted. Therefore, he and many others rarely relied on these programs. Anthony B. truly believed re-entry services had very limited, if any, effectiveness in helping returning citizens build stable lives.

It was at least ten years since Anthony B. was last incarcerated, and he attributed staying out of prison to legal entrepreneurism. He strongly encouraged returning citizens to "open up their own businesses" as a way to contend with the inevitable challenges of re-entry. For Anthony B., an established business offered Black men returning home from prison a level of dignity and autonomy that was typically denied them elsewhere.

Anthony B. also sharply criticized what he perceived was the systematic misuse of parole violations. He was convinced that Wilmington's high recidivism rate was ensured by Delaware's criminal legal system, specifically Delaware's Office of Probation and Parole. In fact, Anthony B. claimed parole officers were monetarily incentivized to violate parolees (i.e., cite them for parole violations). "I really haven't seen any . . . positive things come out of most re-entry programs. All I see is like re-entry to come back to jail. . . . It's not no re-entry program to come back in society and be a productive citizen. They want to . . . keep you on parole so they can violate you for any reason. It could be small or big, . . . they keep adding the time on. Now a brother can start from level two probation and catch a technical violation and get bumped up to level three . . . all the way up to level four, which is home confinement. . . . Every time you get violated, the probation officer gets a bonus in his check. The more people they violate, the more money comes in their pocket. They want to keep you on parole. . . . I don't see no re-entry program helping anybody!"

Anthony B. makes a point that is often missed in the re-entry literature—that there are formal and informal incentives for keeping returning citizens under court surveillance. Black men across the country have widely reported how probation/parole officers "violate" or sanction returning citizens for minor infractions, holding them to unreasonable expectations to pay fees and fines they cannot afford, to adhere to rigid curfews, and to avoid so-called known felons in communities where large numbers of Black men have felony convictions.[36] While "client's resistance to services" is cited as a significant factor in the lack of re-entry success, research shows that many returning citizens avail themselves of re-entry programs but find them sorely inadequate.[37] Trimbur concludes: "Ironically, men who trust the system to help them reenter fare much worse by their own estimation than those who do not, and, in a sense, remain much more vulnerable to the social injury of unmet expectations."[38]

Experiencing Re-entry: "The War," Rugged Individualism, and the Role of Black Women

To avoid returning to prison, even temporarily, returning citizens employed a range of adaptive strategies that were shaped by gender and age. These strategies were fluid approaches to obtaining material and emotional support, and they included utilizing re-entry services and the streets. Jamar (age 29) resided in Southbridge, and he explained that unemployment and low-wage work were most predictive of violence and recidivism. Given his previous incarceration, Jamar believed it was nearly impossible for returning Black men to avoid all of the social-structural traps embedded in Southbridge. He boldly said that returning citizens faced a personal, social, and structural "war." He determined that sheer willpower was required to escape "the battle" with unemployment, violence, and recidivism. Rugged individualism is the belief that people can succeed mostly through self-reliance or largely without the support of government assistance. Rugged individualism was foundational for how Jamar and others approached re-entry, whether they pursued legal or illegal opportunities: "Every day . . . is a war, man, and you can't lose that battle, especially if you unemployed. But losing the battle was to give up hope, for me. I mean, you go to these programs . . . and you fill out all these applications, and don't nobody call you back. But you can't give up, because if you give up, you're like, . . . 'I'm goin' back to the block.' [Then] you lost . . . the war. The flipside of the war is you got n—as warring [gun violence] . . . popping [shooting] at each other. You got n—as that did shit last summer, that's gonna be killed this summer for it. It's [three] wars. And the war within yourself is the biggest war."

According to Jamar, there were at least three "wars," or major barriers facing Black men who came home from prison: (1) *structural wars*, or blocked opportunity; (2) *internal wars*, or challenges with psychological and emotional well-being; and (3) *street wars*, or interpersonal violence. For Jamar, re-entry programs were most effective when they recognized these three wars and offered services through the context of returning citizen's racial-ethnic and cultural backgrounds. Given that Black men and women have unique experiences with incarceration, re-entry providers needed an in-depth understanding of the Eastside and Southbridge's cultural values and structural conditions. Most in the streets were deeply concerned about the structural needs of returning citizens: 75% agreed that "it was financially tough" for returning citizens, 75% agreed that "stable employment would reduce incarceration rates," and 72% believed that returning citizens had difficulty with housing.

BLACK WOMEN AND RE-ENTRY. Only five interviewed women admitted to being jailed, but 34% of those surveyed reported being incarcerated. Also, of the surveyed incarcerated women, 55% reported that selling narcotics was their primary hustle before being incarcerated. Other activities included prostitution, theft, and robbery. About 76% agreed that "parents returning home from prison find it challenging to reconnect with their children" and 82% agreed "it was difficult for fathers, returning home from prison, to provide for their children." Interviewed women also recognized the economic and emotional strain incarceration placed on families, and especially between daughters and their fathers.

These women's experiences with their incarcerated fathers were also socially reproduced in their relationships with the men in their adult lives. In general, women's experiences with re-entry revolved around supporting returning boys and men. Black women, especially mothers, qualified more easily for public assistance. Thus, women were more stable and more readily had access to social services. The men's needs, however, still overwhelmed what were already structurally fragile homes. But the women persevered, at least when they could. Some were embittered about having to be their family's anchor. Others were motivated to formally organize for better re-entry programs. And despite the recidivism of so many Black men, most women we spoke with still found ways to keep their families afloat.

After losing Dayveair to gun violence, Yadira still had two younger children to raise. Dayveair's father Roger was incarcerated when Dayveair was killed, so Yadira had to work hard to take care of her children, be responsive to other family members, and update Roger. Yadira also noted that even if Roger were not incarcerated, most likely he would have been unemployed due to his criminal record, or otherwise unable to meaningfully contribute to his son's funeral. Yadira further argued that "the State of Delaware" actively prevents Black men with a felony from re-entering the legal economy. She also believed that street-identified Black men were eager to be rehabilitated, but poor employment, unstable housing, and ineffective schooling permanently sealed a large segment of Black men into poverty: "They don't have no resources. He can't find a job! . . . He may want to be rehabilitated and want to change his life, but when he gets out into the community, where is he going to find a job? Where is he going to go to get the education? Because once you're labeled a felon, that's it in the state of Delaware."

Yadira's frustrations clarified why Black men reverted to the streets as a re-entry strategy. Local residents did not always fault the men for recidivating either. They, too, understood well the lowly structural positions they were forced into. Yadira and many others were convinced that Black men with felonies were blocked from legal work; thus, crime was generally understood to be a means to an economic end, and sometimes even worth the risk of recidivism.

Rennie Rox and Re-entry: Redemption through Rugged Individualism

Although many were aware that structural forces caused recidivism, returning Black men still drew on a re-entry strategy based on personal responsibility and a hard work ethic. "Giving up," or not striving for a middle-class existence, was incomprehensible, even in the face of obvious structural violence. Returning citizens who were able to avoid recidivism more often had family support or stronger social or professional networks.[39] Returning citizens who did not have this support but somehow managed to avoid the streets and returning to prison generally had to endure bouts of extreme poverty. This was more common among older participants, most of whom had previously recidivated at least once and now drew on families and religious communities to avoid returning to prison.

Rennie Rox (age 35) was from the Eastside and subscribed to self-reliance as a core re-entry strategy. Based on a traumatic experience with recidivism, Rennie has now decided to work long hours for low pay, and he has stomached periods of hard poverty to survive his re-entry. By age 14, Rennie had sold drugs and committed armed robberies, and at age 19, he was sentenced to ten years for a felony drug conviction. Released at age 28, Rennie recidivated after just five months and was sentenced to another four and a half years. "I'm laying up on [the top] bunk . . . after doing eight years and then getting locked back up five months later. It felt like . . . somebody had a belt around my neck and was turning it from underneath the bunk, like it was killing me. . . . The biggest regret was me coming home and realizing that a life could be lived . . . I really could have just chilled out. I really could of kept trying and pushing, and I could still be home. . . . Now I'm in this position again."

After his second incarceration, Rennie's re-entry strategy was grounded in legal entrepreneurism. Self-employment gave him the chance to circumvent some degree of hiring discrimination. Business ownership also afforded Rennie the social distinction and respect he craved, flexibility in his daily schedule, and potential earnings generally denied returning citizens. For Rennie, a strategy born out of the principles of self-determination was the only available legal response to hardened systemic barriers. Even as a two-time felon who lived in a community saturated with low-income Black men, Rennie had to believe he could beat the structural odds. Rennie was very aware of the structural barriers facing returning citizens and even realized they were excluded from the professional networks needed to succeed. However, he still insisted it was possible for him and others to overcome existing structural challenges: "You get shot down everywhere you go, when you got felonies . . . unless you absolutely know somebody that's already working there that can get you in. But a lot of places . . . their policies are so tight. . . . even if you work for a temp service. . . . I don't use that as a cop-out, to say, 'I'm not going get a job.' It's just that it's hard to find a job."

Rennie shared a disheartening experience with a re-entry program to explain why self-determination was the elixir for a brutal structural violence complex. In the last year of Rennie's second incarceration, he was selected for a coveted "specialized" re-entry program as a part of his formal discharge plan. However, Rennie claimed he never received any of the job training, employment, housing, counseling, or educational opportunity "promised" after his release. Although disappointed, Rennie refused to be embittered, and instead internalized and employed principles of rugged individualism to re-enter the Eastside:

> There wasn't no job leads! There wasn't no education leads! It wasn't, "Go here if you need your driver's license again . . . [or] assistance with food." . . . Everything was left on my own. You have a program that's in place and it's not doing what it's supposed to be doing. . . . [People] depend on these programs to get their self together. . . . I realized when I came home . . . [that] I can't depend on no re-entry program! I can't depend on probation and parole. . . . I'm not even looking for none of these people to help me do anything because it's just going to be a disappointment and cause me to [recidivate] out of frustration because I done put all my faith in . . . these people. . . . I can't wait on them to give me an opportunity!

Returning citizens were disappointed but not surprised about Wilmington's poor re-entry services. Consequently, Rennie and others measured re-entry programs for their relative worth, pinching out whatever opportunities they could. Most found real value in connecting with constructive people in these spaces. Direct services were generally poor, but an informal network of returning citizens and some trusted service providers sometimes led to day-work or stable employment, housing, and counseling opportunities.

Returning citizens able to leave the streets and not recidivate generally did so by enduring a life of dis-opportunity and extreme poverty. With the structural deck firmly stacked against him, Rennie still insisted it was possible to contend with a negative re-entry experience. To accomplish this goal, Rennie decided to work long hours in "ninety-degree heat" to build his landscaping business: "I had to get my brother's lawnmower. . . . $20 front and back. I'm trying to do three, four houses a day in ninety-degree heat. . . . [I'm] the same cat that would run in your house and take all your drugs, pistol-whip your whole family, and shoot somebody if they don't give it up. I was the same dude that'll stand on the corner trying to sell a thousand dimes [$10 worth] a day of cocaine. . . . I can't do that no more. . . . I got to . . . feed my family and try to contribute to these bills, . . . And I don't let these felonies hold me back!"

For Rennie, an honorable life was now achieved by cutting three to four lawns per day for $20 each. Although he lauded this kind of work ethic, we actually wondered to what extent his general well-being was affected. Even if Rennie realized $80 per day, or $560 per week (assuming he worked seven days), what would this mean for his psychological, physical, and spiritual health in five to ten years, for instance? Rennie's lofty goal of $560 per week under the most distressing conditions possible also did not account for travel, gas, and the maintenance of his car and landscaping materials. Nor did he account for vacation or sick days, health insurance, retirement, or local, state, and federal taxes. These additional costs meant that Rennie actually made less than minimum wage. To the larger society, Rennie's strategy was delusional, but for Rennie, this approach was empowering.

CONTRARY TO CONVENTIONAL WISDOM, the streets cared deeply about people returning home from prison, largely believed in their potential to thrive after incarceration, and often provided support to returning citizens. It is in this racial-ethnic and cultural space of well-being where re-entry programs would benefit from the insight of street-identified Black men and women.

Re-entry programs were largely considered to be complicit in the widespread system of structural oppression. The criminal legal system, from arrest to re-entry, was framed as a profit-generating industry designed to ensure enduring inequality. Felony convictions, parole violations, unemployment, and poor housing were noted as key features of a larger structural violence complex.

According to some, successful re-entry in a context of structural violence required a philosophy of firm discipline that tolerated little material return over a prolonged period of time. In reality, and largely because they were boxed into disenfranchisement, most used a range of illegal and legal strategies to navigate re-entry.

ACTION AND RE-ENTRY IN MURDER TOWN, USA

The streets of Wilmington recognized that disrupting the structural violence complex required aggressive, grassroots mobilization. But the streets were clearly the missing piece in efforts to organize against power. They had the social capital and a functional network to quickly mobilize a small city, but they needed the platforms and skills to organize that part of the community that no one else could reach, the most disenfranchised part of Wilmington: persons active in the streets, the unemployed, the homeless, runaways or severely traumatized youth, students pushed out of schools, and incarcerated and returning citizens. As a core segment of Wilmington, these vulnerable and deeply neglected populations and their loved ones comprised the largest number of Black residents in Wilmington. Most of this disaffected group had given up on leadership a long time ago. But we knew that if anyone could rally this group together, it was the Street PAR Associates.

The Wilmington Street PAR project was a timely, decentralized model of grassroots research activism that demanded Wilmington focus on employment initiatives, particularly for its returning citizens.[40] For us, there was no other way to deal with the painful concerns of Black Wilmington. In light of our collective advocacy and the energy stirred in the city, at the end of his term in 2012, Mayor James Baker issued an executive order for a "Ban the Box" policy in Wilmington. The "Box" refers to the checkbox on some job applications where the applicant must indicate whether they have a criminal record. Mayor Baker's executive order required the removal of all criminal justice inquiries, particularly for "nonuniformed city jobs," to improve returning citizen's chances of being employed. One limitation of the order, however, was that it did not prevent criminal background checks once a conditional offer was made.[41] In 2014, Governor Jack Markell also signed Ban the Box into state law.[42]

Yet, following Ban the Box, there were very few new opportunities related to employment, poverty, housing, schooling, or re-entry in the Eastside and Southbridge. Ban the Box had proven to be just a loud, symbolic victory in Wilmington. Many were offended by leadership's "benign neglect" policy and clever dismissal of Wilmington's tug-of-war with violence and recidivism.

The Delaware Center for Justice and the "Remaking" of Re-entry in Murder Town

DCJ was among the leading re-entry organizations in Delaware. Under the leadership of Executive Director Ashley Biden, they skillfully challenged leadership while remaining dedicated to community-centered approaches. Dedicated to criminal legal reform, DCJ's long legacy was steeped in "service to justice-involved citizens and crime victims."[43]

A large chunk of DCJ's work took place in Wilmington, but DCJ also offered services in their offices in central and south Delaware. With a staff of twenty, DCJ combined private and public funding for "research, direct services, advocacy, and policy work to support youth and adult offenders and crime victims."[44]

DCJ's organizational structure included "Programs and Services," which focused on youth and adults, and "Policy and Advocacy," which tackled advocacy for vulnerable communities and policy reform. DCJ prided itself on the hands-on case management they provided to youth in communities, schools, and detention facilities. Other noteworthy concerns taken on by DCJ were employment, violence prevention, abolishing the death penalty, conditions of confinement, and re-entry.

Ashley passionately led DCJ, and because of her liberal fury, she was beloved by many in the streets. But many in Delaware's establishment perceived that Ashley was far too progressive. As a young, vibrant, influential, and progressive white woman, she pushed the limits on behalf of so many who needed her boldness. Ashley tried. She really did care. And for this, she took her lashes while also learning a grave lesson about the true intentions and retributive strength of Wilmington's corporatocracy.

DCJ's main office was located in the heart of Downtown Eastside in the Community Service Building (CSB) on West Tenth Street between Shipley and Orange Streets. CSB was in the middle of Wilmington's thriving banking district, and on any given day, this part of Tenth Street was busy with white professionals. Directly across from the CSB were the back entrances to the towering DuPont Building. The CSB was led by Thère du Pont, an executive director of the Longwood Foundation (nonprofit of the DuPont Corporation). Established in 1997, the CSB holds over sixty nonprofit organizations in Wilmington.

Despite its stated mission "to improve the quality of life for current and future generations of the State of Delaware," most in the Eastside and Southbridge either did not know where the CSB was or did not consider it a welcoming space.[45] The CSB's negative appeal was partly explained by the fact that most nonprofits had leased the below-market office space for accommodating its core staff, not necessarily for meeting with residents or even their clients. A few agencies did open their doors for daily walk-ins, and some did open their office space to public events. But when working with residents, most agencies in the CSB dispatched their community-friendly staff to public spaces identified inside or near their neighborhoods.

DCJ's organizational model was top-heavy, with a sterling board of directors who oversaw an underpaid, overworked, yet motivated executive director and agency staff. Like the HOPE Commission, DCJ was largely underresourced and often announcing fundraisers. Its board, however, was stuffed with various politicians, bankers, lawyers, university professors, and executives.

The offices in DCJ reflected the unique identities of a staff of mostly young progressive white women. Several employees had once been affected by the same challenges DCJ vowed to reform. Some staff had substance abuse histories, a few were formerly incarcerated, others were recent college graduates—but the majority were qualified employees who demanded real structural change. Many staff members were trusted inside Eastside and Southbridge because their own past experiences with drug use or violence made them relatable. DCJ's staff were a spirited bunch of justice warriors who were deeply concerned for poor Black Wilmington.

Kirstin Cornnell, director of operations, was a driven, young white woman from nearby Philadelphia. Kirstin was also Ashley's right-hand woman and could be counted on to maintain a tight ship. Kailyn Richards was a lively Black woman in her early twenties and a recent graduate of the University of Delaware. Formerly an assistant for then House Representative candidate Lisa Blunt-Rochester, Kailyn was now an office coordinator and communications assistant at DCJ. Sitting at the front desk, new visitors were usually met by this bubbly and inquisitive person. Isaac Dunn was a grassroots-oriented Black man and program manager for DCJ's gun violence program, Student Warriors against Guns and Gangs (SWAGG). SWAGG offered case management to street-identified youth and instructional classes on violence in Ferris Detention Center, Delaware's largest juvenile facility. Isaac was also very confident, always professional, and a well-read Black man in his mid-thirties. His long, thick braided locks, a scruffy but full beard, and African-centered tattoos signaled to youth he understood their concerns. Cindy McDaniel, an older white woman, was program coordinator for the School Offense Diversion Program (SODP). SODP worked with youth arrested at school, as an alternative to the juvenile court process. Cindy cared deeply for these kids, and some felt she cared too much. She could break down in tears in a heartbeat and in the next moment, deliver advocacy that was hard as nails.

In 2014, Ashley Biden hired Corry Wright (Associate) as an intensive case manager for the SWAGG and truancy reduction programs. After being under Isaac's tutelage for three years, Corry was promoted to program coordinator of SWAGG. Corry had also independently launched two other programs for street-identified youth, one of which was Community Outreach Recreation Education (CORE). CORE redirected the addictive "thrill of the streets" by training youth to repair mountain bikes, mopeds, and motorcycles to use in exploring the backwoods of Delaware. Corry also went back to college and completed a bachelor of art's degree at Wilmington University and a master of arts degree at the University of Delaware.

ASHLEY AND I SAT on a number of panels in Wilmington at historic venues like the Baby Grand, Wilmington Country Club, and The Queen. We were quite the one-two punch on structural violence and unified condemnation of its treacherous effects on Black Wilmington. In April 2015, DCJ awarded the Wilmington Street PAR Program the coveted William A. Vrooman Exemplar of Justice Award. Named after a DCJ founder, the Vrooman award ceremony was a major event in Delaware. This annual award was "a tribute to individuals who have devoted their time and energy to improving the quality of justice in Delaware."[46] Each year, this grand ball happened in Greenville, a wealthy, secluded section of Wilmington. For one night, this affair overflowed with public officials alongside a cadre of returning citizens and their families. That night was magical for my family, close friends, and the Wilmington Street PAR program. And we made sure to use the microphone to spread our uncompromising message about structural violence.

DCJ also hosted other timely community programs that were spectacular affairs with a hodgepodge of people from wealthy, working-class, and street-identified communities. Their justice-centered events were always down-to-earth and especially chic. Wine, cheese, fruit, exquisite desserts, and fancy hors d'oeuvres were carried on elegant silver trays. At the center of these magnificent programs was always a provocative message on justice.

In January 2019, DCJ debuted a curated an art show, *UNWARRANTED: The Human Cost of Fines*, at the Christina Cultural Arts Center in Downtown Eastside. On the walls of the center's second floor, *UNWARRANTED* displayed art that spoke powerfully to the excessive court fees and fines leveraged against poor Black Delawareans. Delaware issued "nearly 45,000 warrants for failure to pay a fine or fee associated with non-felony crimes."[47] In a state of under 1 million where Blacks accounted for 22% of the population, that number of warrants could not easily be ignored.

So many in Delaware wanted to know why so many were being shaken down by the state. *UNWARRANTED* adeptly spotlighted Delaware's brewing concerns over civil asset forfeiture, or the process in which police seized assets (e.g., cash, jewelry) from persons suspected of but not charged with a crime. According to Ronald Fraser, "Delaware state and local law enforcement agencies fattened their budgets in 2016 by more than $1.2 million through this practice [civil asset forfeiture], including the: Delaware State Police, $348,474; Dover Police Department, $60,705; Newark Police Department, $272,144; Wilmington Police Department, $238,881; the Smyrna Police Department, $23,772; and the New Castle County Division of Police, $121,434."[48] *UNWARRANTED* skillfully exposed the relationship between structural violence and crime. In March, two months later, the state legislature re-examined its policy on excessive court fees and fines.[49]

The Remaking Murdertown *Podcast*

Short Order Production House and DCJ's 2016 podcast series *Remaking Murdertown: Poverty, Punishment, and Possibility* shook Delaware's structural order.[50] The podcast contained four gripping episodes on the nexus of poverty, violence, and re-entry. It came two years after Jones's controversial *Newsweek* "Murder Town USA" article, and both the article and the podcast were sore spots that undermined the establishment's framing of Wilmington as "A Place to be Somebody."[51] The streets generally agreed with Jones's and DCJ's larger message that Wilmington was a unique, two-taled city of white wealth and Black structural failure.

Ashley received major backlash from Wilmington's corporatocracy for the *Murdertown* podcast.[52] Wilmington was supposed to be known as a progressive city, not a place characterized by Black suffering. Leadership pressured Ashley to discontinue the podcast, but she weathered their vitriol. Ashley wanted (needed) the stories of the streets to be authentically told and folded into the official record: "It's difficult for me to even use the term 'Murdertown' to describe our city . . . but we [DCJ] think it's important to address this misnomer head-on. We want to explore the real issues facing Wilmington and the real people experiencing them. Wilmington, without a doubt, has its problems: a poverty problem, an opportunity problem and a trauma problem. We cannot ignore that. But we must also lift up our neighbors and acknowledge one another's stories in order to identify solutions."[53]

Ashley risked her professional career with the *Murdertown* podcast, which for several months captured Delaware's attention with its dramatic, saga-like appeal. The final episode, "Swimming Upstream," was aired before a live audience at The Queen in Downtown Eastside. Following the airing was a ninety-minute panel discussion and Q&A hosted by the podcast's narrator and producer, Zach Phillips. Two Street PAR Associates sat on this panel.

Ricky Reyes was the podcast's protagonist. Ricky lived in the Westside and now was an upstanding member of SWAGG. Ricky admitted that without real time and structural support, it would have been impossible for him to let go of the streets. From ages 8 to 16, Ricky was in and out of detention centers. At age 16, he was shot, and after getting out of the hospital, Ricky admitted, "That whole week I was looking for him [the shooter]. I was out there with my crutches, and I had a gun on my back. . . . God works in mysterious ways." Ricky was arrested a week later. "If I would have seen him, we wouldn't be having this conversation." For Ricky, at least in this instance, gun violence, or holding the person that shot him accountable by the standards of the streets, was a valid way to ensure his physical and social survival in Wilmington.

In 2017, Wilmington was declared the teenage capital of homicide in the United States, and street youth like Ricky were the reason why Wilmington was, at times, so volatile.[54] In 2017, about 3,000 juveniles were arrested in Delaware, a state with a total of 210,000 juveniles. Translated, this was an arrest rate of fifteen arrests per 1,000 juveniles.[55] In 2017, 256 juveniles in Delaware were arrested for a Part I violent charge (e.g., homicide, forcible rape, robbery, aggravated assault), and detained youth were remanded to one of four detention centers.

Despite the difficulties, Ashley was the captain of the DCJ ship, and she steered it over rough waters. Bonilla-Silva claimed that privileged whites were unable to be fully "racially tolerant," or willing and accepting enough to make any significant changes to the structural order.[56] Undoing Black poverty meant undoing white wealth, because the wealth was invariably tied to the poverty. In a cutthroat capitalistic system, it was not possible to have one without the other, or wealth without poverty. White privilege as a social-structural advantage was predicated on a racial caste system that devalued Black skin. Bonilla-Silva argued in the midst of this structural reality that it was possible for Blacks to forge alliances with working-class white women. For Bonilla-Silva, working-class white women had their "limits," but they were the most "racially progressive" white subgroup to sincerely support real racial justice.[57]

Ashley was not working class, but she was a young white woman and "racially progressive," and her audacious advocacy caught Delaware's establishment off guard:

We had a lot of people coming to us about the "Murder Town" title. *And I stand by it!* The reason I stand by it is because we currently have an issue . . . with gun violence. Unless we look at the root causes, we're not going to get anywhere. If businesses really want to get rid of the "Murder

Town" kind of perception, I'm asking all those businesses to invest money, into violence prevention [and] violence intervention and economic development and community revitalization within the community. My dad [Joe Biden] has an expression, "If you want to know what someone values, look at their budget." Where is the money going into violence intervention and prevention? We [DCJ] are running the only gun violence intervention program in the state.... Where do we get our money from? ... a foundation in New York City. It's a great thing that we are doing things on the Riverfront and on Market Street, but you can't then have, two blocks away, communities with abject poverty. My hope, through this podcast, is that we have now addressed the elephant in the room. "Now it's time to put your money where your mouth is." As frustrated as I am, and as saddened as I am at times, I'm also extremely hopeful.... We are at a moment where we can take this *Newsweek* title of "Murder Town" and do something really positive with it. To be able to say, "Look (at) what we did. We implemented evidence-based programming to address this issue. We are putting our money into economic development—into education." I refuse to maintain the status quo. I won't do it! I will address the elephant in the room. Because we are talking about people's lives. We are talking about human beings.[58]

Ashley had the attention of real power and unapologetically told them what they refused to hear. She voiced what an heir to Delaware's aristocracy was never supposed to admit—that it was no longer acceptable for the state to snatch Black bodies and ruin Black lives for the making of white wealth.

In March 2019, Ashley resigned as executive director of DCJ.[59] Her departing Facebook message aptly noted, "Together we have changed the landscape of justice reform, violence intervention, and victim services for the State of Delaware." And "we" did. The epic *Murdertown* podcast in May 2016, the *UNWARRANTED* art show in January 2019, and Ashley's final speech at DCJ's annual celebration (Vrooman Awards) in April 2019 were the triumvirate pillars of her indictment of Delaware's white ruling elite.

Ashley was tired, burned out. About two months after she resigned, she had a farewell lunch with thirty to forty of her closest friends. Three weeks later, she and I had lunch, and then shortly after she left town to recover.

PART THREE

Street Agency

Coping with and Ending the Structural Violence Complex

Chapter 7

"Brenda's Got a Baby"

COMPETING ROLES OF BLACK WOMEN
AS MATRIARCHS AND HUSTLERS

> Black women living in conditions of imposed marginality bear the disproportionate brunt of . . . political and economic processes. . . . Increasing social inequality is inflected by and in turn influences how race, gender, and social class are experienced in everyday struggles. . . . We often overlook how women of color are deeply affected by, challenge, and successfully resist—at least temporarily—how unemployment, mass incarceration, and state disinvestment . . . impact their communities.
>
> —João Costa Vargas, *Catching Hell in the City of Angels*

STREET-IDENTIFIED BLACK WOMEN were an active population in Wilmington. Both optimistic about their futures and hardened by disappointment, these women drew on the streets to cope with their tough sociostructural realities. Fury and resentment also situated much of their lived experience.[1] They were angry with parents and male partners (especially their fathers and their children's fathers), close friends, and extended family members. They also had contentious relationships with service providers and institutions. Social service programs and schools generally treated them with great suspicion and used bureaucratic barriers to stall them. School officials framed them as irresponsible parents, while providers treated them as beggars or as if they were ungrateful. Both institutions generally characterized them as social pariahs dependent on handouts.

Caught between poverty and navigating institutional mazes, some Black women used street life as a site of resilience because many "come of age in the same distressed neighborhoods as those of [their] male counterparts."[2] In the Eastside and Southbridge, older women largely modeled for younger street generations social characteristics that grounded how they emotionally, psychologically, and structurally survived.[3]

Black women played an integral role in the social scene of Wilmington's street life. Many attended parties or bars, participated in social clubs such as motorcycle or car clubs, socialized on street corners, and organized neighborhood events. Illegal activities exhibited by these women included acts of violence, sex work, preparing drugs for sale, selling or holding drugs or drug money for others, facilitating drug deals, gambling, and bookkeeping.[4] LeBlanc used the term "millworkers" to describe women who were involved in the drug trade as preparers and holders of illegal narcotics.[5] These women are often girlfriends, ex-girlfriends, or relatives of the men who sell drugs, and are responsible for manufacturing, weighing, packaging and transporting narcotics for sale. Anderson analyzed Black women's participation in the illicit drug economy in four core activities: (1) providing housing and sustenance in female-headed homes; (2) purchasing drugs as users; (3) subsidizing male drug dependency; and (4) participating in drug sales.[6] Some women also assisted with robberies by using the lure of sex to set men up.[7]

Most of the women we encountered in Wilmington were low-income, Black single mothers who were at some point street identified. Oftentimes, these women and their children struggled with housing, childcare, and employment. As Black mothers formerly of the streets, the women were constantly concerned with raising children in neighborhoods hammered by street violence. Their resilience was pronounced in their ability to resist structural assault just enough to provide a way forward for their children, who were their most valuable treasure. In many respects, these women and their extraordinary will to survive challenged traditional analysis of them as "deviant" or "over-sexed." Their behavior was skillful and adaptive as they relied on established relationships to survive the demands of oppressive environments.[8]

These women's lived experiences were also racialized, ethnic, and cultural iterations of the streets and motherhood.[9] How they survived street violence—the manner in which they coped with homicide, for instance—was deeply informed by their racial-ethnic and cultural orientation. Even expressions of grief were enacted through the cultural lens of their Black Americaness. Black women in these two neighborhoods mourned hard and sometimes for years, especially when homicide struck their families. The Eastside and Southbridge's cultural value system allowed Black mothers space to grieve deeply and for long periods. Due to a history of racial oppression, suffering Black women were allowed to publicly cry uncontrollably, scream, or even convulse over the murder of a close family member. These expressions were cathartic and considered a healthy way to work through their outrage.

Social kinship networks of mostly female family members and close friends were also drawn on by Black women to cope with the impact of violence. When possible, these close-knit groups provided a range of supports to grieving women. According to Vargas, the ethics of "sociability and solidarity" forced Black women in South Central to be supportive of each other in moments of social crisis.[10] As low-income Black mothers, they knew it was a matter of time before social problems, in one form or the other, would be at their doorstep, which prompted them to readily help others in great need. Vargas writes, "The sociability and solidarity among women . . . stood at the center of life in our building. Struggling with poverty, unemployment, institutional power, and overwhelming uncertainty, the women in my building organized their lives around kinship relations and household activities. Their extremely volatile domestic lives required mutual aid and assistance, and the material help and affective support they could give each other. Local sociability functioned as an antidote even if only temporary, for overwhelming personal hardships."[11]

Like the women in South Central, Black women in Wilmington realized they needed each other in a world with much disappointment. Their fates as Black women were heavily interdependent or bound together, whether they wanted it or not. In this context, "isolation was maladaptive," or the willingness to be sociable was necessary.[12] Black women bonded over their pain or "shared experiences of suffering against which solidarity was the most effective, if not the only, remedy."[13]

Surviving had a lot to do with the families they lived for and maintained, and especially the children they deeply cared for. Family was everything to women in the Eastside and Southbridge neighborhoods. Pursuing loving relationships with life partners, having healthy children, and successfully guiding and raising those children was what most Black women wanted in Wilmington.

Poignantly, however, Black women, and especially those involved in the streets, were socialized to accept or expect single motherhood, given their experiences in childhood.[14] Nationally, 47% of Black women have never been married (as compared with 28% of white women), and one in three Black households are female headed, with almost three-quarters of births to Black women occurring outside of marriage.[15] Nearly half of Black female–headed homes with children live in poverty, and 31% of Black adults are married.[16]

The national figures are close to what Black women experienced in Wilmington and Delaware as a whole. While less than half of births in Delaware are to unmarried women, about one-fifth of births are to unmarried Black women. Almost three-quarters of those unmarried Black mothers are Medicaid recipients. In addition, among all Black women in Delaware, unmarried Black women accounted for about 70% of births. In Wilmington, about 59% of births were to Black mothers, and nearly three-quarters of births to single mothers in Wilmington were to Black women. Teen pregnancy, in general, has declined in Delaware since the early 2000s, with only about 5% of births to women under twenty years old. In Wilmington, just over 6% of births were to Black women under 20 years old.[17]

While 25% of homes in Wilmington were female headed, 70% of homes in the Eastside and 74% of homes in Southbridge were female headed. Additionally, although a quarter of Wilmington lived below the poverty line, this number reached 40% for both Eastside and Southbridge residents.[18]

The women we encountered were hustlers and former hustlers, mothers, and, ultimately, the glue that held families in these two neighborhoods together. In the midst of structural desperation, they achieved family cohesion, at least in part, by hitting the streets, and many of them were eventually incarcerated for doing so. Over half of women in prison and 80% of women in jails are mothers.[19] Black women account for about one-third of all women incarcerated.[20] Incarceration rates of Black women in Delaware also reflected the disproportionate national incarceration rates of Black women. In Delaware, the overall rate of female incarceration is 44 per 100,000, which is below the national average of 58 per 100,000.[21] Although the rate of imprisonment has continued to decline for Black women and girls since 2000, these women are still incarcerated at twice the rate of white women and girls.[22] Black women and girls are imprisoned largely for nonviolent, drug-related offenses or property offenses.[23] Also, although white women and men are more likely to use and sell illegal narcotics, Black women generally receive harsher punishments for these crimes.[24]

Action Research in Baylor

In November 2010, I presented our Street PAR project to a college class held in Delores J. Baylor Women's Correctional Institution (BWCI). Named after the first Black warden in Delaware, BWCI opened in 1991 and is the only women's prison in Delaware.[25] It employed about 200 people at the time of this study, 91 of whom were considered "permanent guards"; men made up 41% of these guards.[26] Baylor housed approximately 400 inmates, both pretrial and sentenced women, at all security levels.

The students I spoke to at Baylor were a part of the Inside-Out Prison Exchange Program. Established in 1997, Inside-Out is a national and international prison-based program that registers college students and inmates as peers in classrooms held in correctional facilities (www.insideoutcenter.org). For clarity on this program, inmates are referred to as "Inside students" and college students are described as "Outside students."

I arrived at Baylor by 6:00 p.m. An officer at the front desk cross-referenced my driver's license against a list of approved guests. I was then instructed to fill out the log and place the contents of my pockets into trays to be screened. After walking through the metal detector, I took a seat in the nearby waiting space. Ten minutes later, a Black female correctional officer was buzzed into the waiting room. She led me through a set of hallways partitioned by wide, heavy metal doors. Women were busily engaged in various activities. Some cleaned, others were clumped together in small groups, a few women read, and others congregated in recreational spaces. We arrived into a relatively large and active classroom. About twenty students chatted in small groups. Half were inmates and half were undergraduates from the University of

Delaware (UD). UD students were generally white young women, while inmates constituted a more diverse cross-section of white, Latina, and Black women.

Several "Inside" women walked over and introduced themselves while I set up my presentation.

"Hi. So how long have you been a professor at UD?" one woman asked.

"I've been at UD now for about five years."

"What do you teach?"

"I teach classes about crime in the Black community and how to work with these communities to do research and activism."

Another Inside woman said, "We've heard a lot about your project in class and also in the newspapers. What got you into doing this type of research?"

"Street PAR was the way I always thought research in poor Black communities should be done. I actually thought this was how it was being done, prior to becoming a PhD student." Then we both chuckled at my naïveté.

More students listened, others joined in, and then it was time to begin. For ninety minutes, I used our study to talk about theory, methodology, analysis, and activism. I shared survey data and numerous voices that detailed the social and structural traumas experienced in Wilmington. We also discussed the immeasurable impact that one strategic, community-centered research project could have in a small city.

Our time together was best described as a deeply cathartic experience. Inside women were curious and fervently questioned me. They were active, intellectual sponges that soaked up and contributed sound critical analysis of street culture and structural violence. These women were genuinely appreciative of the opportunity to debate widely held assumptions about them and their neighborhoods. We laughed, supported one another, disagreed, and quibbled, and some shared personal stories that were glaring examples of our project's preliminary findings. We viewed photographs of their communities and read the voices of people they knew. Neighborhood images were cherished and pondered in ways Outside students and I took for granted.

In general, Outside students were quiet and listened far more than they spoke. And it was wise for them to be quiet. In my street ethnography course at UD, I often say to graduate students, "Less is more, as a street ethnographer, in the community." Culturally, it made sense that persons eager to learn about street culture should engage slowly. It was the Outside students' turn to listen, particularly if they were genuinely interested in learning about the perspectives of women who were incarcerated.

I closed with a discussion on our project's action agenda items, which included barbecues, street art exhibitions, food and clothes drives, voter registration campaigns, and working with police and city leadership. We also talked about the use of social media and forms of civil disobedience like public protests. Taken by our project's ambition, Inside-Out students weighed in.

An older Inside Black woman said, "You don't think you will piss some people off with this action agenda?"

A younger Inside Black woman warned, "Yeah, you might scare some of them professional people away. Don't you kind of need their support?"

"We might. I suppose it's all possible. We won't know until we try," I replied.

The Inside women were wise, and their warnings conveyed how much they were monitored, controlled, and punished. Their guidance was valuable but foreboding.

An Inside woman continued, "You know, your concept of Street PAR helped us to work on something in Baylor." Inside women giggled, and two or three of them whispered to each other after this woman's comment. I wondered why they laughed. Was she being sarcastic?

"You know, if we could do a Street PAR project in Baylor, we would examine how some women are forced to have sex with COs [corrections officers]." The buzzing energy in the room ground to a halt, and I did not know how to respond.

"If only you knew what some women are going through in here. That's why we created our own survey. We got like 125 women to fill it out," she said excitedly.

Both shocked and inspired, I was still baffled. I wondered what their survey looked like and what kind of questions it asked. An inmate-driven study on a sensitive and volatile subject like sexual assault was potentially explosive. I wondered how safe it was for them to talk about this study with someone like me. What if we were being audio- or video recorded? Apparently, we were not. We were in the room by ourselves, and one CO sat outside the door of our classroom. He monitored us by peeking through the reinforced plexiglass window in the top half of the door.

They changed the conversation and began speaking about scheduling, remaining classes, homework assignments, and the reading groups they held. Outside students chimed in with advice on course-related matters. Soon after, the CO informed us we needed to wrap up the class. Inside women lined up in a particular corner of the room. Outsides departed first and were taken to Baylor's entrance, while Insides were escorted back to their cellblocks.

ABOUT A MONTH LATER, I visited Baylor to attend the Inside-Out course's closing ceremony, which felt more like a formal graduation. The Inside-Out Prison Exchange Program is not a degreed college program; instead, it empowers colleges and correctional facilities to offer courses for college credit. About 100 people attended the closing ceremony for this one course, including civic, religious, political, corporate, correctional, and academic leaders as well as inmates' family and friends. We were delighted to be in each other's company, and our optimism fueled the auditorium's palpable energy.

Baylor's new warden, Wendi Lucas Caple, greeted and addressed the audience. Warden Caple was a Black woman in her late forties. She was conservatively dressed and measured in her remarks. Promising that Baylor would continue to be a stellar example for correctional facilities for women nationwide, she guaranteed that the women would receive quality attention and programming to rehabilitate their lives. Warden Caple then touted the Inside-Out Prison Exchange Program and encouraged UD and Baylor to forge an even stronger relationship. After a warm round of applause, Warden Caple took her seat and basked in the glow of the evening.

About five Inside women closed the program with a well-rehearsed presentation. Formal remarks were powerfully orated from the podium. They proudly announced that they had conducted a study that examined sexual assault in Baylor and they intended on sharing their survey results from about 150 women. Political correctness ruled the moment. Most in the audience just smiled and cheered, as if we did not just hear a group of incarcerated women saying in front of dozens of city and state leaders that they intended to share data on sexual assault in Baylor. Surprisingly, they were allowed to finish. Although this was empowering for the women, it was extremely embarrassing for Baylor.

Their presentation was a scholarly, theatrical, poetic, and spiritual plea for protection, not prosecution of Baylor's culpable COs. They reported that about 40% of their sample had been subjected to unprotected sex with COs at least once, and also that 95% thought condoms should be made available to women in Baylor. Of course the women wanted the sexual abuse to stop, but they generally believed that less would be gained by immediately holding COs accountable. For the women, the problem of sexual violence was deeply structural and reached beyond the behaviors of individual correctional officers. Also, if they had revealed the names of abusive COs during their presentation, these women would have exposed themselves to retribution. They risked this anyway, but I could only assume that harsher treatment would have resulted from the revelations of correctional officers' names.

Sexual abuse was intrinsic to institutions like Baylor, as a social by-product of the space and a lack of policy enforcement. But more accurately, Baylor was a site where rape, violence, coercion, love, and manipulation all intersected or crashed into one another. Some women also came in with experiences that made them more vulnerable to sexual violence than others. Most experienced some variation of sexual violence prior to incarceration, and many came from a life of exotic dancing or stripping, prostitution, and/or drug addiction, which complicated their experiences inside prison. Sadly, sexual indiscretions were encouraged, given that some of the most vulnerable women were locked inside with underappreciated, overworked, and underpaid male correctional officers willing to use heinous methods to reclaim some form of control or perceived dignity. According to Barrish, prison environments like Baylor were toxic with the potential for sexual abuse: "The problem of guards having sex with women behind bars in Delaware goes much deeper than ... criminal cases.... [There is] a longstanding culture where safeguards and oversight are lacking, sex is a commodity to be traded for privileges, and inmates and even other staffers are reluctant to report assaults because they fear retaliation."[27]

The Inside women concluded by pleading for more quality programs inside Baylor and also for re-entry. From their standpoint, idle time—which usually resulted from a lack of programming—increased the potential for women in Baylor to be sexually violated.

Baylor's staff were utterly stunned by the Inside women's presentation. The women cleverly concealed their intentions, because staff certainly would have removed it from the schedule or even canceled the program altogether. This inmate-driven study and presentation on sexual violence was how the women enacted resistance in Baylor, which vindicated them for the moment. Poignantly, these women's victimization was the impetus for a reclaimed expression of resilience, operationalized by a research-activist paradigm. These women were already gifted at figuring out how to craft greatness out of tragedy—this strategy was often used by them in varying ways to navigate the streets and life overall. Here in Baylor, however, their adaptive capacity for thriving and fighting back manifested in a project that left an empirical record of sexual violence. What was more resilient than this? With the opportunity they had available, what would be more piercing, and selfless, than sacrificing their quality of life in Baylor to leave behind systematic analysis of dozens of women being subjected to sexual violence? The Inside women and many other women in Baylor were convinced of the power of research and how their phenomenologically based data could be used by them to increase group cohesion and advance activist-based objectives.

Michelle Fine, four of her graduate students, and seven women incarcerated in Bedford Hills Correctional Facility worked on a multimethod PAR project that examined the impact of college on women in prison, on the larger prison environment, and on women who returned home from prison.[28] Bedford is a maximum-security facility and typically housed women that came from the most trauma-filled homes and poorest communities in New York City. At least 80% of women in Bedford at the time of Fine et al.'s study reported being sexually abused as children and/or adults.

Fine et al. also found that women who attended college in prison were five times less likely to recidivate (7.7%) than those who did not attend college in prison (29.9%). After release from prison, the college-educated women were also more likely to find employment, continue their college education, and even participate in civic causes.[29]

Part of the legacy of research activism is that many institutions have felt threatened by and have aggressively responded to the empirical analysis and "action" generated by PAR.[30] To understand institutional retribution, Fine and Torre explained how the "intimate details" or critical reflections of their Bedford PAR project revealed a severe backlash against many of the incarcerated PAR members.[31] Corrections prevented several women from joining the college prison program at Bedford, and many of the PAR members were threatened with solitary confinement, their cells were "tossed," and their writing contributions were sometimes ripped up and confiscated. Fine and Torre poignantly write: "We learned that many of the women on the prison research team had their cells searched, papers thrown out, poetry destroyed. Some are being threatened with transfer to a prison near the Canadian border, others to Solitary Confinement. Their writings/their selves ripped from them, futures unclear. Demands that they testify against each other in another trumped-up charge just to send chills through the institution. Will never quite understand the sadism of prisons."[32]

The most incidental of perceived infractions eventually became enough for correctional staff to disrupt the Bedford PAR project. In many respects, temperamental COs and constant surveillance made Bedford an inherently hostile environment to conduct PAR.

> We knew that the futures of the program and our collaboration were always in jeopardy. Too many tears, or bringing in too much food could provoke an officer to shut us down. In a research meeting it was common for us to jog between hope/possibility and despair/fear, as our collective unconscious wouldn't allow us to settle on the latter terms for too long. . . . We deliberately stayed clear, . . . keeping "on task" as a way to exert control where little was available. The context and physical environment of our research was harsh, noisy and without privacy, by design.[33]

Although their PAR project was approved by Bedford, the conditions under which Fine et al. operated were still frighteningly oppressive. After four years, Bedford abruptly terminated their study. Ironically, the women in the PAR project in Baylor experienced the same backlash for their analysis on sexual violence in the prison. Women daring to conduct their own research using empirical methods was an affront to racist and misogynist systems of containment. In the case of Bedford in New York, the women documented the positive impact of college in prison, and in the case of Baylor in Delaware, the women bravely documented the sexual violence to which they were subjected. And in both projects, these women were punished for said documentation. As in most oppressive systems, authentic expressions of autonomy over body, mind, and spirit had to be punished.

Oddly enough, the closing ceremony for this Inside-Out course in Baylor ended without a hitch. Everyone *appeared* supportive, and the presentation ended with a polite reception. By the end of the week, however, we heard that Baylor's staff "came down hard" on the Inside women. Their data were seized and the results from the study were never made public. The Inside-Out Prison Exchange Program was also suspended at Baylor.

Five years later, news stories of sexual violence in Baylor erupted in Delaware.[34] At the center of this scandal was the prison's security superintendent, Major Fred Way III. Way was third in command at Baylor, and now he was arrested for having sex on two separate occasions with a 27-year-old woman; Way was being charged with two counts of "sexual relations in a detention facility" and one count of "official misconduct." Way was bailed out with $5,000 on the day he turned himself in for arrest. Ironically, many women had committed less serious crimes and were detained in Baylor because they could not afford to make bail of far less than $5,000. At least seven Baylor guards resigned to avoid prosecution for sexual misconduct between 2006 and 2011, and it was claimed that Warden Patrick J. Ryan had concealed sexual misconduct, even where there was DNA evidence available. There were twenty-two other sexual misconduct complaints made by inmates at Baylor between January 2010 and July 2015. Baylor's rate of "staff-inmate sexual misconduct" was three times higher than the national rate in 2013.[35]

In 2011, legal action taken by the Delaware American Civil Liberties Union resulted in a $287,000 settlement in a case involving a male guard at Baylor sexually assaulting a woman after she showered.[36] The settlement also required Baylor to make major institutional changes, including more training and security cameras. This was slow to happen, and concerns still remain about the extent to which institutional changes were actually implemented in Baylor.

Family, Economic Violence, and the Streets of Wilmington

Street-identified Black women both in the community and in Baylor were generally most active in street life prior to motherhood. As mothers, however, some did participate in "convenient hustles" to supplement their income, from braiding hair and selling home-cooked meals to arranging drug deals and "boosting," or stealing products to resell. Nearly all women interviewed shared the same story of dropping out of school due to pregnancy and becoming single teenage mothers with little assistance from their children's fathers. While almost three-quarters surveyed said that they "cared a lot about their grades in high school," only half obtained a high school diploma, and only 6% completed some college or got a bachelor's degree. Four women interviewed had received a high school diploma, and six obtained a GED. Nearly two-thirds of women surveyed, and more than half interviewed, were unemployed and actively looking for work. Involvement in the streets was interpreted as a viable way to respond to the emotional and structural challenges of poor schooling, joblessness, a lack of material assistance from fathers, and incarceration.

Most women grew up around violence and other forms of crime. In fact, 75% surveyed claimed that "street activity was widespread" where they were raised. Also, of the 34% incarcerated, 55% admitted having sold drugs as their primary hustle before incarceration. Other street activities included prostitution, theft, and robbery.

CAMILLE (AGE 24): "I was always enticed by the streets, you know, just because of who I am, of who I grew up around, where I came from."

CHANTEL (AGE 30): "I've sold the drugs, I done the charges, I done did the jail time and did all that."

Across their life spans, as girls, teenagers, young women, and mothers, their homes and communities were always immersed in crime and inequality. Some used drugs to cope with being single mothers during distressed economic periods, and some sold drugs to help feed their children. Others did both, but most regarded the streets as adaptive, or a "means to an end."

That said, relatively few women in our study repeatedly experienced violent assaults. About 35% surveyed were "threatened with serious physical harm," and 12% were chased by "gangs or individuals." In addition, 40% admitted to being "slapped, punched, or hit by someone" at least once, while 15% said they were stabbed and 14% said they had been shot.

TONI (AGE 18): "Before my son, I was wild, didn't care. [I would have] fought anybody. I've been arrested. I have charges, [I] just didn't care."

CAMILLE (AGE 24): "It used to be unheard of for a girl, like, slicing people up, you know, cutting people up. [Now] it's like that. You got the girls that just go hard [fight aggressively] like [boys]. They don't know what their place is. Like, they don't know what [being] a lady is about."

Like the men, some women framed violence as a form of social capital to be traded or used to maintain personal, group, and family safety. Violence was never perceived to be a "good" or a healthy form of coping, but at times it was a necessary means to survive.

Moreover, most women actually preferred not to be violent; they'd rather spend time with their families. Motherhood was a defining, prioritized, and culturally supported identity in the Eastside and Southbridge. Motherhood was also a positively reinforced achievement that was in reach or within their control. Young Black women in their late teens to mid-twenties were rarely stigmatized for having children, even out of wedlock, particularly if they were deemed to be responsible women. Children were considered to be a "gift from God."[37]

Mothers were most concerned with safely raising their children in neighborhoods that sometimes felt to them like "war zones." It was possible, during "times of war" between street rivals, for children and other innocent bystanders to be unintended victims. These mothers were cursed with the burden of raising sons in communities that easily drew young boys, male partners, and other male loved ones into a whirlwind of street violence.

ANESHIA (AGE 29): "Now you scared to let your child be born. It's a strain . . . when your child goes outside. It's a shame that they can't walk outside because you're afraid. When we first moved [to Southbridge] it was the Wild, Wild West. I mean, the movie scene, they were ducking [bullets] on the basketball courts, and it was like a war zone. Like, they were literally shooting in broad daylight. I thought I was on TV."

In a small city like Wilmington, Black mothers knew firsthand how violence quickly bound residents together, especially the families of perpetrators and victims. Over 53% of women surveyed had a relative who was shot and killed, most of whom were male family members. These women experienced the full totality of violence, not just with the loss of relatives and friends but also as perpetrators, victims, and witnesses, and vicariously through the experiences of family, friends, and other residents. But most often, however, these women were tasked with being the caretakers of victims.

BLACK MOTHERHOOD: EXPERIENCES WITH FATHERS AND MALE PARTNERS

Black men played a critical role in raising Black children, and especially Black boys in Wilmington, and the loss of them to incarceration and homicide greatly destabilized their families and actually increased violence in their neighborhoods.[38] Wilmington's institutional removal of its Black men had caused Black women to draw from a much smaller pool of prospective male partners. Almost 53% of women surveyed were single without significant partners, and only 5% were legally married. None of the women interviewed were married and only a few had significant partners. Nearly two-thirds of women surveyed had children, and all eighteen women interviewed had children. Eight women interviewed had their first child before the age of 18, and three were as young as 14. Thirteen of the women interviewed were raising children without their children's fathers living in the home.

Securing a long-term relationship with a male partner was in many respects an elusive goal. Romantic partnerships and families, for most women, were complicated and adaptive arrangements fitted to the structural realities Black couples faced in Wilmington. Most women in the study had both scorn and love for their children's fathers. The women were concurrently blind to and aware of how their men were blocked from structural opportunity and how that prevented Black families from thriving in Wilmington. But a structural analysis rarely blotted out the pain and betrayal many felt when Black men were unable to emotionally and materially provide. It was useful to know about a structural argument, but usually that was not enough to heal the wounds that came with a "broken" family.

LESLIE (AGE 31): "It makes me feel bad because there's no [help]. It's, like, hard raising 'em [children] all by myself with no help."

TISHA (AGE 27): "It's hard to be a single mother out trying to raise your kids on your own. So, the best thing you can do is just hold them tight and let them know everything's gonna be alright. You know, don't run to the streets."

Aneshia (age 29) was the mother of six children and grandmother of two, and she was very angry with her father and the fathers of her children. Her father was rarely present in her life, and none of the fathers of her children were active in their lives. Aneshia chose to raise her children alone and rejected using the "white man" or judicial system to hold their fathers accountable.

ANESHIA: "If the white man gotta make you take care of my child, then we don't need you. It made me really dislike men, too. . . . It started with my dad. *Yeah*, I'm a male basher! Like, I was hurt by a man, really badly, deeply rooted hurt by a man so that [had] a great impact on me."

Black women held positive and negative attitudes toward their fathers and the fathers of their children. They both loved and hated them. Their formative years, however, were clearly the developmental period when Black girls became "angry Black women" with regard to Black men.

Brandy (age 29) also had a contentious relationship with her father. She lost her mother to complications from HIV/AIDS and dropped out in ninth grade due to her embarrassment about her mother's condition. Her father was in prison for the majority of her life, including when she lost her mother. Although he kept in contact with her as a child, Brandy now refused to speak with and financially support him because of her resentment of him. Brandy shared: "My dad went to jail when I was five years old, got twenty-five years [in prison]. [He] came home when I was 25. I'm 29 now. He got out [of prison] when I was 25, he went back when I was 27 and got life. . . . So basically, I know his first and last name."

Experiences with the father of Brandy's children were very similar to experiences with her own father. According to Brandy, he was far too involved with drug dealing to fully embrace his family. Incensed and jaded, she believed that he wanted no meaningful experiences with his children. In fact, she believed he did not even love them anymore. Brandy said, "My children's father is not around, not in the household, sells drugs every day. 'Like, you live about a twenty-minute walk from Southbridge, and it's been months since you looked my kids in their face. So, no, I don't believe you love them.'"

Gloria (age 29) also grew up without a father, raised in a single mother home. She had a volatile relationship with both her parents, who did not get along with each other. Her father's absence cut the deepest and fueled a hatred she once felt for him. Gloria said, "I loved my father and I can honestly say now that I love my father more. Growing up, [I was like,] 'My dad wasn't there for me,' and I hated him for it. For a very long time. I had to come to grips with that."

Substance abuse, sale of narcotics, and incarceration were common reasons why the women's fathers (and sometimes mothers) were not present in their childhood homes. Dionne's (age 29) father struggled with alcoholism and incarceration for most of her life. In fact, her father was incarcerated at the time of her interview.

DIONNE: "[My relationship with my father] has always been the same . . . [I see] him sometimes. He stays in and out of jail. He's still in jail. He . . . get out of jail, [and] my grandmom would give him a chance, . . . he would come back [home] . . . [but] he kept coming home drunk, and grandmom [would] say, 'The next time you come home drunk, you're not coming back.' And that's how it's always been."

The women confirmed that incarceration and unmet re-entry needs negatively impacted the economic viability of their families. About 76% of women surveyed thought it was extremely challenging for parents returning home from prison to emotionally reconnect with their children, and 82% agreed it was especially difficult for returning fathers to provide for children and their families.

The women's memories of their own fathers not working, being shuffled off by police, or returning from prison were eerily similar to their experiences with their children's fathers. Cursed by an onslaught of debilitating structural forces, Black women in Wilmington, especially those who experienced the streets and deep poverty, seemingly accepted the possibility of not securing a stable nuclear family. Mass incarceration of Black men, welfare policies that make it financially beneficial for Black women to remain single and reside in poor conditions, and high-crime environments all made single motherhood normative for many Black women in Wilmington. Most women were heartbroken by their inability to form meaningful relationships with the men in their lives. They endured by cobbling together what remained of their families. And to cope with so much loss, many relentlessly organized around violence and incarceration.

THE *HOMICIDE ART EXHIBITION*

A little over a year into the project, we were done with the first wave of data collection. Our study began to break in local and regional media. The *News Journal* had just run a one-week front-page series (My Neighborhood) on our project that ran from Sunday, November 21, to Friday, November 26, 2010. Honestly, I was a little nervous about the early attention but very appreciative of the positive press and public support. We still had at least a year and half of work to do in terms of analysis and writing. Institutional partners, however, felt we needed to take advantage of the public momentum and open the project to media coverage. It was still early, and moving too fast could undermine our efforts, but the partners' insistence proved to be wise for public relations and it solidified group morale.

Ms. Raye Jones Avery was the executive director of the Christina Cultural Arts Center (CCAC) in Downtown Eastside and one of our key institutional partners. She led the project's "action" or activism dimension. Ms. Raye is an elegant Black woman deeply committed to Black Wilmington, and she was also well connected to Delaware's establishment class. In truth, she is one of the elite, but she remained rooted in a community-oriented philosophy because she also once struggled with some of the same issues faced by Black women in Wilmington. It was not uncommon for the governor or a bank president or members of the mayor's office to attend one of CCAC's performances at the Baby Grand Theatre in Downtown Eastside.

In December 2010, Ms. Raye, Curator Jenny Bart, and Associates Ashley, Dubard, and Bernard launched the *"Homicide Art Exhibition"* at CCAC.[39] On this evening, a strong community spirit swept the interior of the building. Its hallways, smaller rooms, and main gallery space were all impeccably decorated with local art on gun violence. There was a wide cross-section of Wilmington in attendance, including reporters from the *News Journal*, Rennie Rox and his video team, a diverse group of street-identified Black men and women, Street PAR Associates, city leadership, clergy, residents, and the loved ones of persons lost to gun violence.

For six months, the action subteam's work was featured in CCAC's main gallery. They curated the stories of almost a dozen victims of gun violence. After selecting the stories, the subteam requested written permission from family members to develop their loved ones' stories into artistic representations. They also interviewed friends and family members, collected written accounts of the homicides, and examined community-level data on violence prior to unveiling their artistic stories to the public.

Twelve-year-old Sheila Ferrell's curated biography underscored the historical violence Black girls and women experienced in Wilmington. Sheila was chased and killed by a racist white man named John H. Bailey on Sunday, August 17, 1975.[40] She lived a half block from John and had innocently drifted over to a peach tree in his backyard. Sheila picked two peaches before John bolted out of his back door with a gun. He claimed Sheila and others were stealing "furniture and furnishings" from his back porch and fruit in his backyard. Sheila was shot once in her back and she actually made it home before she died, collapsing on her porch. John was sentenced to thirty years for manslaughter and ten years for a felony weapon offense, and these two sentences ran consecutively. Sheila's death was well over thirty years ago, but Wilmington still struggled with her story.

The life of Jerome "Boomer" Green, Dubard, Kontal, and Tyrin's close friend, was also curated. In February 2008, Boomer was killed in front of his young daughter. Looking at Boomer's giant smile and nearby images of Felicia Austin, Kontal said, "This corner is a little more intimate to me, because I personally know these two people over here. Felicia Austin is Tree Tree's mom, and Jerome Greene, or Boomer, was like one of my best friends. These two people alone, man, left like nine kids behind. And it [homicide] don't really hurt them, it hurts the kids."

In another area of the exhibition, Dubard stood proudly near his makeshift wooden telephone pole, which represented a street memorial. Dubard wanted onlookers to see how the streets memorialized people killed in Wilmington. Dubard meticulously surrounded the improvised stub of wood with two dozen lit candles, a handful of liquor bottles, and stuffed teddy bears. Part of the telephone pole was wrapped with yellow-and-black police tape. Other areas of the pole were wrapped with a collage of images and antiviolence messages.

The main gallery was stuffed with attendees who did their best to squeeze in. After the introductory remarks, Ashley introduced two public service announcements (PSAs) developed by the action subteam. One PSA focused on gun violence and the second grappled with domestic violence. Ashley and Wolf starred in a ten-minute PSA that featured them as a couple struggling with domestic violence. Surprisingly, Ashley and Wolf performed well on screen delivering a complex story of marital abuse inside poor Black Wilmington.

After viewing the PSAs, Bernard introduced *The People's Report Mix CD*.[41] Our communal album, which Bernard directed, contained twenty-two tracks in the forms of poetry, skits, narration, singing, and mostly gangsta rap music. All contributions on the album focused on the relationship between crime and structural violence. We gave away 100 CDs, made closing remarks and then offered a buffet of finger foods and cold beverages.

Lynette Williams, the boisterous woman I met at Dayveair Golden's repast, stopped by the exhibition. Lynette attended with her good friend Ms. Jackie Latson.

"Dr. Yasser? This is my friend Ms. Jackie. We both want to thank you for this evening,"

Ms. Jackie assured me, "This was a proper remembrance of our loved ones."

"Thank you for supporting tonight, but most of the thanks goes to Ms. Raye and the action subteam. We have a blessed Street PAR family."

After chatting, I finally took time to closely examine the art, and then I realized that Lynette's brother and Ms. Jackie's son were among the curated stories.

Resilience and Loss: How Two Black Women Take on Violence and City Officials

Approximately three weeks after the *Homicide Art Exhibition*, we interviewed Lynette and Ms. Jackie together at CCAC. We wanted to better understand their stories, but also Black women's grief overall, with respect to the loss of their loved ones to gun violence. We needed to know more about how Black women in Wilmington coped with this continual tragedy. Lynette and Ms. Jackie were among the most active residents, and they repeatedly called for the development of a homicide unit.[42] Lynette collected about 25,000 signatures for a petition in support of this unit.

Lynette Williams was a 46-year-old, full-figured, dark-skinned woman. She was a native Eastsider but now resided in Wilmington's Riverside neighborhood. Her brother Vaughn Allen Williams was shot and killed in 1998. Lynette found out about his murder one morning while watching the Channel 6 news. After taking a public bus to the scene, she waded through police and residents to confirm the victim was her brother. Vaughn was killed on Third and Madison Street in a car behind the local McDonalds. He was found in the driver's seat with his head leaned back while the radio blared. To date, his murder remains unsolved. According to Lynette, racism and classism explained best why her brother's homicide was a low priority for police: "It's not what you know, it's who you know and how much you got. . . . And it connects to my brother's issue [homicide] because I ain't have enough money for them to properly work on his case."

Lynette was consumed by her brother's homicide. I wondered whether her persistence empowered or ate away at her. Her spirit was cut deeply by his murder, and I wondered if her emotional wound could actually heal. Ms. Jackie sat next to Lynette, held her hand, and sometimes sighed in support. We listened and asked few questions. Like Lynette, Ms. Jackie struggled with the loss her son. To my surprise, 63-year-old Ms. Jackie was more emotional and grief-stricken than Lynette.

Lynette and Ms. Jackie first met each other at a support group called Survivors Addressing Grief Easement (SAGE). SAGE was founded in 2005 by Ms. Edwina Bell Mitchell, and it provided counseling to people grieving over loved ones that had been killed. SAGE lost its funding, and after its closing in 2008, Lynette and Ms. Jackie stayed in touch. According to Ms. Jackie, SAGE was instrumental to her emotional and psychological recovery. Ms. Jackie's grief ran deep and would never be completely cured: "All you can do with grief is address it. You can't close it. You can't shoot it. You can't medicate it. And you can't pray it away." SAGE encouraged her to face her son's murder head-on with the support of other Black women.

Ms. Jackie was a proud, African-centered woman who was in deep love with Black Wilmington. She was one of fourteen children and now lived in the Hilltop section of Wilmington. Raised in extreme poverty, she said, "We weren't even *po* [poor], . . . we were just *p* [sounded out the letter *p*]." Married twice, she had an older son and younger daughter who were eleven years apart.

Ms. Jackie was well known in Wilmington for her seven massive three-ring binders on shootings and homicides since 2002. Each binder contained hundreds of lamented news articles and other clippings. Scores of residents and representatives of organizations visited her home to view them. She even received requests from art museums, libraries, and other institutions to purchase her binders, but she has refused. Her binders were not just how she coped with her son's murder but also one of the ways she resisted or fought city leadership.

Ms. Jackie shared three of the binders with us. Written on their sleeves were the words "Wilmington Shootings" or "Murder in Wilmington" with the corresponding years (e.g., 2005–2006). We huddled around her in a horseshoe. Slowly sliding her hand across the articles, she indicated deep familiarity with and critical examination of each case. Many involved victims and perpetrators that she personally knew. Some stories were of young children or other residents who were unintentionally killed. Whether she knew them or not, Ms. Jackie considered them all to be her "babies." Ms. Jackie was so obsessed with this project that she also chronicled each shooting and homicide in an Excel spreadsheet with the circumstances surrounding each case and the outcome of the victim's funeral. While most funerals were peaceful ceremonies, some, however, erupted into explosive arguments and even physical altercations between family members and friends. Ms. Jackie literally exhausted herself with this activity because it was one of the few coping mechanisms that worked for her.

Ms. Jackie's thirty-one-year-old son Hakeem Iman Cornelius Crawford was killed in 2004 near the intersection of Seventh and Washington Streets. Hakeem was shot at five times and hit by three of the bullets. Two struck him in the back, and the third, which pierced his neck, killed him. If Hakeem had survived, he would have been instantly paralyzed. According to Ms. Jackie, Hakeem was shot because he owed someone $124. "I will never be the same. They say my son was a corner boy. If my son was a corner boy, well, he was the brokest corner boy I know."

Dubard (Associate) asked, "How did you feel about the media's coverage of your son's death?" Greatly dissatisfied with the coverage, Ms. Jackie asserted that his murder was exploited and poorly framed. She also claimed the media never contacted her: "They never got his mother's perspective." Ms. Jackie believed that reporters were more interested in his romantic partners, and she also suspected one may have assisted with his murder: "I don't know if they set him up or not." Street ethnographers with a focus on violence have paid increasing attention to how women have played integral roles in getting men in the streets robbed, assaulted, and even killed.[43]

It was a young Black woman who ran to Ms. Jackie's home on Eighth and Windsor Streets to alert her about Hakeem's death. "I didn't even know her [that well]. I shot out of the house, and when I got there, there was nothing I could do. I never even got a call from the police." There were about "500 people" at the scene of her son's homicide. Police prevented her from approaching her son's body. Devastated, Ms. Jackie screamed, cursed, and collapsed on the pavement. Reliving the moment, and in a shrill voice, she pleaded with us, "You have to understand, he was not raised that way! He would fight you with his fist in a heartbeat, but he would never pull out a gun. He'll beat the living crap out of you. And that's what he had done that day. He had beat that young man. My son owed him $124. My son probably wasn't able to pay, and they got into a disagreement."

Fueled with rage, she was compelled to find out who killed Hakeem. Ms. Jackie drew on her community network and learned of the details surrounding her son's homicide three days after his death. "The streets came and told me. They didn't necessarily tell the police, but they did tell me. When they told me that, I said, 'I got to find him.' Not to kill him. That's not what God put on my heart."

"You are so strong. You are a strong Black woman," Dubard interjected.

"Thank you, baby," she responded. "So, I couldn't tell anybody that I got a phone call about who did it. . . . I was told that he was going to be in the courthouse for a case that had nothing to do with Hakeem. . . . I asked for his name and where his court case would be."

Ms. Jackie looked down, paused for a few seconds, slowly looked up, and stared at us. "I get to the courtroom. I see this young man sitting in the front with his sister. It got very quiet around me. . . . Next thing I heard was the name Dwayne Staats, and everything in my body stopped."

She shook uncontrollably and cried. The pitch of her voice sharpened. Ms. Jackie then cried harder. She shouted, "I didn't realize the boy who killed my son was right in front of me! I sat right behind him all that time and I did not know it. . . . And when I realized, I couldn't move!"

She paused, cried more, and wiped her nose and tears.

"When I got up, I couldn't move my hand. I couldn't move anything. . . . He got up and left, and I followed. I was still quiet."

In the corridor, she walked near him and gently asked, "Are you Dwayne Staats?" He replied, "Yeah." Then she calmly uttered, "I am Hakeem Crawford's mother. God bless you." In response, "He couldn't open his mouth."

They walked outside the courthouse on King Street and Ms. Jackie spoke to the man who murdered her son. "I wasn't scared at all. I didn't have any fear in my heart. I didn't have any vengeance, hatred, jealousy, and he saw that in me, and that's what freaked him out."

Once more, Ms. Jackie exploded in tears, revealing to us that she realized in that moment with Dwayne that she did feel vengeful. Her face and lips quivered, and her voice shook as she screeched, "He was standing right there! . . . The scariest part was when I saw my car across the street. I started shaking. You know why, dear?"

"Why?" replied Dubard.

Ms. Jackie screeched even higher, "If I would have had a gun in that car, I cannot swear I wouldn't have shot him." She cried more and her body convulsed. "That's what scared me more than anything. Seeing him didn't scare me. Talking to him, facing him didn't scare me. What scared me was what if I would have been stupid enough, ungodly enough to kill him."

DWAYNE STAATS (AGE 21) was convicted of first-degree murder of Hakeem Crawford in June 2005.[44] According to news reports, Dwayne's sister screamed in court when her brother was sentenced to life in prison.

"Do you think justice was served?" Dubard asked.

"Yes, I do, dear. However, there is no closure. There is no such thing.... But I have a *peace* of justice."

Ms. Jackie found solace in her son's children—he had twelve children, and she was in contact with seven. Crying and breaking down one more time, Ms. Jackie said, "His baby boy was born on December 25, 2004. He was born on Christmas Day after his father died. My son is probably up there saying, 'Ma, I left you one last one for Christmas.'"

BLACK AMERICAN culture played a critical role in how Ms. Jackie and Lynette coped with street violence. Race and culture deeply shaped their lived experiences, including their spiritual perspectives and the way they bonded, and race and culture deeply informed how they grieved and fought back as Black women. According to Vargas, a "radical Black solidarity" existed among and protected poor Black women from unrelenting social structural challenges.[45]

For all of the pain Ms. Jackie and Lynette felt, it was not enough to stop their ambitious efforts around town. In fact, their pain fueled their activism. Their fearlessness even forced them to walk "to the block to talk to the corner boys." Ms. Jackie begged them to "get off the street. Do you want your mother to be in pain like me?" Ms. Jackie and Lynette took their message to street corners, living rooms, community events, and media—they made their homes available and stormed the offices of city leadership.

Extreme poverty and family instability were the primary causes of gun violence in Wilmington, according to Ms. Jackie. She argued that more opportunity for Black families to improve their socioeconomic realities was the most logical way to reduce violence.

"You've got people who are working in these little penny-annie jobs. They can't afford to pay their electric bills, and their rent, and/or mortgage in the same month anymore. Now, when you find yourself not being able to do that..."

"You will resort to extreme measures," Dubard said.

"*Yeah! You waking up angry!* Wouldn't you?"

Ms. Jackie and Lynette represented how gun violence sharply affected the psychological well-being of Black women in Wilmington. A gnawing pain chased them, and even I was exhausted from the screams and tears that resulted from this chase. I had never been exposed to this level of concentrated sadness in one sitting. I actually felt guilty that I was not able to make their pain go away. They had no expectations for me or us to do so, but I still felt compelled to ease their misery.

A Conversation with Grieving Black Mothers

Because they were the emotional cornerstones of their families and communities, Black women rarely understood their womanhood as separate from the boys and men in their lives. Women as daughters, sisters, mothers, and life partners often suffered out loud from the impact of gun violence on their sons, brothers, fathers, and cousins. They were the nurturers of all, but it was unclear who consoled them in their times of grief.

Many Black women in the Eastside and Southbridge neighborhoods turned to God or to a church or mosque for support. Tabernacle Full Gospel Baptist Church in Wilmington was one of the churches that offered spiritual guidance and coping skills to Black women struggling with the impact of homicide. One Friday evening in Tabernacle, I sat with senior pastor Bishop Aretha E. Morton as she spoke with four Black women grieving over their son's homicides. Sitting in a semicircle near the church's pulpit, Bishop Morton opened the conversation with the reading of Jeremiah 9:20–21: "*Now hear the word of the Lord*: Call for the women who cry for the funerals. Teach your daughters how to cry. Teach your neighbors funeral songs. Death has come through our windows and entered our palaces. Death has cut down the children in the streets and the young men in the marketplaces."

All four Black mothers' heads swung low as we absorbed Bishop Morton's selection. The biblical passages paralleled well the experiences of violence in Wilmington. After reading, Bishop Morton said, "The word of the Lord according to Jeremiah. Never saw it before until all of this [violence] started happening."

Like Lynette and Ms. Jackie, these four mothers wailed for almost two hours. Eddiesha Johnson said her son's homicide "is a pain you can't describe and it doesn't go away." According to Eddiesha, her "spirituality" and this support group at Tabernacle were the most effective mechanisms for coping with her son's death.

Another mother shared that her 17-year-old son Kevin was killed in 2006. She thought Kevin was home when her daughter called her about his murder. Startled by what she thought was a practical joke, she scolded her daughter, "Don't call here playing jokes like that! Kevin is downstairs.... I just seen him." She put the phone down, walked out of her bedroom, and screamed Kevin's name. There was no response, so she ran outside and screamed his name again. She looked over and saw a crowd swelling almost two blocks away, where her son's body lay on the concrete, lifeless and riddled with bullets. Trembling, she remarked that it was unnatural for a mother to bury her son. "You never ever think that you will outlive your children, no matter what type of life they lived. They're still your child. For me to have to bury my kid at 17 years of age—nothing ever could have happen to me in life that hurts *that much*. I live with it each and every day of my life!"

Shontai Moore lost her 18-year-old son Jaiquone in 2008. Trying to find words to describe her experience, Shontai paused, tears filled her eyes, and she slowly said, "I don't know if I will ever be happy again." Shontai's son grew up in a "rough" neighborhood in the Eastside, but she was able to move her children to a safer neighborhood a few years before her son was killed. Attached strongly to his friends and the Eastside community, Jaiquone refused to abandon them; he traveled to his old neighborhood as often as he could. According to Shontai, Jaiquone defended a friend who got into an altercation, and "two days later he [Jaiquone] was shot in his back." Shontai was a registered nurse and very familiar with human anatomy. Crying, she said, "The bullet severed his aorta, his lungs, his liver. He bled out there on the street. There was nothing I could do." Looking away from the group, she also described the enormous loneliness felt by single Black mothers with slain children. "Everyone talks about how strong you are as a mother, but no one is there at night when you cry yourself to sleep. No one is there in the shower when you are breaking down and you are trying to clean yourself up before you leave. No one is there when you are at the cemetery and you don't want to leave the cemetery."

Ms. Trudy Boardley's older son Darryl Lively was shot and killed in 2003 on the Eastside's "notorious" Bennett Street, trying to help his younger brother Robert Teat, who was robbed at gunpoint "for $3 to buy drugs."[46] Darryl loved his brother, and he tried to protect him. Feeling an enormous level of guilt, Ms. Boardley blamed herself for Darryl's death because she believed she had failed him. Tears fell from under her brown glasses as she said, "For years I thought I didn't raise him right. That I wasn't a good mother. That it was my fault."

Black mothers were resilient, but they were survivors of extreme trauma. They reeled with grief, and still many were hopeful and "God fearing." Wholesome conversations and a reliance on God was the way many coped with the seemingly impossible. These women still believed that positive change was probable, and they did not necessarily view their emotional breakdowns as evidence of clinical depression or poor psychological functioning. Extreme grief and long periods of mourning were considered culturally acceptable methods of coping for mothers of children who were killed.

Bishop Morton left us with a prophetic warning. Feeling the women's heavy guilt, she offered a sharp structural analysis as a way for them to relieve their pain. Bishop Morton's synopsis called out city leadership's unwillingness to address the poverty drowning so many Black families. She warned of a conspiracy to undermine Black Wilmington and commanded us to look beyond the symptoms of inequality to the aims of larger systemic forces. Confidently, she taught:

> Every politician will say, "It starts in the home." Would you say that all of what you have gone through is because of the home environment? Or is it the street environment? Or is it because we don't have enough jobs? Is it because we don't have enough money? . . . Poverty? . . . I don't know if you would agree or disagree, *but* it seems as if everything has been designed for us to fail! . . . Everything that we try to touch, all of the gold and the silver . . . that we try to touch, it's designed for us to fail! We either are going to be incarcerated or we are going to be killed one way or the other. And there is a design for that to happen!

ODE TO AFENI SHAKUR

Tupac recorded the smash hit "Brenda's Got a Baby" (also the name of this chapter) on his 1991 debut album, *2Pacalypse Now*. The song gloomily highlights the gut-wrenching experiences many street-identified Black girls and women have with sexual assault, street life, pregnancy, and child rearing in extremely impoverished communities, and many of the heartfelt sentiments raised by Tupac in the song were in fact reflected in the experiences of street-identified Black girls and women in our study. Also, it should be noted that while child rearing was challenging for many of these girls and women, this did not mean they did not desire or treasure having children. In fact, we found that all of the young women in our study (and the fathers of their children and surrounding family members) were extremely grateful for their children.

Furthermore, the late Afeni Shakur was the mother of the late Tupac Shakur, and her life also represented for us the myriad experiences observed among Black women in Wilmington. Afeni was a single Black mother with two children. She lived in low-income environments, was formerly incarcerated, struggled with substance abuse, and lost her son Tupac to gun violence. She was also a community activist, African centered, politically engaged, and very family oriented. Afeni's sister Assata Shakur lives in Cuba and is still wanted by the U.S. government for "eight counts of murder, robbery and assault in a 1973 shootout on the New Jersey Turnpike that left one state trooper dead and another wounded."[47]

Tupac recognized his mother's virtues and limitations and still loved every part of her. In tribute to Afeni, Tupac recorded "Dear Mama," another smash hit released on his 1995 album *Me Against the World*. In this song, set to a melodic rhythm, Tupac hailed his mother as a "Black Queen" who endured the hardship of raising two children.

Black women in Wilmington were various versions of Afeni Shakur. Many were poor single mothers who were at some point involved in the streets. Some had been homeless, others lost children to gun violence, and most had at least one male relative or friend who was killed. These women were also loving and hardworking, enjoyed being mothers, and took pride in their neighborhoods. They loved and hurt hard and were far more complicated than the stereotypical framing of them as women ravaged by urban poverty, welfare dependency, and absent fathers.[48] These women were not "deficient," "delinquent," "deviant," "oversexed," or suffering from "cultural pathology." Their behavior was adaptive, extending out of the demands of oppressive structural environments. While Wilmington's street life was highly gendered and male dominated, homes in these communities were largely female dominated, including the homes of those involved with the streets.[49] Black women traversed gendered networks and acted as vital supports for families, local neighborhoods, and the streets.

CHAPTER 8

"Street Love"

HOW PSYCHOLOGICAL AND SOCIAL
WELL-BEING INTERRUPTS GUN VIOLENCE

> Bumpy [Johnson] would stand up there in the flatbed truck, a benign king dispensing freshly butchered turkeys like benedictions, and poor folk in their tattered clothes would crowd around and grin up at him gratefully and an elegantly attired Bumpy would grin back . . . the Robin Hood of Harlem.
> —Max Allan Collins, *American Gangster*

> He's [J. R., his murdered cousin] not even the person that people make him out to be. He's actually very quiet. . . . He's real relaxed. I mean, everybody who I ever introduced him to was like, "Man, that dude was so cool." I'm talking about people from Eastside. . . . People from Southbridge will be like, "That dude was cool, man." It's been times that I would have friends over to the house where we both lived together and he would take off his shoes and give them his shoes. Or say, "Go to my closet and get whatever you want out of my closet."
> —Aaron (29), study participant

SMALL CITY SIZE was a double-edged sword, in that smallness both negatively and positively affected the social climate in the Eastside and Southbridge. Violence was more concentrated in small cities, but residents in Wilmington also united in times of duress. Black Wilmingtonians were more likely to trust each other first, or for survival's sake—they remained very suspicious of "outsiders." Outside intervention was unreliable and often came in the form of punitive policies. In general, interventions focused on "deviant" behaviors in ways that detached people from their humanity. In Wilmington, violence reduction programs focused on impulse control and cognitive behavior; employment training programs emphasized soft skills, time management, and self-efficacy; schools employed suspensions and expulsions to regulate behavior and stimulate academic performance; and the cornerstones of public safety were arrests and incarcerations.

Rehabilitation programs rarely accounted for the structural oppression that participants and their families had experienced. In fact, the intergenerational impact of structural violence was generally rendered moot by program heads. Community programs, when they did exist, expected people to "get over it," or plow ahead through their pain. Interventions also generally ignored that street-identified Black men and women were the products of loving relationships—that they were also the sons and daughters, siblings, and parents of so many who cared deeply about them. It was also rarely considered that these individuals had dreams too, and in the Eastside and Southbridge, their aspirations were often tied to the well-being of their families and communities.

For generations, Black men and women have drawn on the streets to respond to their socioemotional and identity needs, as well as to secure financial support, acquire protection, and improve social cohesion. Shakur offers rich examples of how he bonded with individual peers and how his "eight-trey" Crip set supported many in his Los Angeles neighborhood. Shakur explained that returning to the community from prison was a time where friends or "brothers" in the street were more likely to be generous with one another.[1] Participants in Patton's ethnography noted that protection was the primary reason why young men and women joined gangs, because "many of them learned at an early age that they were vulnerable if they did not belong to a gang that would protect them when they were threatened by other gang members."[2] According to Horowitz, gangs often maintain complex yet "positive relationships" with local communities. Horowitz explained that it was not uncommon for gangs to serve as the "local police force" by ensuring the safety of all neighborhood residents.[3] Venkatesh also described how "tenant leaders" in Chicago's Robert Taylor Homes worked with gang leaders "to resolve conflicts and, in peaceful periods, force [gang] leaders to live up to their stated desire to 'better the community.'"[4] Gang leaders in Venkatesh's study also escorted senior citizens, provided protection to other residents not affiliated with crime, engaged in "community cleanups," and even reduced how long they socialized in public spaces.

In the Eastside and Southbridge, this communal tradition of giving back was described by some as an expression of "street love." Street love was phenomenological language used by street-identified Black men and women to explain how they bonded and contributed to family, friends, and community.[5] Expressions of street love were abundant in Wilmington, or it was evident that some men who sold crack cocaine or women who prostituted themselves, for instance, were also committed to improving their communities. Street love in Wilmington manifested in three ways: (1) *individual expressions of street love*, or engaging in kind acts on an individual level (e.g., loaning money, offering advice/counsel); (2) *group expressions of street love*, or group-based bonding (e.g., playing pool, going to the local bar); and (3) *communal expressions of street love*, or when individuals and groups in the streets sponsored

8.1. Street Love Theoretical Model

prosocial activities (e.g., giving away free turkeys, community barbecues) (see figure 8.1). Street love was also perceived as activism, or a response to city leadership's inability to create real structural change.

Street Love at Price's Run Park

Jerry Williams was a thirty-six-year-old Black man from the Riverside neighborhood. He invited us to the Third Annual Spring Anti-Violence Rally and BBQ, which he and others hosted at Price's Run Park (or Brown-Burton Winchester Park). "Healing," "love," and a "call to end Wilmington's violence" were the barbecue's core themes. Mothers and children, throngs of teenagers and young adults, older residents, members of the streets, and some professionals filled the park. A small army of food servers from Kingswood Academy Community Center lined up behind seven to ten long tables. Chips, popcorn, cotton candy, water, juice, and a variety of condiments populated the tables. Nearby grills prepared hot dogs, cheeseburgers, and chicken.

The barbecue featured a large stage and a moon bounce for young children. Several mopeds "wheelied" and four-wheelers "peeled out" while basketball games took place in the center of the park. Jerry and his friends did what few professionals were able to—provide a fun afternoon for the community.

"Our goal was to unify the community," Jerry said to me. "Hopefully, this community day can help decrease some of the violence. Today we had spoken word, dancing, and a fashion show. In addition, speeches were made by Pastor D and Pastor Wilmore."

"What's fueling the street violence, and what can be done to end it?"

Speaking louder, over the blaring hip-hop music in the background, Jerry responded, "One of the things that increases street violence is economics. When people cannot get a job, they tend to do what they have to do to take care of their families. We need to come together and find a way to give those who were convicted, a job. And we need to find meaningful work for those who are from low-income families. We need job training, job development, job readiness, and employment."

A DJ played in the middle of the stage while his giant speakers blasted the latest hip-hop, reggae, and R&B music. A woman greeted the audience and hosted a two-hour program of performance, recognition, and protest. The slain were acknowledged, residents received awards, and hip-hop and spoken-word performances were given. A fashion show of children and adult models from Wilmington then dazzled the audience. Wolf tapped my shoulder, pointed to the stage, and said, "Look!" To my surprise, Dubard and Kontal (Associates) walked the runway to the roar of the crowd. Afterward, at least two dozen young children cheerfully danced on stage.

Pastor Derrick Johnson ("Pastor D") of Joshua Harvest Church took to the stage and spoke about the slaying of 33-year-old Salima "Star" Jefferson. On June 8, 2009, Star's body was found in her Cadillac SUV at Forty-First and Tatnall Streets, shot "execution style."[6] Droves of Star's loved ones wore airbrushed T-shirts and hoodies bearing a picture her face and the caption "We Lost a [Star] . . . and We Pray for Peace."

Referring to Star's death, Pastor D claimed her murder was so disturbing that it immobilized Black Wilmington, shocking everyone into inaction. Also, few could relate to the amount of homicides Star's family endured. Star's older sister was killed in New York City in 1981; Star's life partner, Kenneth Davis Sr., was murdered in 1994; Star was murdered in 2009; and Star's son, Kenneth Davis Jr., was shot two days before Jerry's annual barbecue. Pastor D shamed us for tolerating this level of violence to be imposed on one family: "Not long ago, there was a senseless, stupid, crazy murder in this city of a beautiful sister that we call Star. Now Star represents everybody that's been murdered senselessly and needlessly. And the irony is, her son Kenny had already lost his father to murder. And then not more than forty-eight hours ago, somebody shot him [Kenny]."

After berating the audience, Pastor D made sure to scowl at "police" and "politicians" while also castigating the growing audience. Through call-and-response, Pastor D electrified the crowd: "When things get that bad and that crazy and you get triple effect [gun violence] on one family, it's not time for more police! It's not time for more politicians! It's time for us to come together, keep it real, and do something about the way we act towards one another. Am I right about it?" The crowd roared, "Yeah!" in reply.

Ardently, Pastor D continued, "No, am I right about it? Because tomorrow night, it could be you or your child!"

Dropping to his knees, he laid hands and prayer on countless young people at the stage's edge.

What Jerry and his friends accomplished this afternoon extended out of a long intergenerational street tradition in Wilmington. The outpouring of love and healing radically and strongly challenged dominant arguments about the "internalized racism," "low self-esteem," "maladaptiveness," "deviance," "hopelessness," "helplessness," and "poor social cohesion" of the streets and poor Black people. To the contrary, our survey data strongly suggested that most in the Eastside and Southbridge thought highly of themselves, as well as their families and communities. Eighty-five percent reported being "satisfied" with their family life, 83% felt personally "satisfied," 85% were "happy" with their lives, and 94% understood themselves to be "a useful person to have around."

Many in the streets were expected to "give back" in some positive way to the very communities where they committed crime. If portions of illegal earnings circulated back into the community, residents were more likely to reason with or tolerate some level of illegal activity.[7] When those in the streets gave back, most residents believed these activities were genuine displays of support. In fact, everyone we spoke with, including those critical of the concept of street love, described at least one experience of street love, including, taking care of children, paying a loved one's outstanding bill, sponsoring holiday celebrations, or even paying college tuition.

Outsiders instinctively equated street love to a false or overly romanticized concept of honor. For outsiders, the streets were anything but noble, chiefly because of the street violence and the pain, physical injury, and death left behind. It did not matter how many positive activities the streets engaged in, outsiders never acknowledged any positive impact they made. But it didn't matter. Many from the Eastside and Southbridge still deeply appreciated the material support provided by the streets. In the context of extreme poverty, residents were able to make sense out of or tolerate some level of crime as expressions of "subaltern resilience" to withstand the effects of structural exploitation, economic precarity, and social dispossession.[8] Crime was not desirable, but residents and especially the streets also understood that illegal activity was a consequence of adverse lived experiences. As the "wretched of the earth" or a "disposable population," street-identified Black Americans utilized street love as a buffer between these adverse lived experiences and illegal activity.[9] They enacted street love as a form of collective agency in response to oppressive conditions.[10] Their identities are crafted from this collective struggle, and Bracke urges us to reimagine how "subalterns" "continue to be productive" despite the enduring legacy of colonialist capitalism.[11]

Given its many dimensions, street love could be complicated, even for persons in the streets. Many held critical perspectives, but they were often able to distinguish between disingenuous and more authentic actors. The "spirit of the crime" or the intentions behind illegal activity and the social standing of persons involved in the streets were generally weighed before judgment was rendered on someone's moral character.

Sitting in his apartment in the Eastside, Adil (age 18) discussed the ethical contradictions of street love from his perspective as a young person.

WOLF: Do you think the streets genuinely care about their community?
ADIL: To an extent.... They'll look out for each other and their neighbors and stuff. But, you know, they turn around and trash the neighborhood

themselves again, but they look out for each other and keep the community up too.
WOLF: What is your overall opinion about the Eastside?
ADIL: I don't think it's bad. But I don't look at violence as a bad thing . . . but I look at it as people . . . do it because they think it's a necessity.
WOLF: When you say, 'look out for each other,' what do you mean by that? What do they do specifically when they look out for each other?
ADIL: If someone needs money, they help him out. They may do it the wrong way . . . but it's still helping them out.

Banks (age 27) had witnessed "quite a few guys" organize "big barbecues" or "fireworks" displays on the "Fourth of July." He agreed that sales of "crack and dope" were morally wrong and negatively impacted the community, but for Banks, this did not preclude people who "got it" (profited from drug sales) from engaging in prosocial or constructive behavior. Banks and others did not always view persons from the streets as ruthless and being incapable of ethical or kind acts—despite how they were typically regarded by outsiders. Banks believed it was honorable for them to make sure "their hood" was provided for. "Quite a few guys . . . from my side of town gave back: Fourth of July, fireworks, barbecues, DJs . . . down at the park—*big barbecues!* . . . Even if you want to say with the drug aspect, [guys in the street] made sure their hood was okay [provided for]. . . . You have some guys that . . . give back to the community in a good way, even though they . . . doing what they do."

Banks also called on community professionals to recognize that most in the streets wanted quality educational and employment opportunities—a perspective that is rarely the focus of analyses on street-identified Black populations: "You might have a guy that's . . . selling drugs . . . doing what they do, but at the end of the day . . . he might be in the library reading a book or learning about some things, he might be trying to get [his] business [together] to get out the game [or the streets]. . . . I know a lot of guys . . . in the game that . . . I grew up under that's doing real good for their self and they want to give back to the community."

Anthony B. (age 33) owned One Stop, a small but very popular urban clothing, mix CD, DVD, and telecommunications store. One Stop provided an active social networking space for young people who aspired to be part of the entertainment industry. On any given day, young people stood in or outside of One Stop waiting eagerly to meet local and regional hip-hop and R&B artists and filmmakers. Prior to his national success, we saw the Philadelphia-based rapper Meek Mill (or Meek Millz) at One Stop promoting *Meek Mill Flamers 3*, his DJ Drama–hosted mix CD project.

Curating a Black-owned business with in-store signings of "major talent" was Anthony B.'s way of "giving back to the community. . . . How many people can bring major talent to the hood? Or how many . . . are able to put the streets in real proximity to artists like a Meek Millz? This is just one of the ways I give back or do street love. . . . I wanted to come to the city bearing a little bit of fruit. I didn't just want to come with my hands out." For Anthony, these kinds of social gatherings raised the morale of poor Black neighborhoods that might not otherwise be exposed to someone of celebrity status.

Anthony B. argued that many with similar experiences in the streets also felt compelled to give back because they assumed that city leaders were unwilling to do so. Street love was how they responded to the absence of community centers or vital youth programs, for instance. Community professionals and nonprofit organizations in Wilmington were generally viewed as ineffective or more concerned about serving their own institutional interests. He said, "I've seen more of them [the streets] do more than some of the churches. . . . Sometimes [nonprofits] might be doing it for a tax write-off, and some people do it for the love. . . . The hustler might be doing it for the love, and [for] the church people [it] may [be] . . . just a quick tax write-off, a 1099 real quick."

UB9 AND STREET LOVE: TAKING BACK THE EASTSIDE

Banks was a part of the United Brothers of Ninth Street (UB9), a collective of Black men from the Eastside dedicated to neighborhood programming. The name of the group was derived from the street corner, Ninth and Poplar Streets in the Eastside, where original members socialized in the 1990s.

One summer evening while we collected survey data near Poplar, a charged skirmish broke out between five to eight youths. A few older men eventually ran over and ended the conflict. According to T-Warren, violence spiraled out of control because the youth no longer understood the honor and pride people used to feel about growing up on "Ninth and Poplar." Although T-Warren remembered a more cohesive neighborhood in the 1990s, he said the neighborhood still had a very active street culture:

> UB9's name was based on the street we hung out on. Ninth and Poplar meant a lot to us. There were a lot of good and some bad memories on that street. Ninth and Poplar was the "trap" spot, or the drug spot. Not everybody . . . was pumping [selling drugs], though. That corner . . . was a gathering spot for a lot of people. We would hang out there and socialize. You know, drink, smoke. It was a meeting area in the community. It was a lot going on out there. Barbecues. A "numbers spot" [gambling location] was not that far from the corner. A lot went on out there.

Neighborhood-level space was integral to the social identity of street-identified Black men and women in the Eastside and Southbridge neighborhoods. Primarily used to cope and establish resilience, demarcated physical spaces were truly cherished by various street crews in Wilmington. These communal spaces were more than arbitrary locations—they connoted a deeper connection to something beyond the self. Physical space affirmed cultural strength, social status and group capacity. Ninth and Popular Streets was a "physical site of resilience," or a cultural space that greatly helped UB9 members in the 1990s to survive and make meaning out of the world.[12] In a structurally turbulent city, Ninth and Poplar Streets was safe enough for many Black men to be emotionally vulnerable, spiritually affirmed, and socially accomplished. On this urban stretch of land, these men were positively reinforced and recognized as competent and able to create group and communal cohesion.

Ninth and Poplar was a vibrant cultural location that people drew on as an active social space. In the 1990s and early 2000s, T-Warren and others in UB9 safely hustled and socially bonded in meaningful ways on Ninth and Poplar. This did not mean that Ninth and Poplar did not have its fair share of violence. But for T-Warren, the overall experience of Ninth and Poplar and his particular experience with UB9 more so represented a brotherhood committed to the larger neighborhood.

Ninth and Poplar was also a historic location that had its roots in jazz. Wilmington was one of the original three cities (along with Kansas City and New Orleans) where jazz was born, and the musician Clifford Brown was the face of jazz in Wilmington. Brown lived at 1013 Poplar, and in the 1950s he played his horn in Club Baby Grand, also on Ninth and Poplar. Club Baby Grand was a major stop on the jazz "chitlin' circuit." Household names like Sammy Davis Jr., Ray Charles, Dizzy Gillespie (who discovered Clifford Brown), Lester Young, and Jimmy Smith graced the stage at Club Baby Grand. Jimmy Smith also recorded the famous jazz album *Club Baby Grand* (1952) at the Wilmington venue. Each June, the city closes Market Street in Downtown Eastside to host the Clifford Brown Jazz Festival, and in 1996, the city renamed Poplar Street "Clifford Brown Walk."

Echoing UB9's connection to Ninth and Poplar, Harding also claimed that youth in his study strongly identified with particular spaces in their neighborhoods.[13] Harding's work in Boston evaluated how youth and city officials perceived these spaces and neighborhood boundaries differently. According to Harding, neighborhood boundaries were narrowly defined and "socially constructed" by youth, whereas the city set the demarcations of neighborhoods wider than youth understood the boundaries to be. In line with Harding's argument, men and women in the Eastside and Southbridge were also more likely to understand their neighborhood as "the blocks," or the housing developments or local parks they most frequented, which were generally smaller spaces in the Eastside and Southbridge. For UB9 in the Eastside, Ninth and Poplar Street was the neighborhood they proudly claimed.

And it was also over the protection of these localized spaces that many were prepared to be violent if necessary.[14]

Founded by Gerald Spicer, Ernie Thompson, Joe Carson, and Aaron Ghost, the UB9 Flag Football League (1994–1999) was the genesis of the UB9 nonprofit. This league gave countless Black men in New Castle County an opportunity to build community. Prominent teams were the Spotlights, the Gods, and T-Warren's BVDs. Some believed that the UB9 Flag Football League was responsible for Wilmington's lower rates of violence in the 1990s. In fact, Wilmington saw no more than nine homicides per year in the 1990s.[15]

UB9's NONPROFIT OPENED ceremoniously in 2000 and closed prematurely in 2002. At its height, UB9 consisted of almost 100 members and had a formal cabinet including a president, vice president, secretary, treasurer, sergeant of arms, security team, and board of directors. Most members of UB9 were formally street identified and/or involved with the criminal legal system, but were now on a mission to do local programming for youth and returning citizens. Some of UB9's noted activities were their Mother's Day celebration, Clean-Up Day, Easter Egg Hunt, bookbag giveaway, and neighborhood fish fry programs. Doc (age 34), a member of UB9, said, "United Brothers of Ninth Street . . . is trying to give back to this community. . . . On Mother's Day we made sure we went to her [a local politician's] house to give her roses to show that . . . we are in our community, giving back. . . . We even had Easter Egg Hunts. . . . We even had parties for the kids. . . .'Cause if we don't do it as a community, nobody ain't going do it."

Doc also believed that the public framing of UB9 as "gang affiliated" blocked them from receiving city support. The men's relationship with the streets was in some respects an asset, but it made leadership skeptical of their motives. Doc said, "Hopefully, they'll see that we still out here . . . grinding . . . and we [need to] get some sponsors . . . to help us out. . . . This all is being done by guys that live in the community. They working men. . . . You got lawyers, you got probation officers, you got all types . . . that's part of this United Brothers of Ninth Street. I don't want nobody to get it misconstrued and think it's some type of gang, or gang affiliated. Naw! We just brothers who care about our community on the Eastside. We want to help give back to the kids."

Doc further shared that a city councilwoman shut down a July Fourth fireworks display believed to be sponsored by street-identified persons in the Eastside. Doc claimed that she publicly announced to the neighborhood, "There's nothing but drugs [proceeds from selling drugs] . . . up there [fireworks] doing that [in the sky]." While illegal money had been used to sponsor this event, Doc still argued that ending it negatively impacted youth on the Eastside. These young people generally did not have the means to attend the city-sponsored fireworks display and did not feel welcome there. According to Doc, "We had a Fourth of July block party for at least eight years. Firework shows, everything! The city council lady who raised me . . . stopped it and said, 'We not blocking off no streets for no drug dealers.' Okay, there might be some drug dealers helping provide this stuff, but they was giving back! Them kids had a good time. Them kids was getting free food, free music, free dance . . . and you took that from them. And since you took that, July Fourth on the Eastside hadn't been the same since."

Street love as a cultural value challenged the moral centers of individuals and neighborhoods. Most agreed that it was problematic for "drug money" to be used for community programming, and in this respect, it was appropriate for city leadership to dissociate themselves from an illegal funding source. However, their assumption that drug dealers were using "blood money" for programming in communities that were rife with legally funded youth-based activities was wrong. On the contrary, there were so few legal activities for young people that many in the streets felt compelled to organize programs for youth living in extreme poverty. The motivation behind crime was generally well intentioned, and according to Rose and Clear, it was important to recognize "the connections of these young men to children, families, and others in their neighborhoods. . . . Though the gang isolates the young man from prosocial elements of community life, those connections are still seen as valuable by gang members and their families alike, partly due to the mutually supportive relations gang members have with others in their community."[16]

Remembering Derrick "Pretty Ricky" Hoey

Ms. Cecelia Hoey (age 62) was raised in the Eastside, and her shrewd activism emerged from a family lineage that stretched back to the 1930s. Cherished by local residents including the streets, and members of city leadership, Ms. Hoey was driven by love and pain, because her son Derrick Sean Hoey was shot and killed in January 2009. I wondered if Ms. Hoey's quiet demeanor was her natural disposition or a product of her son's homicide. Sometimes I cringed when I was around her, awkwardly searching for the right words. But Ms. Hoey was a nurturing and patient woman who was more concerned about making others feel comfortable.

During an early morning dispute, 41-year-old Derrick Sean Hoey was shot and killed by 25-year-old D'Andre Rogers.[17] D'Andre had accompanied a friend to his ex-girlfriend's apartment on the 200 block of West Thirty-Fifth Street. D'Andre stayed in the car while his friend knocked on her door. Derrick answered the door, and a lengthy argument ensued. Eventually, the two men began to fight. Outside, D'Andre and several neighbors listened to the commotion. Unsure what to do and feeling pressured to support his friend, D'Andre panicked, grabbed a handgun, bolted into the apartment, and shot Derrick four times. Bleeding, Derrick stumbled outside and died.

At trial, D'Andre's attorney, Ralph D. Wilkinson, argued that there was no physical evidence to prove D'Andre shot Derrick.[18] The gun was never recovered, and there was no video recording of Derrick's homicide. D'Andre had confessed when he was first interrogated, but at trial he recanted, and Wilkinson now claimed that he had previously lied to police. D'Andre's "lie" was framed by his attorney as a poor attempt to demonstrate loyalty to the street code against snitching. Wilkinson also argued that forensic evidence strongly suggested that the shooter did not intend to kill Derrick. Thus, he questioned why D'Andre faced a first-degree murder charge, which assumed premeditation. D'Andre's defense was clever, and it may have played a role in reducing his first-degree murder charge to a second-degree murder conviction, which meant he no longer faced a life sentence. On September 24, 2010, D'Andre was sentenced to forty years.

Like his mother, Derrick was beloved and regarded as a community mentor to young Black men trying to leave the streets. Derrick was also a popular member of UB9 and did much of his activism through that organization.

The Brother-to-Brother Annual Walk

In honor of Derrick's birthday and his life, Ms. Hoey launched the Brother-to-Brother Annual 5-Mile Memory Walk nine months after Derrick died. The walk was a fundraiser for the Derrick Sean "Rick" Hoey College Scholarship Fund and an invitation to honor other families struggling with gun violence. We joined the second annual walk in October 2010 at Brandywine Park, located on the banks of Brandywine Creek between Augustine Road and North Market Street. The park's 178 acres were stunningly beautiful on this warm Saturday morning, and there were many people jogging, biking, walking their dogs, or playing with children.

A dark-skinned older woman wearing black shades worked feverishly at the sign-in table. With pride, she registered participants and collected their $25 donations. The line was long, and many registered participants gathered nearby. Photo collages of the slain and their loved ones holding lit candles were displayed on about a dozen tables. At one table, images of three Black men were peppered with photos of the men's children, life partners, mothers, fathers, siblings, and friends. Several photo collages at this table were also attached to the white cloth that stretched down to the grass. One collage read, "Our Hero," and directly below were the words "Pretty Ricky" and a picture of Derrick Hoey.

At least five women surrounded by a dozen or so children and teenagers sat in a blue summer shelter. They wore airbrushed T-shirts in tribute to Derrick with the words "Missing U 4Ever." Dozens more wore airbrushed T-shirts with photos of Derrick and others lost to gun violence. On the back of one little girl's black T-shirt were the words, "Gone but Not Forgotten." Next to her was a little boy wearing a white T-shirt that read "R. I. P. Daddy." He waved at me when I walked by.

At last, Ms. Hoey grabbed the microphone and instructed everyone to assemble at the stage near the sign-in table. From the fingertips of her left hand swung a photo collage titled "Jason's Family." It gently bumped against her thigh as she spoke. A photo of her son's face was imposed on the center of her white T-shirt. Above Derrick's picture was the name, Derrick Sean Hoey, and below his picture on the far right and left sides of the T-shirt were two red, clenched boxing gloves. Across the knuckle of one glove was his birthdate, 10.08.67, and on the other was his passing date, 01.04.09; the ominous words "The Final Bout" lay between the gloves. Ms. Hoey looked exhausted but she was energized by the moment. "This has been a very challenging year for me. I am learning to find a new normal.... 'Son,' as I affectionately called him, is my only boy baby. This is a learning experience for me. The annual walk is what we do to share with you. And you help me by sharing with me. You help me to take my sadness away."

Ms. Hoey introduced her granddaughter, Derrick's 18-year-old daughter Demmi Hoey. Demmi nervously grabbed the microphone. "I'm not shy. I just don't like talking to people. But, ahm, thank all of y'all for coming," she said, and then hurriedly returned the microphone to her grandmother.

Ms. Hoey shook her head, smiled, and said, "She is shy!" and then celebrated her granddaughter's achievements as a finance major at Delaware State University. Looking at her granddaughter, Ms. Hoey also shared that Demmi had promised her father she would graduate from "Del State." Laughter and applause followed. Next, Ms. Hoey and Demmi thanked UB9 for their financial contribution and overall love for Derrick. "Because of your support, we are blessed to officially open the Derrick Sean 'Rick' Hoey Survivors College Scholarship Fund! It's officially open!" Looking into the audience, Ms. Hoey firmly said, "Your children ... are the recipients of this college scholarship fund. So, *Pledge! Pledge! Pledge!* Thank you!"

T-Warren and Pharrell approached the microphone, greeted everyone, and on behalf of UB9 presented Ms. Hoey with an oversized cardboard check for $1,389.00. "Son may have been an only boy baby, but he was blessed to have a lot of brothers and sisters to share in all of his love. And UB9, the United Brothers of Ninth Street, were the first to make the pledge to kick off our second annual Brother-to-Brother 5-Mile Walk."

"This is a donation from UB9," T-Warren remarked. "We started about a year and a half ago, and this is the funds we have left over. Our group actually put up this money.... Everybody worked together.... We had parties. We did things for the community.... We cleaned up the neighborhood. We gave flowers to mothers on Mother's Day. We did a lot of things for the community. And this is what we have left over. We are presenting it to Ms. Hoey for the scholarship fund. And this is what it is all about, giving back for Mr. Derrick 'Rick' Hoey."

U'Gundi Jacobs and Gerald Spicer spoke next. Gerald's black doo rag, tightly wrapped around his head, and bright red UB9 T-shirt commanded our attention. "It's kind of hard for everybody," said Gerald. Many of the homicides highlighted at this event gave him pause. "There are some pictures of people at the table that I didn't even know wasn't here anymore. . . . It's kind of touching, and my heart goes out to the families."

Derrick's best friend U'Gundi advised us, "It's a terrible situation, but I truly thank everyone for coming out. . . . Stay strong." His bald head, thick goatee, and stout figure was a conspicuous billboard for his white Derrick Sean Hoey T-shirt. He promised "Brother Rick" that *"We still here!* We still think about you every day. *You got a lot of love!* And I want to thank everyone for coming out and supporting the scholarship fund. Thank you!"

"It's this kind of love that keeps us standing here," said Ms. Hoey. "We will continue to host this memory walk year after year, even when I am tired." Then pointing to UB9 members and several women, Ms. Hoey trumpeted, "My sons in back of me and my daughters in front of me will continue with this memory walk because we built a scholarship for him [Derrick] to share with your children. This is also your memory walk, too!"

Ms. Hoey found purpose and some peace with a loss she will never recover from. But even more astonishing was her capacity, in the midst of unbearable pain, to stoke up joy and resilience in so many others. After unraveling herself from a web of hugs, Ms. Hoey reminded us of our obligation to end violence in Wilmington. "Violence is very much alive in our neighborhood. . . . I am standing for violence prevention along with the HOPE Commission and the Wilmington Street PAR group from the University of Delaware. We are praying and asking our churches to join with us to stand and pray for our families that are healing. It is not just an effort just for us wounded families, but it is an effort for our entire community to embrace."

THE WALK. The park was beautiful and the walk was meditative. With each step, I thought more deeply about who Derrick was and the factors that led to his homicide.

"Did you know Derrick?" I asked Ms. Raye.

"Yes. And I know his mother, his aunts and uncles. His grandfather and my father were best friends."

"Wow! Really?"

"When we first moved to Delaware from Philadelphia, we moved to the Eastside of Wilmington. My family became friends with the Hoeys and the Hutts. And they still live in the Eastside. They've been living there for well over seventy years."

"What kind of impact do you think Derrick's death had on Wilmington?"

"It had a devastating impact. He was a leader. He was respected. He was a mentor. It was devastating."

"Can I ask a hard question, Ms. Raye?"

"Sure."

"Was Ms. Hoey like this from the very beginning? Did the death of her son precipitate her positive involvement in the community?"

"No, his death did not precipitate her involvement in the community. She was always very involved. I am sure even in her wildest dreams, she couldn't imagine that her son would become a victim of violence. She was always very loving and caring. She has always embraced everybody."

About thirty minutes in, we strolled over a bridge that stood about twenty-five feet over the park. Underneath was a large garden with several rows of tall pink, white, and red roses. Not far from the garden, water poured out of stone sculptures of lions and angels. The mood and energy of the park was profoundly serene, and its stunning beauty was undeniable. I couldn't help but wonder what poor Black people thought about the existence of a magnificently beautiful park that was only a stone's throw away from where they dwelled.

About forty feet from the finish line, Derrick's good friend and UB9 member Clarence (aka Sonny Bono) ran up to Ms. Raye and me after lapping us for a second or maybe a third time. Sonny was a licensed gym trainer and had led stretching activities before the walk. Huffing and puffing, he said, "This walk is for my baaaby, Ricky Ross! Pretty Ricky! We looking for y'all to come back next year."

After passing the finish line, Ms. Raye and I hugged. Her guidance and lessons on Black Wilmington were invaluable. We then turned to three tables filled with bottled water, bananas, and other snacks.

Sonny and his friend Jermaine returned and spoke with me about how homicide had impacted them. I hadn't realized how much pain they were still in, or that they were also recovering from more than just Derrick's homicide. Sonny said, "Some [don't] have the opportunity to come out and speak their minds about someone that got shot from street violence. For instance, my daughter's mom got killed in 1994 in the Jamaican Inn." Sonny paused and then changed the direction of his statement: "It ain't about me. It's about Ms. Hoey and all the other victims. Like my buddy right here [Jermaine], who lost his son."

Clumsily, I asked Jermaine about his son's homicide. Unable to respond to that question, he instead highlighted that this annual walk had motivated so many to organize against gun violence. "It still shows that it is some hope out there. Not everybody giving up. It's easy to say, 'f-ck it!' This walk today shows we still got some hope and some togetherness."

Sonny added to Jermaine's message on resilience and collective efficacy: "Everybody out here can identify with someone out here, and that makes this family a much tighter family. . . . Everybody out here speaking with one another, 'Guess what, I lost my daughter's mother, he lost a son.' . . . We all can identify with the love of somebody we lost." Then, in unison, the two affirmed, "And we just trying to share this day together!"

What Street Love Teaches Us

Street love was the way street-identified Black men and women in Wilmington ensured personal, group, and communal levels of resilience. Although nonprofits modified and co-opted the street's tradition of local barbecues, turkey and bookbag giveaways, and even conflict resolution, community professionals did not have the same level of impact, and their activities generally drew only older residents. The activities the streets organized were guided by their neighborhood's interests and cultural values, which may explain why their programs were typically more successful.

Street love also taught us that street-identified Black men and women were governed by complicated conceptualizations of morality, at least from the traditional perspective of academic scholarship. We found many examples of street-identified Black men and women who were sincerely committed to giving back and ending violence. The literature, however, is filled with negative characterizations and outcomes—so much so that it ignores any analysis of positive dimensions for street-identified Black populations. The literature erects binaries of moral or criminal, street or decent, good or bad, to otherize poor Black populations. Our Street PAR project challenges this dichotomy of people who do not commit crimes being moral versus people who do commit crimes being immoral. If we are truly interested in helping, we must be more thoughtful and willing to incorporate this complex notion of street love into community-level interventions. Much could be learned about how to reach the streets by examining the positive dimensions of their families and exploring their systems of bonding with each other and local communities.

CHAPTER 9

"Winter Is Coming!"

WHITE WALKERS, REVOLUTIONARY CHANGE, AND THE STREETS CALL FOR STRUCTURAL TRANSFORMATION

To be a Negro in this country and to be relatively conscious is to be in a rage almost all the time.
—James Baldwin, "The Negro in American Culture"

Why would these kids want to be leaders? When I go to elementary schools and I ask kids, "Historically, when you are a Black man and you stand up, what happens to you?" . . . Guess what they say? "You die!" You don't think these kids know that shit? Stand up and be Black and successful at the same time? . . . Why would you want to be a King, when you see what happens to Kings? . . . We may hate white supremacy [but] there are a lot of people that benefit . . . off of America being exactly the way that it is. I don't think our leaders will come from somebody who's famous or rich, because they made their money *with it being exactly the way it is right now!*
—David Banner, "David Banner on White Supremacy, Illuminati, the God Box"

COLEY HARRIS was a 44-year-old husband and father, education administrator, street outreach worker who engaged with the "shooters," respected "OG," and a former inmate convicted of manslaughter. He was also close friends with Wolf, and after a fourteen-year stint he returned to Wilmington from James T. Vaughn Correctional Center in Smyrna in 2008. Coley had a serious but calm demeanor, with a sharp focus and level of discipline that distinguished him from others. As accomplished as he was in the streets, he was also an author, poet, actor, and podcast host. Coley could truly light up a stage, and thousands came to see him perform. Wolf insisted and I agreed that we needed him to be a part of our team.

About once a month, we got together for a "cup of joe" on Saturday mornings. With tear-filled eyes, he lamented the pain he felt when observing the poor conditions of some youth he worked with: the hunger, unclean clothing, and the gun violence they had to navigate.

"You know, 'Winter is coming,' Yas. The White Walkers are coming. You know who the White Walkers are, right?"

Coley was an avid fan of the HBO series *Game of Thrones*. "Winter is coming" and "White Walkers" were instrumental references in this cable series' story line.

"I do, but tell me what you think about the White Walkers."

"The White Walkers are the streets and all of the warring factions in *Game of Thrones* are only unified by one thing.... They're only united to destroy the White Walkers. But the White Walkers are coming to hold them and their death-dealing ways accountable."

THE SOCIOPOLITICAL WINDS started shifting to a more structural conversation in Wilmington. Structural violence as a core concept took root and sparked a series of discussions inside neighborhoods. At least in some areas of the city, organizing became more radical, and aggressive civil disobedience increased in the face of structural violence. For most in the Eastside and Southbridge, the tipping point for this forceful community mobilization was the police-involved shooting of Jeremy McDole in 2015.

A FEW DAYS LATER, Coley texted me a Facebook link to a video trailer of him and his son Ahmar's play, *Out of the Ashes*. Their autobiographical, two-person play was about the negative impact incarceration had on Black fathers and their children. Audiences cheered, laughed, and cried across the state of Delaware, and then across the country. The question-and-answer period was equally as powerful as the ninety-minute play, and sometimes lasted as long.

Shortly after I viewed the trailer, Coley texted me another link to a two-minute video clip from HBO's *Game of Thrones*. This short clip was a scene from season 6, episode 5, "The Door." Highlighted in the scene was the explanation of what Coley described over coffee about the meaning of "Winter is coming" and "White Walkers." He followed up with another text: "The Children of the Forest created the White Walkers to protect the earth from the destruction of men. Then the nobility and the free folk banded together to destroy the White Walkers!"

Bran Stark was the lead character in this scene, and after years of searching, he had finally discovered the conditions that created the White Walkers. Bran was a gifted empath, able to tap into the past and future. In "The Door," Bran slipped into a trance and learned that the Children of the Forest kidnapped a member of the "First Men" (humans) with the intention of turning him into the first White Walker. The Children of the Forest were an ancient population on Earth with vast powers that existed long before humans evolved. Troll-like, they were small in stature and almost looked like children, hence their name. The Children greatly feared the First Men's insatiable thirst for war and their need to colonize.[1] The Children ignored the evil ways of the First Men until they no longer could. They tried to win the war by turning the First Men into White Walkers.

White Walkers were the out-caste in the *Game of Thrones*. Physically disfigured, their butchered bodies with dangling flesh were an ominous sight for adversaries. With their ear-splitting howls, the White Walkers were an angry, vile, and especially violent bunch. In their ragged clothing, they rabidly swarmed their prey. If they did not devour you, their contagion transformed what was left of your body into a White Walker. As undesirables, they roamed the outskirts of the seven kingdoms and were restricted to a barren wasteland.[2]

Until Bran's dream, very few knew how the White Walkers were created and why they were so enraged. Most forgot this history, but the White Walkers did not, and they wanted revenge.

Bran's dream also showed a Child of the Forest in a religious ceremony, slowly pushing a knife made of "dragonglass" into the chest of the first human. Out of this ritual came the "Night King," the indomitable leader of the White Walkers.

BRAN STARK: You made the White Walkers.
CHILDREN OF THE FOREST: We were at war. We were being slaughtered. Our sacred trees cut down. We needed to defend ourselves.
BRAN STARK: From whom?
CHILDREN OF THE FOREST: From you. From men.

For Coley, this scene was an excellent allegory or metaphor to understand the experiences and worldviews of street-identified Black men and women in Wilmington. Spoiled by the world's riches, the First Men's lustful greed and increasing menace caused them to fall from grace and be turned into White Walkers. As White Walkers, street-identified Black-Americans are considered a banished people who swelled in numbers but learned to control their anger until they could exact retribution. Fighting the White Walkers was the only interest that united the seven kingdoms (or civilized world).

The *Game of Thrones* story line was a useful way for Coley to think about Wilmington's structural arrangement, particularly how institutions and structural systems negatively impacted its poor Black residents. Privileged communities in Wilmington were representative of the royal families clinging to power in *Game of Thrones*. Wilmington's ruling elite, like the royal families in this series, directly benefited from the structural genocide of communities like the Eastside and Southbridge. More ominously, Coley also saw the royal families' fears of the White Walkers as similar to the deep concerns that Wilmington's ruling elite had about Black men and women in the streets. According to Coley, they were afraid that the streets and other poor Black people would learn why their communities had been made poor—that their community's perpetual destabilization "was the plan," that it was intentional and even necessary for Wilmington's economy to function. The streets of Wilmington had not yet reached the unity exhibited by the White Walkers, but Coley believed that the establishment feared they would, and greatly feared the idea of and the emergence of Black revolutionary activism.

After a long stint in prison, Coley had rebounded and excelled in Delaware. Few with a story like his were able to transition back into society to the degree that he did. The former shooter was now a family man, working professional, public speaker and respected grassroots leader, media darling, artist extraordinaire, and on-the-ground general who used his social capital to stop street rivals from slaughtering each other. Coley was a superstar of sorts in Delaware and especially a giant in Wilmington. But from my perspective, he was so immersed in the community that he couldn't fully appreciate the impact he made. He couldn't see that he was the "Night King," or supreme leader of the White Walkers. Coley, at least for now, was too close to the pain to truly see how magnificent he was.

AFTER POLICE MURDERED MCDOLE in 2015, grassroots activism radiated in Black Wilmington. Discussions of gun violence and inequality were finally a main part of the public discourse. Residents across race and class were frustrated, and city leadership was under pressure to produce the change it always promised yet never delivered.

Mayor Baker's third and final term ended in December 2012, but the city still struggled with homicide and structural violence. Mayor Williams's administration was embattled with conflict from the start, and it was not able to slow the rising rates of gun violence. A one-term mayor, Williams lost the election in November 2016 to Michael Purzycki. Williams's loss incidentally marked the end of a twenty-four-year run of Black male mayors in Wilmington.

Wilmington's 2016 mayoral race was a bruising political contest. Eight candidates clamored for control of this small city. Purzycki went below the belt with then-candidate Eugene Young. It did not go unnoticed that Young, a tall, ambitious, clean-cut, dark-skinned man from the Eastside was treated with condescension by a 72-year-old white man. Although Young lost the race, his run signaled a new progressive start for Wilmington. After serving as an aide to Senator Cory Booker from 2013 to 2015, Young returned to Wilmington in late 2015 and entered the race with an activist platform. Just before the election, Booker came to Wilmington to support Young's campaign. But the kind of change that Young advocated for made traditional leadership nervous. His progressive platform took on prison re-entry, gun violence, educational inequality, and joblessness, and Young also sought to organize a set of neighborhood-based voting blocks to identify a fresh new group of voters and political talent for city and state positions.

Corporate Wilmington would not allow this, and the levers were pulled to ensure a Purzycki victory. Purzycki won with less than a quarter of the total votes, and Young lost by only 234 votes.[3]

Reproaches and Recommendations from the Streets

Many in the Eastside and Southbridge held political leadership responsible for the gun violence, or they held them accountable for the structural devastation that had destroyed their families and ultimately caused the violence. Feeling betrayed and abandoned, they had long determined that serious help was never coming. While officials never actually delivered justice to poor Black Wilmington, they never stopped promising change in new campaigns. In this way, they were similar to scholars studying poor Black people. It didn't matter if research produced substantive change, but with every paper and conference presentation, with every new study, we researchers still claimed we did.[4]

The streets knew they were being exploited by just about every professional they came in contact with. They wisely concluded that it was their lack of power and resources that best explained the poverty, substandard education, punitive policing, overincarceration, and gun violence.

Lambasting Black politicians like President Obama, a very frustrated Byron (age 18) mostly held Black politicians accountable for the isolation and structural failings of Southbridge. "There's nowhere for me to go! Now I'm boxed in. Look at Southbridge, it's kind of like a box . . . with like one little doorway out. Now when you close that, what do you want me to do? Now there's a bunch of n—as out here hungry. . . . These n—as is hungry! *There's kids out there right now, hungry!* . . . Obama talk about 'change.' . . . I was a young guy, silly on his high horse riding with Obama. Obama talk about change, but I ain't seen nothing, to keep it one hundred [i.e., to be honest]. The white man still running the country, whether a Black man in office or not."

The streets of Wilmington were tired and very angry. They had lost hope—not in themselves, but they had given up on city officials who willingly embraced strategies of incrementalism. Street PAR sought to fill this sociopolitical gap and give them a platform to control their message about gun violence and inequality. The streets demanded that community professionals work alongside them; real change required a grassroots presence that connected deeply with the hard circumstances of people's lives.

Tyree (age 18), a close friend of Byron, also blamed politicians for Southbridge's structural standing. He also didn't have any faith that leadership would create safer environments for his son or other Black children. Much of Tyree's life was wracked by family and friends dying from homicide, and he could not imagine how his son's life would be different. According to Tyree, constant exposure to murder also predisposed him to use violence as a strategy to protect and provide for his child.

> When the murder rate rise . . . blame it on the politicians! Don't blame it on us, 'cause we still got to survive. When you [politicians] go home to your Hockessin [nearby wealthy white city] [and] sit back and look at your stars, [that's] what I want to do with my son. I can't take my son outside and lay back and look at the stars . . . I got to look at my son like, "[How am I] going get you some Pampers? Because I know you going to run out." But when I see that n—a ride down, slumped down in his car, and I turn and look at my son, or I look at my niece . . . and I know they need something. What do you think I am going to do?

Violence was so common that Tyree and his friends believed they would be killed before their early twenties. Tyree even admitted they sometimes used "wocky tock" (PCP) to cope with this possibility. Given how prevalent street violence was in Wilmington, Tyree implored politicians to "come to the hood" to walk side by side with residents in the most violent areas of their communities. For Tyree, a ground-level view of poverty and violence would make it difficult for leadership to ignore their tough conditions:

> For n—as in my age group . . . [living until age 20 is] a long time. My peoples was bodied [my close friend was killed] at 17. My [other] peoples was bodied at 18. They didn't get to see they life. . . . I grew up with my n—a [another friend], [and] he bodied right now. There's so many n—as in our age group that's down [killed]. So for us to still be here . . . that's good money. . . . So, I don't know how much change can really come. . . . Politicians talk about wanting change, then why you sitting in the capitol building, doing nothing? You ain't in the hood! You ain't gonna get change in the capitol building. Y'all n—as [politicians] need to come to the hood.

An older young man, Anthony G. (age 26) echoed the same concerns that the younger Tyree (age 18) and Byron (age 18) had. For Anthony, leadership made things too complicated and often developed policy that socially reproduced the inequality.[5] Anthony strongly urged professionals to apply an aggressive hands-on approach that required some level of immersion in the conditions of the Eastside and Southbridge. Soaking themselves in the poverty, food insecurity, and poor housing of these neighborhoods was believed to be a shocking enough experience to compel policymakers to meet the basic needs of poor Black people and especially the concerns of the streets. For Anthony, as well as Byron and Tyree, politicians' refusal to walk side by side with them meant they were not actually interested in change. Anthony said, "Come inside . . . the community and try to reach out and see what's going on with my community, on my side of town. . . . Whether it's housing, food, heat, electric, or whatever. Find out what's going on. . . . As long as I know what's going on, I'm going fix that problem. . . . I think the community need more. . . . Look how many abandoned houses or whatever that's going on around here? There's some single women that need homes for their kids, instead of having them over in the Mission [homeless shelter]."

Black women's narratives about change generally mirrored the men's messages about justice, and most did not believe leadership actually cared, at least not as much as they claimed. What needed to be done was obvious, and for these women, real change began with addressing widespread poverty and unemployment. The women also called for leadership to walk inside their neighborhoods to better understand the kind of help needed to improve their circumstances. Frustrated at leadership and scared for her son's life, Aneshia (age 29) insisted:

> If you get out and you reach out to the community, if everybody reach out, then we won't continue to lose each other. Because right now we are dying. . . . If we all pull together, and we all stand on one accord, then we can move mountains. . . . Where are the people that we voted in? The congressmen, the governor, all of those people, where are they? They keep hollering about these funds. . . . You wonder why the crime rate is so high in young people. . . . If the parents had more help. . . . I have a teenager. . . . I am scared. . . . I don't want to lose him to Delaware. I truly don't.

Black women were much more likely to work with local politicians, other professionals, and even police. Brandy, for instance, challenged her neighborhood coalition in Southbridge to redirect tax funds to benefit families in public housing, not just those with residential or private homes. Brandy recognized the privilege she had over Black men to speak more freely, and she asserted it in this meeting. She also called for the streets and Black Wilmington to storm city council meetings to demand jobs and other opportunities:

> They [the neighborhood coalition] got mad at me because I spoke up for the people who wasn't there. . . . I said to them, "You can't do that to the people in Southbridge. You can't just marginalize the people that don't own homes. . . . Give the money to everybody, do something for everybody. Why don't y'all fix the basketball court up?" They got mad at me . . . but now . . . they respect me. . . . Once you stand up . . . you become empowered. . . . If y'all were to go into city council meetings and say something about the jobs, about your child not getting a job, do you know what that will do?

Brandy understood the advantage poor Black Wilmington and especially the streets had over local politicians. Their capacity to more quickly organize larger numbers of people threatened the traditional balance of power. Being repeatedly disruptive at city council meetings was also a formidable weapon to fight power. In a small city and state, it took just one or two dozen people to shut a meeting down, or a similar number of emails or complaining phone calls to meet with any politician. And of course, only a few hundred votes decided most elections in Wilmington and the state.[6]

To better understand gang violence, Vargas called on ethnographers to examine the "political ecometrics" of local communities, or the "measures of political spaces within neighborhoods that includes who is governing the neighborhood and how."[7] According to Vargas, gang violence thrived in neighborhoods that were destabilized by local politicians. In his study, for instance, the east side of Little Village in Chicago did not have the same political strength as the west side; thus, the east side had higher rates of gun violence.

Many in the Eastside and Southbridge felt similarly about Wilmington's political leadership. City council, the mayor's office, state representatives, and especially professionals in the legal system were ultimately held responsible for the city's rates of gun violence.

Street Uprisings: Civil Disobedience as a Site of Resilience

Frantz Fanon believed that violence was a site of resilience, or a rational means for "colonized peoples" to achieve justice.[8] Fanon also was not surprised that oppressed groups sometimes caused each other harm. To better understand violence against and between members of disadvantaged groups, Fanon argued that all violence—both interpersonal and violent resistance—should be contextualized within a framing of Western imperialism. Fanon's arguments about Black self-hatred, capitalism, false consciousness, cognitive dissonance, and community mobilizing have largely been rebuked by mainstream scholarship but embraced by grassroots leaders, critical race scholars, and more radical PAR scholars.[9]

Fanon called for a deeper awareness of the practical motivations of violent revolt. Most fought the state because it was adaptive to do so, and many felt that their lives literally depended on it: "When we revolt, it's not for a particular culture. We revolt simply because, for many reasons, we can no longer breathe."[10] Fanon further argued that the loss of cultural dignity also played a major role in why oppressed people revolted. For Fanon, violent resistance was "cathartic," or a "cleansing force" that "restored . . . self-respect" or a cultural integrity erased by state oppression.[11]

Rios draws on Fanon's argument to contextualize experiences with violence among street-identified Black and Latino male youth in Oakland, California.[12] Like Fanon, Rios concluded that he observed two distinct expressions of violence: street violence and violent resistance against authorities. Rios refers to violent resistance as "crimes of resistance" and street-identified youth embodying a "resistant identity," particularly when they clashed with police. Rios added that a severe lack of resources and low community standing (i.e., being disrespected) were the driving factors for both street violence and violent resistance.

In Wilmington, the streets knew their families and neighborhoods were being targeted by the structural violence complex, and the deep inequality seeded an environment where gun violence flourished. Every successive generation experienced more poverty, limited public housing, inadequate schooling, and mass incarceration. Unable to sit passively and experience the abusive structural conditions and neighborhood violence, some aggressively responded to public officials. The obvious complicity of officials effectively confirmed for them Galtung's argument about "cultural violence," or the hateful indifference leadership and the wider community had for poor Black people in Wilmington.[13] Angry that their trauma was trivialized and ignored, the streets were now desperate for change, and from their standpoint they had no other choice but to fight back.

After the police-involved shooting of Jeremy McDole in 2015, the streets became radicalized. McDole's family was so angry that they and many others started disrupting public programs, embarrassing leadership and cursing out officials. In a 2016 mayoral debate at Ezion Fair Baptist Church in Southbridge, McDole's sister pounced with a well-timed outburst that humiliated Mayor Williams.

Wilmington was a microcosm of what raged nationwide, particularly after the high-profile murders of Michael Brown in Ferguson (2014), Eric Garner in New York (2014), Laquan McDonald in Chicago (2014), Freddie Gray in Baltimore (2015), and Walter Scott in Charlotte (2015). Other cities where street-identified Black men and women raged in response to police violence included Dallas, Baton Rouge, Los Angeles, and Milwaukee.[14] Many lashed out by taunting police, burning their vehicles, and looting and destroying businesses. Cops were also assaulted, shot, and in a few instances, even killed.[15]

Moreover, a slow-sweeping set of prison uprisings erupted between 2010 and 2020, but the 2016 iteration was the most impactful in this ten-year-period.[16] September 9, 2016, was the forty-fifth anniversary of the 1971 Attica Prison uprising. On this date, upwards of fifty prisons embarked on a nationwide strike. About 200,000 prisoners across "24 states and 40 to 50 prisons pledged to join the national strike."[17] The men at Washington State Penitentiary, Ohio State Penitentiary, William C. Holman Correctional Facility in Alabama, and the Louisiana State Penitentiary at Angola led the strike. They boycotted work and other responsibilities, went on hunger strikes, rioted and started fires, seized sections of the facility, and in some cases assaulted, kidnapped, and killed staff.

Delaware's James T. Vaughn Correctional Center, or "Smyrna," as it's commonly called, joined the nationwide uprising on February 1, 2017. According to a lawsuit brought by Stephen Hampton, prior to and following the uprising at Smyrna, "[inmates] were beaten, tortured and abused—sometimes sexually—by correctional officers and other law enforcement."[18] Governor John Carney, wardens, correctional officers, and other prison officials were named in the lawsuit or held responsible for the conditions that led to the uprising. Inmates claimed they were denied medical care, food, and clean bedding, and that they were subjected to unnecessary anal probes and other dehumanizing practices. They also complained their cells were randomly searched and their property destroyed by guards.

During the eighteen-hour standoff at J. T. Vaughn, three correctional officers were badly beaten and taken hostage. One of the three guards, Lieutenant Steven Floyd, was killed. Floyd, a Black male, was kidnapped by masked men, handcuffed, repeatedly bludgeoned, stabbed, and later slammed into a utility closet, where the 47-year-old bled out.[19] Inmates also seized control over communications and demanded to speak with Gov. Carney. The inmates' demands included improved health care, educational opportunities, programming, and fair treatment by guards and other prison staff.[20]

Eighteen were charged, including sixteen charged with conspiracy, assault, rioting, kidnapping, and murder.[21] But according to Attorney General Denn, trying to convict all eighteen would have been "futile."[22] In the end, only three were convicted. Dwayne Staats—the same person who had killed Ms. Jackie's son, Hakeem, in 2004 (see chapter 7) received two life sentences for murder and an additional 153 years for assault, kidnapping, and rioting. Staats's co-defendant Jarreau Ayers received 123 years for assault, kidnapping, and rioting. For cooperating against Staats and Ayers, Royal Downs received just three years.

Revolt in 2020: COVID-19, George Floyd, and More Homicide

In 2020, the COVID-19 pandemic and its restrictions induced a social crisis in poor Black communities. Structural violence, and homicide in particular, spiked during this period, further destabilizing Black communities. Arguably, these precarious conditions forced more people to the streets to offset unemployment or impending eviction notices. Greater numbers of disaffected young people with greater access to guns and fewer senior leaders to curb violent behavior only aggravated gun violence. At the end of 2020, homicides rates had jumped by 25% over the previous year nationally, and in Wilmington, shootings were up by 52% and homicides by 35%.[23] And by the end of 2021, Wilmington broke another homicide record with thirty-nine homicides (55 homicides per 100,000).[24]

By March 2020, roughly 60 million had filed for unemployment, and by June there was 25% "real unemployment."[25] Of those who found work, most secured temporary, low-skilled or low-wage employment.[26] But this wasn't enough, and massive unemployment, food lines stretching three to five miles, rent strikes, and gun violence converged nationwide by late April.[27]

And then in May 2020, the whip cracked when police killed George Floyd in Minneapolis. Mass protests rippled across the country and then abroad as Floyd's death was the proverbial North Star for the summer of protest that unfolded.[28] Floyd's death lit the fuse, but the nation was also deeply affected by the murders of Ahmaud Arbery in February and Breonna Taylor in March and the release of details in July about the murder of Elijah McClain.[29] Images of Arbery's collapsing body, the bullets that ripped through Taylor's apartment, and the last words of McClain were overwhelming. But Floyd's death was the national tipping point.

For using a $20 counterfeit bill, four police handcuffed and shoved Floyd into the back of their vehicle, from which he either escaped or was forcibly removed. Police then restrained him on the pavement. Two officers held down his legs and back while officer Derek Chauvin kneeled on Floyd's neck for nine minutes and twenty-nine seconds. The fourth officer stood near Chauvin and just watched as Floyd mumbled thirteen times, "I can't breathe," before he died.

> I didn't do nothing serious, man. Please! Please! Please, I can't breathe! . . . Somebody, please, man! *I can't breathe! I can't breathe! . . . I can't breathe!* Please, a knee on my neck, *I can't breathe!* Shit, I will, I can't move! *Mama, mama, I can't.* My knee, my neck. I'm through. . . . I'm claustrophobic. My stomach hurt. My neck hurts. Everything hurts. Some water or something. Please, please. *I can't breathe officer! Don't kill me! They're going to kill me. . . . They're going to kill me. . . .* Sir, please. Please. . . . *I can't breathe!*

Following Floyd's murder, civil unrest erupted in roughly 350 cities, with looting, arson, assault, and even the shooting and murder of civilians—by civilians.[30] According to the Armed Conflict Location and Event Data Project (ACLED): "Between 24 May and 22 August . . . there were more than 10,600 demonstration events across the country. Over 10,100 of these—or nearly 95%—involve peaceful protesters. Fewer than 570—or approximately 5%—involve demonstrators engaging in violence. Well over 80% of all demonstrations are connected to the Black Lives Matter movement or the COVID-19 pandemic."[31]

Thousands of protesters destroyed the CNN building in Atlanta and broke into and looted Macy's in downtown Manhattan and luxury stores in Beverly Hills and Santa Monica. Police departments in Seattle, Portland, and Minneapolis were torched. The uprisings of 2020 were unlike those in the 1960s and 1970s, which erupted mostly in or near poor Black communities. In 2020, protesters targeted white-owned businesses and residential communities, including the homes of politicians and police officers. Whites were harassed in high-end restaurants, taunted while walking, threatened while stopped at red lights, and assaulted for perceived racial indiscretions. Police were pelted with rocks, bottles, and water balloons, and their cars were firebombed. Some officers were beaten, assaulted by mobs, hit by cars, or killed. By August, there had been a 30% upsurge in 2020 in killings of on-duty officers.[32] In September, two officers in Los Angeles were shot in a parked car, presumably in retaliation for killing 29-year-old Dijon Kizzee.[33]

Unfortunately, Wilmington was no different. On May 30, 2020, protesters destroyed Downtown Eastside, Wilmington's business center.[34] By 11:00 A.M. the crowd had grown to 1,000 in Rodney Square, and by 3:00 P.M. they had dissipated and a few hundred headed to I-95 to "shut it down!" I-95 is a major highway system in the Northeast, so stopping traffic in both directions sent a sharp message to city and state leadership. Dozens of state police in riot gear and armed with "long guns" descended. But protesters did not disperse, and their anger swelled. This face-off subsided only when police withdrew their guns. But protesters returned to Wilmington's police headquarters to continue demonstrating. Mayor Purzycki and Chief Tracy tried to address the concerns of a growing crowd. Among the crowd's chief demands was the termination of any officer that supported the murder of George Floyd. And the mayor and chief promptly acknowledged they would terminate any officer that did so.

But by 7:00 P.M., Downtown Eastside was ground zero for an uprising that brought Delaware to its knees. Protesters smashed windows and looted mostly white-owned businesses. Broken shards of glass and debris peppered the pavement. A large trash dumpster blazed as young people surrounded the fire with their fists held aloft in the Black Power salute. The windshields of police SUVs and other cars were smashed in with bricks, bottles, and rocks. At least one news reporter was attacked, "punched in the left eye."[35] La Fia, Bardea, Merchant Bar, and Solid Gold Jewelers were all broken into. According to Hughes et al., "protesters took aim at the long-simmering inequality in Wilmington represented by the recently revitalized Market Street. As they surveyed the damage at Bardea, one of the first to be vandalized, some recalled the beloved—and cheaper—fried chicken eatery it had replaced."[36]

Around 9:00 P.M., Wolf, Derrick, and I jumped on a conference call. Wolf, Derrick, and other Associates were on the ground in various parts of the city, as they felt compelled to protect law-abiding protesters. Wherever they were located, it certainly sounded chaotic. Over the phone, I heard people screaming, rummaging around, and breaking glass.

"Yas, it's crazy out here," Wolf said. "The people ain't standing for it no more. Shit's crazy, but we good, and we ain't going to let nothing happen to these people."

Wolf cut away and yelled, "Ay! Ay! Be safe out here, now! Watch yourself! You run down the street over there and you're going to run right into a bunch of police, with a bunch of guns. Use your head, now."

Then Wolf asked, "Der Der [Derrick], what's going on your side?"

"You know, we got them [we're supporting protesters] over here. We good. It's going down, but we ain't letting nobody touch these people. We ain't going to let that happen. . . . The police are standing down, though."

At 10:00 P.M., an armored police vehicle slowly traveled down Market announcing the protest was over and everyone should leave Market Street or risk arrest for "unlawful assembly."[37] But the uprising continued.

Activism after the Uprising

After Wilmington's last uprising, our team went right to work. We attended and spoke at rallies, participated in and organized marches, increased outreach efforts, checked on families, and utilized media to voice the people's deepest concerns.

Dubard (Associate) was director of the Smart Justice Campaign for the ACLU-DE, and his popular program trained residents to reform criminal legal policy. One morning, Dubard called me for support with an emergency meeting with city and state leadership.

"Yas, I need y'all. I really need the PAR family to come down and support me."

Sounding exasperated, Dubard pleaded for help. Skeptical of the intentions of leadership, he said, "We got this march that's about to happen and they don't want us to do it. They don't! They trying to stop us, Yas."

"They trying to stop the march? Are you sure? A day after Downtown blew up, they went on record that they're going to work with the people."

"Yas, trust me. That's just what they're saying. They not really trying to help nobody out here. . . . Come on, Yas. They just saying that. I feel like I'm like losing my mind. . . . The National Guards came to Coby's house last night to get him to stop the march, because the permit is under his name. . . . I would do it myself, but it's just too crazy for me right now. Please tell everyone to meet me in front of the state building [in Wilmington]."[38]

I sent out a group text, and ten of us joined about twenty other grassroots leaders to meet with the governor and his cabinet secretaries, Mayor Purzykci, Attorney General Kathleen Jennings, and other officials. Surrounded by members of the Black bourgeoise, the governor and mayor—two older white men—sat at each end of a long conference table. Their goal was to stop the upcoming march, and the meeting was also questionably about whether they would employ a militarized response against protesters.

Mayor Purzycki assured everyone that he was working hard against racial injustice. To demonstrate his support to poor Black Wilmington, he even committed the city's unused office space to be utilized for economic development to address the widespread poverty and unemployment in Black Wilmington: "We got 2 million square feet of unused office space. . . . That's 2 million square feet where there are no jobs, there's no economic engine, there's nothing going on."

Other leadership jumped in: "Yes, we have to find a different way than a march. There are enough opportunities to find a better way . . ." He was cut off midsentence by shouts from the crowd.

"Don't let them sweet talk you and steal your freedom, now!"

"Now is the time to stand tall!"

"Don't be scared, now! *Hold the line!*"

A grassroots leader said, "The march isn't going to stop. The march will be peaceful, but it's not going to stop."

"This march is bigger than anyone in the room. . . . It's going to happen. . . . There is nobody in the room that's big enough to stop the march at this point."

Grasping to find something appealing to his audience, Mayor Purzycki then promised police body cameras. Local activist Dion Wilson believed his proposal sounded like "bargaining chips" that were contingent on stopping the march. In response to this concern, the mayor pledged, "I'm not holding up anybody for this. . . . I'm here to give you that commitment, no strings attached."

There was also a request for officials to be on the "front line" at the march. Attorney General Jennings agreed, but the mayor and the governor hesitated. In response to their reluctance, one gentleman said, "No one would loot while standing next to the governor, mayor, attorney general, and our chair of the Delaware Black Caucus."

Not willing to take all the heat, Mayor Purzcyki responded, "As I said, we have these outside guys who come in here and they seem to hijack these things. . . . I don't want to be there as I was the other day in two different episodes where the anger just got focused on me, because I'm the symbol of everything that people are angry about. . . . But if it's part of an expression of contempt for what goes on to Black Americans, I'll be there, I'll be happy to be there."

County councilman Jea Street questioned the mayor's commitment to police body cameras. Street said the state was "basically run by former police officers, and they got a lock on it. . . . State law still has to be changed to make cameras possible. We got to take the fight to Legislative Hall." Street was also very concerned about the safety of protesters. He reminded us of the backlash that resulted from Wilmington's 1968 uprising. "All hell broke loose. . . . There was one city [Wilmington] in the country where the National Guard was on the streets for more than a year. And the fact of the matter is, the city never recovered from that. . . . You're taking a hell of a risk."

Street left, and leadership continued with trying to stop the march. They also did not offer any concrete suggestions for structural change.

Shortly after, I got into a disagreement with Darius Brown, a Black state senator from the Northside of Wilmington. He also led the Delaware Legislative Black Caucus and the Senate Judiciary Committees. And Brown lambasted us—*the people*—saying that we had no clear demands but expected them (i.e., politicians) to explain how *they* planned to address our concerns around structural violence.

I finally addressed the room: "We have been on the ground for the last ten years. My guys were also on the ground during the recent uprisings, helping to keep this city from being torn apart. . . . What program has been more involved at the local level and more accurate about the conditions of poor Black Wilmington?"

Looking to the grassroots leadership, I exclaimed, "We told you this was going to happen!"

Staring at Brown and Purzycki, I said, "When it comes to white corporate interests, they figure it out! They ain't got no problem figuring out how to serve *their* needs. But when it comes to *your* concerns, they're at a loss for suggestions. . . . What's up with the structural violence? How are you going to address that? It's unfair to ask this group to develop bulletproof points in three to five minutes and then you blame them when they fail to do so. You are trained, elected officials! It is your job to figure this out. You know what our priority is!"

Turning to Governor Carney, I said, "We need you to come up with real solutions to deal with this structural violence. We don't need dense or abstract plans for change. What's your plan?"

He did not respond. He even appeared annoyed by my question. The two-and-a-half-hour meeting ended shortly after this exchange. The governor and a few others withdrew to a back room.

We gathered in an area outside the conference room, where State Senator Brown was also standing. Given that Brown was from the Northside, we were surprised at his weak advocacy for Black Wilmington. I hoped that the two of us could come to a common understanding—it made no sense for us to be at odds. I approached Brown and tried to shake his hand, but he rejected it.

I said, "It's not personal. It's just business. It's about the people for me."

Brown exploded, "Yes it is! It is personal! It's always personal with you! That's right, everything is always about you! It's always about you!"

After Brown left, a few of us gathered outside. We were greatly disappointed in him. His elevated stature as a state senator had turned Brown into a shadow of his former himself: a justice-centered city councilman who had challenged the Wilmington Police Department and Delaware's legal system.[39] Nearly one year later, he was arrested for domestic violence for punching his girlfriend in a restaurant.[40]

The march went off without a hitch, and several Associates were among the key organizers and public speakers.[41] The city and state still did everything they could to undermine the march, including cordoning off sections of the city that day, making it nearly impossible to enter the city by car. Still, several thousand marched through the streets, and even more protested in front of the New Castle County Courthouse on King Street. For several hours, we reminded Wilmington and the State of Delaware that they worked for the people, not corporations.

After the protest, the Delaware Legislative Black Caucus (DLBC) held a press conference at Legislative Hall, promising "sweeping changes to police accountability and transparency statewide."[42] In response to what felt like empty platitudes, the Street PAR team released a scathing op-ed criticizing the DLBC.[43]

The "Wilmington 15"

We had traveled a long, ten-year road, and we were only getting started. We were too determined, locally supported, and enmeshed in city and state discourse on criminal legal reform to stop now. Because of our impact and ability to sustain ourselves, Jonathan (Associate) started referring to us as the "Wilmington 15." Jonathan wanted the group to more deeply appreciate our accomplishments and the change that former "shooters" and "hustlers" had made in Wilmington. For Jonathan, we were a special group that needed to recognize how we elevated the city's awareness on gun violence.

Over ten years, our Street PAR program had established itself as an institution and social movement in Wilmington. But sometimes it felt like for every round of accomplishments, we also had at least one painful setback. In the early years, Darryl's son and Dubard's brother were killed in separate incidents. Jonathan was robbed and shot, and now was paralyzed from the waist down. Midway through our journey, Kontal was accidently shot or grazed and arrested for drug possession. Tiana suffered a heart attack, but had recovered. Toward the end of our ten-year journey tragedy returned, this time to the children of one of our Associates. In 2019, Bernard's son was shot and survived, despite doctors warning that he had a "fifty-fifty chance." Then Bernard's daughter died in a car accident in January 2020. And in October 2022, we lost Dennis "Feetz" Watson (Associate).

Five Associates recidivated; Kenyatta was hit the hardest, with an eight-year sentence for possession of drugs and an illegal firearm. Kenyatta was integral to the team, and as a leader on the data collection subteam, he successfully navigated our study through the community. On some occasions, just Kenyatta and I walked the streets and collected survey data in hot sites.

Kenyatta was jailed in 2012 and returned in 2019. While he was incarcerated, I sent him dozens of pictures of the team. When he went in, we were still growing. Much of the news about what he had co-founded he learned in prison and "from the newspaper." In 2014, Kenyatta's facility starting screening *The People's Report*, a documentary that showcased our research-activist movement. Kenyatta was shocked to discover that he was also featured in the documentary.

After his release, I was so happy to see Kenyatta. We had lunch at Big Fish on the Riverfront in Wilmington, a restaurant that had opened while he was incarcerated. Shocked to see how developed the Riverfront was, Kenyatta took a moment to take in the new hotels, condominiums, the movie theater, and dozens of other businesses that now crowded the area.

Kenyatta was a changed man. Most importantly, he was happy and in love with his fiancée, Kristal Wortham. He landed full-time employment as a janitor for the Department of Health and Social Services (DHSS). Kenyatta was done with the streets and content with the simple pleasures of life—a good conversation, having a great meal, and building a stable family. But after working for eight months, Kenyatta was abruptly terminated. DHSS had fallen behind with background checks, and when they finally reviewed his, they fired him, although Kenyatta's performance indicated he was doing well. Confused and angry, he called me to help make this right.

"Yasser, I need your help. . . . These mother-ckers fired me."

"Your job let you go?"

"Yes, these motherf-ckers fired me. For no reason! I need your help . . . and the PAR family's too. This is what PAR is about, right? These people need to know I got back! I need you to email and call my supervisor. And I need you to call and email *his* supervisor."

"I'm on it, bro. And if this don't work out, we will make sure to get you something else. Let me call Wolf. His ties at DHSS are strong. I'm sure he can find you something."

"Yasser, that's cool, but I *need you* to jump on this situation. They can't just take my job like that. I was doing good. . . . I didn't do anything wrong. This is why people go back to the streets."

I called Wolf, and in a few days, he found him a new position. Kenyatta was grateful, but he insisted that I follow his instructions. For Kenyatta, he was more interested in restoring his dignity. I emailed and called his supervisor, and I also spoke with another official at DHSS. I reminded them of their public position on re-entry and that DHSS even funded some of our work. Two weeks later I received a generous text from DHSS affirming that Kenyatta would be reinstated.

Two months later, Kenyatta died from a heart attack. While out of town, he passed away in front of Kristal. COVID-19 restrictions prevented his funeral from taking place, but roughly fifty people attended his viewing.

That September, we held a memorial for Kenyatta at the Center for Structural Equity (CFSE). Darryl was the organization's executive director and they had just gotten the building in July 2020. Kenyatta's fiancée, father, and other family members joined us at CFSE, and we celebrated his life. The walls of the center's large multipurpose room were decorated with pictures of Kenyatta and the PAR family. After giving and listening to formal reflections on Kenyatta's life, we ate soul food, listened to music, had hearty conversations, and posed for photographs.

Like so many other losses, Kenyatta's death was tough for me. He truly deserved another chance, and finally he was empowered with a stable job, a fiancée, closer ties with his daughter and family, a strong network of research-activists, and the ability to give back to his community. The odds were low for someone as street-identified as Kenyatta to make the change he made. But he did. And that's why we celebrated him, and why his passing hurt so much.

Kenyatta was a founding member and integral part of Wilmington's inaugural group. He contributed greatly to what we became in Wilmington. Kenyatta's transformation and even his physical passing, in many ways, symbolized our ten-year trek. He started with us in late 2009, so his memorial marked the beginning of a new cycle for our program.

AT THE BEGINNING OF 2020, all fifteen Associates were employed, and six had enrolled in college. Four of the six Associates enrolled in undergraduate programs, and the two others (who already had their BA degrees) enrolled in MA programs. Also, while on the project, another Associate graduated with a BA and then completed his MA degree. Three Associates in total completed their MAs, and two of these three pursued doctorates. To date, one Associate has completed their doctorate. Also, seven of the original fifteen Associates have launched, between them, eleven community-based programs (see figure 9.1).

By fall 2020, our study had grown considerably and was now housed in the Center for Structural Equity and the Youth Empowered Program Center, which housed six funded studies (including this first study): two YPAR (or youth participatory action research) projects and three other Street PAR projects. In one of these studies, we teamed up with the Center for Justice Innovation in New York City to launch a four-city Street PAR project on gun violence. We also provided consulting on seven other independent PAR projects both in and outside of Delaware. Since fall 2009, we have trained nearly sixty Associates and acquired nearly sixty-five "Honorary Associates" or additional affiliates (see figure 9.1). By late 2020, the Wilmington Street PAR Program comprised more than 150 people including institutional partners, faculty, and students. Clearly, we were here to stay, and Street PAR was the mechanism that grounded our grassroots movement.

A NEW WILMINGTON: RAGE AGAINST THE MACHINE

Since 2009, the Eastside and Southbridge have grown in significant ways. The streets developed a sharper structural awareness and strongly resented service providers, schools, and political leadership. To secure some dignity, young people even disrespected and threatened city leadership. Educators, local politicians, and police were more closely scrutinized and sometimes embarrassed at public forums. They recognized why their families and neighborhoods remained poor, and in June 2020 they demanded serious accountability. The fog of false consciousness was lifting, and now the streets could more easily pinpoint the cruelty of their social, economic, and political reality.

In a context where extreme poverty festered, it made sense for some to engage in various forms of violence, including civil disobedience and even

Institutional Partners	Street PAR Associates
University Partnerships 6 Faculty | 20 Students • University of Delaware • Delaware State University • Wilmington University	**Core Members** 58 Total
Nonprofit Partnerships • The HOPE Commission • Christiana Cultural Arts Center • Wilmington Urban League • United Way Delaware • The Neighborhood House • ChristianaCare Hospital • Mother African Union Church • Delaware Center for Justice • ACLU-DE • Parkway Academy • Center for Count Innovation	**Honorary Members** 65 Total
	Center Locations
	Center for Structural Equity Darryl Chambers Executive Director
State/City Partnerships • Wilmington Mayor's Office • Delaware Department of Health and Social Services • Delaware Department of Services for Children, Youth and Their Families	**Youth Empowerment Program** Coley Harris Executive Director

9.1. Wilmington Street PAR Program: Organization Chart

gun violence, to cope with mounting inequality. For the streets, public disruptions were cathartic acts of resistance that brought attention to their structural oppression and pressured authorities to create real change.

Structural oppression was more than the functional loss of employment or affordable housing; inequality, regardless of its form, also meant the loss of dignity. For cultural reasons, diminishment of social standing was so shameful

Subsidiary Programs

Community Intervention Team
Darryl Chambers

Violence intervention based on community engagement & positive youth development

WIIT
Coley Harris

Local think tank that addresses structural violence & poor political leadership

Out of the Ashes
Coley Harris

Community play on the impact of re-entry on families

Smart Justice, ACLU
Dubard McGriff

Community education on racial disparities in criminal justice

Fathership Foundation
Jonathan Wilson

Nonprofit that supports male parenting, education/training, & community stewardship

The Southwest Philly Street PAR Program
Jonathan Wilson

Street PAR team addressing gun violence in Southwest Philadelphia, PA

SWAGG DCJ
Corry Wright

Violence intervention program that consists of courses at Ferris School for Boys for students sentenced by gun court

CORE Initiative
Corry Wright

An intervention designed to train young people to repair bicycles

Open Eye Radio Show WHGE 95.3 FM
Patrice Gibbs

Local radio show that focuses on the political concerns of Black Wilmington

Alive and Free, Inc.
Bernard Cornish

This LLC owns and markets music, films, books, and other merchandise developed and promoted by Bernard Cornish

Knowledge Is the New Hustle Program
Bernard Cornish

This community-based program trains youth to establish LLC's and use multimedia equipment to record and market music, film, and book projects

9.1. (Continued)

that violence was sometimes viewed as an acceptable means to restore honor. Community interventions rarely recognized the role that culture played in the hard trauma produced by structural violence. Structural oppression could quickly erode a level of family distinction or esteem that may have taken generations to cultivate. In small, poor communities like the Eastside and Southbridge, social standing was the primary currency used to ensure safety and other resources.

Furthermore, most residents insisted that community professionals visit their neighborhoods to see and absorb their oppression firsthand. The assumption was that a greater understanding could yield better policies and resources. Although this rarely occurred, they still called for leadership to see how they lived, outside of the well-planned programs at nonprofits. Orchestrated visits were welcomed, but they wanted officials to venture deeper into their communities to see how poverty interfaced with families in public housing or with young men in the local park.

Street PAR filled the void left between the needs of the streets and the intentions of city leadership. Our team was often the bridge between service providers and everyday people. We were formally a research project, but Street PAR was also a reliable conduit for communication between members of the streets and city officials. Our grassroots efforts also signaled to leadership that our reach inside these communities was authentically strong. Over a ten-year period we engaged in multiple forms of activism, from planning local barbecues and art shows on gun violence to gathering dozens to meet with leadership and mobilizing thousands to march against police violence.

The Eastside and Southbridge needed city leadership to understand that violence—whether in the streets or against authorities—was primarily tied to inequality and daily survival, not "poor choices" or corrupted values. In a context of extreme poverty, gun violence was a trusted site of resilience to settle disputes in the streets. Contrary to dominant arguments raised in the literature about their resilience, the "shooters" wanted the violence to end, and they desperately wanted safer and thriving communities. And perpetrators and victims actually did what they could to achieve this end. It was difficult for officials to comprehend gun violence from this perspective. But interweaving interventions with this alternative, cultural lens was the only way change could be made with Black men and women in the streets of Wilmington.

Conclusion

CALLING FOR A RADICAL STREET
ETHNOGRAPHY: STREET PAR, SOR
THEORY, AND THE BOTTOM CASTE

At the very same time that America refused to give the Negro any land, through an act of Congress, our government was giving away millions of acres of land.... [The United States] was willing to undergird its white peasants from Europe with an economic floor, but not only did they give the land, ... they provided county agents to further their expertise in farming, ... they provided low interest rates in order that they could mechanize their farms. Not only that, today many of these people are receiving millions of dollars in federal subsidies *not to farm*, and they are the very people telling the Black man that he ought to lift himself by his own bootstraps.... Now, when we come to Washington ... we are coming to get our check.
—Martin Luther King Jr., 1968 speech

Women and men need to know what is on the other side of the pain experienced in politicization. We need detailed accounts of the ways our lives are fuller and richer as we change and grow politically, as we learn to live each moment as committed feminists, as comrades working to end domination.
—bell hooks, "Feminism: A Transformational Politic"

WILMINGTON, DELAWARE, WAS A TOUGH TOWN on many fronts, and it contained some of Black America's most active street environments. Street life in the Eastside and Southbridge, however, never represented the larger cultural reality of most Black people in Wilmington. Our study focused on gun violence, but violence did not exemplify Black Wilmington. In fact, on most days there were no displays of violence. Mundane activities like housekeeping, shopping, taking care of children, and attending school accounted for most of residents' daily activities.

Gun violence in Wilmington did occur at a higher rate than in most cities, but the violence was seldom random; it was often targeted or connected to a larger story. If community professionals (including scholars) were to have a real shot at reducing Wilmington's violence, then they needed to learn how its rhythms evolved out of a network of culturally embedded relationships. The violence came with rich stories and a wrath of intergenerational trauma that orchestrated its outcomes.

Professionals often did not understand, nor did they think it was necessary to comprehend, the greater cultural realities of poor Black communities. Instead, it was always more convenient to frame their behaviors as the result of "poor choices." Interventions often undervalued knowing the rich cultural and structural legacy undergirding the spread of gun violence, and in this way scholars were also complicit in the spread of violence in the Eastside and Southbridge. All too often, we wanted a dataset, not a genuine connection with poor Black people and especially men and women active in the streets.

Although gun violence dominated the discourse on Black Wilmington, very few in or out of the streets ever understood their city in this way. Most never identified their city as "Murder Town, USA," but many did appreciate the attention *Newsweek* gave to the structural collapse of Black Wilmington, or how inequality was connected to gun violence. For Abigail Jones, Wilmington was an extremely racialized tale of two cities in which ruthless white wealth thrived at the expense of the gun violence and poverty they ultimately created in communities like the Eastside and Southbridge.[1]

Black Wilmington never defined themselves through either of these tales. For residents of the Eastside and Southbridge, their Black American cultural identity was largely independent of these two dominant perspectives. Most people, including the streets, tied their cultural identity to a religion, religious group, or spirituality, and they also rooted themselves in a historical legacy of Black resistance.

Black Wilmington was a culturally proud, intertwined force that was hardworking, fair-minded, determined, very principled, and grassroots oriented. Black residents of Southbridge founded the country's first major Black social movement in the late 1700s. Their mighty, small-town honor was shaped by key historical events and movements like the Underground Railroad or abolitionist, African Methodist Episcopal, Baptist, Garveyite, Moorish, Nation of Islam, Black Sunni Muslim, and Black Power traditions. And with the exception of the abolitionist movement, all of these traditions have persevered to the present day.

The Wilmington Street PAR program benefited from this strong Black activist legacy. The countless Black families destroyed by structural violence and the Black lives lost pursuing justice were also the fertile grounds that situated our research-activist program. For Black Wilmington, it was impossible to solve gun violence without incorporating the lessons learned from its multicentury race struggle with white supremacy.

The streets of Wilmington forced us to learn these lessons and required that we earn their respect before receiving permission to examine their experiences. Their lessons reminded us how intentional, permanent, and even necessary the inequality was—and also, how they always resisted. Since the period of slavery, a strong contingent of freedom fighters has fought courageously and always informed others about the structural violence created by the ruling elite.

What the Eastside and Southbridge mostly taught us, however, was that gun violence and crime overall were sites of resilience. In a context of extreme racialized structural oppression, both the "shooter" and their victims were resilient.

Gun Violence as a Site of Resilience

Street culture is a worldview guided by a code of ethics based on personal, social, and economic survival. A street identity is also an intergenerational standpoint anchored in a gendered racial-ethnic and cultural orientation. In addition to being a social identity, street culture is also activity based, with illegal and bonding activities as the dominant behaviors enacted by a street identity. Bonding or "street love" activities actually accounted for most of their time in the Eastside and Southbridge, not crime or gun violence. The group itself, group bonding, and attachment to a group identity provided them with emotional security, physical protection, and some semblance of a reliable family structure.

Street love also explained how street-identified Black men and women in the Eastside and Southbridge established social well-being or positively contributed to family, friends, and community. Community-level interventions designed for gun violence need to better understand, recognize, and draw on the generally *high levels of well-being* found in poor Black communities, including the well-being of many involved in street culture. For far too long, scholars and other community professionals have either ignored or just assumed that this part of their social identity is not worth knowing more about. We have also been led to believe that most street-identified young people have poor psychological well-being, or that most in the streets are "self-serving" and struggle with "low self-esteem," "self-defeating behavior," or a "negative self-concept." But we actually have little solid evidence to support this claim of poor psychological well-being. It is important for researchers and service providers to work with street-identified young people from the cultural standpoint that they also long for social acceptance, a loving family, stable home life, quality employment, good schooling, and a solid opportunity to make a positive contribution to broader society.

Street love was also perceived to be a response to structural oppression and the inadequacies of public leadership. Some even believed that violence against the state was sometimes necessary. For instance, after police brazenly murdered the paraplegic Jeremy McDole in 2015, some residents of the Eastside and Southbridge responded with aggressive civil disobedience to send a stiff and contemptuous message to city and state leadership. From their perspective, their backs were against the wall, and they had no choice but to risk their lives by challenging the establishment.

There is a danger in presuming that resilience exists only when it is classified as a "positive outcome" or "neutral behavior." To exclude street life or gun violence and violent resistance as a site of resilience because they are not lawful behavior ignores the complex functions of resiliency. This faulty argument suggests that certain values should prevail while others are inappropriate, and scholars have alerted us to the perils of this logic.[2] Gordon and Song note that the outcomes we label as resilience, resistance, invincibility, and so forth are relative, situational, and attributional.[3] Thus, the assumed meaning of resilience may have greater significance for the researchers who define or investigate it than for the person or persons who experience it. If you think I am a "loser," and I think I am a "winner," whose classification is to apply?[4]

Some "deviant" behaviors should be reframed as acts of resistance in service of resilience.[5] Robin Kelley, for example, argues that the Black working class in the mid-twentieth century engaged in "infrapolitics," or subtle and not so subtle acts of resistance.[6] For Kelley, infrapolitics represent the "daily confrontations, evasive actions, and stifled thoughts that often inform organized political movements. . . . Political history of oppressed people cannot be understood without reference to infrapolitics, for these daily acts have a cumulative effect on power relations."[7] Kelley illustrates the infrapolitics of resistance by describing how young Black people, on late weekend nights, would intentionally disturb white bus passengers. Categorizing behavior as "delinquent," "deviant," or "maladaptive" may, in fact, be a misinterpretation of adaptive and goal-oriented behavior. From the perspective of street-identified Black men and women, much of their attitudes and behavior is an act of resistance in service of resilience.

Fanon argued that the same desperation that caused oppressed people to harm one another was what also caused them to revolt against the state.[8] Loss of dignity or cultural standing and extreme poverty was largely what drove their participation in violence. For Fanon, violence was practical and its ethical implications were "relative." Rigid definitions of "right" and "wrong" were oversimplified binaries to understand violence. To better understand why violent resistance made sense, Fanon underscored that "in the colonial countries the peasants alone are revolutionary, for they have nothing to lose and everything to gain. The starving peasant, outside the class system, is the first among the exploited to discover that only violence pays. For him there is no compromise, no possible coming to terms; colonization and decolonization is simply a question of relative strength."[9]

The factors that influenced violent resistance were also responsible for street violence in the Eastside and Southbridge. Black people in these communities were desperate for economic relief, and some determined that crime was the best method to acquire resources and the respect typically denied them and their families. Gun violence was inevitable in an excruciating context of poverty and crime. At some point in an environment with little opportunity, rivals will come to an impasse that from their standpoint can be solved only by gun violence. In fact, not only was gun violence understood as a site of resilience for perpetrators in Wilmington, but also victims were considered to be resilient before, during, and after recovery. In their relentless pursuit for resources, perpetrators and victims were caught in a quandary. They either chose a life of humiliating poverty or risked injury, incarceration, and death.

Knowing more deeply the cultural dynamics around gun violence is the missing link in effectively reducing gun violence in Wilmington. Street PAR methodology allowed us to work directly with perpetrators and victims—often, the same people were both. Our data revealed that most people in the Eastside and Southbridge struggled far more with their exposure to violence than with being personally victimized. Observing and hearing about other people's victimization and losing family and close friends to gun violence were a much greater concern than fear of personally being harmed in the streets. Although people outside Black Wilmington were flooded with stories of gun violence, most study participants had never been shot, and only a small group were repeatedly victimized. We also found that positive attitudes toward economic well-being were predictive of fewer experiences with violence, and this relationship was mediated by their psychological and social well-being.[10] At least for us, this suggested that economic mobility was the answer to solving gun violence in Wilmington. Better understanding the positive implications of their well-being, particularly the racial-ethnic cultural dimensions of this well-being, were key to developing an intervention the streets could buy into.

MANY IN THE STREETS OF WILMINGTON were organized in dozens of small, fluid collectives nestled across the city. These collectives were usually interconnected, constantly morphing, family and neighborhood based, and generationally grounded. Also, there were at least three core factors that drove them to the streets: anger, group bonding, and securing an economic future. Wilmington's small city context hyperaccelerated these factors into gun violence.

Tribalism also thrived in small cities like Wilmington. This dynamic was best understood through groups, cliques, core families, and then lone individuals. Most people strongly identified with a community (e.g., Southbridge), and just about everyone we encountered was very proud of Wilmington. But deeper than this neighborhood and city allegiance was a fidelity to, and firm reliance on, their networks of support. The way to navigate Wilmington was through group membership or by moving with a group with some level of gravitas or capital. One's neighborhood was important, but being a member of a group with high social standing could be more significant. Street life was born out of disenfranchised neighborhoods, and the group people associated with was how they survived violent crime and extreme poverty.

If public leadership was unwilling to empower them, then they were going to adapt accordingly.

IN ANOTHER CONVERSATION, Coley conceded that Wilmington's street youth "could be very violent," but he believed their violence was no longer tied to the drug trade: "They're not making any money from the drugs anyway." After the tragedy of 9/11, there was a significant increase in wholesale and retail drug prices across the country.[11] Due to increased border control, it is harder for drugs like cocaine and heroin to be trafficked, and the penalties for using were harsher. The 2001 Patriot Act, for instance, allowed drug traffickers to be charged as "terrorists."[12]

In this post-9/11 climate, low-level, street-identified Black youth in small cities were largely priced out of the drug market. And while the drug market shrank considerably in Wilmington, what increased was the rage and extreme poverty experienced by youth. Thus, the violence was the "new product," or in the absence of a viable underground market, the primary hustle became the violence itself, especially for young people in Wilmington.[13] On this point, we were deeply saddened one Saturday afternoon to hear from someone in Southbridge that for street youth, "the going rate for a body [i.e., for killing someone] is $300 to $500." Cheap street bounties underscored the precarity of Black life in the face of bleak economic prospects.

Furthermore, the lack of guidance in the streets due to the incarceration of established street leadership created a series of violent power vacuums.[14] Spawned from impoverished conditions, increased access to guns, and fury emanating from those vacuums, some Black youth resorted to violence to solve their disputes.

Coley reached an epiphany about how to significantly reduce the violence, which he needed Wilmington to heed: "We can pay them out of the violence!"

I responded, "We can pay them out of the violence? Break that down for me."

"Look, basically, they're shooting in these streets because they're hungry and they're angry. You should see some of these kids that I work with, Yas. Listen, there's this kid at my center that just got shot twelve times. He's alive, and he didn't even snitch."

Coley was now an executive working with street-identified youth at the Youth Empowerment Program Center in Wilmington. With tears in his eyes, he continued, "Shit like this f-cks with me. Because at the bottom of all of this is that these kids are broke. They living in crazy situations. The poverty is driving them crazy. And don't nobody give a f-ck!"

Coley further explained that even a modest stipend program tied to job training and school performance for poor Black youth would greatly reduce gun violence, "They don't need a lot of money. Just a few dollars to take care of their day-to-day needs. That's all. That's all we need to bring the city's violence down."

This structural approach to gun violence worked in Richmond, California, another small city that once struggled with elevated murder rates.[15] After providing counseling, life skills training, a monthly stipend, chances to go back to school, and stable employment to young people at risk for gun violence, Richmond saw a 77% drop in homicides over a three-year period.

Recommendations for Radical Ethnography on Gun Violence

There are scores of violence prevention and intervention programs, but very few seriously focus on street-identified Black men and women's adaptive resilience. Instead, most theoretical models undergirding these programs are more interested in "criminalizing" their clients, presumably to correct their moral failings.[16] Conservative resilience strategies adapted for street-identified populations, like grit,[17] mindfulness,[18] and cognitive behavioral therapy,[19] have five major problems: (1) they are primarily interested in assimilating clients to a middle-class white cultural orientation; (2) they lack racial-ethnic and cultural competence; (3) they have an ahistorical stance; (4) they value an individualized perspective that holds the person solely responsible; and (5) they fail to incorporate a structural violence analysis.

Violence intervention programs like the Boston Gun Project Working Group or Operation Ceasefire, Focused Deterrence or Pulling Levers, Group Violence Intervention (GVI), and in some instances the Cure Violence program not only have these five problems but also are willing to work closely with police departments to incarcerate the very people they presumably are trying to help. Although these programs have gained considerable notoriety over the last decade, most of the support for them comes from formal leadership, not from local residents, who typically feel betrayed by the programs.[20]

In 2014, ChristianaCare Hospital set up a meeting in Delaware between our team and program directors employed with the Chicago Cure Violence program. Cure Violence (formerly Cease Violence) develops chapters across the country to recruit "violence interrupters" in their neighborhoods to stop gun violence. At the meeting, we inquired about their support for or association with Operation Ceasefire, Focused Deterrence, or GVI, which follow the approach of their founder, David Kennedy, in working directly with police to identify perpetrators of gun violence. The appeal of Kennedy's programs for police departments is that they provide the departments with the cover needed to incarcerate large swathes of young people. To accomplish this goal, these violence outreach programs were skilled at surrounding themselves with the social capital of the streets, or generally persons who were formerly incarcerated, and other community members. At least in Wilmington, GVI worked closely with probation and parole offices in requiring probationers and parolees with a history of violence to attend a "call in," a required group meeting, or be in violation of their probation or parole. This unethical mandate to attend the "call in" was developed after GVI started receiving severe backlash from communities about the program's direct cooperation with police.

In 2019, the GVI program began in Wilmington. And in June 2021, to the dismay of many residents, Chief Robert Tracy boldly credited GVI with the arrest of fourteen alleged members of North Pak, a local Wilmington gang, on 120 charges, including six homicides.[21] Chief Tracy proudly announced at a press conference: "Through the implementation of evidence-based, proven crime reduction strategies, we have had great success identifying those responsible for driving gun violence in our city and throughout Delaware. Indictments like these . . . [send] a clear and powerful message that gun violence and illegal gun possession will not be tolerated. . . . Through GVI, we . . . attempt to direct individuals away from crime and violence driven by senseless conflicts. Those who heed those warnings are provided support, while those who continue to engage in violence are held responsible through our enforcement efforts."[22]

Street PAR rejects working with police to identify and incarcerate local residents, and we also strongly call on the field of street ethnography to not participate in this kind of community policing approach. This strategy is treacherously unethical because it manipulates the trust of communities and especially the streets, and it puts residents at great risk for violent retribution for their complicity or direct cooperation in getting people incarcerated.

Based on our study in the Eastside and Southbridge, we make five recommendations for ethnographers and other community professionals to reduce gun violence: (1) lead structural awareness campaigns inside local neighborhoods, (2) bring more empirical attention to the racial wealth gap and its role in gun violence, (3) become more deeply immersed in distressed neighborhoods, (4) utilize the arts for activism, and (5) expand use of the Street PAR methodology.

Structural Awareness Campaign

Major structural change is required for gun violence to be eliminated, and a lack of awareness about structural violence will only ensure the continuance of gun violence. Poor Black communities need to be taught firsthand about the expansive, intentional, and "permanent" nature of their structural positioning.[23] Valentine's iconic ethnography, *Hustling and Other Hard Work*, argues that "economic and political forces" are directly responsible for the grave poverty found in poor Black communities.[24] Most of the participants in Valentine's study had to creatively string together three components in order to survive in a minimal or basic manner: (1) welfare or public assistance, (2) minimum-wage employment, and (3) hitting the streets. Valentine argues that the frightening socioeconomic conditions of Blackstone (a fictionalized name) could be addressed only through a massive social-structural overhaul. Valentine says:

> The problems of employment, education, health care, housing, welfare—of making the system work—are structural and institutional issues whose solutions are beyond the individual. Their resolution must involve massive change in society.
>
> The American economic system as it is currently organized leaves a significant portion of the population periodically or permanently unemployed. Because of racism, most of the men and women in Blackstone who are able to find work are limited to marginal, fluctuating, low-paid work. At the same time, they are required to pay high rents for substandard housing and inflated prices for low-quality food and consumer goods.[25]

In theoretical alignment with Valentine's argument on inequality, we call on street ethnographers to teach structural violence and critical race theories to poor Black communities to ultimately reduce gun violence. Generally, residents understand that structural violence is socially engineered, but typically they are unable to critically comprehend the total impact of systemic injustice in their personal lives. Critical race scholar Michelle Alexander argues that the U.S. economy erects a "racial caste system" that requires a racial outgroup, and Black Americans are designated to this bottom-caste position.[26] This level of structural awareness is liberating, not disempowering, because it distills for poor Black people the abstractness of inequality so that they can connect the structural dots to their daily circumstances and begin organizing accordingly.

Our research program took on the responsibility of teaching these theories in Black Wilmington. We found in one workshop after another that residents were eager to learn about the intentional permanence of inequality. Through the lens of these theories, we taught participants the history of dis-opportunity and how inequality was ultimately tied to gun violence in and outside of Black Wilmington.

Closing the Racial Wealth Gap

Oliver and Shapiro coined the term "racial wealth gap" after emergent data revealed a striking wealth disparity between racial groups in the United States.[27] Oliver and Shapiro's analysis strongly supported Bell's[28] "racial realism" and Alexander's[29] "racial-caste" arguments by confirming that Black

Americans were, in fact, cemented onto the bottom rung of the U.S. economic system.

According to Traub et al., "the racial wealth gap [is] the absolute difference in wealth holdings between the median household among populations grouped by race or ethnicity."[30] Wealth is not income or employment, but wealth represents the value of an individual's or group's total assets (e.g., property or savings).[31]

As such, we implore street ethnographers to examine gun violence in relation to the *racial-ethnic* wealth gap. Analyses must move beyond just race to examine how wealth (or lack thereof) is monopolized by particular racial-ethnic groups. Levels of poverty, joblessness, and economic well-being are useful indicators to understand people involved with gun violence, but racial-ethnic wealth standing is a superior way to measure the role inequality plays in homicide rates.

Black Americans, as a group, have always had little access to real wealth. The U.S. economy totals about a $110 trillion, and white Americans control nearly 90% of that, while Black Americans have about 4%.[32] About 75% of Black America's wealth is controlled by 10% of the Black community, leaving upward of 60% of Black people at or near zero dollars in wealth. The average Black family has about $1,700 in wealth, while the average white family has about $117,000.[33]

With this said, race by itself, or sometimes what's referred to as a pan-ethnic designation (e.g., Latino or Asian) or pan-racial group (e.g., Black or white) is used to hide the inequality or the wealth acquired by particular racial-ethnic groups (e.g., British Americans, Cuban Americans, Nigerian Americans, Chinese Americans, or Jewish Americans). Racial-ethnic designation provides a more accurate portrayal of wealth holdings than racial groups alone, and the racial-ethnic analysis of wealth is even more troubling at the city level. In Boston, Black Americans had $8 in liquid wealth, while the average white family had $247,000.[34] In Miami, Black Americans had $11 in liquid assets, while whites had about $11,000 liquid and $107,000 in household wealth.[35] Miami's Caribbean Blacks, Cubans, and Puerto Ricans all fared better than Black Americans, having $2,000, $3,200, and $200 in liquid wealth, respectively. In Los Angeles, the average white family had about $330,000 in wealth with $110,000 in liquid assets, while Black Americans had $4,000 in wealth with about $200 in liquid assets.[36] African immigrants in Los Angeles had about $60,000 in liquid wealth.

In 2017, our research program and other advocates called for a racial-ethnic wealth gap analysis in Wilmington. Due to rising interest in the topic and concurrent discussions of Black reparations, the Metropolitan Wilmington Urban League co-hosted a well-attended forum on the wealth gap titled "50 Years Since MLK's Poor People Campaign—Where Are We Now?," which featured Dr. Darrick Hamilton, one of the most esteemed economists in the racial wealth gap literature.[37]

After this event, JP Chase Morgan strategically got in front of the racial wealth gap argument in Wilmington by conducting a race-focused (not racial-ethnic) analysis.[38] Their findings were, at best, misleading. The report conveniently used the language of "race and ethnicity" but never conducted a racial-ethnic analysis. The nondisaggregated analysis concealed how specific groups and sections of neighborhoods fared with respect to wealth holdings. The report collapsed all areas of the city, which glossed over the complexity that Wilmington includes some of the poorest as well as some of the wealthiest communities in the country. For example, this report draws on aggregate city-level racial data to conclude:

> White households earn a median income of $60,772, Black households make half of that at $30,034, and Latino households earn a median of $32,976. Asian households in Wilmington have the highest median income of $70,461. . . . The city's white income poverty rate of seven percent is less than a third of the income poverty rate of Black (26.9%) and Latino (25.3%) families, which is also true across the country. . . . The median property value for white homeowners is $189,000 in Wilmington and $200,000 nationally, while the property value for Black homeowners is $125,000 in Wilmington and $138,000 nationwide.[39]

A robust Black reparations plan is the only intervention that can realistically counter the entrenched poverty and resultant gun violence revealed by the racial wealth gap literature.[40] The appeal for Black reparations is a call for a comprehensive, multitrillion-dollar package of resources and wealth for Black American descendants of the slaveholding South. And it is time for street ethnographers who study homicide to make an ethnographic case for Black reparations.

Discussions of Black reparations have soared across social media and dozens of popular podcasts including *Tariq Radio*, *The Black Authority* (TBA), *Professor Black Truth*, *Breaking Brown*, and *Tone Talks*. Jason Black's (TBA) "Cut the Check!" and Tariq Nasheed's "Tangibles2020" were the battle cries that resonated strongly in poor Black communities and during the 2020 presidential race. Passionate calls for reparations also reached the tumultuous 2020 mayor's race in Wilmington, and some openly connected the violence and poverty in Black Wilmington to the significant lack of wealth in these neighborhoods.

Immersion of Community Professionals

We strongly support our participants' call for community professionals, including ethnographers who study gun violence, to immerse themselves more deeply in the communities we service and research. A well-designed outreach and community support program embedded with community professionals would confirm a real commitment to these neighborhoods. Closely working in distressed neighborhoods means visiting street corner vigils, spending time with victims and their families, attending funerals, creating authentic community research programs, and deeply canvassing neighborhoods with residents. Neighborhood residents also want professionals to participate in prosocial activities like attending local birthdays and barbecues, sponsoring neighborhood sports leagues, and organizing programs that celebrate Black fathers, mothers, or the Black family. Not closely working inside neighborhoods potentially signals community professionals' ill intent or exploitative interests.

"Africana activists" or other ground-level scholars competent in Black culture are able to develop stronger partnerships because of their awareness of these neighborhoods' core values.[41] Cultural scripts streamline the group's goals, and given that a group's priorities are not necessarily linear or easily predicted, immersion is required to have some systematic understanding of the group's cultural dynamics. Social science courses have largely failed to identify useful methods to analyze culture, and we have not trained students well to work inside communities.[42]

Mastery of culture is an ethical practice, and this sacred knowledge should never be leveraged to further exploit distressed communities. The purpose of knowing culture should always be to help communities. For McDougal, Africana activists organize community projects to "indirectly and directly save[e] lives, improv[e] people's overall wellbeing or chang[e] the way people think about critical issues."[43] Bowman also recommends four "adaptive strategies" to ethically enter distressed Black communities: (1) work with local or "indigenous interviewers"; (2) identify local advisers or "community consultants and groups"; (3) establish transparent "trade off and exchange arrangements" to ensure a reciprocal relationship; and (4) routinely discuss with residents the study's "relevance to community needs."[44]

Moreover, participants believed that a sustained presence on the ground in poor Black communities—what some scholars call "long-term ethnographic immersion"[45] or "embodied ethnography"[46]—would refine community professionals' awareness of the social and structural dimensions of their lives. For the residents of the Eastside and Southbridge, truly understanding their experience with gun violence meant full involvement or direct neighborhood participation by professionals. For participants, it's only possible to understand and advocate on their behalf by deeply experiencing the cultural totality of their communities. According to Schliewe,

> Embodied ethnography invites us to see human experience as including material, sensorial, and affective involvement in the world. Thus, it highlights a dimension often marginalized, as researchers favor talk and observation alone. . . . Science prefers to avoid ambiguous experiences. . . . The "material presence" of the people we study tends to be forgotten, as verbal accounts and "meaning-making" have become the prime lens for our qualitative research. However, this creates a rather distorted picture of the lifeworlds that we actually live in. Everyday human experience is

much more than just words or observable actions. It is also feeling the summer sun on our skin, going to art museums, eating ice cream, and giving hugs to loved ones.[47]

The streets in particular needed leadership to personally observe and feel, to truly experience and absorb how much they actually wanted to work; how deeply they loved their children, families, and neighborhoods; and how desperate they were for structural change. The streets believed that drenching themselves in the people's poverty and pain was the kind of professional development scholars and service providers needed to do in order to better advocate for them. As noted in chapter 9, participants like Tyree wanted politicians to "come to the hood," or walk with them in the poorest and most violent areas of their community. The assumption was that this close view of their poverty would strike a chord with their humanity and prompt leadership to urgently respond.

We were critical of this recommendation. On its face, it was a naïve strategy; in the absence of something substantive to bargain with, residents would certainly get little change. But this strategy could be useful, particularly if a well-thought-out follow-up response was planned after a neighborhood visit.

Arts for Activism

The arts are another effective way to not only raise awareness about structural violence but also teach community members how to fight against inequality. PAR projects have increasingly used art-based methods to galvanize the public, report and disseminate findings, and do grassroots organizing.[48] M. Brinton Lykes's extensive body of PAR work has drawn on the arts as a form of action in combination with archival, policy, and also survey- and interviewing-based methods.[49] Much of her work is focused on parenting, immigration, human rights, and the overall resilience of women and children throughout Central America. Lykes's project "Creative Arts and Photography in Participatory Action Research in Guatemala" worked with the Association of Maya Ixil Women–New Dawn (ADMI) by using photo voice methodology to examine how these women created change in a former war environment. Photo voice is an arts-based research method and form of analysis that draws on photography and video to document the social hardships of a group to ultimately trigger grassroots activism in marginalized communities.[50]

In Wilmington, we organized two street art exhibitions—the *Homicide Art Exhibition* (see chapter 7) and the *Wilmington Trap Stars Street Art Exhibition*—to teach local residents about the inherent relationship between inequality and crime. These exhibitions attracted thousands of Delawareans. Building on the *Homicide Art Exhibition* at the Christiana Cultural Arts Center in 2010, in 2014 we curated the *Wilmington Trap Stars Street Art Exhibition* at the Delaware Center for Contemporary Arts (DCCA). The DCCA is a high-end art center located on the Riverfront in Wilmington. Maiza Hixson (chief curator at

DCCA), Michael Kalmbach (executive director of Creative Vision Factory, an art-based drop-in center in Wilmington), the Action subteam (Raye Jones Avery, executive director of Christiana Cultural Arts Center, and four Street PAR Associates) and I recruited about fifty untrained local artists who produced nearly 300 pieces of art across various mediums (i.e., graffiti, oil paintings, pencil sketches, sneaker art, photography, collages, music, and video). Satirical images of the Wilmington Police Department, striking paintings of impoverished row homes, and photographs of Blood gang members toting guns, along with funeralized pictures of gang members were on shocking display. Also, an interactive feature of the exhibition included two enlarged chalkboards with the ominous words "Before I Die . . ." Underneath these words were a series of blank lines in which attendees could write the last activities they desired to experience before they passed away. And no line was left blank. Moreover, these amazing artworks were on full display in DCCA's main gallery for a three-month period, from March 22 to June 15, 2014. Further, while DCCA's full capacity is 500 people, nearly 1,000 attended the opening night, and thousands more visited over the three months. Artists were able to sell their art, and some breakout talent were scheduled for their own show at DCCA. Interspersed throughout this three-month period was additional programming on structural violence and crime. Further, it should be underscored that art compliments well the multidimensional theories and empirical data discussed in our structural awareness workshops. In fact, we often showed images from our art exhibitions in our structural awareness workshops and academic presentations.

On the opening weekend of the *Wilmington Trap Stars Street Art Exhibition*, we also featured a musical showcase of about twenty-five performers of poetry, dance, hip-hop, and R&B; much of the music is recorded on the mixtape project located on the *People's Report* website. Daroun "Rev" Jamison (a new Street PAR Associate) hosted and performed at this jam-packed showcase. After completing a seventeen-year sentence for attempted homicide, Daroun became a great example of a high-achieving returning citizen. In addition to joining our second Street PAR project in the Northside and Westside sections of Wilmington, Daroun found full-time employment, enrolled in college, and authored two self-published book projects. On the first night of our opening weekend, Daroun gloriously introduced the headliner, Robert Teat (or local rap giant "Bobby Dimes"), who brought the crowd to a thunderous roar with his smash hit "Out Delaware." Then–presidential candidate Joe Biden even played "Out Delaware" at campaign events in Delaware. But like so many before him, Robert would also succumb to the streets of Wilmington. Just over two years after the *Wilmington Trap Stars Street Art Exhibition*, Robert was shot and killed in November 2016.[51] Robert was the son of Ms. Trudy Boardley, a woman we interviewed about her older son Darryl Lively being shot and killed while defending Robert from being robbed (see chapter 7).

More Street PAR

Our research program demonstrates that street-identified persons and groups are willing to be trained in Street PAR and other community-based methodology. In most instances, however, when recruited for research, residents generally are confined to data collection for formal researchers, under the guise of full participation in a study.[52] For us, this approach is also deeply unethical and highly deceptive. We heartily reject this representation of PAR and strongly encourage researchers to train members of the streets in theory, methods, analysis, and local organizing. Data from poor Black people are invaluable, and residents just have to be trained to access it and to analyze and profit from their own information. Serious instruction on scholarly reading and writing, quantitative and qualitative methods, and public speaking is the only kind of experience that would offset the poor academic and criminal backgrounds that many in the streets have. Training that includes formal presentations and publications will also ensure that participants receive favorable attention from colleges and employers, as well as admiration from their families and communities.

We underestimated the impact that Street PAR would have in a small city like Wilmington. Small cities are ideal environments for Street PAR to thrive because they offer cultural intimacy and a set of close relationships that are necessary to quickly mobilize large swathes of the community.

The PAR literature often places emphasis on research (and mostly theoretical arguments), with less attention on a well-designed action agenda. Grassroots organizing is at the heart of Street PAR, as the priority of this methodology is to use analysis to guide local activism. Constant neighborhood programming is chiefly how we connected with the Eastside and Southbridge. We strongly encourage ethnographers and other scholars, service providers, and residents (including the streets) to view Street PAR as an organizing tool and ultimately as a sociopolitical project.

bell hooks calls for Black feminists to return to "small group" conversations in local neighborhoods to invoke "consciousness-raising" and activism.[53] Small organizing groups generally do not attract the same attention and resources as more commercialized forms of activism, but for hooks, smaller groups are typically more effective at reaching the hearts of the community and more committed to carrying out justice-centered work. hooks wrote:

> It would be useful to promote anew the small group setting as an area for education for critical consciousness, so that women and men might come together in neighborhoods. . . .
>
> Small groups . . . coming together to engage . . . in dialectical struggle make a space where the "personal is political" as a starting point for education for critical consciousness can be extended to include politicization of the self that focuses on creating understanding of the ways sex, race,

and class come together to determine our individual lot and our collective experience. . . . This individual commitment, when coupled with engagement in collective discussion, provides a space for critical feedback which strengthens our efforts to change and make ourselves anew.[54]

Small tactical groups with focused agendas have always been the guiding post for successful social movements, and Street PAR provides an empirically based approach for small and large groups to strategically mobilize against gun violence. In an effort to stop the violence, persons with high social capital who sit on the cusp between the streets and making a positive change must be identified to participate in the socioeconomic and political affairs of their communities. The streets have the attention and the hearts of the community and the trust and cultural mastery to engage the people most involved with gun violence. They just lack the formal skill set (but not the ability to comprehend it) and access to key resources to achieve this goal.

To empower the streets, new, useful, and innovative methods for working with them and skills to train them in must be identified. Their cultural ways and forms of knowing must be properly integrated not only to teach and learn a new skill, but also to demonstrate its utility for them and their community. For instance, many in the streets need culturally competent training to conduct GIS (geographic information system) analysis on gun violence or gang networks in their neighborhoods, or training in participatory budgeting and power mapping, along with guidance on turning these results into publications, presentations, and programming.

THE STREETS ARE THE ANSWER to ending gun violence, and through forging a truly reciprocal partnership with them, broader society will learn how to connect more deeply with its own humanity. The entrenched problems of inequality and gun violence have always been bigger than the individual behaviors of Black men and women in the streets. In fact, we argue that the stripping away of vital resources and key institutions by political and corporate forces are far more responsible for the poverty and homicide rates found in Black America.

The defining civil rights fight in the twenty-first century is a battle over resources or wealth, and access to opportunity. And this fight is the only fight that ever mattered in terms of justice and liberation, or in this instance, reducing gun violence. Street PAR designs give street-identified groups a skill set to organize around and the opportunity to control their own narratives or data; and profit from what they know best—*the nuances of the streets*.

More than anything, we learned that no sociopolitical climate or local environment can withstand the growing and disciplined drumbeat of an intellectually based grassroots movement situated on its street corners. As we found with our project, at some point, the establishment will be forced to concede.

Notes

Introduction

Epigraphs: Martin Luther King Jr., "The Three Evils of Society," speech delivered at the First Annual National Conference on New Politics, Chicago, August 31, 1967, https://www.nwesd.org/ed-talks/equity/the-three-evils-of-society-address-martin-luther-king-jr/; Angela Davis, interview, *Frontline*, PBS, 1997, https://www.pbs.org/wgbh/pages/frontline/shows/race/interviews/davis.html; Timothy Black, *When a Heart Turns Rock Solid: The Lives of Three Puerto Rican Brothers on and off the Streets* (New York: Vintage Books, 2009), xxxiii.

1. Although most people refer to them as "neighborhoods" (and in this book I sometimes do as well), Eastside and Southbridge are technically "sections," with smaller neighborhoods inside them. However, these "sections" are relatively small (Eastside with a population of 5,000 and Southbridge with 1,900) because Wilmington is a small city. There are five major sections of Wilmington, with forty-four recognized neighborhoods.
2. Cris Barrish, "Study: 8 in 10 Released Inmates Return to Del. Prisons," *USA Today*, July 31, 2013, https://www.usatoday.com/story/news/nation/2013/07/31/delaware-prison-recidivism/2603821/.
3. Christopher Wink, "64% of Fortune 500 Firms Are Delaware Incorporations: Here's Why," Technical.ly, September 23, 2014, https://technical.ly/delaware/2014/09/23/why-delaware-incorporation/.
4. Abigail Jones, "Murder Town USA (aka Wilmington, Delaware)," *Newsweek*, December 9, 2014, https://www.newsweek.com/2014/12/19/wilmington-delaware-murder-crime-290232.html; Brittany Horn et al., "Wilmington: Most Dangerous Place in America for Youth," *News Journal* (Wilmington, DE), September 9, 2017, https://www.delawareonline.com/story/news/crime/2017/09/08/our-babies-killing-each-other/100135370/; "NeighborhoodScout's Most Dangerous Cities—2022," NeighborhoodScout, January 3, 2022, https://www.neighborhoodscout.com/blog/top100dangerous.
5. U.S. Census Bureau, "2008–2010 ACS 3-Year Estimates," Census.gov, 2011, https://www.census.gov/programs-surveys/acs/technical-documentation/table-and-geography-changes/2010/3-year.html.
6. Yasser Arafat Payne and Tara Marie Brown, "'I'm Still Waiting on That Golden Ticket': Attitudes toward and Experiences with Opportunity in the Streets of Black America," *Journal of Social Issues* 72, no. 4 (2016): 789–811.
7. Jones, "Murder Town USA."
8. Waverly Duck, *No Way Out: Precarious Living in the Shadow of Poverty and Drug Dealing* (Chicago: University of Chicago Press, 2015); Rick A. Matthews, Michael O. Maume, and William J. Miller, "Deindustrialization, Economic Distress, and Homicide Rates in Midsized Rustbelt Cities," *Homicide Studies* 5, no. 2 (2001): 83–113.
9. Duck, *No Way Out*.

10. Horn et al., "Wilmington."
11. Robert Vargas, *Wounded City: Violent Turf Wars in a Chicago Barrio* (New York: Oxford University Press, 2016).
12. Duck, *No Way Out*; William Julius Wilson, *When Work Disappears: The World of the New Urban Poor* (New York: Vintage Books, 1996).
13. Robert Agnew, "Strain Theory and Violent Behavior," in *The Cambridge Handbook of Violent Behavior and Aggression*, ed. D. J. Flannery, A. T. Vazsonyi, and I. D. Waldman (New York: Cambridge University Press, 2007), 519–529; Charis E. Kubrin and Ronald Weitzer, "Retaliatory Homicide: Concentrated Disadvantage and Neighborhood Culture," *Social Problems* 50, no. 2 (2003): 157–180.
14. Stephen W. Baron, "General Strain, Street Youth, and Crime: A Test of Agnew's Revised Theory," *Criminology* 42, no. 2 (2004): 460.
15. Yasser Arafat Payne, "Site of Resilience: A Reconceptualization of Resiliency and Resilience in Street Life–Oriented Black Men," *Journal of Black Psychology* 37, no. 4 (2011): 426–451; Yasser Arafat Payne and Angela Bryant, "Street Participatory Action Research in Prison: A Methodology to Challenge Privilege and Power in Correctional Facilities," *The Prison Journal* 98, no. 4 (2018): 449–469.
16. Sarah Bracke, "Is the Subaltern Resilient? Notes on Agency and Neoliberal Subjects," *Cultural Studies* 30, no. 5 (2016): 839–855; Wilson, *When Work Disappears*.
17. Michelle Alexander, *The New Jim Crow: Mass Incarceration in the Age of Colorblindness* (New York: New Press, 2010); Randol Contreras, *The Stickup Kids: Race, Drugs, Violence, and the American Dream* (Berkeley: University of California Press, 2013).
18. Ed Diener, Jeffrey J. Sapyta, and Eunkook Suh, "Subjective Well-Being Is Essential to Well-Being," *Psychological Inquiry* 9, no. 1 (1998): 33–37.
19. Diener, Sapyta, and Suh, 34.
20. Robin D. G. Kelley, *Yo' Mama's Disfunktional! Fighting the Culture Wars in Urban America* (Boston: Beacon Press, 1998).
21. Aimé Césaire, *Discourse on Colonialism* (1972; repr., New York: Monthly Review Press, 2000).
22. Kelley, *Yo' Mama's Disfunktional!*, 25.
23. Alexander, *New Jim Crow*; Eduardo Bonilla-Silva, *Racism without Racists: Color-Blind Racism and the Persistence of Racial Inequality in America* (Lanham, MD: Rowman & Littlefield, 2014); Kimberlé Crenshaw, Neil Gotanda, Gary Peller, and Kendall Thomas, *Critical Race Theory: The Key Writings That Formed the Movement* (New York: New Press, 1995).
24. Contreras, *Stickup Kids*.
25. David J. Harding, *Living the Drama: Community, Conflict, and Culture among Inner-City Boys* (Chicago: University of Chicago Press, 2010); Wilson, *When Work Disappears*.
26. Wilson, *When Work Disappears*, 70–71.
27. Duck, *No Way Out*.
28. Duck, 47.
29. Payne, "Site of Resilience."
30. Contreras, *Stickup Kids*; Duck, *No Way Out*; John L. Jackson, *Harlemworld: Doing Race and Class in Contemporary Black America* (Chicago: University of Chicago Press, 2001); Payne, "Site of Resilience"; Vargas, *Wounded City*; James Diego Vigil, *A Rainbow of Gangs: Street Cultures in the Mega-City* (Austin: University of Texas Press, 2002).
31. Fox Butterfield, *All God's Children: The Bosket Family and the American Tradition of Violence* (New York: Harper Perennial, 1995); Adrian Nicole LeBlanc, *Random Family: Love, Drugs, Trouble, and Coming of Age in the Bronx* (New York: Scribner, 2003).
32. Claude Brown, *Manchild in the Promised Land* (New York: Touchstone-Simon, 1965); Sanyika Shakur, *Monster: The Autobiography of an L. A. Gang Member* (New York: Grove Press, 1993).

33. Jackson, *Harlemworld*.
34. Jackson, 60.
35. W. E. B. Du Bois, *The Philadelphia Negro* (Philadelphia: Schocken Books, 1899).
36. Sean Patrick Griffin, *Black Brothers, Inc.: The Violent Rise and Fall of Philadelphia's Black Mafia* (Preston, UK: Milo Books, 2005).
37. Anderson J. Franklin, "Invisibility Syndrome and Racial Identity Development in Psychotherapy and Counseling African American Men," *The Counseling Psychologist* 27, no. 6 (1999): 761–793; Cheryl Lynette Keyes, *Rap Music and Street Consciousness* (Urbana: University of Illinois Press, 2002).
38. Contreras, *Stickup Kids*; Duck, *No Way Out*; Philippe I. Bourgois, *In Search of Respect: Selling Crack in El Barrio* (New York: Cambridge University Press, 1995).
39. Johan Galtung, "Violence, Peace, and Peace Research," *Journal of Peace Research* 6, no. 3 (1969): 167–191; Johan Galtung, "A Structural Theory of Imperialism," *Journal of Peace Research* 8, no. 2 (1971): 81–117.
40. Garry M. Leech, *Capitalism: A Structural Genocide* (London: Zed Books, 2012).
41. Michael Hardt and Antonio Negri, *Empire* (Cambridge, MA: Harvard University Press, 2000).
42. Edward E. Baptist, *The Half Has Never Been Told: Slavery and the Making of American Capitalism* (New York: Basic Books, 2016); Eric Eustace Williams, *Capitalism and Slavery* (Chapel Hill: University of North Carolina Press, 1994).
43. Alexander, *New Jim Crow*.
44. Edward L. Ayers, *Vengeance and Justice: Crime and Punishment in the Nineteenth-Century American South* (New York: Oxford University Press, 1984).
45. Galtung, "Violence"; Galtung, "Structural Theory"; Johan Galtung, "Cultural Violence," *Journal of Peace Research* 27, no. 3 (1990): 291–305.
46. Galtung, "Violence," 170.
47. Galtung, "Structural Theory."
48. Rajkumar Bobichand, "Understanding Violence Triangle and Structural Violence," Kangla Online, July 30, 2012, http://kanglaonline.com/2012/07/understanding-violence-triangle-and-structural-violence-by-rajkumar-bobichand/.
49. Galtung, "Cultural Violence."
50. Bobichand, "Understanding Violence."
51. Cedric J. Robinson, *Black Marxism: The Making of the Black Radical Tradition* (Chapel Hill: University of North Carolina Press, 1983).
52. Robert Agnew, "Experienced, Vicarious, and Anticipated Strain: An Exploratory Study on Physical Victimization and Delinquency," *Justice Quarterly* 19, no. 4 (2002): 603–632; Agnew, "Strain Theory"; Baron, "General Strain"; Richard A. Cloward and Lloyd E. Ohlin, *Delinquency and Opportunity: A Theory of Delinquent Gangs* (London: Routledge, 1960).
53. Derrick Bell, *Faces at the Bottom of the Well: The Permanence of Racism* (New York: Basic Books, 1992); Ruth Wilson Gilmore, *Golden Gulag: Prisons, Surplus, Crisis, and Opposition in Globalizing California* (Berkeley: University of California Press, 2007).
54. Michael J. Lynch and Raymond J. Michalowski, *Primer in Radical Criminology: Critical Perspectives on Crime, Power and Identity* (Monsey, NY: Criminal Justice Press, 2006).
55. LIFERS, "Ending the Culture of Street Crime," *The Prison Journal* 84, no. 4 (2004): 48–68; Payne and Bryant, "Street Participatory Action Research"; Stephen C. Richards, "The New School of Convict Criminology Thrives and Matures," *Critical Criminology* 21, no. 3 (2013): 375–387; Stephen C. Richards and Jeffrey Ian Ross, "Introducing the New School of Convict Criminology," *Social Justice* 28, no. 1 (2001): 177–190.
56. LIFERS, "Ending the Culture."
57. LIFERS, 51.

58. Yasser Arafat Payne, "'Street Life' as a Site of Resiliency: How Street Life–Oriented Black Men Frame Opportunity in the United States," *Journal of Black Psychology* 34, no. 1 (2008): 3–31.
59. Throughout this book, Darryl's street names "Wolfie" and "Wolf" will be used interchangeably with his legal name.
60. Ira Porter, "Delaware Crime: Program's First Grads Put Hope to Work—Participants to Research Crime and Its Causes in Communities," *News Journal*, December 24, 2009.
61. Gavin Mueller, "Be the Street: On Radical Ethnography and Cultural Studies," *Viewpoint Magazine*, September 10, 2012, https://www.viewpointmag.com/2012/09/10/be-the-street-on-radical-ethnography-and-cultural-studies/.
62. Contreras, *Stickup Kids*.
63. Lory Janelle Dance, *Tough Fronts: The Impact of Street Culture on Schooling* (New York: Routledge, 2002).
64. Dance, 17; emphasis in original.
65. Jones, "Murder Town USA."
66. Jones.
67. Esteban Parra, Jessica Reyes, and Karl Baker, "Police Charge Death Was Gang-Related," *News Journal*, June 23, 2016, https://www.delawareonline.com/story/news/crime/2016/06/23/four-indicted-murder-15-year-old-brandon-wingo/86283700/.
68. Mimi Doll et al., "Perspectives of Community Partners and Researchers about Factors Impacting Coalition Functioning over Time," *Journal of Prevention & Intervention in the Community* 40, no. 2 (2012): 87–102; Peter Mendel et al., "Partnered Evaluation of a Community Engagement Intervention: Use of a 'Kickoff' Conference in a Randomized Trial for Depression Care Improvement in Underserved Communities," *Ethnicity and Disease* 21, no. 3, suppl. 1 (2011); Kenneth B. Wells et al., "Building an Academic-Community Partnered Network for Clinical Services Research: The Community Health Improvement Collaborative (CHIC)," *Ethnicity and Disease* 16, no. 1, suppl. 1 (2006): S3–S17.
69. Wade W. Nobles, "Extended Self: Rethinking the So-Called Negro Self-Concept," *Journal of Black Psychology* 2, no. 2 (1976): 15–24.

Chapter 1 A City of Banks

Epigraphs: Neil MacFarquhar, "After Centuries of Obscurity, Wilmington Is Having a Moment," *New York Times*, January 19, 2021, https://www.nytimes.com/2020/12/06/us/after-centuries-of-obscurity-wilmington-is-having-a-moment.html; Jessica Bies, "Wilmington: One of the Hardest Places to Achieve the American Dream," *News Journal*, October 4, 2018, https://www.delawareonline.com/story/news/2018/10/03/wilmington-one-hardest-places-achieve-american-dream-united-states/1490481002/.

1. Esteban Parra, "Death Penalty, Life in Prison in Eden Park Shootout," *News Journal*, September 4, 2015, http://www.delawareonline.com/story/news/crime/2015/09/04/two-sentenced-friday-eden-park-shootout/71693874/.
2. Brittany Horn, Esteban Parra, Christina Jedra, and Jessica Reyes, "Delaware's Economy Suffers from Wilmington's Violence," *News Journal*, September 10, 2017, https://www.delawareonline.com/story/news/crime/2017/09/08/delawares-economy-suffers-wilmingtons-violence/102562232/.
3. Eugene Young, personal communication with author, August 21, 2020.
4. João H. Costa Vargas, *Catching Hell in the City of Angels: Life and Meanings of Blackness in South Central Los Angeles* (Minneapolis: University of Minnesota Press, 2006).

5. Karl Baker, "Shooting outside Southbridge Bar," *News Journal*, November 3, 2015, http://www.delawareonline.com/story/news/2015/11/03/shooting-outside-southbridge-bar/75078540/.
6. Yasser Arafat Payne, *The People's Report: The Link between Structural Violence and Crime in Wilmington, Delaware* (Wilmington, DE: self-published, 2013), http://thepeoplesreport.com/images/pdf/The_Peoples_Report_final_draft_9-12-13.pdf.
7. Dennis P. Williams, "Dennis P. Williams: City Is Overcoming Adversity," *News Journal*, December 12, 2015, http://www.delawareonline.com/story/opinion/contributors/2015/12/11/dennis-williams-city-overcoming-adversity/77169302/.
8. Carol E. Hoffecker, *Corporate Capital: Wilmington in the Twentieth Century* (Philadelphia: Temple University Press, 1983).
9. Anon., "Tough Wilmington," *Evening Journal*, August 20, 1889, 3.
10. Hoffecker, *Corporate Capital*; Charles Tilly, Wagner D. Jackson, and Barry Kay, *Race and Residence in Wilmington, Delaware* (New York: Teachers College, Columbia University, 1965).
11. Hoffecker, *Corporate Capital*, 28.
12. Newark Free Community, "Wilmington: White Oppression, Black Despair," *The Heterodoxical Voice* 1, no. 3 (1968): 3, Chris Oakley Collection of Alternative Press, Special Collections, University of Delaware Library, https://exhibitions.lib.udel.edu/1968/exhibition-item/wilmington-white-oppression-black-despair-the-heterodoxical-voice-1968-july-august-volume-1-number-5-page-3/.
13. James Phelan and Robert Pozen, *The Company State* (New York: Grossman, 1973), 13.
14. Hoffecker, *Corporate Capital*.
15. Hoffecker, 65.
16. Hoffecker.
17. Phelan and Pozen, *Company State*.
18. Hoffecker, *Corporate Capital*.
19. Jake Blumgart and Gregory Scruggs, "Fortune 500 Companies, a Central Location and Low Taxes Can't Fix Wilmington," Next City, November 18, 2013, https://nextcity.org/features/fortune-500-companies-a-central-location-and-low-taxes-cant-fix-wilmington; Wink, "64% of Fortune 500 Firms."
20. Blumgart and Scruggs, "Fortune 500 Companies"; Leslie Wayne, "How Delaware Thrives as a Corporate Tax Haven," *New York Times*, June 30, 2012, https://www.nytimes.com/2012/07/01/business/how-delaware-thrives-as-a-corporate-tax-haven.html.
21. Wayne, "How Delaware Thrives."
22. Nicholas Shaxson, *Treasure Islands: Uncovering the Damage of Offshore Banking and Tax Havens* (New York: St. Martin's Press, 2011), 120.
23. Wayne, "How Delaware Thrives."
24. Karl Baker, "SEC Fraud Investigators Demand to Know Who Is behind Delaware LLCs," *News Journal*, December 1, 2017, https://www.delawareonline.com/story/money/business/2017/12/01/sec-fraud-investigators-demand-know-who-behind-delaware-llcs/908586001/; Christina Jedra, "Civic Groups Want 'Independent Counsel' to Look at Delaware's LLC Law," *News Journal*, August 7, 2018, https://www.delawareonline.com/story/news/2018/08/06/citizens-petition-ag-matt-denn-investigate-abuse-delaware-llcs/898036002/; Wayne, "How Delaware Thrives."
25. Baker, "SEC Fraud"; Jessica Masulli Reyes, "Reports: Del. Company May Be Linked to El Chapo," *News Journal*, January 15, 2016, https://www.delawareonline.com/story/news/local/2016/01/15/reports-del-company-may-linked-el-chapo/78859144/.
26. Christopher Wink, "Why Do So Many Banks Have Offices in Wilmington?," Technical.ly, November 18, 2016, https://technical.ly/delaware/2016/11/18/many-banks-headquartered-wilmington-delaware/.
27. Wink.

28. Wink.
29. Jones, "Murder Town USA."
30. Kubrin and Weitzer, "Retaliatory Homicide."
31. Anon., "Tough Wilmington."
32. Anon., 3.
33. Anon.
34. Hoffecker, *Corporate Capital*, 112.
35. Hoffecker, 96.
36. Hoffecker, 127.
37. Hoffecker, 159.
38. Griffin, *Black Brothers, Inc.*; Elizabeth Hinton and DeAnza Cook, "The Mass Criminalization of Black Americans: A Historical Overview," *Annual Review of Criminology* 4 (2021): 261–286.
39. Anon., "Tough Wilmington."
40. Harry Themal, "Harry Themal: New Castle County's Gruesome 1903 Lynching by Fire," *News Journal*, January 9, 2017, https://www.delawareonline.com/story/opinion/columnists/harry-themal/2017/01/09/harry-themal-new-castle-countys-gruesome-1903-lynching-fire/96253932/.
41. Allen Kim and Sheena Jones, "Delaware Removes Whipping Post outside Courthouse," CNN, July 1, 2020, https://www.cnn.com/2020/07/01/us/whipping-post-georgetown-delaware-trnd/index.html.
42. Virginia Postrel, "The Consequences of the 1960s Race Riots Come into View," *New York Times*, December 30, 2004, https://www.nytimes.com/2004/12/30/business/the-consequences-of-the-1960s-race-riots-come-into-view.html.
43. Hoffecker, *Corporate Capital*, 187–190.
44. Hoffecker, 188.
45. Hoffecker.
46. Hoffecker.
47. Jason Bourke, "Urban Governance and Economic Development: An Analysis of the Changing Political Economy of Wilmington, Delaware, 1945–2017" (PhD diss., University of Delaware, 2018).
48. Hoffecker, *Corporate Capital*.
49. Say Burgin, "The 1968 Occupation of Black Wilmington," African American Intellectual History Society/Black Perspectives, October 8, 2018, https://www.aaihs.org/the-1968-occupation-of-black-wilmington/.
50. TyLisa C. Johnson, "Etched in Memory," *Philadelphia Inquirer*, December 7, 2018, https://www.inquirer.com/news/a/wilmington-del-riots-occupation-martin-luther-king-jr-national-guard-20181207.html.
51. Hoffecker, *Corporate Capital*.
52. Cassie Owens, "What Can Happen When the National Guard Is Called into a City over Riots," Next City, April 29, 2015, https://nextcity.org/urbanist-news/city-riots-baltimore-wilmington-national-guard-in-cities.
53. Owens, "What Can Happen."
54. Hoffecker, *Corporate Capital*.
55. Hoffecker.
56. Hoffecker.
57. Hoffecker, 184.
58. Evelyn Scocas et al., *Wilmington Shootings 1996: A Comparative Study of Victims and Offenders in Wilmington, Delaware* (Dover, DE: Statistical Analysis Center and the Criminal Justice Council, 1997), https://www.ojp.gov/ncjrs/virtual-library/abstracts/wilmington-shootings-1996-comparative-study-victims-and-offenders.
59. Scocas et al.
60. Scocas et al.

61. Richard J. Harris and John P. O'Connell, *Operation Safe Streets Governor's Task Force: Review and Impact* (Dover: Delaware Criminal Justice Council Statistical Analysis Center, 2004).
62. Alejandro A. Alonso, "Racialized Identities and the Formation of Black Gangs in Los Angeles." *Urban Geography* 25, no. 7 (2004): 668.
63. Jones, "Murder Town USA"; "The Economic Cost of Gun Violence in Delaware," Giffords Law Center, 2018, https://giffords.org/wp-content/uploads/2018/11/The-Economic-Cost-of-Gun-Violence-in-Delaware-11.18.pdf.
64. Ryan Grim and David Dayen, "Tom Carper and the Rise and Fall of the Delaware Way," The Intercept, August 29, 2018, https://theintercept.com/2018/08/29/tom-carper-delaware-way-kerri-harris/.

CHAPTER 2   "WELCOME TO WILMINGTON—A PLACE TO BE SOMEBODY"

Epigraphs: James Baldwin, *The Fire Next Time* (1962; reprint, New York: Vintage Books, 1991), 5; Joshua M. Price, "Conflict over Approaches to Social Science Research—Participatory Action Research as Disruptive? A Report on a Conflict in Social Science Paradigms at a Criminal Justice Agency Promoting Alternatives to Incarceration," *Contemporary Justice Review* 11, no. 4 (2008): 388–389.

1. The City of Wilmington, Delaware, "City History," n.d., https://www.wilmingtonde.gov/about-us/about-the-city-of-wilmington/city-history.
2. James E. Newton, "Black Americans in Delaware: An Overview," in *History of African Americans of Delaware and Maryland's Eastern Shore*, ed. Carole C. Marks (Wilmington: Delaware Heritage Commission, 1997), 13–33.
3. "The Port of Wilmington," World Port Source, 2020, http://www.worldportsource.com/ports/review/USA_DE_The_Port_of_Wilmington_158.php.
4. Newton, "Black Americans."
5. Edward L. Ayers, *Vengeance and Justice: Crime and Punishment in the Nineteenth-Century American South* (New York: Oxford University Press, 1984); Newton, "Black Americans."
6. Ayers, *Vengeance and Justice*.
7. "History Matters: Wilmington's Southbridge Neighborhood," Delaware Public Media, February 15, 2015, https://www.delawarepublic.org/post/history-matters-wilmingtons-southbridge-neighborhood; Newton, "Black Americans."
8. "History Matters."
9. City of Wilmington, Delaware, "City History."
10. M. Chalmers and Esteban Parra, "Two Views on Violence: Wilmington Ranks Third in Violent Crime for U.S. Cities Its Size," *News Journal*, October 2, 2011, A1.
11. Ira Porter, "Hope Where Others See None: Project Goes Straight to the People to Cut Crime, Poverty," *News Journal*, November 21, 2010.
12. Oliver K. Roeder et al., *What Caused the Crime Decline?*, Brennan Center for Justice, New York University School of Law, February 12, 2015, https://www.brennancenter.org/our-work/research-reports/what-caused-crime-decline; Mason Johnson, "FBI's Violent Crime Statistics for Every City in America," CBS Chicago, October 22, 2015, http://chicago.cbslocal.com/2015/10/22/violent-crime-statistics-for-every-city-in-america/.
13. Reza Bakhshandeh et al., "Degrees of Separation in Social Networks," in *Proceedings of the International Symposium on Combinatorial Search* 2, no. 1, Fourth Annual Symposium on Combinatorial Search (2011), https://ojs.aaai.org/index.php/SOCS/article/view/18200; Jon Kleinberg, "The Small-World Phenomenon: An Algorithmic Perspective," in *Proceedings of the Thirty-Second Annual ACM Symposium on Theory of Computing* (New York: Association for Computing Machinery, 2000), 163–170.

14. Andrew V. Papachristos, Anthony A. Braga, and David M. Hureau, "Social Networks and the Risk of Gunshot Injury," *Journal of Urban Health* 89, no. 6 (2012): 992–1003.
15. Carole Harris, "Gangs in Wilmington," PowerPoint lecture and personal communication with author, 2016.
16. Matthew Desmond, "Relational Ethnography," *Theory and Society* 43, no. 5 (2014): 547–579; Carla L. Reeves, "A Difficult Negotiation: Fieldwork Relations with Gatekeepers," *Qualitative Research* 10, no. 3 (2010): 315–331.
17. Kathy Canavan, "Meet the Mayor: Mike Purzycki," *Delaware Business Times*, November 21, 2016, https://delawarebusinesstimes.com/news/features/meet-mayor-mike-purzycki/.
18. Canavan.
19. Canavan.
20. Darren Weaver, "This Tiny Building in Wilmington, Delaware Is Home to 300,000 Businesses," *Business Insider*, December 27, 2018, https://www.businessinsider.com.au/building-wilmington-delaware-largest-companies-ct-corporation-2017-4.
21. Weaver.
22. Newton, "Black Americans."
23. Angela Bryant and Yasser Payne, "Evaluating the Impact of Community-Based Learning: Participatory Action Research as a Model for Inside-Out," in *Turning Teaching Inside Out*, ed. Simone Weil Davis and Barbara Sherr Roswell (New York: Palgrave Macmillan, 2013), 227–239; Payne and Bryant, "Street Participatory Action Research."
24. Phillip J. Bowman, "Race, Class, and Ethics in Research: Belmont Principles to Functional Relevance," in *Black Psychology*, ed. R. L. Jones (Berkeley, CA: Cobb & Henry, 1991), 747–766; Tara M. Brown, "ARISE to the Challenge: Partnering with Urban Youth to Improve Educational Research and Learning," *Penn GSE Perspectives on Urban Education* 7, no. 1 (2010): 4–14; Tara M. Brown, "'Hitting the Streets': Youth Street Involvement as Adaptive Well-Being," *Harvard Educational Review* 86, no. 1 (2016): 48–71; Nathan Caplan, "The Indigenous Anchorman: A Solution to Some Ghetto Survey Problems," *The Analyst* 1 (1969): 20–34; Michelle Fine et al., *Changing Minds: The Impact of College in a Maximum-Security Prison* (New York: Leslie Glass Foundation and the Open Society Institute, 2001), https://www.prisonpolicy.org/scans/changing_minds.pdf.; Michelle Fine et al., "'Anything Can Happen with Police Around': Urban Youth Evaluate Strategies of Surveillance in Public Places," *Journal of Social Issues* 59, no. 1 (2003): 141–158; Andrew C. Greene, "Sociopolitical Tales of Cultivating Spirituality, Collective Hope, and Emotional Vulnerabilities through a Community-Specific (Grassroots Movement Praxis) Approach to Youth Development" (PhD diss., City University of New York Graduate Center, 2020); Brooklynn Hitchens, "Stress and Street Life: Black Women, Urban Inequality, and Coping in a Small Violent City" (PhD diss., Rutgers University, 2020); LIFERS, "Ending the Culture"; Damion Morgan et al., "Youth Participatory Action Research on Hustling and Its Consequences: A Report from the Field," *Children Youth and Environments* 14, no. 2 (2004): 201–228; Leith Mullings and Alaka Wali, *Stress and Resilience: The Social Context of Reproduction in Central Harlem* (Boston: Springer, 2001); Yasser Arafat Payne, "Participatory Action Research," in *The Wiley Blackwell Encyclopedia of Social Theory* (Hoboken, NJ: Wiley-Blackwell, 2017), 1694–1708; Payne and Brown, "I'm Still Waiting"; Payne and Bryant, "Street Participatory Action Research"; Hans Toch, "The Study of Man: The Convict as Researcher," *Trans-action* 4, no. 9 (1967): 72–75.
25. Bryant and Payne, "Evaluating the Impact"; Payne, *People's Report*.
26. Fran Baum, Colin MacDougall, and Danielle Smith, "Participatory Action Research," *Journal of Epidemiology and Community Health* 60, no. 10 (2006): 854.
27. Baum et al.

28. John A. Rich and Courtney M. Grey, "Pathways to Recurrent Trauma among Young Black Men: Traumatic Stress, Substance Use, and the 'Code of the Street,'" *American Journal of Public Health* 95, no. 5 (2005): 816–824.
29. Rich and Grey, 816, 819, 821.
30. Robert Bogdan and Sari Knopp Biklen, *Qualitative Research for Education: An Introduction to Theory and Methods* (Boston: Pearson / Allyn and Bacon, 2007).
31. Diane Turner, "The Interview Technique as Oral History in Black Studies," in *Handbook of Black Studies*, ed. Molefi Asante and Maulana Karenga (Thousand Oaks, CA: Sage, 2006), 329–332; Adeniyi Coker, "Film as Historical Method in Black Studies: Documenting the African Experience," in Asante and Karenga, *Handbook of Black Studies*, 352–366.
32. Bruce W. Tuckman, *Conducting Educational Research* (Fort Worth, TX: Harcourt Brace College Publishers, 1999).
33. Ann Arnett Ferguson, *Bad Boys: Public Schools in the Making of Black Masculinity* (Ann Arbor: University of Michigan Press, 2001).
34. J. Benjamin Hinnant, Marion O'Brien, and Sharon R. Ghazarian, "The Longitudinal Relations of Teacher Expectations to Achievement in the Early School Years," *Journal of Educational Psychology* 101, no. 3 (2009): 662; Robert Rosenthal and Lenore Jacobsen, *Pygmalion in the Classroom: Teacher Expectation and Pupils' Intellectual Development* (New York: Holt, Rinehart and Winston, 1968).
35. Rosenthal and Jacobsen, *Pygmalion in the Classroom*.
36. Yasser Arafat Payne and Tara M. Brown, "The Educational Experiences of Street Life–Oriented Black Boys: How Black Boys Use Street Life as a Site of Resilience in High School," *Journal of Contemporary Criminal Justice* 26, no. 3 (2010): 316–338; Payne and Brown, "I'm Still Waiting."

CHAPTER 3 "MURDER TOWN, USA"

Epigraphs: James Gilligan, "Dr. James Gilligan on Violence," YouTube, October 20, 2010, https://www.youtube.com/watch?v=HmZjm7yOHwE; Zach Phillips, in "Tidal Wave," episode 3 of *Remaking Murdertown: Poverty, Punishment, and Possibility*, podcast series sponsored by the Delaware Center for Justice and produced by Zach Phillips (Wilmington, DE: Short Order Production House, 2016), June 13, 2016, http://remaking.murdertown.us/episodes/2016/season-one/tidal-wave.

1. Maggie Bowers, "Two Local Cities Land on the List of 'Unfriendliest' in the Country," NBC10 Philadelphia, August 8, 2014, http://www.nbcphiladelphia.com/entertainment/the-scene/Local-Cities-Ranked-Least-Friendly-in-the-US-270398061.html; Maggie Hiufu Wong, "Friendliest/Unfriendliest U.S. Cities, according to *Condé Nast Traveler*," CNN Travel, August 7, 2014, http://www.cnn.com/travel/article/us-unfriendliest-friendliest-cities/index.html; Jones, "Murder Town USA"; *Parenting*, "Top 10 Most Dangerous Cities in America," *Parenting*, June 2012; Andrew Staub, "Wilmington Ranked Most Dangerous City on Crime Rate," *News Journal*, August 22, 2012, http://www.delawareonline.com/article/20120822/NEWS/120822013/Wilmington-rankedmost-dangerous-city-crime-rate.
2. Juliet Linderman et al., "Growing Up under Fire: Wilmington, Delaware, Leads U.S. in Teen Shootings," *USA Today*, September 8, 2017, https://www.usatoday.com/story/news/2017/09/08/wilmington-delaware-leads-u-s-teen-shootings/619458001/.
3. Jones, "Murder Town USA."
4. Ryan Cormier, "Murder Town TV Show 'Probably Dead at This Point,'" *News Journal*, August 12, 2016, http://www.delawareonline.com/story/entertainment/2016/08/12/murder-town-tv-show-probably-dead-point/88614690/.
5. Phillips, "Tidal Wave."

6. Ferguson, *Bad Boys.*
7. Steven Sumner et al., *Elevated Rates of Urban Firearm Violence and Opportunities for Prevention—Wilmington, Delaware: Final Report* (Washington, DC: Division of Violence Prevention, National Center for Injury Prevention and Control, Centers for Disease Control and Prevention, 2015), http://www.dhss.delaware.gov/dhss/cdc finalreport.pdf; Jones, "Murder Town USA."
8. John Watson, "No Escaping Wilmington Violence in 2013," WHYY, December 26, 2013, https://whyy.org/articles/no-escaping-wilmington-violence-in-2013/; Richard J. Harris, Jim Salt, and Charles Huenke, *Delaware Shootings 2012: An Overview of Incidents, Suspects, and Victims in Delaware* (Dover: Delaware Criminal Justice Council Statistical Analysis Center, 2013), https://sac.delaware.gov/wp-content/uploads/sites/64/2017/04/2012StatewideShootingReportNovember-2013.pdf.
9. Christina Jedra, Esteban Parra, and Adam Duvernay, "Wilmington's Deadliest Year: Mayor Withholds 'Serious Concern' until Plan Takes Hold," Delaware Online, January 5, 2018, https://www.delawareonline.com/get-access/?return=https%3A%2F%2Fwww.delawareonline.com%2Fstory%2Fnews%2Flocal%2F2018%2F01%2F05%2Fwilmington-mayor-record-shootings-homicides-not-yet-cause-serious-concern-wilmington-mayor-record-sh%2F984347001%2F.
10. Jones, "Murder Town USA."
11. Jones.
12. Alonso, "Racialized Identities."
13. Alonso, 668.
14. Bruce A. Jacobs, *Robbing Drug Dealers: Violence beyond the Law* (London: Routledge, 2001); Vargas, *Wounded City.*
15. Sudhir Alladi Venkatesh, *Gang Leader for a Day: A Rogue Sociologist Takes to the Streets* (New York: Penguin Books, 2008).
16. Venkatesh, 209.
17. Duck, *No Way Out.*
18. 6-ABC, "Brothers Arrested in Wilmington Homicide," ABC Philadelphia, December 10, 2009, http://6abc.com/archive/7162927/.
19. Thomas Abt, *Bleeding Out: The Devastating Consequences of Urban Violence—and a Bold New Plan for Peace in the Streets* (New York: Basic Books, 2019).
20. William Darity et al., *What We Get Wrong about Closing the Racial Wealth Gap* (Durham, NC: Samuel DuBois Cook Center on Social Equity, 2018), https://socialequity.duke.edu/sites/socialequity.duke.edu/files/site-images/FINAL%20COMPLETE%20REPORT_.pdf.
21. Yann Ranaivo, "Wilmington Police Homicide Unit Coming Soon," *News Journal*, October 14, 2014, http://www.delawareonline.com/story/news/local/2014/10/13/wilmington-police-homicide-unit-coming-soon/17230097/.
22. German Lopez, "The Great Majority of Violent Crime in America Goes Unsolved," Vox, March 1, 2017, https://www.vox.com/policy-and-politics/2017/3/1/14777612/trump-crime-certainty-severity; Wesley Lowery, Kimbriell Kelly, and Steven Rich, "Murder with Impunity: An Unequal Justice," *Washington Post*, July 25, 2018, https://www.washingtonpost.com/graphics/2018/investigations/black-homicides-arrests/?noredirect=on&utm_term=.1edacfb85163.
23. Vinny Vella and Jason Nark, "Is Wilmington Really 'Murder Town'?," *Philadelphia Inquirer*, December 23, 2015, http://articles.philly.com/2015-12-23/news/69240133_1_cousin-shot-city-council-city-officials; Wilmington Public Safety Strategies Commission, *Crime Analysis and CAD Incident Analysis (2010–2014)* (Wilmington, DE: Wilmington Public Safety Strategies Commission, 2015).
24. Vargas, *Catching Hell*; Harding, *Living the Drama.*
25. Thomas Abt, "The Surge in Violent Crime Is Overblown—but Here's How to Combat It," Vox, September 30, 2016, https://www.vox.com/2016/9/30/13115224/crime-violent-reduce-ferguson-murder-fbi-ucr; Abt, *Bleeding Out.*

26. Duck, *No Way Out*.
27. Janine M. Jones, "Exposure to Chronic Community Violence: Resilience in African American Children," *Journal of Black Psychology* 33, no. 2 (2007): 125–149; Nancy Romero-Daza, Margaret Weeks, and Merrill Singer, "'Nobody Gives a Damn If I Live or Die': Violence, Drugs, and Street-Level Prostitution in Inner-City Hartford, Connecticut," *Medical Anthropology* 22, no. 3 (2003): 233–259; Wilson, *When Work Disappears*.
28. Michael A. Yonas et al., "Neighborhood-Level Factors and Youth Violence: Giving Voice to the Perceptions of Prominent Neighborhood Individuals," *Health Education & Behavior* 34, no. 4 (2007): 669–685.
29. Leith Mullings and Alaka Wali, *Stress and Resilience: The Social Context of Reproduction in Central Harlem* (Boston: Springer, 2001); Alford A. Young, *Minds of Marginalized Black Men: Making Sense of Mobility, Opportunity, and Future Life Chances* (Princeton, NJ: Princeton University Press, 2004).
30. Jones, "Exposure to Chronic Community Violence."
31. Jones.
32. Teresa Masterson, "Teen Arrested for Hit-and-Run Death of Boy," NBC10 Philadelphia, February 3, 2010, http://www.nbcphiladelphia.com/news/local/Teen-Arrested-for-Hit-and-Run-Death-of-Boy-83487837.html.
33. Mark Nardone, "Wilmington Crime: A City That Bleeds—Part One in a Series Explains Why Violent Crime Has Increased in Wilmington," *Delaware Today*, April 23, 2015, http://www.delawaretoday.com/Delaware-Today/May-2015/Wilmington-Crime-A-City-That-Bleeds/.
34. Tucker v. State of Delaware, Cr. I.D. No. 1109012280A, Supr. Ct. No. 685, 2013 (Del. Supr. Ct. Nov. 21, 2014), http://cases.justia.com/delaware/supreme-court/2014-685-2013.pdf?ts=1416834064.
35. Minnie Chalmers and Terri Sanginiti, "Mom in Mourning Leans on Faith: 19-Year-Old Son Collapses in His Mother's Arms after Being Shot in the Chest," *News Journal*, September 15, 2011; Nardone, "Wilmington Crime."

CHAPTER 4   "I'M STILL WAITING MAN . . . ON THAT GOLDEN TICKET!"

Epigraph: Byron Allen, "Byron Allen Billionaire Talks Black Wealth with Antonio Moore," YouTube, April 4, 2016, https://www.youtube.com/watch?v=8WyxXMZ9IXI.

Section epigraph: Martin Luther King Jr., "The Three Evils of Society," speech delivered at the First Annual National Conference on New Politics, Chicago, August 31, 1967, https://www.nwesd.org/ed-talks/equity/the-three-evils-of-society-address-martin-luther-king-jr/.

1. Matt Bittle, "Delaware's U.S. Senators Are Members of 'Top 1 Percent' in Income," *Delaware State News*, June 29, 2015, https://baytobaynews.com/stories/delawares-us-senators-are-members-of-top-1-percent-in-income,911?.
2. Payne, *People's Report*.
3. Chris Coons, "Senator Coons to Launch Conversation on Fight against Urban Unemployment," Chris Coons, February 18, 2014, https://www.coons.senate.gov/news/press-releases/senator-coons-to-launch-conversation-on-fight-against-urban-unemployment.
4. Chris Coons, "Senator Coons Hosts Opening Discussion in Series on Urban Unemployment," Chris Coons, February 19, 2014, https://www.coons.senate.gov/news/press-releases/senator-coons-hosts-opening-discussion-in-series-on-urban-unemployment.
5. Oscar Lewis, "The Culture of Poverty," *Scientific American* 215, no. 4 (1966): 19–25.
6. Coons, "Senator Coons Hosts Opening."

7. Delaware Public Media, "Sen. Coons Taps Experts, Community to Help Fight Urban Employment," Delaware Public Media, February 19, 2014, https://www.delawarepublic.org/2014-02-19/sen-coons-taps-experts-community-to-help-fight-urban-unemployment.
8. Delaware Public Media.
9. Michael Barry Katz, *Improving Poor People: The Welfare State, the "Underclass," and Urban Schools as History* (Princeton, NJ: Princeton University Press, 1995); Martin Gilens, *Why Americans Hate Welfare: Race, Media, and the Politics of Antipoverty Policy* (Chicago: University of Chicago Press, 2000).
10. Alexander, *New Jim Crow*.
11. The White House, "Remarks by the President in State of the Union Address," The White House, January 24, 2012, https://www.whitehouse.gov/the-press-office/2012/01/24/remarks-president-state-union-address.
12. John H. McWhorter, *Losing the Race: Self-Sabotage in Black America* (New York: Simon and Schuster, 2000); Lewis, "Culture of Poverty"; Orlando Patterson, "Try on the Outfit and Just See How It Works: The Psychocultural Responses of Disconnected Youth to Work," in *The Cultural Matrix: Understanding Black Youth*, ed. Orlando Patterson (Cambridge, MA: Harvard University Press, 2015), 415–443.
13. Bureau of Labor Statistics, *Labor Force Statistics from the Current Population Survey: Employment Status of the Civilian Noninstitutional Population by Sex, Age, and Race* (Washington, DC: U.S. Department of Labor, 2014).
14. Black, *When a Heart Turns Rock Solid*; Todd R. Clear, Dina R. Rose, and Judith A. Ryder, "Incarceration and the Community: The Problem of Removing and Returning Offenders," *Crime & Delinquency* 47, no. 3 (2001): 335–351; Payne and Brown, "I'm Still Waiting."
15. "Racial Wealth Equity Network," Prosperity Now, 2019, https://prosperitynow.org/get-involved/racial-wealth-equity.
16. Rakesh Kochhar and Richard Fry, "Wealth Inequality Has Widened along Racial, Ethnic Lines since End of Great Recession," *Pew Research Center* 12, no. 104 (2014): 121–145.
17. A. Sum, "Jobless Rate for Poor Black Teen Dropouts? Try 95 Percent," interview by Paul Solman, *PBS NewsHour*, July 5, 2013.
18. Wilson, *When Work Disappears*.
19. Peter B. Edelman, Harry J. Holzer, and Paul Offner, *Reconnecting Disadvantaged Young Men* (Washington, DC: Urban Institute, 2006); William J. Wilson, *More than Just Race: Being Black and Poor in the Inner City* (New York: Norton, 2009); Young, *Minds of Marginalized Black Men*.
20. Stephen Edgell, *The Sociology of Work: Continuity and Change in Paid and Unpaid Work* (London: Sage, 2012).
21. U.S. Department of Labor, "Occupations with the Most Openings" (Washington, DC: U.S. Department of Labor, 2015).
22. Edelman, Holzer, and Offner, *Reconnecting Disadvantaged Young Men*; Lily Fernandes and Nora Hadi Q. Alsaeed, "African Americans and Workplace Discrimination," *European Journal of English Language and Literature Studies* 2, no. 2 (2014): 56–76; Sherry N. Mong and Vincent J. Roscigno, "African American Men and the Experience of Employment Discrimination," *Qualitative Sociology* 33, no. 1 (2010): 1–21.
23. Wilson, *More than Just Race*, 10.
24. Wilson.
25. Wilson.
26. Douglas S. Massey, *Categorically Unequal: The American Stratification System* (New York: Russell Sage Foundation, 2007).
27. Clearinghouse for Economic Well-Being in Social Work Education, "Working Definition of Economic Well-Being," Council of Social Work Education (CSWE),

Notes to Pages 96–102

October 2016, https://www.cswe.org/centers-initiatives/economic-wellbeing-clearinghouse/working-definition-of-economic-wellbeing/.
28. Daniel P. Mears, Xia Wang, and William D. Bales, "Does a Rising Tide Lift All Boats? Labor Market Changes and Their Effects on the Recidivism of Released Prisoners," *Justice Quarterly* 31, no. 5 (2014): 822–851.
29. Clearinghouse for Economic Well-Being in Social Work Education, "Working Definition."
30. Payne, "Site of Resilience."
31. American Bar Association, "National Inventory of Collateral Consequences of Conviction," 2013; Anthony C. Thompson, *Releasing Prisoners, Redeeming Communities: Reentry, Race, and Politics* (New York: New York University Press, 2008).
32. Alexander, *New Jim Crow.*
33. William G. Howell, "Results of President Obama's Race to the Top," *Education Next* 15, no. 4 (2015): 58–67.
34. Howell.
35. Matthew Albright, "Brown v. Board, 60 Years Later: Are We Better Off?," *News Journal*, May 18, 2014, http://www.delawareonline.com/story/news/education/2014/05/16/sunday-preview-brown-v-board-years-later/9196775/.
36. Jessica Bies and Matthew Albright, "Ex-Delaware Education Secretary: Union Blocked Progress," Delaware Online, April 12, 2017, https://www.delawareonline.com/story/news/education/2017/04/12/former-ed-secretary-says-he-lost-teachers-union/100374092/.
37. Albright, "Brown v. Board."
38. Ann Beaudry, John H. Jackson, and Michelle Alexander, *Black Lives Matter: The Schott 50 State Report on Public Education and Black Males* (Cambridge, MA: Schott Foundation for Public Education, 2015).
39. The Schott Foundation for Public Education, *Black Lives Matter: The Schott 50 State Report on Public Education and Black Males*, February 11, 2015, https://schottfoundation.org/resource/black-lives-matter-the-schott-50-state-report-on-public-education-and-black-males/.
40. Susan Ferriss, "The School-to-Court Pipeline: Where Does Your State Rank?," *Reveal*, April 11, 2015, https://revealnews.org/article/the-school-to-court-pipeline-where-does-your-state-rank/; Cassie Powell, "'One of the Worst': The School-to-Prison Pipeline in Richmond, Virginia," RVAGOV, University of Richmond, 2016, https://scholarship.richmond.edu/cgi/viewcontent.cgi?article=1128&context=law-student-publications.
41. Arthur Garrison and Christian Kervick, *Analysis of City of Wilmington Violence and Social/Economic Data* (Wilmington, DE: Criminal Justice Council, 2006).
42. Adam Taylor and Ira Porter, "Growing Audacity amongst City Gunmen: Residents Fear They'll Be Innocent Victims," Delaware Online, September 20, 2009, http://www.delawareonline.com/article/20090920/NEWS01/909200364/Growing-audacity-amongcity-gunmen.
43. Ira Porter, "Anthony Logan—My Neighborhood: A Special *News Journal* Report Special," *News Journal*, November 22, 2010.
44. Saranac Hale Spencer, "Christina Seeks Answers to School Discipline Issues," *News Journal*, May 26, 2016, https://www.delawareonline.com/story/news/education/2016/05/25/christina-seeks-answers-school-discipline-issues/84929680/.
45. Spencer.
46. Wilmington Education Improvement Commission, *Strengthening Wilmington: An Action Agenda*, 2015, https://bpb-us-w2.wpmucdn.com/sites.udel.edu/dist/7/3504/files/2015/08/weac-final-book-2015-web-uxn0ge.pdf.
47. Larry Nagengast, "When Will Public Schools Get Better?," *Delaware Today*, June 7, 2017, https://delawaretoday.com/uncategorized/when-will-public-schools-get-better/.

48. Matthew Albright and Saranac Hale Spencer, "Legislators Push Back Redistricting Vote to Next Year," *News Journal*, July 2, 2016, https://www.delawareonline.com/story/news/2016/06/30/legislators-push-back-redistricting-until-next-year/86576406/.
49. Jessica Bies, "Delaware Student Test Results Confirm Plight of Low-Income Students," *News Journal*, July 28, 2017, https://www.delawareonline.com/story/news/education/2017/07/28/state-test-results-confirm-plight-delawares-low-income-students/512992001/.
50. Signithia Fordham and John U. Ogbu, "Black Students' School Success: Coping with the Burden of 'Acting White,'" *Urban Review* 18, no. 3 (1986): 176–206; Eric A. Stewart and Ronald L. Simons, "Race, Code of the Street, and Violent Delinquency: A Multilevel Investigation of Neighborhood Street Culture and Individual Norms of Violence," *Criminology* 48, no. 2 (2010): 569–605.
51. Nilda Flores-González, *School Kids / Street Kids: Identity Development in Latino Students* (New York: Teachers College Press, 2002); Nikki Jones, *Between Good and Ghetto: African American Girls and Inner-City Violence* (New Brunswick, NJ: Rutgers University Press, 2010); Payne and Brown, "Educational Experiences."
52. Pedro Mateu-Gelabert and Howard Lune, "Street Codes in High School: School as an Educational Deterrent," *City & Community* 6, no. 3 (2007): 173–191.
53. Gaston Alonso et al., *Our Schools Suck: Students Talk Back to a Segregated Nation on the Failures of Urban Education* (New York: New York University Press, 2009); Ferguson, *Bad Boys*.
54. Aviles Ann de Bradley, *From Charity to Equity: Race, Homelessness, and Urban Schools* (New York: Teachers College Press, 2015); Brown, "Hitting the Streets"; Vigil, *Rainbow of Gangs*.
55. Avelardo Valdez, *Mexican American Girls and Gang Violence: Beyond Risk* (New York: Palgrave Macmillan, 2009); Jones, *Between Good and Ghetto*; Richard Spano, William Alex Pridemore, and John Bolland, "Specifying the Role of Exposure to Violence and Violent Behavior on Initiation of Gun Carrying: A Longitudinal Test of Three Models of Youth Gun Carrying," *Journal of Interpersonal Violence* 27, no. 1 (2012): 158–176.
56. Dance, *Tough Fronts*, 47.
57. Victor M. Rios, *Punished: Policing the Lives of Black and Latino Boys* (New York University Press, 2011).
58. Tyrone C. Howard and Richard Milner, *Handbook of Urban Education* (New York: Routledge, 2014).
59. Jessica Masulli Reyes, "Wilmington Shooting Leads to Prison Sentence," *News Journal*, September 8, 2016, https://www.delawareonline.com/story/news/crime/2016/09/08/wilmington-shooting-leads-prison-sentence/89997840/.
60. Adam Taylor, Terri Sanginiti, and Sean O'Sullivan, "US DE: Riverside Mourns Slain 'Ghetto Icon,'" Media Awareness Project, October 23, 2005, http://www.mapinc.org/drugnews/v05/n1678/a03.html.
61. Robin Brown, "Man Killed in Wilmington Shooting," *News Journal*, April 3, 2014, https://www.delawareonline.com/story/news/crime/2014/04/02/wilmington-police-scene-shooting/7223057/.
62. Ferguson, *Bad Boys*; Yasser Arafat Payne and Tara Marie Brown, "It's Set Up for Failure, and They Know This: How the School-to-Prison Pipeline Impacts the Educational Experiences of Street-Identified Black Youth and Young Adults," *Villanova Law Review* 62 (2017): 307; Rios, *Punished*.
63. Lauren Musu-Gillette et al., *Indicators of School Crime and Safety: 2017* (Washington, DC: National Center for Education Statistics, U.S. Department of Education, 2018), https://nces.ed.gov/pubs2018/2018036.pdf.
64. Randall Chase, "Teens Face Judge in Deadly Delaware School Restroom Fight Case," NBC10 Philadelphia, April 4, 2017, https://www.nbcphiladelphia.com/news/local/amy-joyner-francis-high-school-bathroom-death/11147/.

Notes to Pages 110–116

65. Baker, "SEC Fraud."
66. Parra, Reyes, and Baker, "Police Charge"; Xerxes Wilson and Nick Perez, "Two Sentenced in Murder of 15-Year-Old Brandon Wingo," *News Journal*, January 31, 2020, https://www.delawareonline.com/story/news/crime/2020/01/31/two-sentenced-murder-15-year-old-brandon-wingo/4564219002/.
67. Wilson and Perez, "Two Sentenced."
68. Wilson and Perez.
69. Horn et al., "Wilmington."
70. Wilson, *More than Just Race*.

CHAPTER 5 "F-CK THE POLICE!"

Epigraph: William L. Patterson, Ossie Davis, Jarvis Tyner, and U.S. Civil Rights Congress, eds., *We Charge Genocide: The Historic Petition to the United Nations for Relief from a Crime of the United States Government against the Negro People* (New York: Civil Rights Congress, 1951), 8.

1. Cris Barrish, "Shootings Rise in Wilmington in 2019 as Homicide Clearance Rate Drops Sharply," *News Journal*, December 26, 2019, https://whyy.org/articles/shootings-rise-in-wilmington-in-2019-as-homicide-clearance-rate-drops-sharply/; Vella and Nark, "Is Wilmington Really 'Murder Town'?"; Wilmington Public Safety Strategies Commission, *Crime Analysis*.
2. Barrish, "Shootings Rise"; Adam Duvernay, "Gun Murders, Especially in Wilmington, Continue to Be Toughest to Solve," *News Journal*, August 22, 2018, https://www.delawareonline.com/story/news/crime/2018/08/22/gun-murders-especially-wilmington-continue-toughest-solve/999185002/.
3. Robert J. Durán, "Legitimated Oppression: Inner-City Mexican American Experiences with Police Gang Enforcement," *Journal of Contemporary Ethnography* 38, no. 2 (2009): 149.
4. U.S. Department of Justice, Civil Rights Division, *Investigation of the Ferguson Police Department* (Washington, DC: U.S. Department of Justice, Civil Rights Division, 2015), https://www.justice.gov/sites/default/files/opa/press-releases/attachments/2015/03/04/ferguson_police_department_report.pdf.
5. U.S. Department of Justice, Civil Rights Division.
6. U.S. Department of Justice, Civil Rights Division, *Investigation of the Baltimore City Police Department* (Washington, DC: U.S. Department of Justice, Civil Rights Division, 2016), https://civilrights.baltimorecity.gov/sites/default/files/20160810_DOJ%20BPD%20Report-FINAL.pdf.
7. Wilmington Public Safety Strategies Commission, *Crime Analysis*.
8. Mike Maciag, "Police Employment, Officer Per Capita Rates for U.S. Cities," *Governing*, May 7, 2014, http://www.governing.com/gov-data/safety-justice/police-officers-per-capita-rates-employment-for-city-departments.html.
9. Wilmington Public Safety Strategies Commission, *Crime Analysis*.
10. Federal Bureau of Investigation, *Crime in the United States 2013*, accessed January 4, 2023, https://ucr.fbi.gov/crime-in-the-u.s/2013/crime-in-the-u.s.-2013.
11. Wilmington Public Safety Strategies Commission, *Crime Analysis*; Federal Bureau of Investigation, *Crime in the United States 2013*.
12. Jenna Pizzi, "Shotspotter: Wilmington Gunshots Decrease 42 Percent," *News Journal*, July 8, 2015, https://www.delawareonline.com/story/news/crime/2015/07/06/wilm-officials-fewer-gunshots-detected-downtown/29793477/.
13. Esteban Parra and Adam Wagner, "Wilmington Unveils Public Safety Initiative," *News Journal*, January 26, 2015, https://www.delawareonline.com/story/news/local/2015/01/26/wilmington-unveils-public-safety-initiative/22345323/.

14. Jenna Pizzi, "Wilmington Police Disband Community Policing Unit," *News Journal*, January 12, 2016, https://www.delawareonline.com/story/news/local/2016/01/11/wilmington-police-disband-community-policing-unit/78660918/.
15. Ranaivo, "Wilmington Police Homicide."
16. 6-ABC, "Brothers Arrested."
17. Brittany Horn, "13 Gang Members Face 91 Charges, Including Murder," *News Journal*, September 11, 2015, https://www.delawareonline.com/story/news/crime/2015/09/11/gang-members-indicted-charges-including-murder/72080642/.
18. Yasser Arafat Payne, "Jobs, Not Jail, the Answer to Wilmington Violence," *News Journal*, June 7, 2015, https://www.delawareonline.com/story/opinion/contributors/2015/06/07/jobs-jail-answer-wilmington-violence/28661195/.
19. Wilmington Public Safety Strategies Commission, *Crime Analysis*. Although to some extent a misnomer, this commission was often colloquially referred to as the "crime commission"—a widely publicized group assembled by Governor Jack Markell to primarily create major police reform in the City of Wilmington.
20. Adam Wagner, "Williams Doesn't Back Down on Police Recommendations," *News Journal*, April 15, 2015, https://www.delawareonline.com/story/news/2015/04/15/wilmington-mayor-dennis-williams-meets-crime-consultants/25795369/; Wilmington Public Safety Strategies Commission, *Crime Analysis*.
21. Esteban Parra, Jessica Reyes, and Karl Baker, "Police Charge Death Was Gang-Related," *News Journal*, June 23, 2016, https://www.delawareonline.com/story/news/crime/2016/06/23/four-indicted-murder-15-year-old-brandon-wingo/86283700/; Xerxes Wilson, "Councilman Street: Crime-Reduction Efforts Have Failed," *News Journal*, October 23, 2015, https://www.delawareonline.com/story/news/2015/10/21/councilman-street-crime-reduction-efforts-have-failed/74345110/; Brittany Horn, "Wilmington Rapper's Mom Sees Killing as Retaliation," *News Journal*, November 30, 2016, http://www.delawareonline.com/story/news/crime/2016/11/30/wilmington-rappers-mom-sees-killing-retaliation/94667130/.
22. Horn, "Wilmington Rapper's Mom."
23. Parra, Reyes, and Baker, "Police Charge."
24. Jessica Reyes, Jenna Pizzi, and Esteban Parra, "Wilmington Residents Say Rift with Police Growing Worse," *News Journal*, October 2, 2015, https://www.delawareonline.com/story/news/local/2015/10/02/city-residents-say-rift-police-growing-worse/73241752/.
25. Victor M. Rios, *Punished: Policing the Lives of Black and Latino Boys* (New York: New York University Press, 2011), 121.
26. Payne, "Site of Resilience," 439.
27. Rios, *Punished*.
28. Rios.
29. Payne, "Participatory Action Research."
30. Rod K. Brunson and Brian A. Wade, "'Oh Hell No, We Don't Talk to Police': Insights on the Lack of Cooperation in Police Investigations of Urban Gun Violence," *Criminology & Public Policy* 18, no. 3 (2019): 623–648.
31. Karl Baker and Esteban Parra, "'Hidden from View': The Ongoing Battle for More Police Transparency in Delaware," *News Journal*, June 20, 2020, https://www.delawareonline.com/story/news/2020/06/18/delaware-police-records-private-what-does-mean-reform/3208401001/.
32. Kimberly Kindy, "Fatal Police Shootings in 2015 Approaching 400 Nationwide," *Washington Post*, May 30, 2015, https://www.washingtonpost.com/national/fatal-police-shootings-in-2015-approaching-400-nationwide/2015/05/30/d322256a-058e-11e5-a428-c984eb077d4e_story.html; Anne Nordberg et al., "Exploring

Minority Youths' Police Encounters: A Qualitative Interpretive Meta-synthesis," *Child and Adolescent Social Work Journal* 33, no. 2 (2016): 137–149.
33. James Comey, "Hard Truths: Law Enforcement and Race," FBI, February 12, 2015, https://www.fbi.gov/news/speeches/hard-truths-law-enforcement-and-race; Kindy, "Fatal Police Shootings."
34. Angela Hattery and Earl Smith, *Policing Black Bodies: How Black Lives Are Surveilled and How to Work for Change* (Lanham, MD: Rowman & Littlefield, 2018).
35. Kindy, "Fatal Police Shootings"; Wesley Lowery, "Aren't More White People than Black People Killed by Police? Yes, but No," *Washington Post*, October 11, 2016, https://www.washingtonpost.com/news/post-nation/wp/2016/07/11/arent-more-white-people-than-black-people-killed-by-police-yes-but-no/?utm_term=.a4ea598d95ed.
36. Yasser Arafat Payne, Brooklyn K. Hitchens, and Darryl L. Chambers, "'Why I Can't Stand Out in Front of My House?' Street-Identified Black Youth and Young Adult's Negative Encounters with Police," *Sociological Forum* 32 (2017): 874–895.
37. Contreras, *Stickup Kids*; Bourgois, *In Search of Respect*; Payne, "Site of Resilience"; Rios, *Punished*.
38. Darryl L. Chambers, *Cease Violence Wilmington: First Year Implementation, Evaluation, and Initial Impact Assessment* (Wilmington: Center for Drug and Health Studies, University of Delaware, 2016).
39. An Honorary Associate is an Associate who never received methods training or participated as a Research Associate on a Street PAR project. Honorary Associates (who are generally from the streets) are also a secondary group of Associates who in varying ways have supported the Wilmington Street PAR program.
40. Center for Structural Equity, accessed February 3, 2023, https://www.structuralequity.org/.
41. Jen Rini, "Cold Case: Wilmington Man Indicted for 2008 Murder," *News Journal*, October 13, 2015, http://www.delawareonline.com/story/news/crime/2015/10/12/wilmington-man-indicted-2008-cold-case-murder/73843200/.
42. Duck, *No Way Out*.
43. Esteban Parra, "Murder Suspect's Facebook Page Down after Comments Posted," *News Journal*, April 2, 2016, https://www.delawareonline.com/story/news/crime/2016/04/02/murder-suspect-facebook-page-down-after-comments-posted/82550998/.
44. Xerxes Wilson, "Wilmington Man Gets 90 Years after Wishing Victim a Happy Birthday, Shooting Him Dead," *News Journal* / Delaware Online, July 21, 2018, https://www.delawareonline.com/story/news/2018/07/20/defendant-wilmington-nightclub-death-birthday-celebrant-gets-90-years/802664002/.

CHAPTER 6 "I DON'T LET THESE FELONIES HOLD ME BACK!"

Epigraphs: Corry Wright in "Swimming Upstream," episode 4 of *Remaking Murdertown*, August 4, https://remaking.murdertown.us/episodes/2016/season-one/swimming-upstream; Jamie J. Fader, *Falling Back: Incarceration and Transitions to Adulthood among Urban Youth* (New Brunswick, NJ: Rutgers University Press, 2013), 100–101.

1. Delaware Department of Correction, *FY 2017 Annual Report* (Dover: Delaware Department of Correction, 2017), https://doc.delaware.gov/assets/documents/annual_report/DOC_2017AnnualReport.pdf; U.S. Department of Justice, National Institute of Corrections, "Delaware 2017," 2017, https://nicic.gov/state-statistics/2017/delaware-2017.
2. Delaware Department of Correction, *FY 2017 Annual Report*.
3. Cris Barrish, "Sex behind Bars: Women Violated in Delaware Prison," *News Journal*, July 31, 2015, http://www.delawareonline.com/story/news/local/2015/07/31/sex-behind-bars-women-violated-prison/30944001/.

4. Christian Kervick and Thomas MacLeish, *Recidivism in Delaware: An Analysis of Prisoners Released in 2008 through 2010* (Dover: Delaware Criminal Justice Council Statistical Analysis Center, 2014).
5. Kervick and MacLeish.
6. Wilmington HOPE Commission, *Southbridge HOPE Zone Pilot Project: Second Year Implementation Report (July 2008 to June 2009)* (Wilmington, DE: Wilmington HOPE Commission, June 2009); Wilmington HOPE Commission. *The State of Reentry in Wilmington: Annual Report* (Wilmington, DE: Wilmington HOPE Commission, 2011).
7. Mark Berman, "These Prosecutors Won Office Vowing to Fight the System. Now, the System Is Fighting Back," *Washington Post*, November 9, 2019, https://www.washingtonpost.com/national/these-prosecutors-won-office-vowing-to-fight-the-system-now-the-system-is-fighting-back/2019/11/05/20d863f6-afc1-11e9-a0c9-6d2d7818f3da_story.html.
8. Phil Hall, "Beau Biden's Fight against Big Banks," *National Mortgage Professional*, June 1, 2015, https://nationalmortgageprofessional.com/news/54276/beau-bidens-fight-against-big-banks.
9. Hall.
10. Carl L. Hart, "How the Myth of the 'Negro Cocaine Fiend' Helped Shape American Drug Policy," *The Nation*, June 29, 2015, https://www.thenation.com/article/archive/how-myth-negro-cocaine-fiend-helped-shape-american-drug-policy/.
11. Ayers, *Vengeance and Justice*; Hart, "How the Myth."
12. Harrison Narcotics Tax Act, 1914, https://www.naabt.org/documents/Harrison_Narcotics_Tax_Act_1914.pdf.
13. Hart, "How the Myth"; Edward Huntington Williams, "Negro Cocaine 'Fiends' Are a New Southern Menace; Murder and Insanity Increasing among Lower Class Blacks Because They Have Taken to 'Sniffing' since Deprived of Whisky by Prohibition," *New York Times*, February 8, 1914, https://www.nytimes.com/1914/02/08/archives/negro-cocaine-fiends-are-a-new-southern-menace-murder-and-insanity.html.
14. U.S. Drug Enforcement Agency, "The Early Years," accessed January 3, 2023, https://www.dea.gov/sites/default/files/2018-05/Early%20Years%20p%2012-29.pdf.
15. German Lopez, "Joe Biden's Long Record Supporting the War on Drugs and Mass Incarceration, Explained," Vox, April 25, 2019, https://www.vox.com/policy-and-politics/2019/4/25/18282870/joe-biden-criminal-justice-war-on-drugs-mass-incarceration.
16. U.S. Sentencing Commission, *Special Report to the Congress: Cocaine and Federal Sentencing Policy* (Washington, DC: U.S. Sentencing Commission, 1995), https://www.ussc.gov/sites/default/files/pdf/news/congressional-testimony-and-reports/drug-topics/199502-rtc-cocaine-sentencing-policy/1995-Crack-Report_Full.pdf; U.S. Sentencing Commission, *Report to the Congress: Cocaine and Federal Sentencing Policy* (Washington, DC: U.S. Sentencing Commission, 2007), https://www.ussc.gov/sites/default/files/pdf/news/congressional-testimony-and-reports/drug-topics/200705_RtC_Cocaine_Sentencing_Policy.pdf.
17. Katheryn Russell-Brown, *The Color of Crime: Racial Hoaxes, White Fear, Black Protectionism, Police Harassment, and Other Macroaggressions* (New York: New York University Press, 2009).
18. Brian Naylor, "How Federal Dollars Fund Local Police," NPR, June 9, 2020, https://www.npr.org/2020/06/09/872387351/how-federal-dollars-fund-local-police; Lauren-Brooke Eisen, "The Federal Funding That Fuels Mass Incarceration," Brennan Center for Justice, June 7, 2021, https://www.brennancenter.org/our-work/analysis-opinion/federal-funding-fuels-mass-incarceration.
19. Justin Wolfers, David Leonhardt, and Kevin Quealy, "The Methodology: 1.5 Million Missing Black Men," *New York Times*, April 20, 2015, https://www.nytimes.com/2015/04/21/upshot/the-methodology-1-5-million-missing-black-men.html.

20. Brady Heiner, "The Procedural Entrapment of Mass Incarceration: Prosecution, Race, and the Unfinished Project of American Abolition," *Philosophy & Social Criticism* 42, no. 6 (2016): 594–631.
21. E. Ann Carson, *Prisoners in 2016* (Washington, DC: Bureau of Justice Statistics, 2018), https://bjs.ojp.gov/library/publications/prisoners-2016.
22. Carson.
23. Carson.
24. Danielle Kaeble, *Probation and Parole in the United States, 2016* (Washington, DC: Bureau of Justice Statistics, 2018), https://bjs.ojp.gov/library/publications/probation-and-parole-united-states-2016.
25. Kaeble.
26. Mariel Alper, Matthew R. Durose, and Joshua Markman, *2018 Update on Prisoner Recidivism: A 9-Year Follow-Up Period (2005–2014)* (Washington, DC: Department of Justice, Bureau of Justice Statistics, 2018), https://bjs.ojp.gov/library/publications/2018-update-prisoner-recidivism-9-year-follow-period-2005-2014.
27. Yasser A. Payne and Tara M. Brown, "'I Don't Let These Felonies Hold Me Back!' How Street-Identified Black Men and Women Use Resilience to Radically Reframe Reentry," *Race and Justice*, December 21, 2021, https://journals.sagepub.com/doi/abs/10.1177/21533687211047948.
28. Elizabeth Panuccio and Johnna Christian, "Work, Family, and Masculine Identity: An Intersectional Approach to Understanding Young, Black Men's Experiences of Reentry," *Race and Justice* 9, no. 4 (2019): 407–433.
29. Fader, *Falling Back*; John Halushka, "Work Wisdom: Teaching Former Prisoners How to Negotiate Workplace Interactions and Perform a Rehabilitated Self," *Ethnography* 17, no. 1 (2016): 72–91; Andrea Leverentz, "Being a Good Daughter and Sister: Families of Origin in the Reentry of African American Female Ex-prisoners," *Feminist Criminology* 6, no. 4 (2011): 239–267.
30. Joyce A. Arditti and Tiffaney Parkman, "Young Men's Reentry after Incarceration: A Developmental Paradox," *Family Relations* 60, no. 2 (2011): 205–220.
31. Fader, *Falling Back*; Panuccio and Christian, "Work, Family, and Masculine Identity"; Lucia Trimbur, "'Me and the Law Is Not Friends': How Former Prisoners Make Sense of Reentry," *Qualitative Sociology* 32, no. 3 (2009): 259–277.
32. Connie Wun, "Unaccounted Foundations: Black Girls, Anti-Black Racism, and Punishment in Schools," *Critical Sociology* 42, no. 4–5 (2016): 737–750.
33. Thompson, *Releasing Prisoners*.
34. Devah Pager, *Marked: Race, Crime, and Finding Work in an Era of Mass Incarceration* (Chicago: University of Chicago Press, 2009).
35. Alice O'Connor, Chris Tilly, and Lawrence Bobo, *Urban Inequality: Evidence from Four Cities* (New York: Russell Sage Foundation, 2001); Payne and Brown, "I'm Still Waiting."
36. Fader, *Falling Back*; Ricardo Y. Smith, "No Way Out: Giving Voice to the Post-Prison Experiences of African-American Men in Two Ohio Counties" (PhD diss., Union Institute and University, 2014).
37. Shelli B. Rossman, "Case-Managed Reentry and Employment: Lessons from the Opportunity to Succeed Program," *Justice Research and Policy* 5, no. 2 (2003): 75–100.
38. Timbur, "Me and the Law."
39. Panuccio and Christian, "Work, Family, and Masculine Identity"; Christy A. Visher, "Incarcerated Fathers: Pathways from Prison to Home," *Criminal Justice Policy Review* 24, no. 1 (2013): 9–26; Christy A. Visher, Pamela K. Lattimore, Kelle Barrick, and Stephen Tueller, "Evaluating the Long-Term Effects of Prisoner Reentry Services on Recidivism: What Types of Services Matter?," *Justice Quarterly* 34, no. 1 (2017): 136–165.
40. Payne and Brown, "I'm Still Waiting."
41. Frank Gerace, "Mayor Baker Issues 'Ban the Box' Executive Order," WDEL, December 10, 2010, http://www.wdel.com/story.php?id=47654.

42. Shirley Min, "Delaware Is Latest State to 'Ban the Box,'" WHYY, May 9, 2014, https://whyy.org/articles/delaware-is-latest-state-to-ban-the-box/.
43. Delaware Center for Justice, "Executive Summary," n.d., accessed January 3, 2023, https://philanthropydelaware.org/resources/Documents/DCJ%20ED%20Position%20Description%20FINAL%20FULL.pdf.
44. Delaware Center for Justice, "About DCJ," n.d., accessed January 3, 2023, https://dcjustice.org/.
45. Community Service Building, "Our Mission," n.d., accessed January 3, 2023, https://www.csbcorp.org/our-mission.
46. Delaware Center for Justice, "Delaware Center for Justice Annual Celebration 2022," n.d., accessed January 3, 2023, https://dcjustice.org/delaware-center-for-justice-annual-celebration-2022/.
47. Xerxes Wilson, "Delaware Democrats Take Aim at Laws They See as Unfairly Hurting Minorities, Poor," *News Journal*, March 18, 2019, https://www.delawareonline.com/story/news/2019/03/15/delaware-reforms-address-criminal-fines-inequality-sentencing/3161130002/.
48. Ronald Fraser, "How Delaware Cops Prey on Private Property," *News Journal / Delaware Online*, April 26, 2017, https://www.delawareonline.com/story/opinion/2017/04/26/how-delaware-cops-prey-private-property/100940132/.
49. Wilson, "Delaware Democrats."
50. *Remaking Murdertown: Poverty, Punishment, and Possibility*, podcast series sponsored by the Delaware Center for Justice and produced by Zach Phillips (Wilmington, DE: Short Order Production House, 2016), http://remaking.murdertown.us/; Rana Fayez, "A New Podcast on Poverty, Punishment and Possibility: The Kitchen's Zach Phillips Is Producing a Compelling New Podcast: Remaking Murdertown," Technical.ly, June 21, 2016, https://technical.ly/professional-development/remaking-murdertown-zach-phillips/.
51. Jones, "Murder Town USA."
52. Jessica Masulli Reyes, "Reports: Del. Company May Be Linked to El Chapo," *News Journal*, January 16, 2016, https://www.delawareonline.com/story/news/local/2016/01/15/reports-del-company-may-linked-el-chapo/78859144/.
53. Reyes.
54. Linderman et al., "Growing Up under Fire."
55. Delaware Juvenile Justice Advisory Group, *Annual Report and Recommendations to Governor John Carney and the Delaware State Legislature* (Wilmington: Delaware Juvenile Justice Advisory Group, 2019), https://cjc.delaware.gov/wp-content/uploads/sites/61/2019/06/Delaware-2018-JJAG-ReportvPRINTER.pdf.
56. Bonilla-Silva, *Racism without Racists*.
57. Bonilla-Silva.
58. Ashley Biden in "Swimming Upstream," episode 4 of *Remaking Murdertown*.
59. Esteban Parra, "Ashley Biden Leaves Job, Adds to Speculation over Joe Biden 2020 Presidential Campaign," Delaware Online, March 8, 2019, https://www.delawareonline.com/get-access/?return=https%3A%2F%2Fwww.delawareonline.com%2Fstory%2Fnews%2F2019%2F03%2F08%2Fashley-biden-leaves-job-adds-speculation-over-dad-joe-bidens-presidential-decision%2F3102891002%2F.

Chapter 7 "Brenda's Got a Baby"

Epigraph: Vargas, *Catching Hell*, 85.

1. Vargas, *Catching Hell*.
2. Jones, *Between Good and Ghetto*, 20.
3. Brooklynn K. Hitchens and Yasser Arafat Payne, "'Brenda's Got a Baby': Black Single Motherhood and Street Life as a Site of Resilience in Wilmington, Delaware," *Journal of Black Psychology* 43, no. 1 (2017): 50–76.

Notes to Pages 158–160

4. Stephanie Bush-Baskette, *Misguided Justice: The War on Drugs and the Incarceration of Black Women* (Bloomington, IN: iUniverse, 2010); Hitchens and Payne, "'Brenda's Got a Baby.'"
5. LeBlanc, *Random Family*.
6. Tammy L. Anderson, "Dimensions of Women's Power in the Illicit Drug Economy," *Theoretical Criminology* 9, no. 4 (2005): 371–400; Eloise Dunlap, Bruce D. Johnson, and Lisa Maher, "Female Crack Sellers in New York City: Who They Are and What They Do," *Women & Criminal Justice* 8, no. 4 (1997): 25–55.
7. Randol Contreras, "'Damn, Yo—Who's That Girl?' An Ethnographic Analysis of Masculinity in Drug Robberies," *Journal of Contemporary Ethnography* 38, no. 4 (2009): 465–492; Contreras, *Stickup Kids*; Shakur, *Monster*.
8. Vargas, *Catching Hell*.
9. Hitchens and Payne, "'Brenda's Got a Baby'"; Vargas, *Catching Hell*.
10. Vargas, *Catching Hell*, 64.
11. Vargas, 64.
12. Vargas, 64.
13. Vargas, 92.
14. Kathryn Edin and Laura Lein, *Making Ends Meet: How Single Mothers Survive Welfare and Low-Wage Work* (New York: Russell Sage Foundation, 1997).
15. Sam Roberts, "51% of Women Are Now Living without Spouse," *New York Times*, January 16, 2007, https://www.nytimes.com/2007/01/16/us/16census.html; Daphne Lofquist, Terry Lugaila, Martin O'Connell, and Sarah Feliz, *Households and Families: 2010*, report C2010BR-14 (Washington, DC: U.S. Census Bureau, 2012), https://www.census.gov/content/dam/Census/library/publications/2012/dec/c2010br-14.pdf; U.S. Census Bureau, "Marital Status: 2015 American Community Survey 1-Year Estimate," 2015, https://www.census.gov/programs-surveys/acs/technical-documentation/table-and-geography-changes/2015/1-year.html.
16. Joan Entmacher, Katherine G. Robbins, Julie Vogtman, and Anne Morrison, *Insecure and Unequal: Poverty and Income among Women and Families 2000–2012* (Washington, DC: National Women's Law Center, 2013); Eurpub, "Why the African-American Divorce Rate Is 70%: What We Can do to Fix It," EUR, March 26, 2017, http://www.eurweb.com/2017/03/african-american-divorce-rate-70-can-fix-video/; U.S. Census Bureau, "Marital Status."
17. Delaware Health Statistics Center, *Delaware Vital Statistics Annual Report 2016* (Dover: Delaware Health Statistics Center, 2016), https://dhss.delaware.gov/dph/hp/files/ar2016_print.pdf.
18. Garrison and Kervick, "Analysis of City of Wilmington"; Rachel M. Shattuck and Rose M. Kreider, *Social and Economic Characteristics of Currently Unmarried Women with a Recent Birth*, American Community Survey report 21 (Washington, DC: U.S. Census Bureau, 2013), https://www2.census.gov/library/publications/2013/acs/acs-21.pdf.
19. Wendy Sawyer, "Bailing Moms Out for Mother's Day," Prison Policy Initiative, May 8, 2017, https://www.prisonpolicy.org/blog/2017/05/08/mothers-day/.
20. Marc Mauer, *The Changing Racial Dynamics of Women's Incarceration* (Washington, DC: Sentencing Project, 2013).
21. Sentencing Project, "Incarcerated Women and Girls," Sentencing Project fact sheet, updated 2020, http://www.sentencingproject.org/wp-content/uploads/2016/02/Incarcerated-Women-and-Girls.pdf.
22. Carson, *Prisoners in 2016*.
23. Sentencing Project, "Incarcerated Women and Girls."
24. Alexander, *New Jim Crow*; Marc Mauer, *The Changing Racial Dynamics of the War on Drugs* (Washington, DC: Sentencing Project, 2009); Natasha A. Frost, Judith Greene, and Kevin Pranis, *Hard Hit: The Growth in the Imprisonment of Women, 1977–2004* (New York: Institute on Women and Criminal Justice, 2006), http://www.csdp.org/research/HardHitReport4.pdf.

25. State of Delaware, "Baylor Women's Correctional Institution," Delaware.gov, n.d., accessed January 7, 2023, https://doc.delaware.gov/views/baylor.blade.shtml.
26. State of Delaware.
27. Barrish, "Sex behind Bars."
28. Fine et al., *Changing Minds*; Michelle Fine and María Elena Torre, "Intimate Details: Participatory Action Research in Prison," *Action Research* 4, no. 3 (2006): 253–269.
29. Fine et al., *Changing Minds*.
30. Payne and Bryant, "Street Participatory Action."
31. Fine and Torre, "Intimate Details."
32. Fine and Torre, 256.
33. Fine and Torre, 261.
34. Cris Barrish and Brittany Horn, "Baylor Security Boss Arrested for Sex with Female Inmate," *News Journal*, July 7, 2015, http://www.delawareonline.com/story/news/local/2015/07/07/prison-security-boss-suspended-inmate-sex-probe/29817969/.
35. Allen J. Beck et al., *Sexual Victimization in Prisons and Jails Reported by Inmates, 2011–12* (Washington, DC: Bureau of Justice Statistics, 2014), https://bjs.ojp.gov/content/pub/pdf/svpjri1112.pdf.
36. Barrish and Brittany Horn, "Baylor Security Boss Arrested."
37. Kathryn Edin and Maria Kefalas, *Promises I Can Keep: Why Poor Women Put Motherhood before Marriage* (Berkeley: University of California Press, 2005).
38. Hitchens and Payne, "'Brenda's Got a Baby.'"
39. Ryan Cormier, "Showcase Chronicles Lives Claimed by Gun Violence," *News Journal*, December 4, 2010.
40. Bailey v. State of Delaware, 363 A.2d 312 (1976), http://law.justia.com/cases/delaware/supreme-court/1976/363-a-2d-312-3.html.
41. The *People's Report Mix CD* can be found at thepeoplesreport.com.
42. Ranaivo, "Wilmington Police Homicide Unit."
43. Contreras, *Stickup Kids*; Duck, *No Way Out*; Jacobs, *Robbing Drug Dealers*.
44. Staats v. State of Delaware, Cr. I.D. No. IN04-09-0107 and 0108, Supr. Ct. No. 501, 2005 (Del. Supr. June 29, 2006), https://caselaw.findlaw.com/de-supreme-court/1011939.html; Staats v. State of Delaware, Cr. I.D. No. 0408028022, Supr. Ct. No. 501, 2005 (Del. Supr. May 17, 2012), https://caselaw.findlaw.com/de-supreme-court/1011939.html.
45. Vargas, *Catching Hell*.
46. Horn, "Wilmington Rapper's Mom."
47. Judy Russell, "Assata Shakur Convicted of Murder in 1977," *Daily News* (New York), March 24, 2017, https://www.nydailynews.com/news/crime/assata-shakur-convicted-murder-1977-article-1.3008371.
48. Linda M. Burton and M. Belinda Tucker, "Romantic Unions in an Era of Uncertainty: A Post-Moynihan Perspective on African American Women and Marriage," *Annals of the American Academy of Political and Social Science* 621, no. 1 (2009): 132–148.
49. Anderson, "Dimensions of Women's Power."

CHAPTER 8 "STREET LOVE"

Epigraph: Max A. Collins, *American Gangster* (New York: Tom Doherty Associates, 2007), 2.

1. Shakur, *Monster*.
2. Peter L. Patton, "The Gangstas in Our Midst," *The Urban Review* 30, no. 1 (1998): 49–76.
3. Ruth Horowitz, "Sociological Perspectives on Gangs: Conflicting Definitions and Concepts," in *Gangs in America*, ed. C. Ronald Huff (Thousand Oaks, CA: Sage, 1990), 37–54.
4. Venkatesh, *Gang Leader for a Day*.

Notes to Pages 182–203

5. Payne, *People's Report*; Yasser Arafat Payne and Hanaa A. Hamdi, "'Street Love': How Street Life–Oriented US-Born African Men Frame Giving Back to One Another and the Local Community," *The Urban Review* 41, no. 1 (2009): 29–46.
6. Adam Taylor, "Slaying of Mom Latest in Long Line of Tragedy for Wilmington Family," Delaware Open Carry, June 9, 2009, http://www.delawareopencarry.org/forums/viewtopic.php?f=30&t=2055.
7. Wilson, *When Work Disappears*; Duck, *No Way Out*.
8. Bracke, "Is the Subaltern Resilient?"
9. Frantz Fanon, *The Wretched of the Earth* (New York: Grove Press, 1963).
10. Bracke, "Is the Subaltern Resilient?"
11. Bracke, 852.
12. Payne, "Site of Resilience."
13. Harding, *Living the Drama*.
14. Harding.
15. Mark Nardone, "Wilmington Crime: Hope for the Hood—Part Two in a Series Explains How Men Who've Survived Life on the Streets Intend to Curb the Violence in Wilmington," *Delaware Today*, May 26, 2015, http://www.delawaretoday.com/Delaware-Today/June-2015/Wilmington-Crime-Hope-for-the-Hood/.
16. D. R. Rose and T. R. Clear, "Incarceration, Social Capital, and Crime: Implications for Social Disorganization Theory," *Criminology* 36, no. 3 (1998): 441–480.
17. Sean O'Sullivan, "Wilmington, DE: Delaware Courts: Prosecutor Says Mentor Killed over Woman," *News Journal*, May 14, 2010, http://intimateviolencedeathnews.blogspot.com/2010/05/wilmington-de-delaware-courts.html.
18. Rogers v. State of Delaware, Cr. ID. No. 0901003188 (Del. Super. Ct. Mar. 9, 2016), http://law.justia.com/cases/delaware/superior-court/2016/0901003188.html.

CHAPTER 9 "WINTER IS COMING!"

Epigraphs: James Baldwin, "The Negro in American Culture: A Group Discussion (Baldwin, Hughes, Hansberry, Capouya, Kazin)," YouTube, January 17, 2016, https://www.youtube.com/watch?v=jNpitdJSXWY&feature=youtu.be; David Banner, "David Banner on White Supremacy, Illuminati, the God Box (Full Interview)," YouTube, August 10, 2017, https://www.youtube.com/watch?v=w5McPO11XLU.

1. Dave Trumbore, "'Game of Thrones': The Children of the Forest Explained," Collider, August 6, 2017, http://collider.com/game-of-thrones-children-of-the-forest-explained/#first men.
2. Jess Joho, "Who Are the Children of the Forest on 'Game of Thrones,' and Why Do They Matter?," Mashable, August 7, 2017, http://mashable.com/2017/08/07/children-of-the-forest-game-of-thrones/#LHm7dGMUpiqu.
3. Adam Duvernay, "Wilmington Mayoral Candidates Take Aim at Each Other," *News Journal*, June 20, 2016, https://www.delawareonline.com/story/news/2016/07/19/mayor-candidates-square-off-final-debate/86987108/.
4. Wade W. Nobles, "Extended Self: Rethinking the So-Called Negro Self-Concept," *Journal of Black Psychology* 2, no. 2 (1976): 15–24; Payne, "Site of Resilience"; Richard Delgado, "The Imperial Scholar: Reflections on a Review of Civil Rights Literature," in *Critical Race Theory: The Key Writings That Formed the Movement*, edited by Kimberle Crenshaw, Neil Gotanda, Gary Peller, and Kendall Thomas (New York: New Press, 1995), 46–57.
5. Jay MacLeod, *Ain't No Makin' It: Aspirations and Attainment in a Low-Income Neighborhood* (Boulder, CO: Westview Press, 2008); Rios, *Punished*.
6. Eugene Young, personal communication with author, August 21, 2020.
7. Vargas, *Catching Hell*, 174.

8. Frantz Fanon, *Black Skin, White Masks* (1952; repr., New York: Grove Press, 2008); Fanon, *Wretched of the Earth*.
9. Hussein M. Adam, "Frantz Fanon as a Democratic Theorist," *African Affairs* 92, no. 369 (1993): 499–518; Josué R. López, "Participatory Action Research in Education: A Fanonian Medicine of the People," *Philosophical Studies in Education* 51 (2020): 54–70; Josh Pallas, "Fanon on Violence and the Person," *Critical Legal Thinking* (blog), January 20, 2016, https://criticallegalthinking.com/2016/01/20/fanon-on-violence-and-the-person/; Rios, *Punished*.
10. Fanon, *Black Skin, White Masks*, 65.
11. Fanon, *Wretched of the Earth*.
12. Rios, *Punished*; Fanon, *Wretched of the Earth*.
13. Galtung, "Cultural Violence."
14. Niraj Chokshi and Christopher Mele, "National Guard Deployed in Milwaukee amid Unrest over Fatal Police Shooting," *New York Times*, August 14, 2016, https://www.nytimes.com/2016/08/14/us/violent-crowd-confronts-police-in-milwaukee-after-fatal-shooting.html; Manny Fernandez, Richard Perez-Pena, and Jonah Engel Bromwich, "Five Dallas Officers Were Killed as Payback, Police Chief Says," *Boston Globe*, July 8, 2016, https://www.bostonglobe.com/news/nation/2016/07/07/shots-fired-protest-dallas/1PrIf4FU4gOojlF9PTaaRN/story.html; Joe Marusak et al., "Charlotte Faces Aftermath of Protests Ignited by Fatal Police Shooting; 16 Officers Injured," *Charlotte Observer*, September 20, 2016, https://www.charlotteobserver.com/news/local/crime/article103009432.html; Steph Solis, "Protests Break Out after Baton Rouge Police Fatally Shoot Man," *USA Today*, July 6, 2016, https://www.usatoday.com/story/news/nation/2016/07/05/baton-rouge-alton-sterling-police-shooting/86738368/.
15. Fernandez, Perez-Pena, and Bromwich, "Five Dallas Officers."
16. Alice Speri, "The Largest Prison Strike in U.S. History Enters Its Second Week," *The Intercept*, September 16, 2016, https://theintercept.com/2016/09/16/the-largest-prison-strike-in-u-s-history-enters-its-second-week/.
17. Speri.
18. Brittany Horn, "Lawsuit Claims Vaughn Inmates Were Beaten, Tortured after 2017 Prison Riot Ended," *News Journal*, October 31, 2018, https://www.delawareonline.com/story/news/crime/2018/10/31/lawsuit-vaughn-inmates-were-beaten-tortured-after-prison-riot-ended/1808724002/.
19. Horn.
20. Horn.
21. Ian Gronau, "Inmates Sentenced in Vaughn Prison Riot Case," *Delaware State News*, September 13, 2019, https://delawarestatenews.net/news/inmates-sentenced-in-vaughn-prison-riot-case/.
22. Xerxes Wilson, "Delaware Prison Riot Charges Dropped; More Trials Would Be 'Futile,' AG Says," *News Journal*, June 12, 2019, https://www.delawareonline.com/story/news/2019/06/12/remaining-charges-dropped-vaughn-prison-riot-murder-steven-floyd/1432628001/.
23. German Lopez, "2020's Historic Surge in Murders, Explained," Vox, March 25, 2021, https://www.vox.com/22344713/murder-violent-crime-spike-surge-2020-covid-19-coronavirus; First State Update, "Wilmington Shootings up 52%, Murder up 35%, Overall Crime down 16% over Three-Year Period," First State Update, February 1, 2021, http://firststateupdate.com/2021/02/wilmington-shootings-up-52-murder-up-35-over-crime-down-16-over-three-year-period/.
24. Amy Cherry, "Wilmington Eclipses 2017 Gun Violence Record with Latest Fatal Shooting," WDEL 101.7FM, November 15, 2021, https://www.wdel.com/news/wilmington-eclipses-2017-gun-violence-record-with-latest-fatal-shooting/article_9c33181c-4636-11ec-a95a-f7bf8aafe88b.html; News Journal Editorial / USA TODAY Network Atlantic Group Editorial Board, "Our View: Wilmington's

Wounds—39 Dead in Gun Violence—Are Unbearable. It's Time to Act," *News Journal* / Delaware Online, December 10, 2021, https://www.delawareonline.com/story/opinion/editorials/2021/12/10/39-dead-wilmington-gun-violence-unbearable-its-time-act/6452869001/; Cris Barrish, "'Different Temperature' on Wilmington Streets: Gun Homicides Down Sharply after 2021's Record Carnage," WHYY, July 31, 2022, https://whyy.org/articles/wilmington-gun-homicides-down-after-record-2021/.

25. Jack Kelly, "Jobless Claims: 57.4 Million Americans Have Sought Unemployment Benefits since Mid-March—Over 1 Million People Filed Last Week," *Forbes*, August 20, 2020, https://www.forbes.com/sites/jackkelly/2020/08/20/jobless-claims-574-million-americans-have-sought-unemployment-benefits-since-mid-marchover-1-million-people-filed-last-week/#22a4d9126d59; Greg Iacurci, "Here's Why the Real Unemployment Rate May Be Higher than Reported," CNBC, June 5, 2020, https://www.cnbc.com/2020/06/05/heres-why-the-real-unemployment-rate-may-be-higher-than-reported.html.

26. Michael Ettlinger, "COVID-19 Economic Crisis: By State," Carsey School of Public Policy, University of New Hampshire, October 2, 2020, https://carsey.unh.edu/COVID-19-Economic-Impact-By-State.

27. Sam Van Pykeren, "These Photos Show the Staggering Food Bank Lines across America," *Mother Jones*, April 13, 2020, https://www.motherjones.com/food/2020/04/these-photos-show-the-staggering-food-bank-lines-across-america/; Michelle Singletary, "Perspective | FAQ: Rent Strikes during the Pandemic," *Washington Post*, May 7, 2020, https://www.washingtonpost.com/business/2020/05/07/rent-strike-faq/.

28. Colleen Long, Kat Stafford, and R. J. Rico, "Summer of Protest: Chance for Change, but Obstacles Exposed," AP News, September 6, 2020, https://apnews.com/article/9035ecdfc58d5dba755185666ac0ed6d.

29. McClain died in August 2019, but the details of the case weren't released publicly until July 2020.

30. Mohammed Haddad, "Mapping US Cities Where George Floyd Protests Have Erupted," Al Jazeera, June 2, 2020, https://www.aljazeera.com/news/2020/6/2/mapping-us-cities-where-george-floyd-protests-have-erupted.

31. Roudabeh Kishi and Sam Jones, *Demonstrations & Political Violence in America: New Data for Summer 2020* (Madison, WI: Armed Conflict Location and Event Data Project [ACLED], 2020), https://acleddata.com/acleddatanew/wp-content/uploads/2020/09/ACLED_USDataReview_Sum2020_SeptWebPDF_HiRes.pdf.

32. Bill Hutchinson, "Police Officers Killed Surge 28% This Year and Some Point to Civil Unrest and Those Looking to Exploit It," ABC News, July 22, 2020, https://abcnews.go.com/US/police-officers-killed-surge-28-year-point-civil/story?id=71773405.

33. Artemis Moshtaghian and Amir Vera, "2 Los Angeles County Deputies Are out of Surgery after Ambush Shooting in Compton," CNN, September 13, 2020, https://www.cnn.com/2020/09/12/us/los-angeles-county-officers-shot-compton/index.html.

34. Isabel Hughes et al., "Wilmington Protest for Floyd Turns Violent; Police Order People off the Streets," Delaware Online, May 31, 2020, https://www.delawareonline.com/story/news/2020/05/30/wilmington-protests-george-floyd-turn-violent-night/5295496002/.

35. Hughes et al.
36. Hughes et al.
37. Hughes et al.
38. Coby Owens was a young Black man running for city council in Wilmington and the permit holder for the upcoming march in Wilmington.
39. Ashley Biden and Darius Brown, "Prison Is No Longer the Go-To Response to Crime," Delaware Online, May 10, 2015, https://www.delawareonline.com/story/opinion/contributors/2015/05/10/prison-longer-go-response-crime/27098913/.

40. D. J. McAneny, "Wilmington State Senator Charged with Punching Woman in Restaurant," WDEL 101.7FM, May 19, 2021, https://www.wdel.com/news/wilmington-state-senator-charged-with-punching-woman-in-restaurant/article_8bec1200-b8ca-11eb-a4fc-83edba69bbdc.html.

41. Meredith Newman, Karl Baker, and Jeanne Kuang, "Despite Heavy Rain, Protesters March in Wilmington Friday, Including with Police at End," Delaware Online, June 5, 2020, https://www.delawareonline.com/story/news/2020/06/05/wilmington-protest-george-floyds-breonna-taylor/3158389001/.

42. Sarah Gamard, "Will the Delaware General Assembly Grant Protesters' Wishes to Change Policing Laws?," Delaware Online, June 11, 2020, https://www.delawareonline.com/story/news/politics/2020/06/11/delaware-general-assembly-agree-what-protesters-want/5312262002/.

43. Community Advocates for Black Life, "Delaware Legislative Black Caucus Plan Doesn't Go Far Enough," Delaware Online, August 4, 2020, https://www.delawareonline.com/story/opinion/2020/08/04/delaware-legislative-black-caucus-plan-doesnt-go-far-enough/5571540002/.

Conclusion

Epigraphs: Martin Luther King Jr., unidentified 1968 speech, video clip, 1:13; see Laura Belin, "A Must-Watch MLK, Jr. Clip for Iowans," *Bleeding Heartland* (blog), January 17, 2022, https://www.bleedingheartland.com/2022/01/17/a-must-watch-mlk-jr-clip-for-iowans/; bell hooks, "Feminism: A Transformational Politic," in *Race, Class and Gender in the United States: An Integrated Study*, ed. P. S. Rothenberg and S. Munshi (New York: Worth Publishers, 2016).

1. Jones, "Murder Town USA."
2. Diener, Sapyta, and Suh, "Subjective Well-Being"; Edmund W. Gordon and L. D. Song, "Variations in the Experience of Educational Resilience," in *Educational Resilience in Inner-City America: Challenges and Prospects*, ed. Margaret C. Wang and Edmund W. Gordon (New York: Routledge, 1994), 27–43; M. Brinton Lykes, "Speaking against the Silence: One Maya Woman's Exile and Return," in *Women Creating Lives: Identities, Resilience, and Resistance*, ed. Carol E. Franz, 97–114 (New York: Routledge, 1994), 97–114; Linda Tuhiwai Smith, *Decolonizing Methodologies: Research and Indigenous Peoples* (1992; repr., London: Zed Books, 2012).
3. Gordon and Song, "Variations in the Experience."
4. Gordon and Song, 31.
5. Caplan, "Indigenous Anchorman"; Robin D. G. Kelley, "Kickin' Reality, Kickin' Ballistics: Gangsta Rap and Postindustrial Los Angeles," in *Droppin' Science: Critical Essays on Rap Music and Hip-Hop Culture*, ed. W. W. Perkins (Philadelphia: Temple University Press, 1994); Seymour Parker and Robert J. Kleiner, "Social and Psychological Dimensions of the Family Role Performance of the Negro Male," *Journal of Marriage and the Family* 31, no. 3 (1969): 500–506.
6. Kelley, "Kickin' Reality."
7. Kelley, 8.
8. Fanon, *Wretched of the Earth*.
9. Fanon, 61.
10. Payne and Brown, "I Don't Let These Felonies Hold Me Back!"
11. Peter Andreas, "A Tale of Two Borders: The U.S.-Mexico and U.S.-Canada Lines after 9/11," working paper 77, Center for Comparative Immigration Studies, University of California, San Diego, May 2003, https://ccis.ucsd.edu/_files/wp77.pdf.
12. Melissa Bell, "Patriot Act Used to Fight More Drug Dealers than Terrorists," *Washington Post*, September 7, 2011, https://www.washingtonpost.com/blogs/blog

post/post/patriot-act-used-to-fight-more-drug-dealers-than-terrorists/2011/09/07/gIQAcmEBAK_blog.html.
13. Shakur, *Monster*.
14. Alonso, "Racialized Identities."
15. Jason Motlagh, "A Radical Approach to Gun Crime: Paying People Not to Kill Each Other," *Guardian*, June 9, 2016, https://www.theguardian.com/us-news/2016/jun/09/richmond-california-ons-gun-crime.
16. Rios, *Punished*.
17. Chidike I. Okeem, "On Criminogenic Grit and Theoretical Criminology," *Journal of Theoretical & Philosophical Criminology* 12 (2020): 98–115.
18. June P. Tangney et al., "Is There a Dark Side to Mindfulness? Relation of Mindfulness to Criminogenic Cognitions," *Personality and Social Psychology Bulletin* 43, no. 10 (2017): 1415–1426.
19. Patrick Clark, *Preventing Future Crime with Cognitive Behavioral Therapy* (Washington, DC: National Institute of Justice, 2010); Thomas Feucht and Tammy Holt, "Does Cognitive Behavioral Therapy Work in Criminal Justice? A New Analysis from CrimeSolutions.gov," *National Institute of Justice Journal*, issue 277 (September 2016), https://www.ojp.gov/pdffiles1/nij/249825.pdf.
20. Elliot Davis, "Local Activists Not Happy with How St. Louis Has Rolled Out Cure Violence Program," Fox2Now, November 9, 2020, https://fox2now.com/news/missouri/local-activists-not-happy-with-how-st-louis-has-rolled-out-cure-violence-program; Kayla Drake, "Cure Violence Advocates Defect from St. Louis Program, Claim 'Sabotage' by City Leaders," St. Louis Public Radio, August 11, 2020, https://news.stlpublicradio.org/law-order/2020-08-11/cure-violence-advocates-defect-from-st-louis-program-claim-sabotage-by-city-leaders; Meg O'Connor, "This Anti-violence Strategy May Be Coming to St. Louis, but Activists See Red Flags," The Appeal: Political Report, April 5, 2021, https://theappeal.org/politicalreport/st-louis-mayoral-election-focused-deterrence/.
21. Associated Press, "AG: 14 Indicted on More than 120 Charges Linked to Gang," *U.S. News and World Report*, June 21, 2021, https://www.usnews.com/news/best-states/delaware/articles/2021-06-21/ag-14-indicted-on-more-than-120-charges-linked-to-gang.
22. City News, "Mayor Purzycki, Police Chief Tracy Share Important Announcement from Delaware Attorney General Jennings about NorthPak Gang Indictment," City of Wilmington, June 21, 2021, https://www.wilmingtonde.gov/Home/Components/News/News/5540/225.
23. Bell, *Faces at the Bottom*.
24. Bettylou Valentine, *Hustling and Other Hard Work: Life Styles in the Ghetto* (New York: Free Press, 1978).
25. Valentine, 132.
26. Alexander, *New Jim Crow*.
27. Melvin L. Oliver and Thomas M. Shapiro, "A Sociology of Wealth and Racial Inequality," in *Redress for Historical Injustices in the United States: On Reparations for Slavery, Jim Crow, and Their Legacies*, ed. Michael T. Martin and Marilyn Yaquinto (Durham, NC: Duke University Press, 1995), 91–119.
28. Bell, *Faces at the Bottom*.
29. Alexander, *New Jim Crow*.
30. Amy Traub et al., "The Racial Wealth Gap: Why Policy Matters," Demos, June 21, 2016, https://www.demos.org/research/racial-wealth-gap-why-policy-matters.
31. Robert C. Kelly, "Wealth," Investopedia, April 24, 2021, https://www.investopedia.com/terms/w/wealth.asp.
32. USA Facts, "White People Own 86% of Wealth and Make Up 60% of the Population," USA Facts, 2020, https://usafacts.org/articles/white-people-own-86-wealth-despite-making-60-population/.

33. Niall McCarthy, "Racial Wealth Inequality in the U.S. Is Rampant," *Forbes*, September 14, 2017, https://www.forbes.com/sites/niallmccarthy/2017/09/14/racial-wealth-inequality-in-the-u-s-is-rampant-infographic/?sh=3b72825234e8.
34. Akilah Johnson, "That Was No Typo: The Median Net Worth of Black Bostonians Really Is $8," *Boston Globe*, December 11, 2017, https://www.bostonglobe.com/metro/2017/12/11/that-was-typo-the-median-net-worth-black-bostoniansreally/ze5kxC1jJelx24M3pugFFN/story.html.
35. Alan A. Aja et al., *The Color of Wealth in Miami*, Ohio State University, Duke University, and the Insight Center of Community Economic Development, 2019, https://socialequity.duke.edu/wp-content/uploads/2019/10/The-Color-of-Wealth-in-Miami-Metro.pdf.
36. Antonio Moore, "The Middle Black Family in Los Angeles Is Only Worth $200.00 Liquid," *Los Angeles Sentinel*, December 21, 2017, https://lasentinel.net/the-middle-black-family-in-los-angeles-is-only-worth-200-00-liquid.html.
37. Cassandram, "Wilmington: 50 Years after MLK," Blue Delaware, March 27, 2018, https://bluedelaware.com/2018/03/27/wilmington-50-years-after-mlk/.
38. Lillian Singh and Ebony White. "Racial Wealth Divide in Wilmington," Prosperity Now, March 2019, https://prosperitynow.org/get-involved/racial-wealth-equity.
39. Singh and White.
40. William A. Darity and Andrea Kirsten Mullen, *From Here to Equality: Reparations for Black Americans in the Twenty-First Century* (Chapel Hill: University of North Carolina Press, 2020); Rashawn Ray and Andre M. Perry, "Why We Need Reparations for Black Americans," Policy 2020 Brookings Institution, April 15, 2020, https://www.brookings.edu/policy2020/bigideas/why-we-need-reparations-for-black-americans/.
41. Serie McDougal, *Research Methods in Africana Studies* (New York: Peter Lang, 2014).
42. Wilson, *More than Just Race*.
43. McDougal, *Research Methods*, 3.
44. Phillip. J. Bowman, "Race, Class, and Ethics in Research: Belmont Principles to Functional Relevance," in *Black Psychology*, edited by R. L. Jones (Berkeley, CA: Cobb & Henry, 1991), 755–756.
45. Neil Turner, "Long-Term Ethnographic Immersion," Perspectives in Anthropology, January 21, 2015, https://perspectivesinanthropology.com/2015/01/21/long-term-ethnographic-immersion/.
46. Sanna Schliewe, "Embodied Ethnography in Psychology: Learning Points from Expatriate Migration Research," *Culture & Psychology* 26, no. 4 (2020): 803–818.
47. Schliewe.
48. M. Brinton Lykes, "Creative Arts and Photography in Participatory Action Research in Guatemala," in *Handbook of Action Research*, ed. Peter Reason and H. Bradbury (Thousand Oaks, CA: Sage, 2001), 363–371; Lykes, "Silence(ing), Voice(s) and Gross Violations of Human Rights: Constituting and Performing Subjectivities through PhotoPAR," *Visual Studies* 25, no. 3 (2010): 238–254; Alice McIntyre, "Constructing Meaning about Violence, School, and Community Participatory Action Research with Urban Youth," *The Urban Review* 32, no. 2 (2000): 123–154; Morgan et al., "Youth Participatory Action Research"; Torrance T. Stephens, Ronald L. Braithwaite, and Sandra E. Taylor, "Model for Using Hip-Hop Music for Small Group HIV/AIDS Prevention Counseling with African-American Adolescents and Young Adults," *Patient Education and Counseling* 35 (1998): 127–137.
49. Lykes, "Creative Arts and Photography"; Lykes, "Silence(ing), Voice(s)"; Lykes, "Speaking against the Silence."
50. Lykes, "Creative Arts and Photography"; Morgan et al., "Youth Participatory Action Research."
51. Brittany Horn and Alonzo Small, "Man Fatally Shot in Wilmington Was Well-Known Rapper," *News Journal* / Delaware Online, November 29, 2016, https://www

.delawareonline.com/story/news/crime/2016/11/29/man-fatally-shot-wilmington-well-known-rapper-delaware/94622346/; Xerxes Wilson, "B-Wills, Bobby Dimes and a Story of Murder on Wilmington's East Side," *News Journal* / Delaware Online, January 22, 2020, https://www.delawareonline.com/story/news/2020/01/22/jury-convicts-local-drug-kingpin-murder-hire-plot/4456628002/.
52. Gary Anderson et al., *Participatory Action Research and Educational Policy*, Handbook of Educational Policy Research, American Educational Research Association (New York: Routledge, in press).
53. hooks, "Feminism."
54. hooks, 620.

Bibliography

Abt, Thomas. *Bleeding Out: The Devastating Consequences of Urban Violence—and a Bold New Plan for Peace in the Streets.* New York: Basic Books, 2019.

Abt, Thomas. "The Surge in Violent Crime Is Overblown—but Here's How to Combat It." Vox, September 30, 2016. https://www.vox.com/2016/9/30/13115224/crime-violent-reduce-ferguson-murder-fbi-ucr.

Adam, Hussein M. "Frantz Fanon as a Democratic Theorist." *African Affairs* 92, no. 369 (1993): 499–518.

Agnew, Robert. "Experienced, Vicarious, and Anticipated Strain: An Exploratory Study on Physical Victimization and Delinquency." *Justice Quarterly* 19, no. 4 (2002): 603–632.

Agnew, Robert. "Strain Theory and Violent Behavior." In *The Cambridge Handbook of Violent Behavior and Aggression*, edited by D. J. Flannery, A. T. Vazsonyi, and I. D. Waldman, 519–529. New York: Cambridge University Press, 2007.

Aja, Alan A., Gretchen Beesing, Daniel Bustillo, Danielle Clealand, Mark Paul, Khaing Zaw, Anne Price, William Darity, and Darrick Hamilton. *The Color of Wealth in Miami.* Ohio State University, Duke University, and the Insight Center of Community Economic Development, 2019. https://socialequity.duke.edu/wp-content/uploads/2019/10/The-Color-of-Wealth-in-Miami-Metro.pdf.

Albright, Matthew. "Brown v. Board, 60 Years Later: Are We Better Off?" *News Journal* (Wilmington, DE), May 18, 2014. http://www.delawareonline.com/story/news/education/2014/05/16/sunday-preview-brown-v-board-years-later/9196775/.

Albright, Matthew, and Saranac Hale Spencer. "Legislators Push Back Redistricting Vote to Next Year." *News Journal*, July 2, 2016. https://www.delawareonline.com/story/news/2016/06/30/legislators-push-back-redistricting-until-next-year/86576406/.

Alexander, Michelle. *The New Jim Crow: Mass Incarceration in the Age of Colorblindness.* New York: New Press, 2010.

Allen, Byron. "Byron Allen Billionaire Talks Black Wealth with Antonio Moore." YouTube, April 4, 2016. https://www.youtube.com/watch?v=8WyxXMZ9IXI.

Alonso, Alejandro A. "Racialized Identities and the Formation of Black Gangs in Los Angeles." *Urban Geography* 25, no. 7 (2004): 658–674.

Alonso, Gaston, Noel S. Anderson, Celina Su, and Jeanna Theoharis. *Our Schools Suck: Students Talk Back to a Segregated Nation on the Failures of Urban Education.* New York: New York University Press, 2009.

Alper, Mariel, Matthew R. Durose, and Joshua Markman. *2018 Update on Prisoner Recidivism: A 9-Year Follow-Up Period (2005–2014).* Washington, DC: Department of Justice, Bureau of Justice Statistics. https://bjs.ojp.gov/library/publications/2018-update-prisoner-recidivism-9-year-follow-period-2005-2014.

American Bar Association. "National Inventory of Collateral Consequences of Conviction." 2013.

Anderson, Gary, Tara M. Brown, Kathryn Herr, and Yasser A. Payne. *Participatory Action Research and Educational Policy*. Handbook of Educational Policy Research. American Educational Research Association. New York: Routledge, in press.

Anderson, Tammy L. "Dimensions of Women's Power in the Illicit Drug Economy." *Theoretical Criminology* 9, no. 4 (2005): 371–400.

Andreas, Peter. "A Tale of Two Borders: The U.S.-Mexico and U.S.-Canada Lines after 9/11." Working paper 77, Center for Comparative Immigration Studies, University of California, San Diego, May 2003. https://ccis.ucsd.edu/_files/wp77.pdf.

Anon. "Tough Wilmington." *Evening Journal*, August 20, 1889, 3.

Arditti, Joyce A., and Tiffaney Parkman. "Young Men's Reentry after Incarceration: A Developmental Paradox." *Family Relations* 60, no. 2 (2011): 205–220.

Associated Press. "AG: 14 Indicted on More than 120 Charges Linked to Gang." *U.S. News and World Report*, June 21, 2021. https://www.usnews.com/news/best-states/delaware/articles/2021-06-21/ag-14-indicted-on-more-than-120-charges-linked-to-gang.

Ayers, Edward L. *Vengeance and Justice: Crime and Punishment in the Nineteenth-Century American South*. New York: Oxford University Press, 1984.

Baker, Karl. "SEC Fraud Investigators Demand to Know Who Is behind Delaware LLCs." *News Journal*, December 1, 2017. https://www.delawareonline.com/story/money/business/2017/12/01/sec-fraud-investigators-demand-know-who-behind-delaware-llcs/908586001/.

Baker, Karl. "Shooting outside Southbridge Bar." *News Journal*, November 3, 2015. http://www.delawareonline.com/story/news/2015/11/03/shooting-outside-southbridge-bar/75078540/.

Baker, Karl, and Esteban Parra. "'Hidden from View': The Ongoing Battle for More Police Transparency in Delaware." *News Journal*, June 20, 2020. https://www.delawareonline.com/story/news/2020/06/18/delaware-police-records-private-what-does-mean-reform/3208401001/.

Bakhshandeh, Reza, Mehdi Samadi, Zohreh Azimifar, and Jonathan Schaeffer. "Degrees of Separation in Social Networks." In *Proceedings of the International Symposium on Combinatorial Search* 2, no. 1, Fourth Annual Symposium on Combinatorial Search (2011), https://ojs.aaai.org/index.php/SOCS/article/view/18200.

Baldwin, James. *The Fire Next Time*. 1962. Reprint, New York: Vintage Books, 1991.

Baldwin, James. "'The Negro in American Culture': A Group Discussion (Baldwin, Hughes, Hansberry, Capouya, Kazin)." YouTube, January 17, 2016. https://www.youtube.com/watch?v=jNpitdJSXWY&feature=youtu.be.

Banner, David. "David Banner on White Supremacy, Illuminati, the God Box (Full Interview)." YouTube, August 10, 2017. https://www.youtube.com/watch?v=w5McPO11XLU.

Baptist, Edward E. *The Half Has Never Been Told: Slavery and the Making of American Capitalism*. New York: Basic Books, 2016.

Baron, Stephen W. "General Strain, Street Youth, and Crime: A Test of Agnew's Revised Theory." *Criminology* 42, no. 2 (2004): 457–484.

Barrish, Cris. "'Different Temperature' on Wilmington Streets: Gun Homicides Down Sharply after 2021's Record Carnage." WHYY, July 31, 2022. https://whyy.org/articles/wilmington-gun-homicides-down-after-record-2021/.

Barrish, Cris. "Sex behind Bars: Women Violated in Delaware Prison." *News Journal*, July 31, 2015. http://www.delawareonline.com/story/news/local/2015/07/31/sex-behind-bars-women-violated-prison/30944001/.

Barrish, Cris. "Shootings Rise in Wilmington in 2019 as Homicide Clearance Rate Drops Sharply." *News Journal*, December 26, 2019. https://whyy.org/articles/shootings-rise-in-wilmington-in-2019-as-homicide-clearance-rate-drops-sharply/.

Barrish, Cris. "Study: 8 in 10 Released Inmates Return to Del. Prisons." *USA Today*, July 31, 2013. https://www.usatoday.com/story/news/nation/2013/07/31/delaware-prison-recidivism/2603821/.

Barrish, Cris, and Brittany Horn. "Baylor Security Boss Arrested for Sex with Female Inmate." *News Journal*, July 7, 2015. http://www.delawareonline.com/story/news/local/2015/07/07/prison-security-boss-suspended-inmate-sex-probe/29817969/.

Baum, Fran, Colin MacDougall, and Danielle Smith. "Participatory Action Research." *Journal of Epidemiology and Community Health* 60, no. 10 (2006): 854–857.

Beaudry, Ann, John H. Jackson, and Michelle Alexander. *Black Lives Matter: The Schott 50 State Report on Public Education and Black Males*. Cambridge, MA: Schott Foundation for Public Education, 2015.

Beck, Allen. J., Marcus Berzofsky, Rachel Caspar, and Christopher Krebs. *Sexual Victimization in Prisons and Jails Reported by Inmates, 2011–12*. Washington, DC: Bureau of Justice Statistics, 2014. https://bjs.ojp.gov/content/pub/pdf/svpjri1112.pdf.

Belin, Laura. "A Must-Watch MLK, Jr. Clip for Iowans." *Bleeding Heartland* (blog), January 17, 2022. https://www.bleedingheartland.com/2022/01/17/a-must-watch-mlk-jr-clip-for-iowans/.

Bell, Derrick. *Faces at the Bottom of the Well: The Permanence of Racism*. New York: Basic Books, 1992.

Bell, Melissa. "Patriot Act Used to Fight More Drug Dealers Than Terrorists." *Washington Post*, September 7, 2011. https://www.washingtonpost.com/blogs/blogpost/post/patriot-act-used-to-fight-more-drug-dealers-than-terrorists/2011/09/07/gIQAcmEBAK_blog.html.

Berman, Mark. "These Prosecutors Won Office Vowing to Fight the System. Now, the System Is Fighting Back." *Washington Post*, November 9, 2019. https://www.washingtonpost.com/national/these-prosecutors-won-office-vowing-to-fight-the-system-now-the-system-is-fighting-back/2019/11/05/20d863f6-afc1-11e9-a0c9-6d2d7818f3da_story.html.

Biden, Ashley, and Darius Brown. "Prison Is No Longer the Go-To Response to Crime." Delaware Online, May 10, 2015. https://www.delawareonline.com/story/opinion/contributors/2015/05/10/prison-longer-go-response-crime/27098913/.

Bies, Jessica. "Delaware Student Test Results Confirm Plight of Low-Income Students." *News Journal*, July 28, 2017. https://www.delawareonline.com/story/news/education/2017/07/28/state-test-results-confirm-plight-delawares-low-income-students/512992001/.

Bies, Jessica. "Wilmington: One of the Hardest Places to Achieve the American Dream." *News Journal*, October 4, 2018. https://www.delawareonline.com/story/news/2018/10/03/wilmington-one-hardest-places-achieve-american-dream-united-states/1490481002/.

Bies, Jessica, and Matthew Albright. "Ex-Delaware Education Secretary: Union Blocked Progress." Delaware Online, April 12, 2017. https://www.delawareonline.com/story/news/education/2017/04/12/former-ed-secretary-says-he-lost-teachers-union/100374092/.

Bittle, Matt. "Delaware's U.S. Senators Are Members of 'Top 1 Percent' in Income." *Delaware State News*, June 29, 2015. https://baytobaynews.com/stories/delawares-us-senators-are-members-of-top-1-percent-in-income,911?.

Black, Timothy. *When a Heart Turns Rock Solid: The Lives of Three Puerto Rican Brothers on and off the Streets*. New York: Vintage Books, 2009.

Blumgart, Jake, and Gregory Scruggs. "Fortune 500 Companies, a Central Location, and Low Taxes Can't Fix Wilmington." Next City, November 18, 2013. https://nextcity.org/features/fortune-500-companies-a-central-location-and-low-taxes-cant-fix-wilmington.

Bobichand, Rajkumar. "Understanding Violence Triangle and Structural Violence." Kangla Online, July 30, 2012. http://kanglaonline.com/2012/07/understanding-violence-triangle-and-structural-violence-by-rajkumar-bobichand/.

Bogdan, Robert, and Sari Knopp Biklen. *Qualitative Research for Education: An Introduction to Theory and Methods*. Boston: Pearson / Allyn and Bacon, 2007.

Bonilla-Silva, Eduardo. *Racism without Racists: Color-Blind Racism and the Persistence of Racial Inequality in America*. Lanham, MD: Rowman & Littlefield, 2014.

Bourgois, Philippe I. *In Search of Respect: Selling Crack in El Barrio*. New York: Cambridge University Press, 1995.

Bourke, Jason. "Urban Governance and Economic Development: An Analysis of the Changing Political Economy of Wilmington, Delaware, 1945–2017." PhD diss., University of Delaware, 2018.

Bowers, Maggie. "Two Local Cities Land on the List of 'Unfriendliest' in the Country." NBC10 Philadelphia, August 8, 2014. http://www.nbcphiladelphia.com/entertainment/the-scene/Local-Cities-Ranked-Least-Friendly-in-the-US-270398061.html.

Bowman, Phillip. J. "Race, Class, and Ethics in Research: Belmont Principles to Functional Relevance." In *Black Psychology*, edited by R. L. Jones, 747–766. Berkeley, CA: Cobb & Henry, 1991.

Bracke, Sarah. "Is the Subaltern Resilient? Notes on Agency and Neoliberal Subjects." *Cultural Studies* 30, no. 5 (2016): 839–855.

Brown, Claude. *Manchild in the Promised Land*. New York: Touchstone-Simon, 1965.

Brown, Robin. "Man Killed in Wilmington Shooting." *News Journal*, April 3, 2014. https://www.delawareonline.com/story/news/crime/2014/04/02/wilmington-police-scene-shooting/7223057/.

Brown, Tara M. "ARISE to the Challenge: Partnering with Urban Youth to Improve Educational Research and Learning." *Penn GSE Perspectives on Urban Education* 7, no. 1 (2010): 4–14.

Brown, Tara M. "'Hitting the Streets': Youth Street Involvement as Adaptive Well-Being." *Harvard Educational Review* 86, no. 1 (2016): 48–71.

Brunson, Rod K., and Brian A. Wade. "'Oh Hell No, We Don't Talk to Police': Insights on the Lack of Cooperation in Police Investigations of Urban Gun Violence." *Criminology & Public Policy* 18, no. 3 (2019): 623–648.

Bryant, Angela, and Yasser Payne. "Evaluating the Impact of Community-Based Learning: Participatory Action Research as a Model for Inside-Out." In *Turning Teaching Inside Out*, edited by Simone Weil Davis and Barbara Sherr Roswell, 227–239. New York: Palgrave Macmillan, 2013.

Bureau of Labor Statistics. *Labor Force Statistics from the Current Population Survey: Employment Status of the Civilian Noninstitutional Population by Sex, Age, and Race*. Washington, DC: U.S. Department of Labor, 2014.

Burgin, Say. "The 1968 Occupation of Black Wilmington." African American Intellectual History Society / Black Perspectives, October 8, 2018. https://www.aaihs.org/the-1968-occupation-of-black-wilmington/.

Burton, Linda M., and M. Belinda Tucker. "Romantic Unions in an Era of Uncertainty: A Post-Moynihan Perspective on African American Women and Marriage." *Annals of the American Academy of Political and Social Science* 621, no. 1 (2009): 132–148.

Bush-Baskette, Stephanie. *Misguided Justice: The War on Drugs and the Incarceration of Black Women*. Bloomington, IN: iUniverse, 2010.

Butterfield, Fox. *All God's Children: The Bosket Family and the American Tradition of Violence*. New York: Harper Perennial, 1995.

Canavan, Kathy. "Meet the Mayor: Mike Purzycki." *Delaware Business Times*, November 21, 2016. https://delawarebusinesstimes.com/news/features/meet-mayor-mike-purzycki/.

Caplan, Nathan. "The Indigenous Anchorman: A Solution to Some Ghetto Survey Problems." *The Analyst* 1 (1969): 20–34.

Carson, E. Ann. *Prisoners in 2016*. Washington, DC: Bureau of Justice Statistics, 2018. https://bjs.ojp.gov/library/publications/prisoners-2016.

Cassandram. "Wilmington: 50 Years after MLK." Blue Delaware, March 27, 2018. https://bluedelaware.com/2018/03/27/wilmington-50-years-after-mlk/.

Césaire, Aimé. *Discourse on Colonialism*. 1972. Reprint, New York: Monthly Review Press, 2000.

Chalmers, M., and Esteban Parra. "Two Views on Violence: Wilmington Ranks Third in Violent Crime for U.S. Cities Its Size." *News Journal*, October 2, 2011, A1.

Chalmers, Minnie, and Terri Sanginiti. "Mom in Mourning Leans on Faith: 19-Year-Old Son Collapses in his Mother's Arms after Being Shot in the Chest." *News Journal*, September 15, 2011, B1, B9.

Chambers, Darryl L. *Cease Violence Wilmington: First Year Implementation, Evaluation, and Initial Impact Assessment*. Wilmington: Center for Drug and Health Studies, University of Delaware, 2016.

Chase, Randall. "Teens Face Judge in Deadly Delaware School Restroom Fight Case." NBC10 Philadelphia, April 4, 2017. https://www.nbcphiladelphia.com/news/local/amy-joyner-francis-high-school-bathroom-death/11147/.

Cherry, Amy. "Wilmington Eclipses 2017 Gun Violence Record with Latest Fatal Shooting." WDEL 101.7FM, November 15, 2021. https://www.wdel.com/news/wilmington-eclipses-2017-gun-violence-record-with-latest-fatal-shooting/article_9c33181c-4636-11ec-a95a-f7bf8aafe88b.html.

Chokshi, Niraj, and Christopher Mele. "National Guard Deployed in Milwaukee amid Unrest over Fatal Police Shooting." *New York Times*, August 14, 2016. https://www.nytimes.com/2016/08/14/us/violent-crowd-confronts-police-in-milwaukee-after-fatal-shooting.html.

City News. "Mayor Purzycki, Police Chief Tracy Share Important Announcement from Delaware Attorney General Jennings about NorthPak Gang Indictment." City of Wilmington, June 21, 2021. https://www.wilmingtonde.gov/Home/Components/News/News/5540/225.

The City of Wilmington, Delaware. "City History." n.d. https://www.wilmingtonde.gov/about-us/about-the-city-of-wilmington/city-history.

Clark, Patrick. *Preventing Future Crime with Cognitive Behavioral Therapy*. Washington, DC: National Institute of Justice, 2010.

Clear, Todd R., Dina R. Rose, and Judith A. Ryder. "Incarceration and the Community: The Problem of Removing and Returning Offenders." *Crime & Delinquency* 47, no. 3 (2001): 335–351.

Clearinghouse for Economic Well-Being in Social Work Education. "Working Definition of Economic Well-Being." Council of Social Work Education (CSWE), October 2016. https://www.cswe.org/centers-initiatives/economic-wellbeing-clearinghouse/working-definition-of-economic-wellbeing/.

Cloward, Richard A., and Lloyd E. Ohlin. *Delinquency and Opportunity: A Theory of Delinquent Gangs*. London: Routledge, 1960.

Coker, Adeniyi. "Film as Historical Method in Black Studies: Documenting the African Experience." In *Handbook of Black Studies*, edited by Molefi Asante and Maulana Karenga, 352–366. Thousand Oaks, CA: Sage, 2006.

Collins, Max A. *American Gangster*. New York: Tom Doherty Associates, 2007.

Comey, James. "Hard Truths: Law Enforcement and Race." FBI, February 12, 2015. https://www.fbi.gov/news/speeches/hard-truths-law-enforcement-and-race.

Community Advocates for Black Life. "Delaware Legislative Black Caucus Plan Doesn't Go Far Enough." Delaware Online, August 4, 2020. https://www.delawareonline.com/story/opinion/2020/08/04/delaware-legislative-black-caucus-plan-doesnt-go-far-enough/5571540002/.

Community Service Building. "Our Mission." n.d. Accessed January 3, 2023. https://www.csbcorp.org/our-mission.

Contreras, Randol. "'Damn, Yo—Who's That Girl?' An Ethnographic Analysis of Masculinity in Drug Robberies." *Journal of Contemporary Ethnography* 38, no. 4 (2009): 465–492.

Contreras, Randol. *The Stickup Kids: Race, Drugs, Violence, and the American Dream*. Berkeley: University of California Press, 2013.

Coons, Chris. "Senator Coons Hosts Opening Discussion in Series on Urban Unemployment." Chris Coons, February 19, 2014. https://www.coons.senate.gov/news/press-releases/senator-coons-hosts-opening-discussion-in-series-on-urban-unemployment.

Coons, Chris. "Senator Coons to Launch Conversation on Fight against Urban Unemployment." Chris Coons, February 18, 2014. https://www.coons.senate.gov/news/press-releases/senator-coons-to-launch-conversation-on-fight-against-urban-unemployment.

Cormier, Ryan. "Murder Town TV Show 'Probably Dead at This Point.'" *News Journal*, August 12, 2016. http://www.delawareonline.com/story/entertainment/2016/08/12/murder-town-tv-show-probably-dead-point/88614690/.

Cormier, Ryan. "Showcase Chronicles Lives Claimed by Gun Violence." *News Journal*, December 4, 2010.

Crenshaw, Kimberlé, Neil Gotanda, Gary Peller, and Kendall Thomas. *Critical Race Theory: The Key Writings That Formed the Movement*. New York: New Press, 1995.

Dance, Lory Janelle. *Tough Fronts: The Impact of Street Culture on Schooling*. New York: Routledge, 2002.

Darity, William, Darrick Hamilton, Mark Paul, Alan Aja, Anne Price, Antonio Moore, and Caterina Chiopris. *What We Get Wrong about Closing the Racial Wealth Gap*. Durham, NC: Samuel DuBois Cook Center on Social Equity, 2018. https://socialequity.duke.edu/sites/socialequity.duke.edu/files/site-images/FINAL%20COMPLETE%20REPORT_.pdf.

Darity, William A., and Andrea Kirsten Mullen. *From Here to Equality: Reparations for Black Americans in the Twenty-First Century*. Chapel Hill: University of North Carolina Press, 2020.

Davis, Angela. Interview. *Frontline*, PBS, 1997. https://www.pbs.org/wgbh/pages/frontline/shows/race/interviews/davis.html.

Davis, Elliot. "Local Activists Not Happy with How St. Louis Has Rolled Out Cure Violence Program." Fox2Now, November 9, 2020. https://fox2now.com/news/missouri/local-activists-not-happy-with-how-st-louis-has-rolled-out-cure-violence-program.

De Bradley, Aviles Ann. *From Charity to Equity: Race, Homelessness, and Urban Schools*. New York: Teachers College Press, 2015.

Delaware Center for Justice. "About DCJ." n.d. accessed January 3, 2023. https://dcjustice.org/.

Delaware Center for Justice. "Delaware Center for Justice Annual Celebration 2022." n.d. Accessed January 3, 2023. https://dcjustice.org/delaware-center-for-justice-annual-celebration-2022/.

Delaware Center for Justice. "Executive Summary." n.d. Accessed January 3, 2023. https://philanthropydelaware.org/resources/Documents/DCJ%20ED%20Position%20Description%20FINAL%20FULL.pdf.

Delaware Department of Correction. *FY 2017 Annual Report*. Dover: Delaware Department of Correction, 2017. https://doc.delaware.gov/assets/documents/annual_report/DOC_2017AnnualReport.pdf.

Delaware Health Statistics Center. *Delaware Vital Statistics Annual Report 2016*. Dover: Delaware Health Statistics Center, 2016. https://dhss.delaware.gov/dph/hp/files/ar2016_print.pdf.

Delaware Juvenile Justice Advisory Group. *Annual Report and Recommendations to Governor John Carney and the Delaware State Legislature*. Wilmington: Delaware Juvenile Justice Advisory Group, 2019. https://cjc.delaware.gov/wp-content/uploads/sites/61/2019/06/Delaware-2018-JJAG-ReportvPRINTER.pdf.

Delaware Public Media. "History Matters: Wilmington's Southbridge Neighborhood." Delaware Public Media, February 15, 2015. https://www.delawarepublic.org/post/history-matters-wilmingtons-southbridge-neighborhood.

Delaware Public Media. "Sen. Coons Taps Experts, Community to Help Fight Urban Employment." Delaware Public Media, February 19, 2014. https://www.delawarepublic.org/2014-02-19/sen-coons-taps-experts-community-to-help-fight-urban-unemployment.

Delgado, Richard. "The Imperial Scholar: Reflections on a Review of Civil Rights Literature." In *Critical Race Theory: The Key Writings That Formed the Movement*, edited by Kimberle Crenshaw, Neil Gotanda, Gary Peller, and Kendall Thomas, 46–57. New York: New Press, 1995.

Desmond, Matthew. "Relational Ethnography." *Theory and Society* 43, no. 5 (2014): 547–579.

Diener, Ed, Jeffrey J. Sapyta, and Eunkook Suh. "Subjective Well-Being Is Essential to Well-Being." *Psychological Inquiry* 9, no. 1 (1998): 33–37.

Doll, Mimi, Gary W. Harper, Grisel M. Robles-Schrader, Jason Johnson, Audrey K. Bangi, Sunaina Velagaleti, and Adolescent Medicine Trials Network for HIV/AIDS Interventions. "Perspectives of Community Partners and Researchers about Factors Impacting Coalition Functioning over Time." *Journal of Prevention & Intervention in the Community* 40, no. 2 (2012): 87–102.

Drake, Kayla. "Cure Violence Advocates Defect from St. Louis Program, Claim 'Sabotage' by City Leaders." St. Louis Public Radio, August 11, 2020. https://news.stlpublicradio.org/law-order/2020-08-11/cure-violence-advocates-defect-from-st-louis-program-claim-sabotage-by-city-leaders.

Du Bois, W. E. B. *The Philadelphia Negro*. 1899. Reprint, Philadelphia: Schocken Books, 1967.

Duck, Waverly. *No Way Out: Precarious Living in the Shadow of Poverty and Drug Dealing*. Chicago: University of Chicago Press, 2015.

Dunlap, Eloise, Bruce D. Johnson, and Lisa Maher. "Female Crack Sellers in New York City: Who They Are and What They Do." *Women & Criminal Justice* 8, no. 4 (1997): 25–55.

Durán, Robert J. "Legitimated Oppression: Inner-City Mexican American Experiences with Police Gang Enforcement." *Journal of Contemporary Ethnography* 38, no. 2 (2009): 143–168.

Duvernay, Adam. "Gun Murders, Especially in Wilmington, Continue to Be Toughest to Solve." *News Journal*, August 22, 2018. https://www.delawareonline.com/story/news/crime/2018/08/22/gun-murders-especially-wilmington-continue-toughest-solve/999185002/.

Duvernay, Adam. "Wilmington Mayoral Candidates Take Aim at Each Other." *News Journal,* June 20, 2016. https://www.delawareonline.com/story/news/2016/07/19/mayor-candidates-square-off-final-debate/86987108/.

Edelman, Peter B., Harry J. Holzer, and Paul Offner. *Reconnecting Disadvantaged Young Men.* Washington, DC: Urban Institute Press, 2006.

Edin, Kathryn, and Maria Kefalas. *Promises I Can Keep: Why Poor Women Put Motherhood before Marriage.* Berkeley: University of California Press, 2005.

Edin, Kathryn, and Laura Lein. *Making Ends Meet: How Single Mothers Survive Welfare and Low-Wage Work.* New York: Russell Sage Foundation, 1997.

Edgell, Stephen. *The Sociology of Work: Continuity and Change in Paid and Unpaid Work.* London: Sage, 2012.

Eisen, Lauren-Brooke. "The Federal Funding That Fuels Mass Incarceration." Brennan Center for Justice, June 7, 2021. https://www.brennancenter.org/our-work/analysis-opinion/federal-funding-fuels-mass-incarceration.

Entmacher, Joan, Katherine G. Robbins, Julie Vogtman, and Anne Morrison. *Insecure and Unequal: Poverty and Income among Women and Families 2000–2012.* Washington, DC: National Women's Law Center, 2013.

Ettlinger, Michael. "COVID-19 Economic Crisis: By State." Carsey School of Public Policy, University of New Hampshire, October 2, 2020. https://carsey.unh.edu/COVID-19-Economic-Impact-By-State.

Eurpub. "Why the African American Divorce Rate Is 70%—What We Can Do to Fix It." EUR, March 26, 2017. http://www.eurweb.com/2017/03/african-american-divorce-rate-70-can-fix-video/.

Fader, Jamie J. *Falling Back: Incarceration and Transitions to Adulthood among Urban Youth.* New Brunswick, NJ: Rutgers University Press, 2013.

Fanon, Frantz. *Black Skin, White Masks.* 1952. Reprint, New York: Grove Press, 2008.

Fanon, Frantz. *The Wretched of the Earth.* New York: Grove Press, 1963.

Fayez, Rana. "A New Podcast on Poverty, Punishment and Possibility: The Kitchen's Zach Phillips Is Producing a Compelling New Podcast: Remaking Murdertown." Technical.ly, June 21, 2016. https://technical.ly/professional-development/remaking-murdertown-zach-phillips/.

Ferguson, Ann Arnett. *Bad Boys: Public Schools in the Making of Black Masculinity.* Ann Arbor: University of Michigan Press, 2001.

Fernandes, Lily, and Nora Hadi Q. Alsaeed. "African Americans and Workplace Discrimination." *European Journal of English Language and Literature Studies* 2, no. 2 (2014): 56–76.

Fernandez, Manny, Richard Perez-Pena, and Jonah Engel Bromwich. "Five Dallas Officers Were Killed as Payback, Police Chief Says." *Boston Globe,* July 8, 2016. https://www.bostonglobe.com/news/nation/2016/07/07/shots-fired-protest-dallas/1PrIf4FU4gOojlF9PTaaRN/story.html.

Ferris, Susan. "The School-to-Court Pipeline: Where Does Your State Rank?" Reveal, April 11, 2015. https://revealnews.org/article/the-school-to-court-pipeline-where-does-your-state-rank/.

Feucht, Thomas, and Tammy Holt. "Does Cognitive Behavioral Therapy Work in Criminal Justice? A New Analysis from CrimeSolutions.gov." *National Institute of Justice Journal,* issue 277 (September 2016). https://www.ojp.gov/pdffiles1/nij/249825.pdf.

Fine, Michelle, Nick Freudenberg, Yasser Payne, Tiffany Perkins, Kersha Smith, and Katya Wanzer. "'Anything Can Happen with Police Around': Urban Youth Evaluate Strategies of Surveillance in Public Places." *Journal of Social Issues* 59, no. 1 (2003): 141–158.

Fine, Michelle, and María Elena Torre. "Intimate Details: Participatory Action Research in Prison." *Action Research* 4, no. 3 (2006): 253–269.

Fine, Michelle, Maria E. Torre, Kathy Boudin, Iris Bowen, Judith Clark, Donna Hylton, Migdalia Martinez, Rosemarie Roberts, and Pamela Smart. *Changing Minds: The Impact of College in a Maximum-Security Prison.* New York: Leslie Glass Foundation and the Open Society Institute, 2001. https://www.prisonpolicy.org/scans/changing_minds.pdf.

First State Update. "Wilmington Shootings Up 52%, Murder Up 35%, Overall Crime Down 16% over Three-Year Period." First State Update, February 1, 2021. http://firststateupdate.com/2021/02/wilmington-shootings-up-52-murder-up-35-over-crime-down-16-over-three-year-period/.

Flores-González, Nilda. *School Kids / Street Kids: Identity Development in Latino Students.* New York: Teachers College Press, 2002.

Fordham, Signithia, and John U. Ogbu. "Black Students' School Success: Coping with the Burden of 'Acting White.'" *The Urban Review* 18, no. 3 (1986): 176–206.

Franklin, Anderson J. "Invisibility Syndrome and Racial Identity Development in Psychotherapy and Counseling African American Men." *The Counseling Psychologist* 27, no. 6 (1999): 761–793.

Fraser, Ronald. "How Delaware Cops Prey on Private Property." *News Journal / Delaware Online*, April 26, 2017. https://www.delawareonline.com/story/opinion/2017/04/26/how-delaware-cops-prey-private-property/100940132/.

Frost, Natasha A., Judith Greene, and Kevin Pranis. *Hard Hit: The Growth in the Imprisonment of Women, 1977–2004.* New York: Institute on Women and Criminal Justice, 2006. http://www.csdp.org/research/HardHitReport4.pdf.

Galtung, Johan. "Cultural Violence." *Journal of Peace Research* 27, no. 3 (1990): 291–305.

Galtung, Johan. "A Structural Theory of Imperialism." *Journal of Peace Research* 8, no. 2 (1971): 81–117.

Galtung, Johan. "Violence, Peace, and Peace Research." *Journal of Peace Research* 6, no. 3 (1969): 167–191.

Gamard, Sarah. "Will the Delaware General Assembly Grant Protesters' Wishes to Change Policing Laws?" Delaware Online, June 11, 2020. https://www.delawareonline.com/story/news/politics/2020/06/11/delaware-general-assembly-agree-what-protesters-want/5312262002/.

Garrison, Arthur, and Christian Kervick. *Analysis of City of Wilmington Violence and Social/Economic Data.* Wilmington, DE: Criminal Justice Council, 2006.

Gerace, Frank. "Mayor Baker Issues 'Ban the Box' Executive Order." WDEL, December 10, 2010. http://www.wdel.com/story.php?id=47654.

Giffords Law Center. "The Economic Cost of Gun Violence in Delaware." Giffords Law Center, 2018. https://giffords.org/wp-content/uploads/2018/11/The-Economic-Cost-of-Gun-Violence-in-Delaware-11.18.pdf.

Gilens, Martin. *Why Americans Hate Welfare: Race, Media, and the Politics of Antipoverty Policy.* Chicago: University of Chicago Press, 2000.

Gilligan, James. "Dr. James Gilligan on Violence." YouTube, October 20, 2010. https://www.youtube.com/watch?v=HmZjm7yOHwE.

Gilmore, Ruth Wilson. *Golden Gulag: Prisons, Surplus, Crisis, and Opposition in Globalizing California.* Berkeley: University of California Press, 2007.

Gordon, Edmund W., and L. D. Song. "Variations in the Experience of Educational Resilience." In *Educational Resilience in Inner-City America: Challenges and Prospects,* edited by Margaret C. Wang and Edmund W. Gordon, 27–43. New York: Routledge, 1994.

Greene, Andrew C. "Sociopolitical Tales of Cultivating Spirituality, Collective Hope, and Emotional Vulnerabilities through a Community-Specific (Grassroots Movement Praxis) Approach to Youth Development." PhD diss., City University of New York Graduate Center, 2020.

Griffin, Sean Patrick. *Black Brothers, Inc.: The Violent Rise and Fall of Philadelphia's Black Mafia*. Preston, UK: Milo Books, 2005.

Grim, Ryan, and David Dayen. "Tom Carper and the Rise and Fall of the Delaware Way." The Intercept, August 29, 2018. https://theintercept.com/2018/08/29/tom-carper-delaware-way-kerri-harris/.

Gronau, Ian. "Inmates Sentenced in Vaughn Prison Riot case." *Delaware State News*, September 13, 2019. https://delawarestatenews.net/news/inmates-sentenced-in-vaughn-prison-riot-case/.

Haddad, Mohammed. "Mapping US Cities Where George Floyd Protests Have Erupted." Al Jazeera, June 2, 2020. https://www.aljazeera.com/news/2020/6/2/mapping-us-cities-where-george-floyd-protests-have-erupted.

Hall, Phil. "Beau Biden's Fight against Big Banks." *National Mortgage Professional*, June 1, 2015. https://nationalmortgageprofessional.com/news/54276/beau-bidens-fight-against-big-banks.

Halushka, John. "Work Wisdom: Teaching Former Prisoners How to Negotiate Workplace Interactions and Perform a Rehabilitated Self." *Ethnography* 17, no. 1 (2016): 72–91.

Harding, David J. *Living the Drama: Community, Conflict, and Culture among Inner-City Boys*. Chicago: University of Chicago Press, 2010.

Hardt, Michael, and Antonio Negri. *Empire*. Cambridge, MA: Harvard University Press, 2000.

Harris, Richard J., and John P. O'Connell. *Operation Safe Streets Governor's Task Force: Review and Impact*. Dover: Delaware Criminal Justice Council Statistical Analysis Center, 2004.

Harris, Richard J., Jim Salt, and Charles Huenke. *Delaware Shootings 2012: An Overview of Incidents, Suspects, and Victims in Delaware*. Dover: Delaware Criminal Justice Council Statistical Analysis Center, 2013. https://sac.delaware.gov/wp-content/uploads/sites/64/2017/04/2012StatewideShootingReportNovember-2013.pdf.

Hart, Carl L. "How the Myth of the 'Negro Cocaine Fiend' Helped Shape American Drug Policy." *The Nation*, June 29, 2015. https://www.thenation.com/article/archive/how-myth-negro-cocaine-fiend-helped-shape-american-drug-policy/.

Hattery, Angela, and Earl Smith. *Policing Black Bodies: How Black Lives Are Surveilled and How to Work for Change*. Lanham, MD: Rowman & Littlefield, 2018.

Heiner, Brady. "The Procedural Entrapment of Mass Incarceration: Prosecution, Race, and the Unfinished Project of American Abolition." *Philosophy & Social Criticism* 42, no. 6 (2016): 594–631.

Hinnant, J. Benjamin, Marion O'Brien, and Sharon R. Ghazarian. "The Longitudinal Relations of Teacher Expectations to Achievement in the Early School Years." *Journal of Educational Psychology* 101, no. 3 (2009): 662.

Hinton, Elizabeth, and DeAnza Cook. "The Mass Criminalization of Black Americans: A Historical Overview." *Annual Review of Criminology* 4 (2021): 261–286.

Hitchens, Brooklynn. "Stress and Street Life: Black Women, Urban Inequality, and Coping in a Small Violent City." PhD diss., Rutgers University, 2020.

Hitchens, Brooklynn K., and Yasser Arafat Payne. "'Brenda's Got a Baby': Black Single Motherhood and Street Life as a Site of Resilience in Wilmington, Delaware." *Journal of Black Psychology* 43, no. 1 (2017): 50–76.

Hoffecker, Carol E. *Corporate Capital: Wilmington in the Twentieth Century*. Philadelphia: Temple University Press, 1983.

Horn, Brittany. "Lawsuit Claims Vaughn Inmates Were Beaten, Tortured after 2017 Prison Riot Ended." *News Journal*, October 31, 2018. https://www.delawareonline.com/story/news/crime/2018/10/31/lawsuit-vaughn-inmates-were-beaten-tortured-after-prison-riot-ended/1808724002/.

Horn, Brittany. "13 Gang Members Face 91 Charges, Including Murder." *News Journal*, September 11, 2015. https://www.delawareonline.com/story/news/crime/2015/09/11/gang-members-indicted-charges-including-murder/72080642/.

Horn, Brittany. "Wilmington Rapper's Mom Sees Killing as Retaliation." *News Journal*, November 30, 2016. http://www.delawareonline.com/story/news/crime/2016/11/30/wilmington-rappers-mom-sees-killing-retaliation/94667130/.

Horn, Brittany, Esteban Parra, Christina Jedra, and Jessica Reyes. "Delaware's Economy Suffers from Wilmington's Violence." *News Journal*, September 10, 2017. https://www.delawareonline.com/story/news/crime/2017/09/08/delawares-economy-suffers-wilmingtons-violence/102562232/.

Horn, Brittany, Jessica Masulli Reyes, Esteban Parra, Christina Jedra, and Larry Fenn. "Wilmington: Most Dangerous Place in America for Youth." *News Journal*, September 9, 2017. https://www.delawareonline.com/story/news/crime/2017/09/08/our-babies-killing-each-other/100135370/.

Horn, Brittany, and Alonzo Small. "Man Fatally Shot in Wilmington Was Well-Known Rapper." *News Journal* / Delaware Online, November 29, 2016. https://www.delawareonline.com/story/news/crime/2016/11/29/man-fatally-shot-wilmington-well-known-rapper-delaware/94622346/.

Horowitz, Ruth. "Sociological Perspectives on Gangs: Conflicting Definitions and Concepts." In *Gangs in America*, edited by C. Ronald Huff, 37–54. Thousand Oaks, CA: Sage, 1990.

Howard, Tyrone C., and Richard Milner. *Handbook of Urban Education*. New York: Routledge, 2014.

Howell, William G. "Results of President Obama's Race to the Top." *Education Next* 15, no. 4 (2015): 58–67.

Hughes, Isabel, Jeanne Kuang, Meredith Newman, and Sarah Gamard. "Wilmington Protest for Floyd Turns Violent; Police Order People off the Streets." Delaware Online, May 31, 2020. https://www.delawareonline.com/story/news/2020/05/30/wilmington-protests-george-floyd-turn-violent-night/5295496002/.

Hutchinson, Bill. "Police Officers Killed Surge 28% This Year and Some Point to Civil Unrest and Those Looking to Exploit It." ABC News, July 22, 2020. https://abcnews.go.com/US/police-officers-killed-surge-28-year-point-civil/story?id=71773405.

Iacurci, Greg. "Here's Why the Real Unemployment Rate May Be Higher than Reported." CNBC, June 5, 2020. https://www.cnbc.com/2020/06/05/heres-why-the-real-unemployment-rate-may-be-higher-than-reported.html.

Jackson, John L. *Harlemworld: Doing Race and Class in Contemporary Black America*. Chicago: University of Chicago Press, 2001.

Jacobs, Bruce A. *Robbing Drug Dealers: Violence beyond the Law*. London: Routledge, 2001.

Jedra, Christina. "Civic Groups Want 'Independent Counsel' to Look at Delaware's LLC Law." *News Journal*, August 7, 2018. https://www.delawareonline.com/story/news/2018/08/06/citizens-petition-ag-matt-denn-investigate-abuse-delaware-llcs/898036002/.

Jedra, Christina, Esteban Parra, and Adam Duvernay. "Wilmington's Deadliest Year: Mayor Withholds 'Serious Concern' until Plan Takes Hold." Delaware Online, January 5, 2018. https://www.delawareonline.com/get-access/?return=https%3A%2F%2Fwww.delawareonline.com%2Fstory%2Fnews%2Flocal%2F2018%2F01%2F05%2Fwilmington-mayor-record-shootings-homicides-not-yet-cause-serious-concern-wilmington-mayor-record-sh%2F984347001%2F.

Johnson, Akilah. "That Was No Typo: The Median Net Worth of Black Bostonians Really Is $8." *Boston Globe*, December 11, 2017. https://www.bostonglobe.com/metro/2017/12/11/that-was-typo-the-median-net-worth-black-bostonians-really/ze5kxC1jJelx24M3pugFFN/story.html.

Johnson, Mason. "FBI's Violent Crime Statistics for Every City in America." CBS Chicago, October 22, 2015. http://chicago.cbslocal.com/2015/10/22/violent-crime-statistics-for-every-city-in-america/.

Johnson, TyLisa C. "Etched in Memory." *Philadelphia Inquirer*, December 7, 2018. https://www.inquirer.com/news/a/wilmington-del-riots-occupation-martin-luther-king-jr-national-guard-20181207.html.

Joho, Jess. "Who Are the Children of the Forest on 'Game of Thrones,' and Why Do They Matter?" Mashable, August 7, 2017. http://mashable.com/2017/08/07/children-of-the-forest-game-of-thrones/#LHm7dGMUpiqu.

Jones, Abigail. "Murder Town USA (aka Wilmington, Delaware)." *Newsweek*, December 9, 2014. https://www.newsweek.com/2014/12/19/wilmington-delaware-murder-crime-290232.html.

Jones, Janine M. "Exposure to Chronic Community Violence: Resilience in African American Children." *Journal of Black Psychology* 33, no. 2 (2007): 125–149.

Jones, Nikki. *Between Good and Ghetto: African American Girls and Inner-City Violence*. New Brunswick, NJ: Rutgers University Press, 2010.

Kaeble, Danielle. *Probation and Parole in the United States, 2016*. Washington, DC: Bureau of Justice Statistics, 2018. https://bjs.ojp.gov/library/publications/probation-and-parole-united-states-2016.

Katz, Michael Barry. *Improving Poor People: The Welfare State, the "Underclass," and Urban Schools as History*. Princeton, NJ: Princeton University Press, 1995.

Kelley, Robin D. G. "Kickin' Reality, Kickin' Ballistics: Gangsta Rap and Postindustrial Los Angeles." In *Droppin' Science: Critical Essays on Rap Music and Hip-Hop Culture*, edited by W. W. Perkins, 117–158. Philadelphia: Temple University Press, 1994.

Kelley, Robin D. G. *Yo' Mama's Disfunktional! Fighting the Culture Wars in Urban America*. Boston: Beacon Press, 1998.

Kelly, Jack. "Jobless Claims: 57.4 Million Americans Have Sought Unemployment Benefits since Mid-March—Over 1 Million People Filed Last Week." *Forbes*, August 20, 2020. https://www.forbes.com/sites/jackkelly/2020/08/20/jobless-claims-574-million-americans-have-sought-unemployment-benefits-since-mid-marchover-1-million-people-filed-last-week/#22a4d9126d59.

Kelly, Robert C. "Wealth." Investopedia, April 24, 2021. https://www.investopedia.com/terms/w/wealth.asp.

Kervick, Christian, and Thomas MacLeish. *Recidivism in Delaware: An Analysis of Prisoners Released in 2008 through 2010*. Dover: Delaware Criminal Justice Council Statistical Analysis Center, 2014.

Keyes, Cheryl Lynette. *Rap Music and Street Consciousness*. Urbana: University of Illinois Press, 2002.

Kim, Allen, and Sheena Jones. "Delaware Removes Whipping Post outside Courthouse." CNN, July 1, 2020. https://www.cnn.com/2020/07/01/us/whipping-post-georgetown-delaware-trnd/index.html.

Kindy, Kimberly. "Fatal Police Shootings in 2015 Approaching 400 Nationwide." *Washington Post*, May 30, 2015. https://www.washingtonpost.com/national/fatal-police-shootings-in-2015-approaching-400-nationwide/2015/05/30/d322256a-058e-11e5-a428-c984eb077d4e_story.html.

King, Martin Luther, Jr. "The Three Evils of Society." Speech delivered at the First Annual National Conference on New Politics, Chicago, August 31, 1967. https://www.nwesd.org/ed-talks/equity/the-three-evils-of-society-address-martin-luther-king-jr/.

Kishi, Roudabeh, and Sam Jones. *Demonstrations and Political Violence in America: New Data for Summer 2020*. Madison, WI: Armed Conflict Location and Event Data Project (ACLED), 2020. https://acleddata.com/acleddatanew/wp-content/uploads/2020/09/ACLED_USDataReview_Sum2020_SeptWebPDF_HiRes.pdf.

Kleinberg, Jon. "The Small-World Phenomenon: An Algorithmic Perspective." In *Proceedings of the Thirty-Second Annual ACM Symposium on Theory of Computing*, 163–170. New York: Association for Computing Machinery, 2000.

Kochhar, Rakesh, and Richard Fry. "Wealth Inequality Has Widened along Racial, Ethnic Lines since End of Great Recession." *Pew Research Center* 12, no. 104 (2014): 121–145.

Kubrin, Charis E., and Ronald Weitzer. "Retaliatory Homicide: Concentrated Disadvantage and Neighborhood Culture." *Social Problems* 50, no. 2 (2003): 157–180.

LeBlanc, Adrian Nicole. *Random Family: Love, Drugs, Trouble, and Coming of Age in the Bronx*. New York: Scribner, 2003.

Leech, Garry M. *Capitalism: A Structural Genocide*. London: Zed Books, 2012.

Leovy, Jill. *Ghettoside: A True Story of Murder in America*. New York: Spiegel & Grau, 2015.

Leverentz, Andrea. "Being a Good Daughter and Sister: Families of Origin in the Reentry of African American Female Ex-Prisoners." *Feminist Criminology* 6, no. 4 (2011): 239–267.

Lewis, Oscar. "The Culture of Poverty." *Scientific American* 215, no. 4 (1966): 19–25.

LIFERS. "Ending the Culture of Street Crime." *The Prison Journal* 84, no. 4 (2004): 48–68.

Linderman, Juliet, Brittany Horn, Esteban Parra, and Larry Fenn. "Growing Up under Fire: Wilmington, Delaware, Leads U.S. in Teen Shootings." *USA Today*, September 8, 2017. https://www.usatoday.com/story/news/2017/09/08/wilmington-delaware-leads-u-s-teen-shootings/619458001/.

Lofquist, Daphne, Terry Lugaila, Martin O'Connell, and Sarah Feliz. *Households and Families: 2010*. Report C2010BR-14. Washington, DC: U.S. Census Bureau, 2012. https://www.census.gov/content/dam/Census/library/publications/2012/dec/c2010br-14.pdf.

Long, Colleen, Kat Stafford, and R. J. Rico. "Summer of Protest: Chance for Change, but Obstacles Exposed." AP News, September 6, 2020. https://apnews.com/article/9035ecdfc58d5dba755185666ac0ed6d.

Lopez, German. "The Great Majority of Violent Crime in America Goes Unsolved." Vox, March 1, 2017. https://www.vox.com/policy-and-politics/2017/3/1/14777612/trump-crime-certainty-severity.

Lopez, German. "Joe Biden's Long Record Supporting the War on Drugs and Mass Incarceration, Explained." Vox, April 25, 2019. https://www.vox.com/policy-and-politics/2019/4/25/18282870/joe-biden-criminal-justice-war-on-drugs-mass-incarceration.

Lopez, German. "2020's Historic Surge in Murders, Explained." Vox, March 25, 2021. https://www.vox.com/22344713/murder-violent-crime-spike-surge-2020-covid-19-coronavirus.

López, Josué R. "Participatory Action Research in Education: A Fanonian Medicine of the People." *Philosophical Studies in Education* 51 (2020): 54–70.

Lowery, Wesley. "Aren't More White People than Black People Killed by Police? Yes, but No." *Washington Post*, October 11, 2016. https://www.washingtonpost.com/news/post-nation/wp/2016/07/11/arent-more-white-people-than-black-people-killed-by-police-yes-but-no/?utm_term=.a4ea598d95ed.

Lowery, Wesley, Kimbriell Kelly, and Steven Rich. "Murder with Impunity: An Unequal Justice." *Washington Post*, July 25, 2018. https://www.washingtonpost.com

/graphics/2018/investigations/black-homicides-arrests/?noredirect=on&utm_term=.1edacfb85163.

Lykes, M. Brinton. "Creative Arts and Photography in Participatory Action Research in Guatemala." In *Handbook of Action Research*, edited by Peter Reason and H. Bradbury, 363–371. Thousand Oaks, CA: Sage, 2001.

Lykes, M. Brinton. "Silence(ing), Voice(s) and Gross Violations of Human Rights: Constituting and Performing Subjectivities through Photo PAR." *Visual Studies* 25, no. 3 (2010): 238–254.

Lykes, M. Brinton. "Speaking against the Silence: One Maya Woman's Exile and Return." In *Women Creating Lives: Identities, Resilience, and Resistance*, edited by Carol E. Franz, 97–114. New York: Routledge, 1994.

Lynch, Michael J., and Raymond J. Michalowski. *Primer in Radical Criminology: Critical Perspectives on Crime, Power, and Identity*. Monsey, NY: Criminal Justice Press, 2006.

MacFarquhar, Neil. "After Centuries of Obscurity, Wilmington Is Having a Moment." *New York Times*, January 19, 2021. https://www.nytimes.com/2020/12/06/us/after-centuries-of-obscurity-wilmington-is-having-a-moment.html.

Maciag, Mike. "Police Employment, Officer per Capita Rates for U.S. Cities." *Governing*, May 7, 2014. http://www.governing.com/gov-data/safety-justice/police-officers-per-capita-rates-employment-for-city-departments.html.

MacLeod, Jay. *Ain't No Makin' It: Aspirations and Attainment in a Low-Income Neighborhood*. Boulder, CO: Westview Press, 2008.

Marusak, Joe, Ely Portillo, Mark Price, and Adam Bell. "Charlotte Faces Aftermath of Protests Ignited by Fatal Police Shooting: 16 Officers Injured." *Charlotte Observer*, September 20, 2016. https://www.charlotteobserver.com/news/local/crime/article103009432.html.

Massey, Douglas S. *Categorically Unequal: The American Stratification System*. New York: Russell Sage Foundation, 2007.

Mateu-Gelabert, Pedro, and Howard Lune. "Street Codes in High School: School as an Educational Deterrent." *City & Community* 6, no. 3 (2007): 173–191.

Matthews, Rick A., Michael O. Maume, and William J. Miller. "Deindustrialization, Economic Distress, and Homicide Rates in Midsized Rustbelt Cities." *Homicide Studies* 5, no. 2 (2001): 83–113.

Mauer, Marc. *The Changing Racial Dynamics of the War on Drugs*. Washington, DC: Sentencing Project, 2009.

Mauer, Marc. *The Changing Racial Dynamics of Women's Incarceration*. Washington, DC: Sentencing Project, 2013.

McAneny, DJ. "Wilmington State Senator Charged with Punching Woman in Restaurant." WDEL 101.7FM, May 19, 2021. https://www.wdel.com/news/wilmington-state-senator-charged-with-punching-woman-in-restaurant/article_8bec1200-b8ca-11eb-a4fc-83edba69bbdc.html.

McCarthy, Niall. "Racial Wealth Inequality in the U.S. Is Rampant." *Forbes*, September 14, 2017. https://www.forbes.com/sites/niallmccarthy/2017/09/14/racial-wealth-inequality-in-the-u-s-is-rampant-infographic/?sh=3b72825234e8.

McDougal, Serie. *Research Methods in Africana Studies*. New York: Peter Lang, 2014.

McIntyre, Alice. "Constructing Meaning about Violence, School, and Community Participatory Action Research with Urban Youth." *The Urban Review* 32, no. 2 (2000): 123–154.

McWhorter, John H. *Losing the Race: Self-Sabotage in Black America*. New York: Simon and Schuster, 2000.

Mears, Daniel P., Xia Wang, and William D. Bales. "Does a Rising Tide Lift All Boats? Labor Market Changes and Their Effects on the Recidivism of Released Prisoners." *Justice Quarterly* 31, no. 5 (2014): 822–851.

Mendel, Peter, Victoria K. Ngo, Elizabeth Dixon, Susan Stockdale, Felica Jones, Bowen Chung, Andrea Jones, Zoe Masongsong, and Dmitry Khodyakov. "Partnered Evaluation of a Community Engagement Intervention: Use of a 'Kickoff' Conference in a Randomized Trial for Depression Care Improvement in Underserved Communities." *Ethnicity & Disease* 21, no. 3, suppl. 1 (2011): 78–88.

Min, Shirley. "Delaware Is Latest State to 'Ban the Box.'" WHYY, May 9, 2014. https://whyy.org/articles/delaware-is-latest-state-to-ban-the-box/.

Mong, Sherry N., and Vincent J. Roscigno. "African American Men and the Experience of Employment Discrimination." *Qualitative Sociology* 33, no. 1 (2010): 1–21.

Moore, Antonio. "The Middle Black Family in Los Angeles Is Only Worth $200.00 Liquid." *Los Angeles Sentinel*, December 21, 2017. https://lasentinel.net/the-middle-black-family-in-los-angeles-is-only-worth-200-00-liquid.html.

Morgan, Damion, Victor Pacheco, Chiedza Rodriguez, Elsie Vazquez, Marlene Berg, and Jean Schensul. "Youth Participatory Action Research on Hustling and Its Consequences: A Report from the Field." *Children Youth and Environments* 14, no. 2 (2004): 201–228.

Moshtaghian, Artemis, and Amir Vera. "2 Los Angeles County Deputies Are Out of Surgery after Ambush Shooting in Compton." CNN, September 13, 2020. https://www.cnn.com/2020/09/12/us/los-angeles-county-officers-shot-compton/index.html.

Motlagh, Jason. "A Radical Approach to Gun Crime: Paying People Not to Kill Each Other." *Guardian*, June 9, 2016. https://www.theguardian.com/us-news/2016/jun/09/richmond-california-ons-gun-crime.

Mueller, Gavin. "Be the Street: On Radical Ethnography and Cultural Studies." *Viewpoint Magazine*, September 10, 2012. https://www.viewpointmag.com/2012/09/10/be-the-street-on-radical-ethnography-and-cultural-studies/.

Mullings, Leith, and Alaka Wali. *Stress and Resilience: The Social Context of Reproduction in Central Harlem*. Boston: Springer, 2001.

Musu-Gillette, Lauren, Anlan Zhang, Ke Wang, Jizhi Zhang, Jana Kemp, Melissa Diliberti, and Barbara A. Oudekerk. *Indicators of School Crime and Safety: 2017*. Washington, DC: National Center for Education Statistics, U.S. Department of Education, 2018. https://nces.ed.gov/pubs2018/2018036.pdf.

Nagengast, Larry. "When Will Public Schools Get Better?" *Delaware Today*, June 7, 2017. https://delawaretoday.com/uncategorized/when-will-public-schools-get-better/.

Nardone, Mark. "Wilmington Crime: A City That Bleeds—Part One in a Series Explains Why Violent Crime Has Increased in Wilmington." *Delaware Today*, April 23, 2015. http://www.delawaretoday.com/Delaware-Today/May-2015/Wilmington-Crime-A-City-That-Bleeds/.

Nardone, Mark. "Wilmington Crime: Hope for the Hood—Part Two in a Series Explains How Men Who've Survived Life on the Streets Intend to Curb the Violence in Wilmington." *Delaware Today*, May 26, 2015. http://www.delawaretoday.com/Delaware-Today/June-2015/Wilmington-Crime-Hope-for-the-Hood/.

Naylor, Brian. "How Federal Dollars Fund Local Police." NPR, June 9, 2020. https://www.npr.org/2020/06/09/872387351/how-federal-dollars-fund-local-police.

NeighborhoodScout. "NeighborhoodScout's Most Dangerous Cities—2022." NeighborhoodScout, January 3, 2022. https://www.neighborhoodscout.com/blog/top100dangerous.

Newark Free Community. "Wilmington: White Oppression, Black Despair." *The Heterodoxical Voice* 1, no. 3 (1968): 3. Chris Oakley Collection of Alternative Press, Special Collections, University of Delaware Library. https://exhibitions.lib.udel.edu/1968/exhibition-item/wilmington-white-oppression-black-despair-the-heterodoxical-voice-1968-july-august-volume-1-number-5-page-3/.

Newman, Meredith, Karl Baker, and Jeanne Kuang. "Despite Heavy Rain, Protesters March in Wilmington Friday, Including with Police at End." Delaware Online,

June 5, 2020. https://www.delawareonline.com/story/news/2020/06/05/wilmington-protest-george-floyds-breonna-taylor/3158389001/.

News Journal Editorial / USA TODAY Network Atlantic Group Editorial Board. "Our View: Wilmington's Wounds—39 Dead in Gun Violence—Are Unbearable. It's Time to Act." *News Journal* / Delaware Online, December 10, 2021. https://www.delawareonline.com/story/opinion/editorials/2021/12/10/39-dead-wilmington-gun-violence-unbearable-its-time-act/6452869001/.

Newton, James E. "Black Americans in Delaware: An Overview." In *History of African Americans of Delaware and Maryland's Eastern Shore*, edited by Carole C. Marks, 13–33. Wilmington: Delaware Heritage Commission, 1997.

Nobles, Wade W. "Extended Self: Rethinking the So-Called Negro Self-Concept." *Journal of Black Psychology* 2, no. 2 (1976): 15–24.

Nordberg, Anne, Marcus R. Crawford, Regina T. Praetorius, and Schnavia Smith Hatcher. "Exploring Minority Youths' Police Encounters: A Qualitative Interpretive Meta-synthesis." *Child and Adolescent Social Work Journal* 33, no. 2 (2016): 137–149.

O'Connor, Alice, Chris Tilly, and Lawrence Bobo. *Urban Inequality: Evidence from Four Cities*. New York: Russell Sage Foundation, 2001.

O'Connor, Meg. "This Anti-violence Strategy May Be Coming to St. Louis, but Activists See Red Flags." The Appeal: Political Report, April 5, 2021. https://theappeal.org/politicalreport/st-louis-mayoral-election-focused-deterrence/.

Okeem, Chidike I. "On Criminogenic Grit and Theoretical Criminology." *Journal of Theoretical & Philosophical Criminology* 12 (2020): 98–115.

Oliver, Melvin L., and Thomas M. Shapiro. "A Sociology of Wealth and Racial Inequality." In *Redress for Historical Injustices in the United States: On Reparations for Slavery, Jim Crow, and Their Legacies*, edited by Michael T. Martin and Marilyn Yaquinto, 91–119. Durham, NC: Duke University Press, 1995.

O'Sullivan, Sean. "Wilmington, DE: Delaware Courts: Prosecutor Says Mentor Killed over Woman." *News Journal*, May 14, 2010. http://intimateviolencedeathnews.blogspot.com/2010/05/wilmington-de-delaware-courts.html.

Owens, Cassie. "What Can Happen When the National Guard Is Called into a City over Riots." Next City, April 29, 2015. https://nextcity.org/urbanist-news/city-riots-baltimore-wilmington-national-guard-in-cities.

Pager, Devah. *Marked: Race, Crime, and Finding Work in an Era of Mass Incarceration*. Chicago: University of Chicago Press, 2009.

Pallas, Josh. "Fanon on Violence and the Person." *Critical Legal Thinking* (blog), January 20, 2016. https://criticallegalthinking.com/2016/01/20/fanon-on-violence-and-the-person/.

Panuccio, Elizabeth, and Johnna Christian. "Work, Family, and Masculine Identity: An Intersectional Approach to Understanding Young, Black Men's Experiences of Reentry." *Race and Justice* 9, no. 4 (2019): 407–433.

Papachristos, Andrew V., Anthony A. Braga, and David M. Hureau. "Social Networks and the Risk of Gunshot Injury." *Journal of Urban Health* 89, no. 6 (2012): 992–1003.

Parenting. "Top 10 Most Dangerous Cities in America." *Parenting*, June 2012.

Parker, Seymour, and Robert J. Kleiner. "Social and Psychological Dimensions of the Family Role Performance of the Negro Male." *Journal of Marriage and the Family* 31, no. 3 (1969): 500–506.

Parra, Esteban. "Ashley Biden Leaves Job, Adds to Speculation over Joe Biden 2020 Presidential Campaign." Delaware Online, March 8, 2019. https://www.delawareonline.com/get-access/?return=https%3A%2F%2Fwww.delawareonline.com%2Fstory%2Fnews%2F2019%2F03%2F08%2Fashley-biden-leaves-job-adds-speculation-over-dad-joe-bidens-presidential-decision%2F3102891002%2F.

Parra, Esteban. "Death Penalty, Life in Prison in Eden Park Shootout." *News Journal*, September 4, 2015. http://www.delawareonline.com/story/news/crime/2015/09/04/two-sentenced-friday-eden-park-shootout/71693874/.

Parra, Esteban. "Murder Suspect's Facebook Page Down after Comments Posted." *News Journal*, April 2, 2016. https://www.delawareonline.com/story/news/crime/2016/04/02/murder-suspect-facebook-page-down-after-comments-posted/82550998/.

Parra, Esteban, Jessica Reyes, and Karl Baker. "Police Charge Death Was Gang-Related." *News Journal*, June 23, 2016. https://www.delawareonline.com/story/news/crime/2016/06/23/four-indicted-murder-15-year-old-brandon-wingo/86283700/.

Parra, Esteban, and Adam Wagner. "Wilmington Unveils Public Safety Initiative." *News Journal*, January 26, 2015. https://www.delawareonline.com/story/news/local/2015/01/26/wilmington-unveils-public-safety-initiative/22345323/.

Patterson, Orlando. "Try on the Outfit and Just See How It Works: The Psychocultural Responses of Disconnected Youth to Work." In *The Cultural Matrix: Understanding Black Youth*, edited by Orlando Patterson, 415–443. Cambridge, MA: Harvard University Press, 2015.

Patterson, William L., Ossie Davis, Jarvis Tyner, and U.S. Civil Rights Congress, eds. *We Charge Genocide: The Historic Petition to the United Nations for Relief from a Crime of the United States Government against the Negro People*. New York: Civil Rights Congress, 1951.

Patton, Peter L. "The Gangstas in Our Midst." *The Urban Review* 30, no. 1 (1998): 49–76.

Payne, Yasser Arafat. "Jobs, Not Jail, the Answer to Wilmington Violence." *News Journal*, June 7, 2015. https://www.delawareonline.com/story/opinion/contributors/2015/06/07/jobs-jail-answer-wilmington-violence/28661195/.

Payne, Yasser Arafat. "Participatory Action Research." In *The Wiley-Blackwell Encyclopedia of Social Theory*, edited by B. S. Turner, C. Kyung-Sup, C. F. Epstein, P. Kivisto, and W. Outhwaite, 1694–1708. Hoboken, NJ: Wiley-Blackwell, 2017.

Payne, Yasser Arafat. *The People's Report: The Link between Structural Violence and Crime in Wilmington, Delaware*. Wilmington, DE: self-published, 2013. http://thepeoplesreport.com/images/pdf/The_Peoples_Report_final_draft_9-12-13.pdf.

Payne, Yasser Arafat. "Site of Resilience: A Reconceptualization of Resiliency and Resilience in Street Life–Oriented Black Men." *Journal of Black Psychology* 37, no. 4 (2011): 426–451.

Payne, Yasser Arafat. "'Street Life' as a Site of Resiliency: How Street Life–Oriented Black Men Frame Opportunity in the United States." *Journal of Black Psychology* 34, no. 1 (2008): 3–31.

Payne, Yasser Arafat, and Tara M. Brown. "The Educational Experiences of Stree Life–Oriented Black Boys: How Black Boys Use Street Life as a Site of Resilience in High School." *Journal of Contemporary Criminal Justice* 26, no. 3 (2010): 316–338.

Payne, Yasser A., and Tara M. Brown. "'I Don't Let These Felonies Hold Me Back!' How Street-Identified Black Men and Women Use Resilience to Radically Reframe Reentry." *Race and Justice*, December 21, 2021. https://journals.sagepub.com/doi/abs/10.1177/21533687211047948.

Payne, Yasser Arafat, and Tara Marie Brown. "'I'm Still Waiting on That Golden Ticket': Attitudes toward and Experiences with Opportunity in the Streets of Black America." *Journal of Social Issues* 72, no. 4 (2016): 789–811.

Payne, Yasser Arafat, and Tara Marie Brown. "It's Set Up for Failure, and They Know This: How the School-to-Prison Pipeline Impacts the Educational Experiences of Street-Identified Black Youth and Young Adults." *Villanova Law Review* 62 (2017): 307–327.

Payne, Yasser Arafat, and Angela Bryant. "Street Participatory Action Research in Prison: A Methodology to Challenge Privilege and Power in Correctional Facilities." *The Prison Journal* 98, no. 4 (2018): 449–469.

Payne, Yasser Arafat, and Hanaa A. Hamdi. "'Street Love': How Street Life–Oriented US-Born African Men Frame Giving Back to One Another and the Local Community." *The Urban Review* 41, no. 1 (2009): 29–46.

Payne, Yasser Arafat, Brooklyn K. Hitchens, and Darryl L. Chambers. "'Why I Can't Stand Out in Front of My House?' Street-Identified Black Youth and Young Adult's Negative Encounters with Police." *Sociological Forum* 32 (2017): 874–895.

Phelan, James, and Robert Pozen. *The Company State*. New York: Grossman, 1973.

Pizzi, Jenna. "Shotspotter: Wilmington Gunshots Decrease 42 Percent." *News Journal*, July 8, 2015. https://www.delawareonline.com/story/news/crime/2015/07/06/wilm-officials-fewer-gunshots-detected-downtown/29793477/.

Pizzi, Jenna. "Wilmington Police Disband Community Policing Unit." *News Journal*, January 12, 2016. https://www.delawareonline.com/story/news/local/2016/01/11/wilmington-police-disband-community-policing-unit/78660918/.

Porter, Ira. "Anthony Logan—My Neighborhood: A Special News Journal Report." *News Journal*, November 22, 2010.

Porter, Ira. "Delaware Crime: Program's First Grads Put Hope to Work—Participants to Research Crime and Its Causes in Communities." *News Journal*, December 24, 2009.

Porter, Ira. "Hope Where Others See None. Project Goes Straight to the People to Cut Crime, Poverty—My Neighborhood: A Special News Journal Report." *News Journal*, November 21, 2010, A12.

Postrel, Virginia. "The Consequences of the 1960's Race Riots Come into View." *New York Times*, December 30, 2004. https://www.nytimes.com/2004/12/30/business/the-consequences-of-the-1960s-race-riots-come-into-view.html.

Powell, Cassie. "'One of the Worst': The School-to-Prison Pipeline in Richmond, Virginia." RVAGOV, University of Richmond, 2016. https://scholarship.richmond.edu/cgi/viewcontent.cgi?article=1128&context=law-student-publications.

Price, Joshua M. "Conflict over Approaches to Social Science Research—Participatory Action Research as Disruptive? A Report on a Conflict in Social Science Paradigms at a Criminal Justice Agency Promoting Alternatives to Incarceration." *Contemporary Justice Review* 11, no. 4 (2008): 387–412.

Prosperity Now. "Racial Wealth Equity Network." Prosperity Now, 2019. https://prosperitynow.org/get-involved/racial-wealth-equity.

Pykeren, Sam Van. "These Photos Show the Staggering Food Bank Lines across America." *Mother Jones*, April 13, 2020. https://www.motherjones.com/food/2020/04/these-photos-show-the-staggering-food-bank-lines-across-america/.

Ranaivo, Yann. "Wilmington Police Homicide Unit Coming Soon." *News Journal*, October 14, 2014. http://www.delawareonline.com/story/news/local/2014/10/13/wilmington-police-homicide-unit-coming-soon/17230097/.

Ray, Rashawn, and Andre M. Perry. "Why We Need Reparations for Black Americans." Policy 2020, Brookings Institution, April 15, 2020. https://www.brookings.edu/policy2020/bigideas/why-we-need-reparations-for-black-americans/.

Reeves, Carla L. "A Difficult Negotiation: Fieldwork Relations with Gatekeepers." *Qualitative Research* 10, no. 3 (2010): 315–331.

Remaking Murdertown: Poverty, Punishment, and Possibility. Podcast series sponsored by the Delaware Center for Justice and produced by Zach Phillips. Wilmington, DE: Short Order Production House, 2016. http://remaking.murdertown.us/.

Reyes, Jessica, Jenna Pizzi, and Esteban Parra. "Wilmington Residents Say Rift with Police Growing Worse." *News Journal*, October 2, 2015. https://www.delawareonline.com/story/news/local/2015/10/02/city-residents-say-rift-police-growing-worse/73241752/.

Reyes, Jessica Masulli. "Reports: Del. Company May Be Linked to El Chapo." *News Journal*, January 16, 2016. https://www.delawareonline.com/story/news/local/2016/01/15/reports-del-company-may-linked-el-chapo/78859144/.

Rich, John A., and Courtney M. Grey. "Pathways to Recurrent Trauma among Young Black Men: Traumatic Stress, Substance Use, and the 'Code of the Street.'" *American Journal of Public Health* 95, no. 5 (2005): 816–824.

Richards, Stephen C. "The New School of Convict Criminology Thrives and Matures." *Critical Criminology* 21, no. 3 (2013): 375–387.

Richards, Stephen C., and Jeffrey Ian Ross. "Introducing the New School of Convict Criminology." *Social Justice* 28, no. 1 (83 (2001): 177–190.

Rios, Victor M. *Punished: Policing the Lives of Black and Latino Boys*. New York: New York University Press, 2011.

Roberts, Sam. "51% of Women Are Now Living without Spouse." *New York Times*, January 16, 2007. https://www.nytimes.com/2007/01/16/us/16census.html.

Robinson, Cedric J. *Black Marxism: The Making of the Black Radical Tradition*. Chapel Hill: University of North Carolina Press, 1983.

Roeder, Oliver K., Lauren-Brooke Eisen, Julia Bowling, Joseph E. Stiglitz, and Inimai M. Chettiar. *What Caused the Crime Decline?* Brennan Center for Justice, New York University School of Law, February 12, 2015. https://www.brennancenter.org/our-work/research-reports/what-caused-crime-decline.

Romero-Daza, Nancy, Margaret Weeks, and Merrill Singer. "'Nobody Gives a Damn If I Live or Die': Violence, Drugs, and Street-Level Prostitution in Inner-City Hartford, Connecticut." *Medical Anthropology* 22, no. 3 (2003): 233–259.

Rose, D. R., and T. R. Clear. "Incarceration, Social Capital, and Crime: Implications for Social Disorganization Theory." *Criminology* 36, no. 3 (1998): 441–480.

Rosenthal, Robert, and Lenore Jacobsen. *Pygmalion in the Classroom: Teacher Expectation and Pupils' Intellectual Development*. New York: Holt, Rinehart and Winston, 1968.

Rossman, Shelli B. "Case-Managed Reentry and Employment: Lessons from the Opportunity to Succeed Program." *Justice Research and Policy* 5, no. 2 (2003): 75–100.

Russell, Judy. "Assata Shakur Convicted of Murder in 1977." *Daily News* (New York), March 24, 2017. https://www.nydailynews.com/news/crime/assata-shakur-convicted-murder-1977-article-1.3008371.

Russell-Brown, Katheryn. *The Color of Crime: Racial Hoaxes, White Fear, Black Protectionism, Police Harassment, and Other Macroaggressions*. New York: New York University Press, 2009.

Sawyer, Wendy. "Bailing Moms Out for Mother's Day." Prison Policy Initiative, May 8, 2017. https://www.prisonpolicy.org/blog/2017/05/08/mothers-day/.

Schliewe, Sanna. "Embodied Ethnography in Psychology: Learning Points from Expatriate Migration Research." *Culture & Psychology* 26, no. 4 (2020): 803–818.

The Schott Foundation for Public Education. *Black Lives Matter: The Schott 50 State Report on Public Education and Black Males*. February 11, 2015. https://schottfoundation.org/resource/black-lives-matter-the-schott-50-state-report-on-public-education-and-black-males/.

Scocas, Evelyn, Richard Harris, Charles Huenke, and Le'Verne Cecere. *Wilmington Shootings 1996: A Comparative Study of Victims and Offenders in Wilmington, Delaware*. Dover, DE: Statistical Analysis Center and the Criminal Justice Council, 1997. https://www.ojp.gov/ncjrs/virtual-library/abstracts/wilmington-shootings-1996-comparative-study-victims-and-offenders.

Sentencing Project. "Incarcerated Women and Girls." Sentencing Project fact sheet, updated 2020. http://www.sentencingproject.org/wp-content/uploads/2016/02/Incarcerated-Women-and-Girls.pdf.

Shakur, Sanyika. *Monster: The Autobiography of an L.A. Gang Member.* New York: Grove Press, 1993.

Shakur, Tupac A. "Dear Mama." On *Me against the World* (CD). Interscope Records, 1995.

Shattuck, Rachel M., and Rose M. Kreider. *Social and Economic Characteristics of Currently Unmarried Women with a Recent Birth.* American Community Survey report 21. Washington, DC: U.S. Census Bureau, 2013. https://www2.census.gov/library/publications/2013/acs/acs-21.pdf.

Shaxson, Nicholas. *Treasure Islands: Uncovering the Damage of Offshore Banking and Tax Havens.* New York: St. Martin's Press, 2011.

Singh, Lillian, and Ebony White. "Racial Wealth Divide in Wilmington." Prosperity Now, March 2019. https://prosperitynow.org/resources/racial-wealth-divide-wilmington.

Singletary, Michelle. "Perspective | FAQ: Rent Strikes during the Pandemic." *Washington Post*, May 7, 2020. https://www.washingtonpost.com/business/2020/05/07/rent-strike-faq/.

6-ABC. "Brothers Arrested in Wilmington Homicide." ABC Philadelphia, December 10, 2009. http://6abc.com/archive/7162927/.

Smith, Linda Tuhiwai. *Decolonizing Methodologies: Research and Indigenous Peoples.* 1992. Reprint, London: Zed Books, 2012.

Smith, Ricardo. Y. "No Way Out: Giving Voice to the Post-Prison Experiences of African-American Men in Two Ohio Counties." PhD diss., Union Institute and University, 2014.

Solis, Steph. "Protests Break Out after Baton Rouge Police Fatally Shoot Man." *USA Today*, July 6, 2016. https://www.usatoday.com/story/news/nation/2016/07/05/baton-rouge-alton-sterling-police-shooting/86738368/.

Spano, Richard, William Alex Pridemore, and John Bolland. "Specifying the Role of Exposure to Violence and Violent Behavior on Initiation of Gun Carrying: A Longitudinal Test of Three Models of Youth Gun Carrying." *Journal of Interpersonal Violence* 27, no. 1 (2012): 158–176.

Spencer, Saranac Hale. "Christina Seeks Answers to School Discipline Issues." *News Journal*, May 26, 2016. https://www.delawareonline.com/story/news/education/2016/05/25/christina-seeks-answers-school-discipline-issues/84929680/.

Speri, Alice. "The Largest Prison Strike in U.S. History Enters Its Second Week." The Intercept, September 16, 2016. https://theintercept.com/2016/09/16/the-largest-prison-strike-in-u-s-history-enters-its-second-week/.

State of Delaware. "Baylor Women's Correctional Institution," Delaware.gov, n.d. https://doc.delaware.gov/views/baylor.blade.shtml.

Staub, Andrew. "Wilmington Ranked Most Dangerous City on Crime Rate." *News Journal*, August 22, 2012. http://www.delawareonline.com/article/20120822/NEWS/120822013/Wilmington-rankedmost-dangerous-city-crime-rate.

Stephens, Torrance T., Ronald L. Braithwaite, and Sandra E. Taylor. 1998. "Model for Using Hip-Hop Music for Small Group HIV/AIDS Prevention Counseling with African-American Adolescents and Young Adults." *Patient Education and Counseling* 35: 127–137.

Stewart, Eric A., and Ronald L. Simons. "Race, Code of the Street, and Violent Delinquency: A Multilevel Investigation of Neighborhood Street Culture and Individual Norms of Violence." *Criminology* 48, no. 2 (2010): 569–605.

Sum, Andrew. "Jobless Rate for Poor Black Teen Dropouts? Try 95 Percent." Interview by Paul Solman. *PBS NewsHour*, July 5, 2013. https://www.pbs.org/newshour/economy/jobless-rate-for-poor-black-te.

Sumner, Steven, James Mercy, Susan Hillis, Matthew Maenner, and Christina Socias. *Elevated Rates of Urban Firearm Violence and Opportunities for Prevention—Wilmington,*

Delaware: Final Report. Washington, DC: Division of Violence Prevention, National Center for Injury Prevention and Control, Centers for Disease Control and Prevention, 2015. http://www.dhss.delaware.gov/dhss/cdcfinalreport.pdf.

Tangney, June P., Ashley E. Dobbins, Jeffrey B. Stuewig, and Shannon W. Schrader. "Is There a Dark Side to Mindfulness? Relation of Mindfulness to Criminogenic Cognitions." *Personality and Social Psychology Bulletin* 43, no. 10 (2017): 1415–1426.

Taylor, Adam. "Slaying of Mom Latest in Long Line of Tragedy for Wilmington Family." Delaware Open Carry, June 9, 2009. http://www.delawareopencarry.org/forums/viewtopic.php?f=30&t=2055.

Taylor, Adam, and Ira Porter. "Growing Audacity amongst City Gunmen: Residents Fear They'll Be Innocent Victims." Delaware Online, September 20, 2009. http://www.delawareonline.com/article/20090920/NEWS01/909200364/Growing-audacity-amongcity-gunmen.

Taylor, Adam, Terri Sanginiti, and Sean O'Sullivan. "US DE: Riverside Mourns Slain 'Ghetto Icon.'" Media Awareness Project, October 23, 2005. http://www.mapinc.org/drugnews/v05/n1678/a03.html.

Themal, Harry. "Harry Themal: New Castle County's Gruesome 1903 Lynching by Fire." *News Journal*, January 9, 2017. https://www.delawareonline.com/story/opinion/columnists/harry-themal/2017/01/09/harry-themal-new-castle-countys-gruesome-1903-lynching-fire/96253932/.

Thompson, Anthony C. *Releasing Prisoners, Redeeming Communities: Reentry, Race, and Politics*. New York: New York University Press, 2008.

Tilly, Charles, Wagner D. Jackson, and Barry Kay. *Race and Residence in Wilmington, Delaware*. New York: Teachers College, Columbia University, 1965.

Toch, Hans. "The Study of Man: The Convict as Researcher." *Trans-action* 4, no. 9 (1967): 72–75.

Traub, Amy, Catherine Ruetschlin, Laura Sullivan, Tatjana Meschede, Lars Dietrich, and Thomas Shapiro. "The Racial Wealth Gap: Why Policy Matters." Demos, June 21, 2016. https://www.demos.org/research/racial-wealth-gap-why-policy-matters.

Trimbur, Lucia. "'Me and the Law Is Not Friends': How Former Prisoners Make Sense of Reentry." *Qualitative Sociology* 32, no. 3 (2009): 259–277.

Trumbore, Dave. "'Game of Thrones': The Children of the Forest Explained." Collider, August 6, 2017. http://collider.com/game-of-thrones-children-of-the-forest-explained/#first men.

Tuckman, Bruce W. *Conducting Educational Research*. Fort Worth, TX: Harcourt Brace College Publishers, 1999.

Turner, Diane. "The Interview Technique as Oral History in Black Studies." In *Handbook of Black Studies*, edited by Molefi Asante and Maulana Karenga, 329–332. Thousand Oaks, CA: Sage, 2006.

Turner, Neil. "Long-Term Ethnographic Immersion." Perspectives in Anthropology, January 21, 2015. https://perspectivesinanthropology.com/2015/01/21/long-term-ethnographic-immersion/.

USA Facts. "White People Own 86% of Wealth and Make Up 60% of the Population." USA Facts, 2020. https://usafacts.org/articles/white-people-own-86-wealth-despite-making-60-population/.

U.S. Census Bureau. "2008–2010 ACS 3-Year Estimates." Census.gov, 2011. https://www.census.gov/programs-surveys/acs/technical-documentation/table-and-geography-changes/2010/3-year.html.

U.S. Census Bureau American Community Survey Office. "Marital Status: 2015 American Community Survey 1-Year Estimate." 2015. https://www.census.gov/programs-surveys/acs/technical-documentation/table-and-geography-changes/2015/1-year.html.

U.S. Department of Justice, Civil Rights Division. *Investigation of the Baltimore City Police Department*. Washington, DC: U.S. Department of Justice, Civil Rights Division, 2016. https://civilrights.baltimorecity.gov/sites/default/files/20160810_DOJ%20BPD%20Report-FINAL.pdf.

U.S. Department of Justice, Civil Rights Division. *Investigation of the Ferguson Police Department*. Washington, DC: United States Department of Justice, Civil Rights Division, 2015. https://www.justice.gov/sites/default/files/opa/press-releases/attachments/2015/03/04/ferguson_police_department_report.pdf.

U.S. Department of Justice, National Institute of Corrections. "Delaware 2017." 2017. https://nicic.gov/state-statistics/2017/delaware-2017.

U.S. Department of Labor. "Occupations with the Most Openings." Washington, DC: U.S. Department of Labor, 2015.

U.S. Drug Enforcement Agency. "The Early Years." Accessed January 3, 2023. https://www.dea.gov/sites/default/files/2018-05/Early%20Years%20p%2012-29.pdf.

U.S. Sentencing Commission. *Report to the Congress: Cocaine and Federal Sentencing Policy*. Washington, DC: U.S. Sentencing Commission, 2007. https://www.ussc.gov/sites/default/files/pdf/news/congressional-testimony-and-reports/drug-topics/200705_RtC_Cocaine_Sentencing_Policy.pdf.

U.S. Sentencing Commission. *Special Report to the Congress: Cocaine and Federal Sentencing Policy*. Washington, DC: U.S. Sentencing Commission, 1995. https://www.ussc.gov/sites/default/files/pdf/news/congressional-testimony-and-reports/drug-topics/199502-rtc-cocaine-sentencing-policy/1995-Crack-Report_Full.pdf.

Valdez, Avelardo. *Mexican American Girls and Gang Violence: Beyond Risk*. New York: Palgrave Macmillan, 2009.

Valentine, Bettylou. *Hustling and Other Hard Work: Life Styles in the Ghetto*. New York: Free Press, 1978.

Vargas, João H. Costa. *Catching Hell in the City of Angels: Life and Meanings of Blackness in South Central Los Angeles*. Minneapolis: University of Minnesota Press, 2006.

Vargas, Robert. *Wounded City: Violent Turf Wars in a Chicago Barrio*. New York: Oxford University Press, 2016.

Vella, Vinny, and Jason Nark. "Is Wilmington Really 'Murder Town'?" *Philadelphia Inquirer*, December 23, 2015. http://articles.philly.com/2015-12-23/news/69240133_1_cousin-shot-city-council-city-officials.

Venkatesh, Sudhir Alladi. *Gang Leader for a Day: A Rogue Sociologist Takes to the Streets*. New York: Penguin Books, 2008.

Vigil, James Diego. *A Rainbow of Gangs: Street Cultures in the Mega-City*. Austin: University of Texas Press, 2002.

Visher, Christy A. "Incarcerated Fathers: Pathways from Prison to Home." *Criminal Justice Policy Review* 24, no. 1 (2013): 9–26.

Visher, Christy A., Pamela K. Lattimore, Kelle Barrick, and Stephen Tueller. "Evaluating the Long-Term Effects of Prisoner Reentry Services on Recidivism: What Types of Services Matter?" *Justice Quarterly* 34, no. 1 (2017): 136–165.

Wagner, Adam. "Williams Doesn't Back Down on Police Recommendations." *News Journal*, April 15, 2015. https://www.delawareonline.com/story/news/2015/04/15/wilmington-mayor-dennis-williams-meets-crime-consultants/25795369/.

Watson, John. "No Escaping Wilmington Violence in 2013." WHYY, December 26, 2013. https://whyy.org/articles/no-escaping-wilmington-violence-in-2013/.

Wayne, Leslie. "How Delaware Thrives as a Corporate Tax Haven." *New York Times*, June 30, 2012. https://www.nytimes.com/2012/07/01/business/how-delaware-thrives-as-a-corporate-tax-haven.html.

Weaver, Darren. "This Tiny Building in Wilmington, Delaware Is Home to 300,000 Businesses." Business Insider, December 27, 2018. https://www.businessinsider

.com.au/building-wilmington-delaware-largest-companies-ct-corporation-2017-4.

Wells, Kenenth B. et al. "Building an Academic-Community Partnered Network for Clinical Services Research: The Community Health Improvement Collaborative (CHIC)." *Ethnicity and Disease* 16, no. 1, suppl. 1 (2006): S3–S17.

The White House. "Remarks by the President in State of the Union Address." The White House, January 24, 2012. https://www.whitehouse.gov/the-press-office/2012/01/24/remarks-president-state-union-address.

Williams, Dennis P. "Dennis P. Williams: City Is Overcoming Adversity." *News Journal*, December 12, 2015. http://www.delawareonline.com/story/opinion/contributors/2015/12/11/dennis-williams-city-overcoming-adversity/77169302/.

Williams, Edward Huntington. "Negro Cocaine 'Fiends' Are a New Southern Menace; Murder and Insanity Increasing among Lower-Class Blacks Because They Have Taken to 'Sniffing' since Deprived of Whisky by Prohibition." *New York Times*, February 8, 1914. https://www.nytimes.com/1914/02/08/archives/negro-cocaine-fiends-are-a-new-southern-menace-murder-and-insanity.html.

Williams, Eric Eustace. *Capitalism and Slavery*. Chapel Hill: University of North Carolina Press, 1994.

Wilmington Education Improvement Commission. *Strengthening Wilmington: An Action Agenda*. 2015. https://bpb-us-w2.wpmucdn.com/sites.udel.edu/dist/7/3504/files/2015/08/weac-final-book-2015-web-uxn0ge.pdf.

Wilmington HOPE Commission. *Southbridge HOPE Zone Pilot Project: Second Year Implementation Report (July 2008 to June 2009)*. Wilmington, DE: Wilmington HOPE Commission, June 2009.

Wilmington HOPE Commission. *The State of Reentry in Wilmington: Annual Report*. Wilmington, DE: Wilmington HOPE Commission, 2011.

Wilmington Public Safety Strategies Commission. *Crime Analysis and CAD Incident Analysis (2010–2014)*. Wilmington, DE: Wilmington Public Safety Strategies Commission, 2015.

Wilson, William J. *More than Just Race: Being Black and Poor in the Inner City*. New York: Norton, 2009.

Wilson, William Julius. *When Work Disappears: The World of the New Urban Poor*. New York: Vintage Books, 1996.

Wilson, Xerxes. "B-Wills, Bobby Dimes and a Story of Murder on Wilmington's East Side." *News Journal / Delaware Online*, January 22, 2020. https://www.delawareonline.com/story/news/2020/01/22/jury-convicts-local-drug-kingpin-murder-hire-plot/4456628002/.

Wilson, Xerxes. "Councilman Street: Crime-Reduction Efforts Have Failed." *News Journal*, October 23, 2015. https://www.delawareonline.com/story/news/2015/10/21/councilman-street-crime-reduction-efforts-have-failed/74345110/.

Wilson, Xerxes. "Delaware Democrats Take Aim at Laws They See as Unfairly Hurting Minorities, Poor." *News Journal*, March 18, 2019. https://www.delawareonline.com/story/news/2019/03/15/delaware-reforms-address-criminal-fines-inequality-sentencing/3161130002/.

Wilson, Xerxes. "Delaware Prison Riot Charges Dropped; More Trials Would Be 'Futile,' AG Says." *News Journal*, June 12, 2019. https://www.delawareonline.com/story/news/2019/06/12/remaining-charges-dropped-vaughn-prison-riot-murder-steven-floyd/1432628001/.

Wilson, Xerxes. "Wilmington Man Gets 90 Years after Wishing Victim a Happy Birthday, Shooting Him Dead." *News Journal / Delaware Online*, July 21, 2018. https://www.delawareonline.com/story/news/2018/07/20/defendant-wilmington-nightclub-death-birthday-celebrant-gets-90-years/802664002/.

Wilson, Xerxes, and Nick Perez. "Two Sentenced in Murder of 15-Year-Old Brandon Wingo." *News Journal*, January 31, 2020. https://www.delawareonline.com/story/news/crime/2020/01/31/two-sentenced-murder-15-year-old-brandon-wingo/4564219002/.

Wink, Christopher. "64% of Fortune 500 Firms Are Delaware Incorporations: Here's Why." Technical.ly, September 23, 2014. https://technical.ly/delaware/2014/09/23/why-delaware-incorporation/.

Wink, Christopher. "Why Do So Many Banks Have Offices in Wilmington?" Technical.ly, November 18, 2016, https://technical.ly/delaware/2016/11/18/many-banks-headquartered-wilmington-delaware/.

Wolfers, Justin, David Leonhardt, and Kevin Quealy. "The Methodology: 1.5 Million Missing Black Men." *New York Times*, April 20, 2015. https://www.nytimes.com/2015/04/21/upshot/the-methodology-1-5-million-missing-black-men.html.

Wong, Maggie Hiufu. "Friendliest/Unfriendliest U.S. Cities, according to *Condé Nast Traveler*." CNN Travel, August 7, 2014. http://www.cnn.com/travel/article/us-unfriendliest-friendliest-cities/index.html.

World Port Source. "The Port of Wilmington." World Port Source, 2020. http://www.worldportsource.com/ports/review/USA_DE_The_Port_of_Wilmington_158.php.

Wun, Connie. "Unaccounted Foundations: Black Girls, Anti-Black Racism, and Punishment in Schools." *Critical Sociology* 42, no. 4–5 (2016): 737–750.

Yonas, Michael A., Patricia O'Campo, Jessica G. Burke, and Andrea C. Gielen. "Neighborhood-Level Factors and Youth Violence: Giving Voice to the Perceptions of Prominent Neighborhood Individuals." *Health Education & Behavior* 34, no. 4 (2007): 669–685.

Young, Alford A. *Minds of Marginalized Black Men: Making Sense of Mobility, Opportunity, and Future Life Chances*. Princeton, NJ: Princeton University Press, 2004.

Index

Abu Maahir, Imam, 8, 82
abuse, sexual, 163–164
ACLU of Delaware, 100, 166, 214
action plan, 52
action team, 18
active spaces, 9
activism: Africana activists, 228; arts for, 170–172, 229–230; Black revolutionary, 199; militant, 8; research, 164–165; after uprisings, 208–211
adaptive strategies, 228
addiction, 106–111
adult violence, 79
Africana activists, 228
Africanity, 5
African Methodist Episcopal Church (AME), 8
"After Centuries of Obscurity, Wilmington Is Having a Moment" (MacFarquhar), 27
Akil, Faheem, 82
Alexander, Michelle, 11, 225
Alive and Free, Inc., 215
Allen, Byron, 87
Allen, Richard, 8
Allen, Tony, 101
American Gangster (Collins), 181
American Journal of Public Health, 53
American Recovery and Reinvestment Act, 20, 50, 98
American Revolution, 41
American Sociological Association, 19
Anderson, Tammy L., 158
Andrew, Fr. David, 127–128
anti-Black racism, 142

Anti–Drug Abuse Act, 138
Apple, 35
Arbery, Ahmaud, 206
Armed Conflict Location and Event Data Project (ACLED), 206
arts for activism: *Homicide Art Exhibition*, 170–172, 229; *Wilmington Trap Stars Street Art Exhibition*, 229–230
Asante, Molefi Kete, 54
assault, 43
attorney general (AG), 136–137
audience, 52
Austin, Felicia, 172
Avery, Raye Jones, 171, 230
Ayers, Jarreau, 205

Baby Yellow Gang, 44
Bailey, John H., 171
Baker, James, 2, 115, 117, 148–149, 199
Baldwin, James, 41, 196
Baltimore, Maryland, 62, 114, 204
Bank of America, 35, 101
Banner, David, 196
"Ban the Box" policy, 148–149
Barbiarz, John E. (mayor), 38
Barrish, Cris, 163–164
Bart, Jenny, 171
Baum, Fran, 52
Bayard Middle School, 102, 117
Baylor. *See* Delores J. Baylor Women's Correctional Institution
Beals, Michael, 58
Bedford Hills Correctional Facility, 164–165
Bell, Derrick, 225

287

beneficial ownership information, 36
Bethel Villa Apartments, 33, 49
Beth Shalom, 58
Biden, Ashley Blazer, 137, 149, 151–154
Biden, Joseph R., 36, 46, 48, 57, 88, 137–139, 230
Biden, Joseph Robinette "Beau," III, 136–137
Bies, Jessica, 27
Biklen, Sari Knopp, 53–54
"Billionaire Byron Allen Talks Black Wealth with Antonio Moore," 87
Black, Jason, 227
Black, Timothy, 1
Black American culture, 176
Black American experience, 7
Black American Sunni Muslims, 8, 14, 81–82, 130
Black Authority, The (TBA) (podcast), 227
Black Baptist Church, 67
Black boomer generation, 68
Black communities. *See specific topics*
Black entrepreneurship, 128
Black gangs, 38–39
Black Harlem, 7
Blackie Blacks (gang), 39
Black leadership, 68
Black Lives Matter movement, 206
Black Marxism theory, 11
Black masculinity, 61, 66
Black Moors, 8
Blackness, 5
Black progress, 19
Black reparations, 227
Black revolutionary activism, 199
Black wealth, 93
Black women and girls, 37
blight, 34, 37
blood money, 190
Blunt-Rochester, Lisa, 150
Boardley, Trudy, 178, 230
Bogdan, Robert, 53–54
Bonilla-Silva, Eduardo, 153
Booker, Cory, 199
boomer generation, Black, 68

Boston Gun Project Working Group, 223
boundaries, neighborhood, 188
Bowman, Phillip J., 228
Braga, Anthony A., 44
Brandywine Park, 191
Brandywine River, 42
Breaking Brown (podcast), 227
"Brenda's Got a Baby" (Shakur), 179
Brooks, Kenyatta, 15, 211–213
Brother Lamonte X, 66
Brother-to-Brother Annual 5-Mile Memory Walk, 191–195
Brown, Clifford, 188
Brown, Darius, 209–210
Brown, Michael, 204
Brown v. Board of Education, 110
Bureau of Alcohol, Tobacco, Firearms and Explosives, 39

Cam'ron, 133
capital, social, 40, 70–73
capitalism: colonialist, 184; modern, 11
Caple, Wendi Lucas, 163
Carey, Harmon, 42
Carney, John, 102, 204–205, 210
Carr, Trinity, 110
Carson, Joe, 189
Casbar Lounge, 33, 34
caste system, racial, 225
Catching Hell in the City of Angels (Vargas), 157
Center for Count Innovation, 214
Center for Drug and Health Studies, 21
Center for Justice Innovation, 213
Center for Structural Equity (CFSE), 212, 213
Césaire, Aimé, 5
Challenge Program, 90
Chambers, Darryl "Wolfie"/"Wolf," 14–16, 21, 50, 71–72, 79–84, 107, 127
Chambers, Derrick "Der Der," 127
Charles, Ray, 188
Charlotte, South Carolina, 204
Chase Center on the Riverfront, 47
Chauvin, Derek, 206

Chicago, Illinois, 36, 182, 204
ChristianaCare Hospital, 65, 80, 214, 223
Christianity, 8
Christina Cultural Arts Center (CCAC), 13, 151, 171, 214, 229
Christina Landing (neighborhood), 32
Christina River, 42
Christina School District, 100
city leadership, 60–61, 62
City Tavern Bar, 33
civil disobedience, 203–205
Civil War, 11, 39
Clear, T. R., 190
Clifford Brown Jazz Festival, 188
Clifford Brown Walk, 110–111, 188
Clinton, Bill, 139
Clinton, Hillary, 139
Club Baby Grand, 188
Coca-Cola, 35
"Code Blue," 81
"code of the streets," 9
cognitive behavioral therapy, 223
Coker, Adeniyi, 54
Collins, Ella L., 20
Collins, Max Allan, 181
colonialist capitalism, 185
colonization, of Delaware, 41–42
colorblind analysis, 5
Community Intervention Team, 215
Community Outreach Recreation Education (CORE), 151
Community Policing Unit, 116
community professionals, 186–187; immersion of, 227–229
community programs, 182
Community Service Building (CSB), 149
Comprehensive Control Act (1984), 138
Compton Towers, 33, 49
Conducting Educational Research (Tuckman), 54
"Conflict over Approaches to Social Science Research" (Price), 41
Congressional Black Caucus, 139

consciousness-raising, 231
Constitution, U.S., 41
"Constructing and Using Questionnaires and Interview Schedules" (Tuckman), 54
Contreras, Randol, 19
convict lease system, 137
Cool Spring (neighborhood), 3
Coonin, Robert, 110
Coons, Chris Andrew, 58, 87–88, 89–92
Copeland, Kontal "Gates," 130, 133, 172, 184, 211
CORE Initiative, 215
Cornish, Bernard, 215
Cornnell, Kirstin, 150
Corporation Trust Center (CT Center), 49
corrections officers (COs), 162, 163
Costa Vargas, João, 157
Council on Social Work Education, 96
COVID-19 pandemic, 205
cowboy ethnography, 19
crack cocaine, 9, 137
Crawford, Hakeem Iman Cornelius, 173–174, 205
"Creative Arts and Photography in Participatory Action Research in Guatemala" (Lykes), 229
Creative Vision Factory, 230
crime: history of, 34–37; property, 43; of resistance, 203; structural violence and, 60; violent, 39, 43. *See also specific topics*
"Crime Bill," 138
Crime in the United States 2013 (FBI report), 114
Crime Strategies Unit, 136
criminal legal system, 114
critical criminology, 11
cultural competence, 103–104
cultural limitations, education and, 102
cultural prism model, of SOR, 9
cultural scripts, 228
cultural violence, 11
culture: Black American, 176; mastery of, 228; of poverty, 90, 91; street, 13; of violence, 63–65
Cummings, Bobby, 116, 118, 133

Cure Violence program, 223
Curry, Christopher T. (pastor), 67–69
Curry, Herman, 28–31

Dance, L. J., 19, 105
Darul-Amaanah Mosque, 81–82
data analysis team, 18
Daugherty, Mervin, 101
"David Banner on White Supremacy, Illuminati, the God Box" (Banner), 196
Davis, Angela, 1
Davis, Kenneth, Jr., 184
Davis, Kenneth, Sr., 184
Davis, Sammy, Jr., 188
"Dear Mama" (Shakur), 179
death, cultural mores around, 67
deindustrialization, 94
Delaware. *See specific topics*
Delaware American Civil Liberties Union, 100, 166, 214
Delaware Center for Contemporary Arts (DCCA), 229–230
Delaware Center for Justice (DCJ), 136, 149–154, 214
Delaware Department of Education (DDOE), 98, 100
Delaware Department of Services for Children, Youth and Their Families, 214
Delaware Legislative Black Caucus (DLBC), 209, 211
Delaware River, 42
Delaware State Bar Association, 137
Delaware State University, 12, 214
Delaware Way, 40, 44
Dellose, Joseph, 118
Delmarva Peninsula, 42
Delores J. Baylor Women's Correctional Institution (BWCI), 135, 160–166
Denn, Matt, 116, 205
Denver, Colorado, 114
Department of Education, 98, 100
Department of Health and Social Services (DHSS), 212, 214
Department of Labor, 89, 94

Derrick Sean "Rick" Hoey College Scholarship Fund, 191
Diener, Ed, 4
Dietz, Nancy, 81
"dippers" (PCP), 62, 118
direct violence, 11
Discourse on Colonialism (Césaire), 5
disembodied universalism, 5
dis-opportunity, 94–97
disrespect, by police, 121–126
Division of Prevention and Behavioral Health Services, 127
Downs, Royal, 205
Downtown Eastside (neighborhood), 3, 32, 33, 49, 151
"Dr. James Gilligan on Violence" (Gilligan), 57
Dr. Martin Luther King Jr. Breakfast and Statewide Day of Service, 137
dropout rates, 99–100
Drug Enforcement Administration, 39
drug money, 190
Drugs, Organized Crime, and Vice Division, 116
drugs, war on, 137–138
drug trade, 3, 9, 141, 158, 222
Duck, Waverly, 3, 6
Duncan, Arne, 98, 100, 102
Dunn, Isaac, 150
du Pont, Pierre "Pete" S., IV, 36
du Pont, Thère, 150
DuPont Building, 150
du Pont de Nemours, E. I., 35
Duran, Robert J., 114

Eastside (neighborhood). *See specific topics*
economic deprivation, 34
economic violence, 166–168
economic well-being, 95–96
Eden Park, 28–29
education, 112; cultural competence for, 103–104; gender and, 104–106; leaving school and, 102–106; school policy and, 98–102; unemployment and, 94; violence in, 108–111

Index

Elbert Palmer Park, 78
Ellerbe, Jordan, 111
Elm Street Boys (gang), 44
embodied ethnography, 228
empire, 10
employment: barriers to, 91; self-employment, 146. *See also* unemployment
entrepreneurism, legal, 143, 146
entrepreneurship, Black, 128
Episcopal Church of Saints Andrew and Matthew, 127
essentialist gaze, 19
ethics, 51
ethnography, 19–21, 23; embodied, 228; recommendations for, 223–232
exoticism, 19
exposure to violence, victimization versus, 73–76
Ezion Fair Baptist Church, 66, 204

Fader, Jamie, 135
Fairness and Equity in Schools, 100
Falling Back (Fader), 135
family, 159
Fanon, Frantz, 203, 220
fathers, 168–170
Fathership Foundation, 215
Federal Bureau of Investigation (FBI), 39, 114
felony records, 96
feminism, 231
"Feminism" (hooks), 217
Fennell, Drew, 127, 128
Ferguson, Ann Arnett, 61
Ferguson, Missouri, 114, 204
Ferrell, Sheila, 171
Ferris Detention Center, 150
"50 Years Since MLK's Poor People Campaign—Where Are We Now?" (forum), 226
"Film as Historical Method in Black Studies" (Coker), 54
Financial Center Development Act, 36
Fine, Michelle, 164–165
Fire Next Time, The (Baldwin), 41

"First State," Delaware as, 41
Flint, Michigan, 36–37
Flowers, Leonard, 39
Floyd, George, 205–206, 207
Floyd, Steven, 205
Focused Deterrence, 223
Fort Christina, 42
Franklin, Anderson J., 9
Fraser, Ronald, 152
Fraternal Order of Police (FOP), 116
frisked, by police, 126
Frontline (PBS), 1
full model, of SOR, 10
fundamental prism model, of SOR, 7

Galtung, Johann, 11
Game of Thrones (TV series), 196–199
gangs, 44, 203; Black, 38–39; Sure Shot, 29, 30; Vietnamese, 10. *See also specific gangs*
Garner, Eric, 204
Garvey, Marcus, 8
gathering spaces, 9
Gebhart v. Belton, 110
gender: education and, 104–106. *See also* women
general strain theory, 11
geographic information system (GIS), 232
Ghost, Aaron, 189
Gibbs, Patrice, 16, 127, 215
Gillespie, Dizzy, 188
Gilligan, James, 57
girls, Black, 37
Golden, Dayveair Desmond Lamonte, 65–70, 145, 172
Golden, Yadira, 66, 69, 70–73, 145
Google, 35
Gordon, Edmund W., 220
Gotham Nightclub, 107
Governor's Task Force, 39
Gray, Freddie, 204
Great Recession, 88, 94, 136
Greene, Jerome "Boomer," 130–131, 171–172
Gregory, Theo, 133

Grey, Courtney, 53
Griffin, Earvin "Swearve," 16
Griffin, Tyerin A., 129–134
grit, 223
Group Violence Intervention (GVI), 223–224
gun violence, 53, 57–62, 74, 115, 130, 172–177, 199, 218; culture of violence and, 63–65; Dayveair Golden and, 65–70; racial-ethnic wealth gap and, 226; recommendations for radical ethnography on, 223–232; social capital and, 70–73; as SOR, 4, 219–223; Street PAR and, 70–73; white wealth and, 21. *See also specific topics*
Guzmán, Joaquín "El Chapo," 36

Hall, Roger, 69, 71
Hamilton, Darrick, 226
Hampton, Stephen, 204
Handbook of Black Studies (Asante and Karenga), 54
Happy Valley (neighborhood), 46
harassment, by police, 121–126
Harding, David J., 188
Harlem, New York City, 7, 14, 19–20, 65
Harris, Coley, 196–199, 222–223
Harris-Dickerson, Kevon, 111
Harrison Narcotics Tax Act (1914), 137–138
Haven Memorial Cemetery, 82
Hebrew Israelites, 8
Helms, Dominique "Muhammad," 78–84, 113
Henrietta Johnson Medical Center, 29
high-income white neighborhoods, 3
Highland Elementary School, 102
Highlands (neighborhood), 46
Hill Top Boys (gang), 44
hiring discrimination, 94, 142
history: of crime, wealth, and poverty, 34–37; local, 51
Hitchens, Brooklynn K., 21
Hixson, Maiza, 229–230

Hoey, Cecelia, 190, 191–195
Hoey, Demmi, 192
Hoey, Derrick Sean "Pretty Ricky," 190–195
home conditions, 97–98
homelessness, education and, 102
home life, 106–111
homicide, 43, 61, 70, 130, 153; as complex social problem, 4; rates of, 3; social intensity of, 76. *See also* gun violence
Homicide Art Exhibition, 170–172, 229
hooks, bell, 217, 231
HOPE Commission, 2, 13, 14, 48, 50, 69, 136, 214
HOPE Zone (HZ), 71
Horowitz, Ruth, 182
household incomes, median, 33
household wealth, median, 93
House of Wright Mortuary, 66
housing, 37
Housing Authority, 37
Houston, Texas, 73
Howard High School of Technology, 110–111
Howard R. Young Correctional Institution, 77
humanism, 5
Hunt Irving Chapel, 82
Hureau, David M., 44
Hustling and Other Hard Work (Valentine), 224–225

identity: project, 51; social, 4, 187–188; street, 5, 7, 219
illegal drugs, possession of, 43
imperialism, 11
incarceration rates, 140; for women, 160, 170
incentives, 51
infrapolitics, 220
injustice, social, 11
Inside-Out Prison Exchange Program, 160–166
intergenerational poverty, 90, 111
internal wars, 144

"Interview Technique as Oral History in Black Studies, The" (Turner), 54
intimate spaces, 9
Ivy Hall Apartments, 46

Jackson, John L., 7
Jacobs, U'Gundi, 193
Jacobsen, Lenore, 54
James and Jesse's Barber Shop, 15, 129
James T. Vaughn Correctional Center, 196, 204
Jamison, Daroun "Rev," 230
Jayhawkers (gang), 39
jazz, 188
Jefferson, Salima "Star," 184
Jennings, Kathleen, 136, 208, 209
Jesse, Mr., 129
Jim Crow laws, 37
job creation, 34, 88
Job Creation through Innovation Act, 88
joblessness, 3, 22, 90, 95
job spatial mismatch, 95
Johnson, Derrick "Pastor D," 8, 184
Johnson, Eddiesha, 177
Jones, Abigail, 21, 57, 61, 63, 73, 152, 218
Jones, Absalom, 8
Joshua Harvest Church, 184
Journal of Epidemiology and Community Health, 52–53
Joyner-Francis, Amy Inita, 110
JP Morgan Chase, 89, 227
jump-out squads, 115, 123
juvenile violence, 78

Kalmbach, Michael, 230
Karenga, Maulana, 54
Kelley, Robin D. G., 5, 220
Kennedy, David, 223
Kent County, 42
Keyes, Cheryl Lynette, 9
King, Martin Luther, Jr., 1, 38, 111, 217
King Gardens (subsidized apartment complex), 28
Kingswood Academy Community Center, 183

Kizzee, Dijon, 207
Knowledge Is the New Hustle Program, 215

language, street, 18
large neighborhoods, 31
late arrivals, by police, 124–126
Latson, Jackie, 172–177
leadership, 201–203; Black, 68; city, 60–61, 62; public, 115; street, 63–64
LeBlanc, Adrian Nicole, 158
legal entrepreneurism, 143, 146
Lewis, Oscar, 90
limited liability companies (LLCs), 36
lived experience, of women, 157, 158
Lively, Darryl, 178, 230
local community, 31
local history, 51
local interaction order, 6
Logan, Dan, 136
Long Incarcerated Fraternity Engaging Release Studies (LIFERS), 13
long-term ethnographic immersion, 228
Longwood Foundation, 150
Los Angeles, California, 62, 182, 226
Louisiana State Penitentiary, 204
Lune, Howard, 102
Lykes, M. Brinton, 229
lynching, 37

MacDougall, Colin, 52
MacFarquhar, Neil, 27
Madden, Charles, 2, 45–46, 48–50, 69
Malcolm X, 8, 20
male partners, 168–170
Manafort, Paul, 36
Mangrum, Nathaniel T. "Mase," 131–133
manufacturing, 35, 94
Marcus Garvey Soccer Tournament, 29
Markell, Jack, 101–102, 117–118, 127–129, 149
masculinity, Black, 61, 66
mass incarceration, 98
mass protests (2020), 205–207
Mateu-Gelabert, Pedro, 102

Maude's Beauty Shop, 129
McClain, Elijah, 206
McDaniel, Cindy, 151
McDole, Jeremy "Bam Bam," 22, 118–121, 197, 199, 204, 220
McDonald, Laquan, 204
McDougal, Serie, 228
McDowell, Harris, 99
McGriff, Dubard "Dubie," 14, 77–79, 129–130, 172, 208
Me Against the World (Shakur), 179
median household incomes, 33
median household wealth, 93
mental health outcomes, 4
methodological design, 51
Metropolitan Wilmington Urban League, 89, 100, 226
Mexican Americans, undocumented, 10
Miami, Florida, 226
Midtown Brandywine (neighborhood), 3
militant activism, 8
millworkers, 158
mindfulness, 223
Minneapolis, Minnesota, 36
Miro, Joe, 99
Mitchell, Edwina Bell, 173
modern capitalism, 11
Moore, Jaiquone, 178
Moore, Shontai, 178
moral wrong, violence as not, 4
Morton, Aretha E. (bishop), 8, 177, 178
Mother African Union Church, 214
motherhood, 158, 167; fathers and male partners and, 168–170
Mountain Dew Gang, 39
multifamily homes, 97
Murder Town (TV series), 58
"Murder Town USA (aka) Wilmington, Delaware" (Jones), 21, 57, 61, 63, 152, 218
Murphy, Mark, 98–99, 102
Muslims, Sunni, 8, 14, 81–82, 130

NAACP, 58
NASDAQ, 35
Nasheed, Tariq, 227
nation, 5
National Guard, 38
National Mortgage Servicing Settlement, 136
National Network of Hospital-Based Violence Intervention Programs, 127
Nation of Islam, 8
Negritude movement, 5
"Negro in American Culture, The" (Baldwin), 196
neighborhood boundaries, 188
Neighborhood House, 13, 17, 18, 52, 69, 214
neighborhood-level space, 187–188
"Never Would've Made It" (gospel ballad), 67
New Castle County, 42
New Castle County Council, 88
New Haven, Connecticut, 36
New Jersey, 14
News Journal (Wilmington), 107, 170, 171
Newsweek, 21, 57–58, 63, 218
New York City, 7, 14, 19–20, 62, 65, 164–165, 204
New York Stock Exchange, 35
New York Times, 138
Nichols, Zanthea, 90
N——s for Life (NFL), 61
9/11 terrorist attacks, 222
Ninth and Poplar Streets, 187–188
Nobles, Wade, 23
nonprofit organizations, 187
Northeast, the (neighborhood), 3
North Pak (gang), 224

Oakland, California, 120, 203
Obama, Barack, 20, 50, 93, 98, 131, 200
Office for Civil Rights (OCR), 100
Office of Probation and Parole, 143
Ogden, Utah, 114
Ohio State Penitentiary, 204
older women, 157
Olge, Sheldon, 29
Oliver, Melvin L., 225

OMB (Only My Brothers) (gang), 44, 110–111
One Stop, 186
one-stop re-entry center, 48
Open Eye Radio Show, 215
Operation Ceasefire, 223
Operation DISRUPT (Dealing with Issues of Stabilization through Respect, Understanding, and Promoting Trust), 116
Operation Safe Streets, 39
opportunity hoarding, 95
Out of the Ashes (play), 197, 215
outside intervention, 181
overpolicing, 114

Pager, Devah, 142
Palmer, Chris, 29–30
pan-Africanism, 5, 8
Papachristos, Andrew V., 44
Parker, Karen, 80
Parkway Academy, 214
parole, 139–140; violations, 143
"Participatory Action Research" (Baum, MacDougall, and Smith), 52
"Pathway to Recurrent Trauma among Young Black Men" (Rich and Grey), 53
Patriot Act (2001), 222
Patterson, William L., 113
Patton, Peter L., 182
Payne, James, 20
Payne, Yasser Arafat, 2, 18, 21
PCP (phencyclidine), 62, 118, 201
Peacekeepers, 66–67
people, the, 52
People's Report, The (documentary), 88, 211
People's Report Mix CD, The, 172
Perkins, Jerome E., Sr. "J. R. the Beast," 107
Peterson, Karen, 99
Philadelphia, Pennsylvania, 37, 62
Phillips, Jeffrey, 29
Phillips, Otis, 29, 30
Phillips, Zach, 57, 153

physical spaces of resilience, 8–10, 188
planning spaces, 9
Plummer Community Corrections Center (PCCC), 131, 141
police, 22, 113–116; action and, 126–134; attitudes toward, 122; frisked by, 126; given summons by, 126; harassment and disrespect by, 121–126; high-profile murders by, 204–206; late arrivals by, 124–126; McDole and, 118–121; negative contacts with, 126; reporting to, 124–126; stopped by, 126; Wilmington Public Safety Strategies Commission and, 117–118. *See also* Wilmington Police Department
Police Foundation, 117
political ecometrics, 203
population demographics, 3
post-Reconstruction period, 34
poverty, 2, 6, 60, 112, 145, 176; culture of, 90, 91; education and, 102, 109; exposure to, 73; history of, 34–37; home conditions and, 97–98; intergenerational, 90, 111; median household incomes and, 33; of returning citizens, 140–142, 147; street code and, 64; white wealth and, 3, 21, 153. *See also* unemployment
predatory institutions, 11
pregnancy, teen, 159
Price, Joshua M., 41
Price, Louis, 16
Price's Run Park, 183–187
priority schools, 99, 102
prison: incarceration rates, 140, 160, 170; Inside-Out Prison Exchange Program, 160–166; school-to-prison pipeline phenomenon, 99; uprisings, 204–205; for women, 135–136, 160–166
probation, 139–140
Professor Black Truth (podcast), 227
project identity, 51
property crime, 43
protests (2020), 205–207
psychological spaces of resilience, 8–10

public housing, 37, 97
public leadership, 115
Public Safety Office, 126
public schools, racial segregation of, 110
Pulling Levers, 223
Purzycki, Michael, 46–50, 115, 199–200, 208–210
Pygmalion effect, 54

Qualitative Research for Education (Bogdan and Biklen), 54

race riots, 38–39
Race to the Top program, 98–99, 102
racial caste system, 225
racial-ethnic wealth gap, 226
racial realism, 225
racial segregation, of public schools, 110
racial wealth gap, 225–227
racism: anti-Black, 142; structural, 90
radical Black solidarity, 176
radical street ethnography, 19–21; recommendations for, 223–232
Randolph, Ashley, 16, 55
rapport, building: with corporate gatekeeper, 46–50; with partnership, community, and streets, 45–46
Rashad, Mr., 128
Rashad's Barbershop, 128
RAVE Act (2003), 138
Red Clay School District, 101, 127
re-entry, 135–138; action and, 148–149; experiencing, 143–145; one-stop re-entry center, 48; programs, 22, 142–143; remaking of, 149–154; rugged individualism and, 145–148; SOR and, 139–145; women and, 144–145
reflexivity, 19–21
rehabilitation programs, 182
Remaking Murdertown (podcast), 152–154
reparations, Black, 227
reporting, to police, 124–126

Republican Party, 35
research activism, 164–165
residential segregation, 36
resilience. *See* sites of resilience (SOR)
resources, 51
returning citizens, 90–91, 140–142. *See also* re-entry
revolt of 2020, 205–211
revolutionary activism, Black, 199
Reyes, Ricky, 153
Rich, Daniel, 101
Rich, John, 53
Richards, Kailyn, 150
Richmond, California, 223
Rihanna, 132
Rios, Victor M., 105, 120, 203
riots, race, 38–39
Riverfront Development Corporation, 47
Riverside Project's Gang, 44
Robert Taylor Homes, 182
Robinson, Melodie, 2, 16, 70, 123
Rogers, D'Andre, 190–191
Rogers, Joseph, 107
Romans (gang), 39
Rose, D. R., 190
Rosenthal, Robert, 54
rugged individualism, 144, 145–148
Russell, Tianna, 16
Rutgers University, 21
Ryan, Patrick J., 166
Rykard, KaBron, 77

San Francisco, California, 36
Sapyta, Jeffrey J., 4
Saunders, Marlene, 12
Schliewe, Sanna, 228
School Boys, 61
school exclusion, 102
School Offense Diversion Program (SODP), 151
school performance, 109
school policy, 98–102
school-to-prison pipeline phenomenon, 99
school violence, 108–111
Schott Foundation, 99

scientific colonialism, 23
Scott (friend), 28, 30
Second Chance Act (2007), 48
Secret Service, 39
self-determination, 146
self-employment, 146
self-reliance, 142, 146
Senate Judiciary Committees, 209
"separate but equal" doctrine, 110
sexual violence, 163–166
Shabbazz, Malik, 8
Shades of Blue Bar and Lounge, 132
Shakur, Afeni, 179–180
Shakur, Assata, 179
Shakur, Sanyika, 182
Shakur, Tupac, 179
Shapiro, Thomas M., 225
shell companies, 35–36
ShotSpotter, 116
Sills, James, 117
single mothers, 158
sites of resilience (SOR): civil disobedience as, 203–205; cultural fabric and, 7–8; cultural prism model of, 9; full model of, 10; fundamental prism model of, 7; gun violence as, 4, 219–223; psychological and physical, 8–10, 188; re-entry and, 139–145; Street PAR and, 11–18; the streets and, 4–10; structural violence complex and, 10–11; for women, 157
"six degrees of separation," 44
slave labor financial model, 11
slavery, 42
slums, 37
small businesses, 90–91
small group conversations, 231–232
"small-world phenomenon," 44
Smart Justice, ACLU, 215
Smart Justice Campaign, 208
Smith, Danielle, 52
Smith, Jada Pinkett, 58
Smith, Jimmy, 188
Smith, Richard, 58
Smith, Zaahir, 111
snitching, 124

social balance, 6
social capital, 40, 70–73
social cohesion, 3, 65
social identity, 4; neighborhood-level space and, 187–188
social injustice, 11
social kinship networks, 158–159
social science courses, 228
social spaces, 9
social standing, diminishment of, 214–215
social values, dysfunctional, 93
Song, L. D., 220
Southbridge (neighborhood). *See specific topics*
Southbridge–Wilmington Housing Authority, 50
South Central, women in, 158–159
Southwest Philly Street PAR Program, The, 215
Spencer, Peter, 8
Spicer, Gerald, 189, 193
Staats, Dwayne, 175, 176, 205
Staten Island, New York City, 65
state violence, 38–39
STK (Shoot to Kill) (gang), 44, 111
Stompers (gang), 39
stopped, by police, 125
strain theory, 4, 11
Street, Jea, 209
street code, 6, 64
street collectives, 44
street culture, 13
street ethnography, 19–21, 23; recommendations for, 223–232
street hustlers, 9, 45, 64
street identity, 5, 7, 219
street language, 18
street leadership, 63–64
street life, 5–6
street love, 180–181, 219–220; communal expressions of, 182–183; group expressions of, 182; individual expressions of, 182; lessons from, 195; at Price's Run Park, 183–187; theoretical model of, 183; UB9 and, 187–195

Street Participatory Action Research (Street PAR) Project, 11, 40, 45, 70–73, 83–84, 148, 216, 218, 231–232; backgrounds of Associates, 17; interview design of, 12; methods training, 51–56; neighborhood location of Associates, 18; nine dimensions of, 51–56; organization chart for, 214–215; survey design of, 12; team as family, 13–18; team recruitment for, 13
streets, the: building rapport with, 45–46; "code of the streets," 9; reconceptualizing, 4–10; reproaches and recommendations from, 200–205. *See also specific topics*
street uprisings, 203–211
street violence, 37
street wars, 144
Strengthening Wilmington (WEIC), 101
structural awareness campaign, 224–225
structural context, of Eastside and Southbridge, 31–34
structural genocide, 10
structural racism, 90
structural violence, 3, 22, 60–61, 68, 92, 93
structural violence complex, 10–11
structural wars, 144
Student Warriors against Guns and Gangs (SWAGG), 150, 151
subaltern resilience, 185
subjective well-being, 4–5
subsidiary programs, 215
Suh, Eunkook, 4
summons, given by police, 126
Sunni Muslims, Black American, 8, 14, 81–82, 130
Sure Shot (gang), 29, 30
Survivors Addressing Grief Easement (SAGE), 173
Sussex County, 42
SWAGG DCJ, 215
Szczerba, Michael J., 70

Tabernacle Full Gospel Baptist Church, 177
Tariq Radio (podcast), 227
tax code, of Delaware, 36
Taylor, Breonna, 206
Taylor, Diamonte, 111
teacher expectation theory, 54
Teat, Robert "Bobby Dimes," 178, 230
teen pregnancy, 159
territorialism, 40, 44
Terry, Charles, 38
Thernstrom, Stephan and Abigail, 19
Third Annual Spring Anti-Violence Rally and BBQ, 183
Thompson, Ernie, 189
"Three Evils of Society, The" (King), 1, 111
300 Gang, 44
"Tidal Wave" (Phillips), 57
timeline, 51
TMG (Touch Money Gang), 44
Toliver, Oliver, 78
Tommy (pseudonym), 27–28, 30
Tone Talks (podcast), 227
Torre, María Elena, 165
Touch Money Gang (TMG), 116
Tough Fronts (Dance), 19
Tracy, Robert, 224
traditional value system, 6
Traub, Amy, 226
Trayvor, Lynette, 67
tribalism, 221
Trimbur, Lucia, 143
Trouble Makers, 61
Trump, Donald, 36
Tubman, Harriet, 8
Tucker, Lynell, 80–81
Tuckman, Bruce W., 54
Turner, Diane D., 54
27th Street Gang, 44
2Pacalypse Now (Shakur), 179

UB9 Flag Football League, 189
undocumented Mexican Americans, 10
unemployment, 3, 89–92; COVID-19 and, 205; dis-opportunity and, 94–97;

reframing narrative about, 93–94; of returning citizens, 140–142
United Brothers of Ninth Street (UB9), 187–195
United Way of Delaware, 21, 214
universalism, 5
University of California–Davis, 80
University of Delaware (UD), 21, 46, 52, 80, 101, 160–161, 214
UNWARRANTED (art show), 151–152, 154
Upper Eastside (neighborhood), 33
Upper Westside (neighborhood), 34
uprisings: activism after, 208–211; prison, 204–205; street, 203–211
"Upstream" (Wright), 135
urban Black voyeurism, 19
urban unemployment. *See* unemployment
U.S. Marshals Service, 39
U.S. Probation Office, 91

Valdez, Avelardo, 104
Valentine, Bettylou, 224–225
value system, traditional, 6
Vargas, Robert, 158–159, 176, 203
Vaugh, J. T., 205
Venkatesh, Sudhir Alladi, 64, 182
victimization, exposure to violence versus, 73–76
Vietnamese street gangs, 10
violence: adult, 79; cultural, 11; culture of, 63–65; direct, 11; economic, 166–168; exposure versus victimization, 73–76; intervention programs, 223–224; juvenile, 78; McGriff and, 77–79; reduction programs, 84; school, 108–111; sexual, 163–166; state, 38–39; strategic use of, 64; street, 37; structural, 3, 10–11, 22, 60–61, 68, 92, 93. *See also* gun violence
violence interrupters, 223
violent crime, 39, 43
Violent Crime Control and Law Enforcement Act (1994), 138

Walker, Sherry Dorsey, 133
Walmart, 35
Walnut Street, 34
Warner Elementary School, 102
war on drugs, 137–138
Washington State Penitentiary, 204
Watson, Dennis "Feetz," 16, 211
Way, Fred, III, 166
wealth: Black, 93; of du Pont family, 35; gap, 36, 225–227; history of, 34–37; median household, 93; white, 3, 57, 93
weapons, possession of, 43
We Charge Genocide (Patterson), 113
"Welcome to Wilmington: A Place to be Somebody" (slogan), 45
well-being, 219; economic, 95–96; subjective, 4–5
West Center City (neighborhood), 3
When a Heart Turns Rock Solid (Black), 1
whipping posts, 37
White, Tommy, Jr., 78
white educators, 103–104
white elite, 34, 44
white privilege, 153
White Walkers (fictional characters, *Game of Thrones*), 196–199
white wealth, 3, 21, 57, 93, 153
WIIT (think tank), 215
Wilkinson, Ralph D., 191
William A. Vrooman Exemplar of Justice Award, 151, 154
William C. Holman Correctional Facility, 204
William J. Winchester Bridge, 49
Williams, Dennis P., 34, 58, 115–118, 128–129, 204
Williams, Jerry, 183
Williams, Lynette, 69–70, 172–177
Williams, Vaughn Allen, 69, 173
"Wilmington: One of the Hardest Places to Achieve the American Dream" (Bies), 27
Wilmington, Delaware. *See specific topics*
Wilmington Cease Violence program, 127
Wilmington City Council, 58, 126

Wilmington Education Improvement Commission (WEIC), 101–102
Wilmington 15, 211–213
Wilmington Job Corps, 89–90
Wilmington Mayor's Office, 214
Wilmington Police Department (WPD), 37–39, 49, 113, 114, 126, 230
Wilmington Public Safety Strategies Commission, 117–118
Wilmington Trap Stars (gang), 44
Wilmington Trap Stars Street Art Exhibition, 229–230
Wilmington University, 214
Wilmington Urban League, 214
Wilson, Dion, 209
Wilson, Jonathan "Runn," 16, 55, 119, 211
Wilson, William Julius, 6, 95
Wing, Marquis, 65
Wingo, Brandon, 110–111
Wink, Christopher, 36
"Winning the Fight against Urban Unemployment Discussion Series," 89
"wocky tock" (PCP), 62, 201
Wolters Kluwer, 49

women, 23, 157–159, 172–180, 202; action research on, 160–166; Black, 37; economic violence and, 166–168; education and, 104; *Homicide Art Exhibition* and, 170–172; incarceration rates for, 160, 170; motherhood, 158, 167, 168–170; prison for, 135–136, 160–166; re-entry and, 144–145; returning citizens and, 141
working-class jobs, 94
workshop sessions, 52
World War I, 35, 42
Wortham, Kristal, 212
Wright, Corry, 2, 56, 135, 151
Wright, Latika, 78

Yale Divinity School, 88
Yale Law School, 88
Young, Eugene, 199–200
Young, Lester, 188
Youth Emergency Action Council (WYEAC), 38
Youth Empowered Program Center, 213, 222
Youth Rehabilitative Services, 127

About the Authors

YASSER ARAFAT PAYNE is a professor of sociology in the Department of Sociology and Criminal Justice and the Department of Africana Studies at the University of Delaware. He completed his doctorate in social-personality psychology and his postdoctoral fellowship (with the National Institute on Drug Abuse) in New York City's largest jail, Rikers Island. His street ethnographic research program draws on a methodological framework called street participatory action research (Street PAR)—the process of involving members of street-identified populations in research and local activism. His research program also focuses on street culture, gun violence, policing and re-entry, experiences with work and school, and gangsta rap music and culture. He is currently the principal investigator and coprincipal of two National Institutes of Health–funded Street PAR projects in Wilmington, Delaware, and he is coprincipal of a four-city Street PAR project funded by the National Collaborative on Gun Violence Research. This national study examines the culture of gun violence and its relationship with structural violence in Philadelphia, Detroit, New York City, and Wilmington, Delaware.

To learn more about the study that led to *Murder Town, USA*, please visit:

(1) "Walk with Me, a Community Development Effort" (TedX Wilmington), https://www.youtube.com/watch?v=PXNQ2C_d27A.
(2) *The People's Report*: trailer, https://www.youtube.com/watch?v=macYqbAPTR0.
(3) *The People's Report* (full website), thepeoplesreport.com.

BROOKLYNN K. HITCHENS is an assistant professor of criminology and criminal justice at the University of Maryland. She recently completed a postdoc in the department (2020–2021). She is a sociologist and critical criminologist who studies race, class, and gender inequities in crime, urban violence, and trauma, along with urban policing. Using PAR methods, she partners with low-income Black communities to reduce racial disparities in gun violence. Her work is primarily qualitative, using ethnography, interviews, and focus groups, and she also utilizes mixed methods. She is the co–project director of a multineighborhood research team studying violence, health, and opportunity in Wilmington, Delaware. She is also a project director on a four-site research team studying gun acquisition, use, and injury among "high-risk" Black youth ages sixteen to twenty-four in Philadelphia, Detroit, New York City, and Wilmington. And she is the co–principal investigator on a policing study assessing Black perceptions of and attitudes toward the Baltimore Police Department.

DARRYL L. CHAMBERS is the executive director of the Center for Structural Equity in Wilmington, which houses four Street PAR projects, a gun violence prevention and outreach program, and other various youth programs. He is also a research associate at the Center for Drug and Health Studies (CDHS) at the University of Delaware. His responsibilities at CDHS include work on the Strategic Prevention Framework State Incentive Grant project, the Safe Haven Program, the Suicide Prevention Grant, and crime mapping in Wilmington. He was also the senior research associate on the study that led to the development of *Murder Town, USA*.

Available titles in the Critical Issues in Crime and Society series

Laura S. Abrams and Ben Anderson-Nathe, *Compassionate Confinement: A Year in the Life of Unit C*

Laura S. Abrams and Diane J. Terry, *Everyday Desistance: The Transition to Adulthood among Formerly Incarcerated Youth*

Tammy L. Anderson, ed., *Neither Villain nor Victim: Empowerment and Agency among Women Substance Abusers*

Miriam Boeri, *Women on Ice: Methamphetamine Use among Suburban Women*

Christian L. Bolden, *Out of the Red: My Life of Gangs, Prison, and Redemption*

Scott A. Bonn, *Mass Deception: Moral Panic and the U.S. War on Iraq*

Mary Bosworth and Jeanne Flavin, eds., *Race, Gender, and Punishment: From Colonialism to the War on Terror*

Henry H. Brownstein, Timothy M. Mulcahy, and Johannes Huessy, *The Methamphetamine Industry in America: Transnational Cartels and Local Entrepreneurs*

Loretta Capeheart and Dragan Milovanovic, *Social Justice: Theories, Issues, and Movements*, Revised and expanded edition

Kim Cook, *Shattered Justice: Crime Victims' Experiences with Wrongful Convictions and Exonerations*

Alexandra Cox, *Trapped in a Vice: The Consequences of Confinement for Young People*

Anna Curtis, *Dangerous Masculinity: Fatherhood, Race, and Security inside America's Prisons*

Hilary Cuthrell, Luke Muentner, and Julie Poehlmann, *When Are You Coming Home? How Young Children Cope When Parents Go to Jail*

Walter S. DeKeseredy and Martin D. Schwartz, *Dangerous Exits: Escaping Abusive Relationships in Rural America*

Patricia E. Erickson and Steven K. Erickson, *Crime, Punishment, and Mental Illness: Law and the Behavioral Sciences in Conflict*

Jamie J. Fader, *Falling Back: Incarceration and Transitions to Adulthood among Urban Youth*

Luis A. Fernandez, *Policing Dissent: Social Control and the Anti-Globalization Movement*

Angela J. Hattery and Earl Smith, *Way Down in the Hole: Race, Intimacy, and the Reproduction of Racial Ideologies in Solitary Confinement*

Mike King, *When Riot Cops Are Not Enough: The Policing and Repression of Occupy Oakland*

Ronald C. Kramer, *Carbon Criminals, Climate Crimes*

Timothy R. Lauger, *Real Gangstas: Legitimacy, Reputation, and Violence in the Intergang Environment*

Margaret Leigey, *The Forgotten Men: Serving a Life without Parole Sentence*

Andrea Leverentz, *The Ex-Prisoner's Dilemma: How Women Negotiate Competing Narratives of Reentry and Desistance*

Ethan Czuy Levine, *Rape by the Numbers: Producing and Contesting Scientific Knowledge about Sexual Violence*

Clara S. Lewis, *Tough on Hate? The Cultural Politics of Hate Crimes*

Michael J. Lynch, *Big Prisons, Big Dreams: Crime and the Failure of America's Penal System*

Liam Martin, *The Social Logic of Recidivism: Cultural Capital from Prisons to the Streets*

Allison McKim, *Addicted to Rehab: Race, Gender, and Drugs in the Era of Mass Incarceration*

Raymond J. Michalowski and Ronald C. Kramer, eds., *State-Corporate Crime: Wrongdoing at the Intersection of Business and Government*
Susan L. Miller, *Victims as Offenders: The Paradox of Women's Violence in Relationships*
Torin Monahan, *Surveillance in the Time of Insecurity*
Torin Monahan and Rodolfo D. Torres, eds., *Schools under Surveillance: Cultures of Control in Public Education*
Ana Muñiz, *Police, Power, and the Production of Racial Boundaries*
Marianne O. Nielsen and Linda M. Robyn, *Colonialism Is Crime*
Leslie Paik, *Discretionary Justice: Looking Inside a Juvenile Drug Court*
Yasser Arafat Payne, Brooklynn K. Hitchens, and Darryl L. Chambers, *Murder Town, USA: Homicide, Structural Violence, and Activism in Wilmington*
Anthony M. Platt, *The Child Savers: The Invention of Delinquency*, 40th anniversary edition with an introduction and critical commentaries compiled by Miroslava Chávez-García
Lois Presser, *Why We Harm*
Joshua M. Price, *Prison and Social Death*
Heidi Reynolds-Stenson, *Cultures of Resistance: Collective Action and Rationality in the Anti-Terror Age*
Diana Rickard, *Sex Offenders, Stigma, and Social Control*
Jeffrey Ian Ross, ed., *The Globalization of Supermax Prisons*
Dawn L. Rothe and Christopher W. Mullins, eds., *State Crime: Current Perspectives*
Jodi Schorb, *Reading Prisoners: Literature, Literacy, and the Transformation of American Punishment, 1700–1845*
Susan F. Sharp, *Hidden Victims: The Effects of the Death Penalty on Families of the Accused*
Susan F. Sharp, *Mean Lives, Mean Laws: Oklahoma's Women Prisoners*
Robert H. Tillman and Michael L. Indergaard, *Pump and Dump: The Rancid Rules of the New Economy*
Mariana Valverde, *Law and Order: Images, Meanings, Myths*
Michael Welch, *Crimes of Power and States of Impunity: The U.S. Response to Terror*
Michael Welch, *Scapegoats of September 11th: Hate Crimes and State Crimes in the War on Terror*
Saundra D. Westervelt and Kimberly J. Cook, *Life after Death Row: Exonerees' Search for Community and Identity*